Design Anthropology

Design Anthropology

Theory and Practice

Edited by Wendy Gunn, Ton Otto
and Rachel Charlotte Smith

B L O O M S B U R Y

LONDON • NEW DELHI • NEW YORK • SYDNEY

Bloomsbury Academic

An imprint of Bloomsbury Publishing Plc

50 Bedford Square	1385 Broadway
London	New York
WC1B 3DP	NY 10018
UK	USA

www.bloomsbury.com

First published 2013

British Library Cataloguing-in-Publication Data
A catalogue record for this book is available from the British Library.

ISBN: HB: 978-0-8578-5368-4
PB: 978-0-8578-5369-1
ePDF: 978-1-4725-1823-1
ePub: 978-0-8578-5371-4

Library of Congress Cataloging-in-Publication Data
A catalog record for this book is available from the Library of Congress.

Typeset by Apex CoVantage, LLC, Madison, WI, USA
Printed and bound in India

Contents

Illustrations

Contributors

Brendon Clark is a senior researcher and project manager at the Interactive Institute, Sweden. Since working in community development in Bolivia in the late 1990s, he has focused his PhD and postdoctoral work on knowledge reproduction practices in technology and service design processes in both the public and private sectors. He co-led the Design Anthropological Innovation Model (DAIM) project in Denmark and has been developing a contextualized language learning agenda called Language as Participation. He teaches MA-level and PhD-level design ethnography and collaborative design courses in Denmark and Sweden.

Christian Clausen is a professor in design, innovation, and sustainable transition at Aalborg University, Copenhagen. He combines an engineering background within manufacturing engineering with insight in science and technology studies (STS) and organization. He has published widely on social shaping of technology and sociotechnical dimensions of design and innovation.

Adam Drazin is an anthropologist based at University College London, where he coordinates a masters course on the theme of culture, materials, and design. He has conducted anthropological work for design at HP Labs and Intel Digital Health Group around various themes including aging and remembering. His main current research interests are the conduct of design anthropology, the transnational home, and the material culture of meriting.

Ian Ewart worked as an industrial engineer for many years before studying anthropology. He received his DPhil from the University of Oxford in 2012 following fieldwork in the United Kingdom and Borneo. As a research fellow at the University of Reading, his research interests lie at the cultural and material intersections of technical design, production, and use.

Caroline Gatt is a teaching fellow in anthropology at the University of Aberdeen. Her book entitled *An Ethnography of Global Environmentalism: Becoming Friends of the Earth* will be published by Routledge in 2014. Gatt's research with Friends of the Earth is based on nine years of anthropological engagement as a researcher and a project coordinator. From 2001 to 2006 Gatt also worked with two research theater groups, in Malta and in Italy, in practice-based research on improvisation inside structured performance pieces.

Wendy Gunn is an associate professor of design anthropology at Mads Clausen Institute, University of Southern Denmark. Her main research interests are in skilled practice, environmental perception, systems development, and transformation of knowledge. Gunn has extensive experience of collaborative processes and practices of designing as an integral part of research and teaching. Recent publications include *Design and Anthropology* (Ashgate, 2012, with Jared Donovan).

Elizabeth Hallam is a senior research fellow at the Department of Anthropology, University of Aberdeen, and a research associate in the School of Anthropology and Museum Ethnography, University of Oxford. Her research and publications focus on the historical anthropology of the body; death and dying; material and visual cultures; histories of collecting and museums; the anthropology of anatomy; three-dimensional modeling; and mixed-media sculpture.

Joachim Halse is an assistant professor at the Royal Danish Academy of Fine Arts, School of Design. With a combined background in anthropology and interaction design, Joachim's research explores participatory processes of knowing and making in close collaboration with external industry partners and the public sector. In 2008 Joachim earned the PhD degree from the IT University of Copenhagen with the thesis "Design Anthropology: Borderland Experiments with Participation, Performance and Situated Intervention."

Tim Ingold is a professor of social anthropology at the University of Aberdeen. He has carried out ethnographic fieldwork in Lapland and has written on environment, technology, and social organization in the circumpolar North, as well as on evolutionary theory, human-animal relations, language and tool use, environmental perception, and skilled practice. He is currently exploring issues on the interface between anthropology, archaeology, art, and architecture.

Kyle Kilbourn is a senior human factors scientist at Medtronic, Inc. He has worked on research projects in welfare technology innovation, including the Automated Sterilization of Hospital Equipment (DEFU-STEPP) project in Denmark, which partnered the public and private sectors. His research interests include understanding experiences for design, the intersection between design and anthropology, and interaction design for health care.

Mette Gislev Kjærsgaard has worked with design anthropology for nearly fifteen years in industrial as well as academic contexts. In 2011 she received her PhD from the Department of Culture and Society, University of Aarhus, where she is currently conducting postdoctoral research on community-based innovation and social media.

George E. Marcus is the Chancellor's Professor of Anthropology at the University of California, Irvine. On moving to UCI in 2005 after many years at Rice University, he established a center for ethnography dedicated to examining the conditions and prospects of ethnographic research in diverse contemporary settings. The center has been especially interested in the atmospheres and conditions of collaboration, which particularly influence the setting up and course of fieldwork research. Interfaces of ethnography with design practices and thinking have been of special interest to the center, as has the pedagogy of training apprentice ethnographers in their first projects. Recently, Marcus has coedited *Fieldwork Is Not What It Used to Be* (2009) with James Faubion, and contributed to a published series of conversations with Paul Rabinow entitled *Designs for an Anthropology of the Contemporary* (2008).

Crysta Metcalf is the manager of interactive media user research within Motorola Mobility's Applied Research Center and leads a cross-disciplinary team of applied research scientists. Crysta is an applied cultural anthropologist who received her BA from the University of South Florida, and her MA and PhD from Wayne State University. Her specialty areas include design anthropology, economic anthropology, and business and organizational anthropology. She has worked in applied research for Motorola since 2000, on a variety of projects utilizing team-based, transdisciplinary methods for experience innovation and interaction design. Her work has focused on emerging media and communication technologies and on consumers in both the home and mobile spaces. Crysta regularly publishes and speaks about the use of rigorous ethnographic-style research techniques as part of the invention process.

Keith M. Murphy is an assistant professor of anthropology at the University of California, Irvine. His research explores the relationship between language, design, and politics in Sweden and the United States.

Ton Otto is a professor and research leader at James Cook University, Australia, and a professor of anthropology and ethnography at Aarhus University, Denmark. Since 1986, he has conducted ethnographic field research in Papua New Guinea and published widely on issues of social and cultural change. His interests comprise the epistemology and methodology of ethnographic research, including visual anthropology and its relationship to innovation, intervention, and design. His recent publications include the coedited volume *Experiments in Holism: Theory and Practice in Contemporary Anthropology* (Wiley-Blackwell, 2010, with Nils Bubandt) and two codirected films: *Ngat is Dead—Studying Mortuary Traditions: Manus, Papua New Guinea* (DER,

2009, with Christian Suhr Nielsen and Steffen Dalsgaard) and *Unity through Culture* (DER, 2012, with Christian Suhr Nielsen).

Rachel Charlotte Smith is an anthropologist and a PhD research fellow in anthropology and interaction design at Aarhus University, Institute for Culture and Society and Research Centre for Participatory IT, in co-tutelle with James Cook University. Her research focuses on relations between culture, design, and technology, specifically on digital cultures, representation, and design of participatory technologies. She led *Digital Natives*, an interactive research and exhibition project creating new forms of digital cultural heritage.

Elizabeth (Dori) Tunstall is an associate professor of design anthropology at Swinburne University of Technology. Her research focuses on cultures-based innovation. Dori has worked as a user experience strategist in academia and industry for more than ten years. She holds a PhD in anthropology from Stanford University.

Christina Wasson was trained as a linguistic anthropologist. After finishing her PhD, she worked for E-Lab, a design firm that used anthropological research to develop new product ideas. She currently teaches the only course in design anthropology offered through an anthropology department in the United States. Clients for class projects have included Motorola, Microsoft, and the Dallas/Fort Worth International Airport. Wasson was also a founding member of the Ethnographic Praxis in Industry Conference steering committee.

Preface

This volume is an outcome of a panel held at the 11th Biennial European Association of Social Anthropologists Conference at the National University of Ireland Maynooth, in August 2010. The aim of the panel, *Design Anthropology: Intertwining Different Timelines, Scales and Movements*, was to expand the notion of ethnographic practice and contribute toward a research agenda for design anthropology. About half of the chapters were presented in a first version at this panel, whereas the others have been subsequently elicited by the editors.

Design anthropology is an emergent field and is practiced in different ways depending on one's methodological positioning. Design practices attempt to make connections (albeit partial) between past, present, and future. Ideally, in the present you have a vision of the past in order to create a future out of the everyday. Practitioners of design anthropology follow dynamic situations and social relations and are concerned with how people perceive, create, and transform their environments through their everyday activities. This view challenges the idea that design and innovation only refer to the generation of *new* things as being central to processes of social and cultural change. Design anthropology practices occur across different scales and timelines and involve many disciplines, each bringing their own distinct ways of knowing and doing.

Inspired by processual, critical and action orientated approaches in anthropology, the editors of this volume attend to the potential of design anthropology practices as providing places for reflection on combinations of methodology and theory. As such the volume focuses on concepts, tools, and methodology in an attempt to reconsider the relation between theory and practice in design anthropology. Starting with the ambition of carving out a theoretical field, although very preliminary, we sketch the theoretical and methodological issues involved. Considering the theory-practice relation in design anthropology raises the question, Can you develop theory as part of practice? Underpinning many of the contributions in this volume is a demonstration of the situated nature of theory generated during collaborative engagement and the specificity of theory as emergent from field investigations. Moreover, the contributors to this volume have shown how theory generated in this way can be involved within design processes. As editors we argue that theory in design anthropology is continually being built. Perhaps this is one of the reasons why the volume demanded ongoing collaboration between the editors and contributors far beyond the normal remit of editorial input.

In the moment-to-moment interactions between anthropologists and the people they work with, anthropologists make implicit understandings explicit. What the ethnographic method brings is contrast and relation, and it opens up the taken for granted by bringing into the foreground what was in the background. Anthropological theory uses explicit contrast as a way of constructing meaningful difference. Design anthropology is a move to shift the focus from anthropological description to action. In methodological terms, how does this influence the theory-practice relation in this emergent field? What role does anthropological theory play in design anthropology? How is the validity of knowledge in design anthropology established? To address these questions the volume brings together a group of anthropologists who are actively contributing to this field.

The editors and contributors of this volume have collaborated over a two-year period to provide an overview of various positions taken by anthropologists in this emerging field. We want to emphasize that the approaches presented here are constitutive of design anthropology as conceived by anthropologists at a particular moment in time. As such the various positionings are not meant to be definitive examples of *how to do* design anthropology but rather to open lines of inquiry for practitioners of design anthropology to build on. Central to all of these positionings is a concern for the design anthropologist to be involved in some way with instigating change. Ethnography here is not just *a method*; rather engaging *with* people as a form of correspondence (see Gatt and Ingold, this volume) becomes central to transformation. As a result, *methods* of ethnography can be developed that are grounded in processual, holistic approaches that realize the agency of the participants.

The four themes used for structuring the volume were developed at The Cairns Institute, James Cook University, where Otto was working during the preparation of the volume. We are grateful to the Aarhus University Research Foundation and to SPIRE Centre, Mads Clausen Institute, University of Southern Denmark for their financial support of research visits to The Cairns Institute by Gunn (2010) and Smith (2012) to work with Otto on the volume and in preparing the manuscript. Finally we would like to acknowledge the stimulating collaboration with all contributors. The three editors have contributed equally to the task of bringing out this volume, a task that proved considerably greater than anticipated but also very rewarding intellectually.

Wendy Gunn, Ton Otto and Rachel Charlotte Smith, March 2013

Design Anthropology: A Distinct Style of Knowing

Ton Otto and Rachel Charlotte Smith

DESIGN AND ANTHROPOLOGY

This book is about design anthropology, which is a fast-developing academic field that combines elements from design and anthropology. The following chapters comprise innovative case studies and theoretical reflections that provide an introduction to the field from the perspective of anthropologists participating in its development. In this introductory chapter, we sketch the contours of this new field and its emergence from the early uses of ethnography in design in the late 1970s up to the present. We argue that design anthropology is coming of age as a separate (sub)discipline with its own concepts, methods, research practices, and practitioners, in short its own distinct style and practice of knowledge production. But first we discuss the two separate knowledge traditions from which this new discipline has developed.

Design is a pervasive aspect of modern society with a large number of practitioners and a great range of subfields, such as industrial design, architecture, systems design, human-computer interaction design, service design, and strategic design and innovation. Design as a process of thought and planning is often depicted as a universal human capacity that sets humankind apart from nature (Cross 2006; Friedman 2002; Fry 2009; Chapter 8, this volume). To design is to conceive of an idea and plan it out, "give form, structure and function to that idea" (Nelson and Stolterman 2003: 1), before executing it in the world.[1] In this general sense, designing is a universal aspect of human practice, but the way it is carried out varies considerably across different societies and cultures (Chapter 5, this volume). In contemporary (post)industrial and digital societies, design has become a separate domain of activity because economic and organizational developments have engendered a specialist workforce of designers. These specialists create a variety of solutions in different social and economic contexts: they generate ideas for products that are mass produced by industry; they develop digital systems that perform new functions in workplaces as well as private homes; they design services for public sector institutions; they create strategies for innovation in business and marketing; and they develop plans for urban and rural developments and sustainable forms of living. Design professionals are trained in design schools and other higher education institutions, as well as within companies, and are increasingly supported by a range of academically based design studies. In modern societies with their emphasis on innovation and change, which are often considered as intrinsic values (Suchman 2011), design has arguably become one of the major sites of cultural production and change, on par with science, technology, and art.

Anthropology[2] is the comparative study of societies and cultures, based on detailed empirical research in concrete social contexts. When it was established as an academic discipline in the late nineteenth century, its focus was on studying the cultural institutions and practices of non-Western societies. Today anthropologists carry out research in almost every imaginable social context, from high-tech companies and scientific laboratories in urban centers to remote rural villages in developing countries. A key characteristic of the discipline during the twentieth century was the development of *participant observation* as the dominant method of field research. Considered the core of ethnography,[3] which is the description of cultures, participant observation involves the long-term immersion of a researcher in a social setting with the aim to observe and document everyday practices comprehensively and in detail. In order to get access to everyday events and actions and understand their meaning for the participants, the researcher has to spend time with the people and engage with their lives. The result of an ethnographic study is an ethnography—usually a written report or book, but possibly also a film or exhibition—representing a particular social setting and cultural context and producing theoretically informed arguments about it. The term *ethnography* refers thus both to the process of inquiry—the immersion in social life to understand and describe it—and to its product: the final ethnographic representation.

As the comparative study of societies and cultures, anthropology has an obvious and long-standing research interest in processes of social and cultural change, human creativity, and innovation (Barnett 1953; Hallam and Ingold 2007; Liep 2001). This includes design, even if the anthropological study of design as a modern phenomenon is still in its infancy. However, the major relationship between design and anthropology has been through ethnography. From the late 1970s, designers became aware of the value of ethnographic data and methodologies, in particular to get a better understanding of the needs and experiences of users and the contexts in which products and computer systems were used (Blomberg, Burell, and Guest 2003; Reese 2002). But it is not just the usefulness of ethnographic research and information for design that is at stake here; there appears to be a genuine affinity between design and ethnography as processes of inquiry and discovery that includes the iterative way process and product are interconnected and the reflexive in-volvement by researchers and designers (see Chapter 14, this volume). Tim Brown, the CEO of the international design and innovation firm IDEO, clearly acknowledges this affinity when he writes that designers need to go out and observe people's experiences in the real world rather than rely on exten-sive quantitative data to develop their insights. He continues: "As any an-thropologist will attest, observation relies on the quality of one's data, not the quantity" (2011: 382). Like ethnographers, designers have to begin with immersion in real-life situations to gain insight into experiences and mean-ings that form the basis for reflection, imagination, and design (Nelson and Stolterman 2012: 18). Or as Friedman states: "The design process must in-tegrate field-specific knowledge with a larger understanding of the human be-ings for whom design is made, the social circumstances in which the act of design takes place, and the human context in which designed artifacts are used" (2002: 209–210).

There are, of course, also significant differences between design and an-thropology. The main aim of anthropology, like in most academic disciplines, is to produce generalizations and theories about human societies based on but reaching beyond the particularities of ethnographic case studies. Design, on the other hand, is directed toward the future and the creation of specific products and solutions, an "ultimate particular" (Stolterman 2008). Although the design process may start from "wicked" or ill-defined problems (Buchanan 1992; Gaver 2012), integrating processes of observation and reflection simi-lar to anthropology, its purpose is to create products, processes, and services that transform reality. Its success is measured by the material and social im-pact of particular solutions, rather than by the validity of its generalizations.

As the differences between design and anthropology give design anthro-pology its special character, we will now sketch what we see as the major contributions by these two fields to the new subdiscipline. Further details of specific design anthropological practices and concepts are discussed in the final section of this introduction and in the following chapters. Here we only give a brief characterization of the constitutive differences that produce the creative tensions in this new field and set the conditions for both its chal-lenges and its potential.

First, design is clearly *future oriented*; its success is measured by the rel-evance the designed products and conceptual solutions have for people's everyday lives. Although anthropology has an interest in social change and people's imaginations of the future, as a discipline it lacks tools and practices to actively engage and collaborate in people's formation of their futures. One of design anthropology's challenges is to develop such tools and practices of collaborative future making (see especially Sections I and III, this volume). Second, whereas participant observation by anthropologists might be consid-ered a form of intervention, its ultimate purpose is to observe and document rather than to effect change. Generally anthropologists have been quite concerned to minimize their impact on the people among whom they conduct their studies. In design, the situation is radically different, with both process and product aiming specifically at *intervention* in existing realities. Learning from design practice, design anthropologists are developing methods that employ various forms of intervention, both to create contextual knowledge and to develop specific solutions. The field of design anthropology is thus more oriented toward intervention and transforming social reality than traditional anthropology has ever been.[4] Third, design is (almost) always a process of *collaboration* between different disciplines and stakeholders, including designers, researchers, producers, and users. Anthropology still maintains a tradition, which is only slowly changing, of the lone researcher who conducts individual fieldwork and produces a solo piece of scholarship. Design anthropology radically breaks with this tradition as its practitioners work in multidisciplinary teams, acting in complex roles as researchers, facilitators, and cocreators in processes of design and innovation (all chapters but especially Section IV, this volume).

Anthropology also brings three key constitutive elements to design anthropology. First is the key role of theory and cultural interpretation. Whereas ideation, the generation of design concepts, is a central element of design, it does not have a sustained tradition of *theorizing* the context of usage and *interpreting* the cultural meaning of things.[5] This is the forte of anthropology, with a long history of cultural interpretation (Geertz 1973), contextualization (Dilley 1999), and holistic explanation (Otto and Bubandt 2010) through cross-cultural comparison and the development of theoretical concepts. Design anthropology integrates this rich tradition of contextualization and interpretation into the tasks of design, emphasizing the generative role of theory in developing design concepts and critically examining existing, often implicit conceptual frameworks (see Sections I and II, this volume). Second, against design's concern with creation, innovation, and "future-making" (Björgvinsson, Ehn, and Hillgren 2010), anthropology systematically *investigates the past to understand the present*, including its modes of anticipating the future. It is a great challenge for design anthropology to extend the temporal horizon both forward and backward, to anchor images of the future in reliable constructions of the past, thus avoiding the risk of "defuturing" that is inherent in design (Fry 2011) and of generalizing and essentializing modern values of innovation and change (Suchman 2011) (see Chapter 7 and Section III, this volume). Third, especially through its hallmark practice of ethnography, long acclaimed as useful by designers, anthropology endows design anthropology with a unique *sensitivity to the value orientations* of the various groups affected by design projects—including disempowered groups, consumers, producers, and audiences. The task for design anthropology is to integrate and develop these traditional qualities into new modes of research and collaboration, working toward transformation without sacrificing empathy and depth of understanding (see especially Section IV, this volume).

THE EMERGENCE OF DESIGN ANTHROPOLOGY

In this section we point to central historical developments in the collaboration between anthropology and design that reflect our anthropological vantage point and interest in the field.[6] Design and industrial communities have generally been much more prone to adopt approaches of social research, hereunder ethnography, and to invite anthropologists into their fields, than vice versa. Management researchers and designers collaborated with anthropologists in industrial settings as early as the 1930s to study social and physical aspects of workers' productivity, beginning with Lloyd Warner's involvement in the well-known Hawthorne study[7] (Baba 1986; Reese 2002; Schwartzman 1993). The study was the first to show how informal social processes affected the output and efficiency of factory workers. It was followed by a number of anthropological industrial studies through the 1940s and the 1950s, developing techniques for interaction analysis to predict elements of interpersonal behavior and create insights for business management. Industrial anthropologists were involved mainly in business management up until World War II, when new military fields of expertise developed that involved social scientists more extensively in product development through what was termed *engineering psychology* and *human factors analysis* (Reese 2002: 19–20). Such studies focused on behavioral and psychological factors of workers, or pilots, to gain control over the machinery, prevent accidents, and develop various industrial products and equipment. Both in the United States and in Europe, where the influence from labor movements promoted concerns with workers' health and safety (Helander 1997; Reese 2002: 20), research into engineering, human factors, and behavior in the workplace led the way for social scientists' involvement in industrial design and business management.

In the 1980s, the foundational work of Lucy Suchman (1987) and others in the Work Practice and Technology Group at Xerox Palo Alto Research Center (PARC) furthered ethnographic research in software design through the study of human behavior around computers in the workplace (Blomberg, Burrell, and Trigg 1997; Blomberg et al. 1993). From the 1980s, ethnographic research became part of the interdisciplinary design and research communities of computer-supported cooperative work (CSCW) and human-computer interaction (HCI), where social scientists, computer scientists, and system designers shared knowledge about the use of technology in work practices (Wasson 2000: 380). Research in these fields focused mainly on workplace settings of human-computer interaction and system design, with ethnography functioning as a data collection method to gain insights into the *real-world* experiences and needs of users (Bentley et al. 1992; Harper 2000; Heath and Luff 1992). The computer science foundations of CSCW and HCI placed a strong emphasis on the cognitive and behavioral sciences for understanding users in industrial and corporate settings. As a result the dominant ethnographic method developed in this field was the analytical framework of ethnomethodology, with its detailed attention to situated action and observable patterns of human behavior translated into abstract conceptual values and directions for design (Button 2000; Garfinkel 1967, 2002; Shapiro 1994). Suchman's book *Plans and Situated Action* (1987) was one of the first studies dealing specifically with the relationship between design and anthropology, focusing in detail on the interactions between people and computers. Through comprehensive ethnographic investigations, inspired by ethnomethodology and conversation analysis, as well as activity theory (Vygotsky 1978), Suchman mapped out work flows, plans, and situated action and showed how cultural conceptions had effects on the design and reconfigurations of technologies.

In the early 1990s, E-Lab LLC, the Doblin Group, and a number of other U.S. consultancy and design firms, greatly inspired by Xerox PARC, played an important role in introducing ethnographic methods to industrial design and product development. The approach of E-Lab was unique in that it employed an equal number of researchers and designers to work together in teams, using ethnographic methods (participant observation, video recording of everyday consumer behavior, qualitative interviews, and analysis) as its main research strategy (Wasson 2000: 379). Other central figures in the field were Jane Fulton Suri at IDEO and Liz Sanders from SonicRim—still highly influential in the field—who applied creative participatory design methods as well as generative tools and frameworks from experimental psychology to work with users and understand the needs and behavior of consumers. By the mid-1990s, the wave of interest in ethnography in industrial and commercial design had caused many companies in the United States and Europe to employ anthropologists, psychologists, and sociologists to study the behavior and needs of users and consumers. During this period, more fragmented behavioral and psychological approaches were increasingly replaced by holistic and broadly contextual, ethnographic approaches to understanding products and their use (Reese 2002: 21; Wasson 2000).[8]

The praxis and challenges of the use of ethnography in design that developed out of the industrial and corporate collaborations have been addressed by anthropologists and sociologists placed centrally in the field, such as Suchman (1987, 2007, 2011); Blomberg and colleagues (1993, 2003); Suchman, Trigg, and Blomberg (2002); Anderson (1994); Shapiro (1994); Forsythe (1999); Star (1999); Wasson (2000, 2002); and Van Veggel (2005). Common to these contributions and their inherent critiques is that they argue for the relevance of ethnography in and for design as more than simply a methodology for the study of a readily available world of users outside the design studio. They challenge the way data gained from field research have conventionally been collected, analyzed, and transformed into "specifications for end-user requirements" (Anderson 1994: 151), or what Dourish (2006, 2007) critically terms "implications for design," before being handed over to designers, engineers, or other professionals. They further address the challenge of collaboration and the power relations of the corporate settings, in which anthropologists have been drawn into the field of design on an unequal footing with designers, engineers, and other practitioners (Blomberg et al. 2003; Veggel 2005). In these industrial contexts, the expectations toward anthropologists have generally predefined the often limited premises for contributing to the process of design. Wasson's (2002) depiction of the bow tie model, in which the intermediate phase or "knot" between research and design is used to create shared frameworks of understanding and tie the disciplines together, has been widely used as a model for understanding the integration of ethnography into design. Blomberg and colleagues (1993, 2003) have presented a guide to the basic principles of ethnography for design, along with tools such as experience models and user profiles, to facilitate shared analytical frameworks as well as ways of involving users in the process of design. As such, rather than distinguishing between descriptive observational ethnography and creative design work, they suggest uses of scenarios, user profiles, opportunity maps, and experience models as interdisciplinary ways of bridging the contrast between understanding present practices and designing for future ones. In their view, anthropologists and designers collaborate in both research and design activities as "change agents" (Blomberg et al. 1993: 141).

The principle of involving users in processes of design that Blomberg and her colleagues highlight has been most clearly articulated by the field of *participatory design* that emerged mainly in the United States and Europe, especially Scandinavia (Kensing and Blomberg 1998; Muller 2002; Schuler and Namioka 1993; Simonsen and Robertson 2012). The Scandinavian tradition of participatory design (Bjerknes, Ehn, and Kyng 1987; Ehn 1988, 1993; Greenbaum and Kyng 1991) developed out of the 1970s and 1980s trade union projects (DUE, DEMOS, and UTOPIA) that were critical of the negative impact of new technologies on people's working conditions. The most prominent ideal characterizing the Scandinavian tradition was workplace democracy, which focused on the inclusion and active participation of employees in shaping their own working conditions (Bansler 1989; Bjerknes, Ehn, and Kyng 1987). In this political sense, the approach of participatory design advocated technologies and work processes that augmented the skills and tools of the workers and enabled them to control their work practice rather than technologies that aimed to replace the workers (Ehn 1988). Therefore much effort was spent on developing design techniques and methods, such as design games, simulations of work-technology relations, and cooperative prototyping (Bødker

1991; Greenbaum and Kyng 1991), that would enable disempowered groups to actively participate in and contribute to the design processes. Concerns about the loss of these values of user participation due to the rise of commercial interests in user behavior have been frequently voiced (Beck 2002; Kyng 2010). The tradition of participatory design in Scandinavia continues to be refined and developed, partly driven by government-supported research grants for collaborations between academic researchers and public and private organizations (see, for example, Binder et al. 2011; Iversen and Smith 2012). It constitutes an important context for many contributions to this book (see Chapters 3, 4, 7, and 10, this volume) dealing with areas as diverse as product development, public sector health services, waste handling, and museum exhibition practices.

As the field of human-computer interaction design has expanded its scope beyond workplace studies and system development, the turn to values and experiences has occurred more generally within the field of HCI. In response to the rise of industrial and commercial interest in ubiquitous and pervasive computing, academic researchers in this field have addressed the need for integrating human values into critical and reflective approaches to design (Bannon 2005; Dourish 2007; McCarthy and Wright 2004; Sellen et al. 2009; Sengers et al. 2005; Zimmerman 2009). These human-centered approaches move from a technology and system-focused design practice and an understanding of users as end users or evaluators of technology to a more radical practice of design as cocreation that addresses a larger context of social relations, experiences, values, and ethics. These more critical voices echo Suchman's (2007) concerns in their focus on everyday behavior and imagination, rather than cognition and intended practices, as well as their attendance to the ongoing appropriations of technology by people in their daily lives, beyond the traditional focus on usability and interface design. The strong affiliation to participatory design (Muller 2002) informs an outspoken concern with the role of users and how designers can involve and deal with stakeholders and participants in collaborative processes. It also feeds into a concern to create spaces for critical reflexivity and dialogue about human experience more generally (Hunt 2011). Dourish (2006, 2007) makes the link between design and critical reflection, and the potential of anthropology in this, very blatant, as he critiques the limited focus on ethnographic methods in and for design and points to the transformative potential of classical anthropological studies for understanding relations between people and technologies anew.

Interest in users and participatory design more generally has also been well represented in the commercial and corporate contexts of user-centered design and innovation (Brown 2009), as well as in the fields of organizational development and business management. Significant academic contributions connected to these contexts have dealt with ethnography, design, and customer experiences in industrial and corporate cultures (see, e.g., Cefkin

2010; Nafus and Anderson 2006; Sanders 2008; Squires and Byrne 2002; Suri 2011). Squires and Byrne's edited volume *Creating Breakthrough Ideas* has presented one of the most elaborate discussions of the interrelation between anthropology and design in this field, focusing on the value of ethnography and the role of cultural perspectives in applied processes of design, product development, business, and innovation. The work of anthropologists in corporate and commercial settings is clearly related to the long tradition of anthropological studies of organizations and corporate cultures (Gellner and Hirsch 2001; Jiménez 2007; Orr 1996; Schwartzman 1993; Wallman 1979; Wright 1994), as well as business anthropology (Baba 2006; Cefkin 2012; Jordan 2003; Ybema et al. 2009). The term *business anthropology* was used in the 1980s to describe anthropologists working outside academia with consumer behavior and marketing, but now involves "any application of anthropology to business-oriented problems" (Gray 2010: 1). There are many overlaps between the applied anthropological domains described as *business anthropology* and *corporate ethnography*, and design anthropology. A central venue for these corporate and academic fields of interest is the interdisciplinary Ethnographic Praxis in Industry Conference (EPIC), held annually since 2005, to promote ethnographic practices and principles in business and industry.[9]

There is an emerging interdisciplinary body of literature on design and anthropology that focuses on relations between people and objects, production and use. Most notably, Clarke's (2011) edited volume *Design Anthropology: Object Culture in the 21st Century* and Gunn and Donovan's (2012) edited volume *Design and Anthropology* deal with design's turn to the user and what impact this has had on the understanding of objects and products, their creation and use. Clarke's volume, in addition to being strongly rooted in design, builds on anthropological studies of materiality and consumption, objects and taste, and the cultural processes that shape experiences and products (Appadurai 1986; Bourdieu 1979; Gell 1998; Henare, Holbraad, and Wastell 2007; Miller 2005). Gunn and Donovan (2012) shift the focus to the broader contextual relations between designing, producing, and using, and emphasize the social and emergent aspects of creativity in design and the shaping of *things*. They deal with these issues from three different methodological positions in anthropology, design, and philosophy (Ingold 2012; Redström 2012; Verbeek 2012), thus expanding the scope for interdisciplinary collaboration.

Whatever the focus or aim of connecting anthropology and design, the commitment to concrete practice and reflective action is essential to both. This is reflected respectively in the fields of anthropology and design by the pronounced influence of Tim Ingold and Donald Schön, who are now also inspiring practitioners of design anthropology. Ingold's (2000, 2011; Hallam and Ingold 2007) phenomenological notions of *moving along* the lifelines, paths, and flows of social life have been central to understanding creativity, improvisation, and innovation as cultural process, and in this book (Chapter 8). Ingold and Gatt build on this position to conceptualize design (and "anthropology-by-means-of-design") as a practice of correspondence to the ever-changing circumstances and entanglements of people, objects, and environments. Schön's (1987, 1991 [1983]) prominent accounts of design practice as *reflection-in-action*, responding to design situations through a dialogic engagement with the conditions and materials at hand, have, along with Dewey's pragmatism (1980 [1934]) and contributions such as Dourish (2001) and Sennett (2008), furthered the understanding of designing as a reflexive engagement with concrete experience, based on the intrinsic relation between knowing and doing.

A DISTINCT STYLE OF KNOWING

With the emergence of a field of anthropological inquiry linked with design, the question arises whether we can talk about a new field of study characterized by distinct objects, methods, procedures, and training practices. A number of prominent anthropologists, including Paul Rabinow, George Marcus, and Tim Ingold (see Rabinow et al. 2008 and Chapters 8 and 14, this volume), suggest that design provides inspiration for anthropology to develop its research practices in order to be better equipped for the study of the contemporary world. They propose that anthropology as a discipline should change and that design practice and thinking can give direction to this change. Lucy Suchman, who spent a large part of her career working on design teams, takes a different position. Critical of the overly optimistic approach to innovation and change that prevails in a large part of the design world, she argues that "we need less a reinvented anthropology *as* (or for) design than a critical anthropology *of* design" (2011: 3). Rather than aiming to change the practice of anthropology, she wishes to direct the critical potential of this research tradition toward the study and contextualization of design and technological innovation as a specific mode and site of change in modern society.

We take a third position by arguing that design anthropology is coming of age as a *distinct style* of doing anthropology, with specific research and training practices. Evidence for this emerging field includes the growing number of anthropologists working in and with design, PhD theses that identify with the label *design anthropology*,[10] conferences and publications in this field, as well as the increasing number of university courses and research centers dealing with design anthropology (see Chapters 12 and 14, this volume).[11] With Rabinow, Marcus, and Ingold, we hope and expect that this style will have an impact on anthropology more generally. Its development is prompted by challenges in the contemporary world, which put greater emphasis on designerly ways of thinking and planning (see later in this chapter). And like Suchman we intend design anthropology to have a critical impact on design as well, making it a more broadly humane and "decolonized" (see Chapter 13, this volume) practice through the adoption of the specific anthropological attributes we identified earlier. These include the critical use of theory and contextualization; the extension of the time horizon to include the past and long-term future to ensure sustainability; and sensitivity to and not least incorporation of the values and perspectives of the people whose worlds are affected by design.

Our use of the term *style* is inspired by philosopher Ian Hacking and historian of science A.C. Crombie. The latter identified six major "styles of scientific thinking" in the development of the modern sciences and arts (Crombie 1988, 1994). Hacking (1992) prefers the term *styles of reasoning*, since reasoning is done in public as well as in private, by thinking but also by talking and arguing and showing. We have chosen the term *style of knowing* to indicate that the production of knowledge involves more than thinking and reasoning: it also comprises practices of acting on the world that generate specific forms of knowledge, and it is in these practices we see a major shift.[12] According to Hacking, styles have a number of characteristics. To start with, they have a history, that is, they are invented at a certain point in time and develop subsequently—they may also become less popular again or disappear altogether. Second, each style introduces a number of novelties, which could include types of objects studied, forms of evidence used, ways of assessing truth or validity, and the manner in which generalities, modalities, and possibilities are identified. Finally, each style should have a certain stability to be recognized as such, which primarily refers to enduring standards of quality assessment and validation.

Although design anthropology as we describe it is young, we believe it conforms to Hacking's definition of a new style. It introduces a number of novelties that derive from the experimental integration of anthropological and designerly practices. These include interventionist forms of fieldwork and design that work through iterative cycles of reflection and action, and employ methods and tools such as video feedback, scenarios, mock-ups, props, provo- and prototypes, tangible interactions, and various forms of games, performances, and enactment. Design anthropology also comprises various forms of interdisciplinary collaboration inside and outside the design studio to produce concepts and prototypes, the scaffolding of collaboration with stakeholders and various types of publics, and an intentional focus on facilitating and contributing to change. Finally, design anthropology is characterized by a particular use of theory aimed at generating concepts and new frameworks or perspectives.

Later in this chapter, we further develop these style elements of design anthropology under the headings of the four sections of this book: concepts, methods, and practices; the materiality of design; the temporality of design; and the relationality of design. But first we give a tentative sketch of four different modes of the key method of anthropology—ethnographic fieldwork through participant observation—that have developed over time to make it plausible that the new research practices of design anthropology point to an emerging theoretical paradigm and thus to the development of certain, more or less stable, standards of quality assessment and validation, which are characteristic of the style.

Generally credited to Bronislaw Malinowski (but see Stocking 1983, 1991), the early form of ethnographic fieldwork was presented as a way to gather more reliable data than through anthropology's previous dependence on re-ports by travelers, explorers, traders, and resident missionaries. The focus was on firsthand observation and the theoretical context was provided by the dominant positivist paradigm that in Durkheim's formulation looked at "social facts" as things (see Holy 1984). Quality assessment and validation hap-pened through debate within the academic community. A further development of the ethnographic method was grounded in the hermeneutic approach cham-pioned by Clifford Geertz and others in the 1960s, who suggested that culture could be read as a kind of text. Rather than an observable thing, a social fact was seen as a cultural construction in need of interpretation by the anthropol-ogist, and validation had to include the community sharing the cultural tradi-tion. With the postmodern turn in the 1980s and the rise of praxis theory as the dominant theoretical paradigm (Ortner 2006), greater attention was given to the epistemological and political position of anthropologists in relation to the communities they worked with. Social facts were seen as the result of ac-tions by human agents, who by their actions reproduced but also impacted on the structures under which they operated. Deprived from the quasi-objective or distanced position in the field of study, anthropological validation now in-cluded aspects of dialogue, multivocality, and circumstantial activism (Marcus 1998). Part of this development was a continuing methodological reflection on ethnographic fieldwork, in particular the concept of the field itself that com-prises the complex social relations and research questions ethnographers engage in: for example, dealing with multiple field sites and working with spe-cialist informants, as well as using modern forms of interaction and communi-cation such as the Internet (Faubion and Marcus 2009; Rabinow et al. 2008). These reflections have prepared the way for what we see as the next stage of ethnographic methods that are intentionally interventionist.

With the introduction of interventionist strategies as part of design an-thropological fieldwork, we see the possibility of the rise of a new paradigm that gives greater weight to the human capacity for change through inten-tional design. This might be seen as a further development of praxis theory, but with a greater emphasis on the conditions for change. Whereas praxis theory appears more preoccupied with social reproduction than with change, the new paradigm takes the aspect of *emergence* in human social reality seriously (Mead 2002 [1932]). Since the present includes both its past and its future potential, anthropologists have to develop ways to include the anticipation and creation of new forms in their ethnographic descriptions and theorizing. Gatt and Ingold (Chapter 8, this volume) point to a possible way to connect with people's future by "correspondence." Thus a social fact is no longer merely seen as the result of human action as in praxis theory, but as something that carries the potential of change in its very execution. A new criterion of success would be how design anthropologists are able to correspond and collaborate with people as co-creators of desirable futures and to be the facilitators of knowledge and meaningful practices that transform the present.

Designing and intervening in social and cultural contexts is in many ways a large leap for anthropologists. However, we consider this a necessary step in the face of contemporary local-global transformations and the corresponding academic requirement of developing responsive conceptual frameworks and interventionist practices. A growing body of literature addresses the entanglement of culture and design from a more transformative and imaginative stance (Balsamo 2011; Dourish and Bell 2011). What emerges from these interdisciplinary approaches to technology and change is that culture and design are not separate analytical domains or extensions of each other. Rather they are deeply entangled, complex, and often messy formations and transformations of meanings, spaces, and interactions between people, objects, and histories. It appears now an accepted premise that culture is always already an ingrained and situated part of design practices, but the reverse is equally valid and relevant: by designing objects, technologies, and systems, we are in fact designing cultures of the future (Balsamo 2011).

Designerly ways of thinking and acting are competences more and more sought after in contemporary society. There is an increasing focus from creative industries, government organizations, universities, and design schools alike on the potential impact of design and innovation on solving pressing societal issues. This is connected with fundamental shifts in the global economies from the West to the East, the rapid advance and development of information technologies, and the growing ethical, political, social, and ecological concerns of sustainability (Friedman 2012; Fry 2011). These emergent markets for design in different local and global contexts are at once compelling and fraught. Their promise is to create sustainable, innovative, and financially potent solutions to socioeconomic issues around the world. However, as critics point out (Chapter 13, this volume; Hunt 2011; Latour 2008; Suchman 2011), such ventures need to set modest and realistic goals, build upon humanistic approaches, and foster sensitivity to the cultural and socioeconomic contexts and values of local populations to create sustainable and morally justifiable change and to avoid recasting users as natives and replicating forms of colonialism that anthropology was a part of during the twentieth century. It is in this context that design anthropology finds its place, opportunity, and challenge.

ASPECTS OF DESIGN ANTHROPOLOGY

This section discusses key aspects of design anthropology as a style of knowledge production and practical intervention that straddles two separate knowledge traditions with markedly different objectives, epistemic assumptions, and methods. We sketch key aspects of this style of knowing and introduce the following chapters under the four headings that provide the book's overarching structure.

Concepts, Methods, and Practices

As a contrast with classical ethnography, design anthropologists generally do not engage in long-term fieldwork in one particular social and cultural setting, but rather carry out a series of shorter field studies and interventions, often in different social and cultural settings. In addition they have a specific approach to the use of theory and the generation of new concepts. Malinowski pointed to the key role of theoretical concepts in ethnographic research (1922: 9). For him, these concepts should alert the researcher to "foreshadowed problems" that open up for further questioning and investigation.[13] In later methodological literature, these concepts have been named "sensitizing concepts" (Van den Hoonaard 1997). Whereas these concepts guide the empirical research process and ethnographic description, the role of concepts in design anthropology moves beyond analysis and description to the generation of *design concepts*.

Adam Drazin (Chapter 2, this volume) gives a careful analysis of the role of these design concepts and concludes that they occur in a certain phase of the design process. Whereas the data gathering and analysis at the start of a design project is referred to as *information* or *data*, design concepts happen in the next phase, when designers and researchers work together to sketch emerging ideas, group themes together, and discuss possibilities for development. The design concepts in this phase have a transient and material existence, as they are expressed in drawings, network diagrams, and PowerPoint slides. They are continuously in flux and finally give way to the production of prototypes. Drazin's analysis bears similarity with the bow tie model produced by E-Lab and described by Wasson (2002: 82–83, in particular the second model), where there is a clear transition from data gathering and analysis, to frameworks (the knot in the tie), to design concepts, and then to prototypes. But, in contrast to the E-Lab model, Drazin depicts the development of design concepts as a common endeavor of all team members throughout the process of research and design.

Mette Kjærsgaard (Chapter 3, this volume), in her analysis of a design project for playgrounds in Denmark, presents a similar view on the continuing interaction between designers, design anthropologists, and various other specialists. She focuses on the design workshop as a place where the different perspectives, types of information, materials, and interests are brought together to produce common design concepts. She emphasizes that these different "knowledge pieces," as she calls them, do not neatly fit together as in a jigsaw puzzle. Rather, through a ritualized process of creative juxtaposition, debate, and montage, these pieces are transformed into shared design concepts that form the basis for formulating a design strategy and preparing prototypes. Whereas the design anthropologists are part of the whole process, from the gathering of data, to workshopping the "knowledge pieces" and developing prototypes, Kjærsgaard reserves a specific role for them, based on their disciplinary skills and orientation: to identify implicit assumptions and frameworks in the analysis of data and development of design ideas, thus opening up the design process for alternative solutions through a reframing of these assumptions (see also Suchman 2011).

Kyle Kilbourn (Chapter 4, this volume) develops the idea of design anthropology as a different style of knowing. He argues that the difference with other styles—including anthropology and design—can be found in what design anthropologists use to think with, directing our attention to the tools of their engagement with social reality. Kilbourn distinguishes a number of (non-textual) tools that characterize design anthropological modes of intervention in the field. First, he points to forms of conceptual association and synthesis through visual means ("perceptual synthesis"); second, he describes ways of comparing experiences through games and other means ("experience juxtaposing"); and finally, he mentions various forms of performance as ways to explore the social embeddedness of possible future practices ("potential relationing") (see also Chapter 10, this volume). Kilbourn further discusses the specific form of theoretical practice he finds characteristic of design anthropology, through the consecutive movements of the researcher, first into a specific collaboration and context of practice ("moving in"), then to other contexts that relate to the first one ("moving along"), and finally "moving out" to the critical exploration of potentiality. Thus, he describes an important shift in design anthropology, from using theory primarily to analyze and explain to the generation of conceptual alternatives and future possibilities.

The Materiality of Design

The importance of the materiality and even agency of things for understanding human practice and culture has been highlighted in recent anthropological and philosophical theorizing (Henare, Holbraad, and Wastell 2007; Ingold 2007; Latour 1999; Miller 2005; Verbeek 2005). Although this forms an important theoretical backdrop for analyzing the impact and function of material objects in human society, here we are more concerned with the materiality of the design process itself. With this we refer both to how the manipulation of materials and objects are part of and influence the possibilities of design, and to the concrete practices of exchange and interaction that constitute the design process. Earlier we mentioned how design and design anthropology rely on a range of forms to produce and communicate knowledge in addition to language and text, in particular the material practices of visualization, prototyping, and performance (Chapter 4, this volume). The ethnographic descriptions of design processes presented in Chapters 2 and 3 clearly illustrate the centrality of the material dimension in designing: the importance of the design space and its material tools, the use of concrete, material renderings of "knowledge pieces," and generally the material quality of design concepts. The primary products of design anthropological interventions are not necessarily articles or ethnographic monographs—even though these may be welcome products—but design proposals to be carried out in (material) reality.

Chapters 5 and 6 are ethnographic case studies of design processes, rather than examples of design interventions in which anthropologists participate. These chapters add to our theoretical understanding of how design works and contribute to the reflective practice of design anthropology. Ian Ewart (Chapter 5, this volume) investigates the relation between production and design by comparing the construction of two different bridges in the Kelabit highlands of Borneo. One is a bamboo bridge of a type that is built frequently and habitually by villagers on the basis of an embodied and intuitive design rather than an explicit plan. The other is a new kind of suspension bridge, the construction of which started out with an explicit design drawn on paper, but it was modified to a large extent by practical solutions to unforeseen problems. In spite of the obvious differences between the two processes, Ewart argues that common to both is that design happens as part of production "on the go and in the hand," rather than as a separate stage prior to the process of making.

Elizabeth Hallam (Chapter 6, this volume) also highlights the importance of materiality in processes of designing by focusing on the relationship between design and use of anatomical models employed in the teaching of medical students. It is through the ongoing use of these three-dimensional models in teaching that their limitations are revealed, prompting further design activities to improve the models in a dialogic fashion between students and teachers. Hallam shows how the properties of particular materials, in this case hookup wire, inform the design practice both physically and conceptually, through a process in which critical reflection and embodied practice mutually impact on each other.

Chapter 7 by Rachel Charlotte Smith is a case study of a design anthropological intervention. The overall design framework is posed by the challenge that cultural heritage museums, with their traditional focus on material objects, face in the digital age. To tackle this challenge, the design anthropologist and her design collaborators developed an experimental exhibition project to investigate and give shape to the emerging heritage of so-called digital natives—young people fully immersed in the use of information technologies and digital social media. The project facilitated a dialogic design process involving teenagers, anthropologists, and designers and resulted in the material-digital representation of the emerging sense of identity and heritage among the youngsters through various interactive installations. This case challenges conventional distinctions between the material and the virtual, tangible and intangible heritage, and clearly illustrates the crucial importance of design anthropological interventions in a collaborative exhibition project.

The Temporality of Design

As mentioned previously, the robust future orientation of design is a great challenge for design anthropology, both theoretically and methodologically. Understanding how change happens and how it can be directed by human agency is one of its key theoretical undertakings. Therefore, conceptual and methodological frameworks have to move beyond basic notions of causality and the projection of statistic trends into the future to fully capture the emergent character of the present. According to philosopher G.H. Mead's (2002 [1932]) ideas about the present as the *locus of reality*, we only exist in the present, which is always in a state of emergence. This does not mean that Mead diminishes the existence and relevance of the past and the future, but he emphasizes that these are only accessible as dimensions of the present even though we imagine them as independent and irrevocable entities. In the act of giving shape to the future, we thus evoke a past that makes this future possible.[14] This does not imply that anything goes in the sense of designing a future. To the contrary, the envisaged future has to encompass a possible past, one that does not deny the limiting conditions created by past presents. In line with Mead's vision, the following chapters in various ways move design anthropology's gaze toward the future while at the same time allowing for the past to be a key part of future making. This is important to counteract the generic risk of designerly "hubris" (Suchman 2011: 16) and actual "defuturing" (Fry 2011; Hunt 2011), which is the result of the contraction of the time horizon to the immediate future and a shallow past.

In Chapter 8, Caroline Gatt and Tim Ingold address the theoretical and practical challenge of the changed temporal orientation of design anthropology. They argue that *anthropology-by-means-of-ethnography* has to be replaced by *anthropology-by-means-of-design*. They see ethnography as primarily interested in description, which becomes retrospective once it is completed as a product. In contrast, they argue, anthropology-by-means-of-design should be understood as a practice of *correspondence*. *Correspondence* refers to being in accordance with the flow of events, to moving forward with people in the pursuit of their dreams and aspirations rather than dwelling on their past. Correspondence is about improvisation rather than innovation and about foresight rather than prediction. It is a natural part of participant observation, but with an emphasis on what is produced during fieldwork rather than after fieldwork, such as social relations, practical knowledge, and new practices for the people involved (Glowczewski et al. 2013). Gatt and Ingold call these products "dialogically designed anthropological artifacts" that contribute to the transformational effects of participant observation, or rather "observant participation."

Correspondence is not always easy to establish, and people involved in design have differing views about how to anticipate the future. Wendy Gunn and Christian Clausen (Chapter 9, this volume) look at implicit and contrasting forms of temporality brought into play in the design of indoor climate products and control systems. This industrial field is dominated by engineers and manufacturers who privilege quantitative and technical approaches, which differ from design anthropologists' emphasis on improvisation and design in collaboration with the user-cum-producer. Gunn and Clausen analyze the influence and engagement between these different knowledge traditions in a collaborative design project that stretches over three years. Equally steeped in a concrete case study, Joachim Halse (Chapter 10, this volume) asks the question of how design anthropology can be part of transformative actions instead of only studying them. Inspired by Mead and Kapferer, and working within the Scandinavian tradition of participatory design, he focuses on design events as special generic moments of *becoming* in which people experiment with possible futures. He describes the techniques of collaborative doll scenarios and full-scale enactments and shows how these bring the particularities of place and time into the design process. In this way, design anthropology can contribute by developing particular "technologies of the imagination" that assist people to critically assess, contest, and develop new ideas in specific contexts.

The Relationality of Design

An important distinctive feature of design anthropology is the way its practitioners work in multiple relationships and often complex roles with different stakeholders, including designers, researchers from other disciplines, and sponsors, as well as users and publics. Whereas anthropological participant observation always involves entering relationships at different levels—sometimes sensitive or precarious—with sponsors, doorkeepers, and collaborators, the challenge to design anthropologists appears to be compounded because of design's focus on intervention and change. Thus design anthropologists find themselves working (mostly) in multidisciplinary design teams, alternating between being researchers, facilitators, and co-creators in the design process.

Whereas many of the chapters address these complex relationships (see in particular Chapters 3, 4, 7, 8, 9, and 10, this volume), the chapters in this section address some issues of these relationships in particular.

In Chapter 11, Brendon Clark draws attention to the importance of creating publics for design innovations, which can provide critical feedback on the positive and negative implications of the ideas from different social perspectives. Inspired by DiSalvo (2009), Dewey, and Goffman, Clark argues that these publics are not given and that developing the means for generating them can be part of the work of design anthropology. He illustrates this point with a case study of a second language learning project in Sweden. By organizing a series of collaborative design activities that involved various forms of performance, he was able to generate additional experiential information about potential action and directions for design.

Christina Wasson and Crysta Metcalf (Chapter 12, this volume) discuss the challenges that face anthropologists and designers who wish to collaborate across organizations, in particular between industry and universities. They argue that the development of new industry-academic partnership models has not necessarily made this collaboration easier because of specific transaction barriers that have to do with legal and administrative definitions and implementations of intellectual property rights. The chapter builds on their experience of successful collaboration, over seven years and five projects, between a university professor teaching design anthropology and a research scientist and her team in a private company. Interesting, they assert that the model they have used, which is based on personal relations between the lead researchers rather than on contractual obligations, actually works better than the new industry-academic partnership models.

Dori Tunstall (Chapter 13, this volume) criticizes Western design for potentially continuing the neocolonial attitudes that have historically plagued anthropology, thus affirming existing global inequalities. In her view, design anthropology has a major task in developing a methodology that decolonizes design and anthropological engagement and contributes to a genuine and humane transformation of social relations. In particular she understands design anthropology as pursuing anthropology's major quest of defining what it means to be human by focusing on how design can translate values into tangible experiences. Using her involvement in the Aboriginal Smart Art project as an illustration, she develops a program for a decolonized and humane design anthropology driven by values of creating conditions of compassion among human beings in harmony with their wider environments.

In the epilogue, Keith Murphy and George Marcus address another relational issue pertinent to design anthropology as an emerging style of knowing, namely the overall relationship between the two fields of design and anthropology. They observe that this relationship has been historically one-sided with a dominant emphasis on how anthropology, especially ethnography, can support design rather than the other way around. They find that the time has come to turn this around and look at the ways design practice can benefit the development of an anthropology able to meet the complex challenges of the contemporary world. At the Center for Ethnography at the University of California, Irvine, they experiment with applying various design studio methods to transforming ethnographic practice. This feedback of design into the discipline of anthropology is a worthy conclusion to a book that claims design anthropology has come of age as a distinct style of knowing, with implications for both design and anthropology.

ACKNOWLEDGMENTS

We are grateful to Thomas Binder, Wendy Gunn, and Mette Kjærsgaard for their critical comments and useful suggestions concerning an earlier draft of this introduction. All remaining shortcomings and flaws are of course fully our responsibility.

NOTES

1. The word *design* has a long history of use in English, but the brief definition presented here aims to capture the prevalent meaning in modern usage (see *Oxford English Dictionary*, accessed online October 3, 2012).
2. In the following we use *anthropology* to mean social and cultural anthropology, not the other subdisciplines of the four-field approach popular in the United States: biological anthropology, archaeology, and linguistics.
3. Ethnography also includes other methods such as different forms of interviewing and systematic research of artifacts and documents.
4. There are some notable exceptions, including action research (Huizer 1979; Tax 1952), strands of applied and development anthropology (Gardner and Lewis 1996; Van Willigen, Rylko-Bauer, and McElroy 1989), and the movement to decolonize anthropology (Harrison 2010). See also Flyvbjerg (2001).
5. We are aware that we are making some broad generalizations in this brief introduction for the sake of clarity of our argument. Here and elsewhere it is possible to find exceptions to these general characterizations. In the present case, one can point to architectural theory and critical design, among others.
6. See also Wasson (2000) and Reese (2002) for historical overviews of the collaboration between ethnography and design, particularly in the fields of industrial design, business ethnography, and user-driven innovation.

7. In the Hawthorne studies, anthropologist Lloyd Warner and psychiatrist Elton Mayo collaborated with staff from Harvard University and the Western Electric Company, Chicago. They later founded the Committee on Human Relations in Industry at the University of Chicago and the social research consulting firm Social Research Inc., focusing on business management (Reese 2002).
8. Intel Corporation, IBM, Microsoft, Xerox, and Sapient Corporation employ large numbers of anthropologists in their labs and research units of user experience. Well-known examples of this include anthropologist Melissa Cefkin, employed by IBM, and anthropologist Genevieve Bell, employed by Intel since 1998, who now directs the User Experience Group within Intel Corporation's Digital Home Group in Portland, Oregon.
9. It continues to expand its scope from academic and industrial contexts to corporations and nongovernmental organizations (NGOs) and governmental organizations, as well as partnerships with core institutions such as the American Anthropological Association (AAA) and the National Association of Practicing Anthropologists (NAPA).
10. In Denmark we can mention Clark (2007), Pedersen (2007), Halse (2008), Kilbourn (2010), Kjærsgaard (2011), and Vangkilde (2012).
11. At the time of writing courses in design anthropology were offered by a number of universities including Swinburne University of Technology, University of Aberdeen, University of North Texas, University of Southern Denmark (Mads Clausen Institute), Aarhus University, Harvard Graduate School of Design, as well as the MA in culture, material, and design at University College London (UCL), and the MSc course in design ethnography at University of Dundee. In addition, numerous courses provided by design, architecture, and art schools, introduce various forms of ethnographic research methods, experience research, and social science approaches as part of their curricula.
12. Kwa (2011), who has developed and popularized Crombie's history of scientific thinking, also opts for the term *styles of knowing*.
13. Theoretical concepts should be carefully distinguished from uncritical assumptions, which actually hinder research, as Malinowski makes clear: "Preconceived ideas are pernicious in any scientific work, but foreshadowed problems are the main endowment of a scientific thinker, and these problems are first revealed to the observer by his theoretical studies" (1922: 9).
14. The following quote expresses it beautifully: "Given an emergent event, its relations to antecedent processes become conditions or causes. Such a situation is a present. It marks out and in a sense selects what has made its peculiarity possible. It creates with its uniqueness a past and a future" (Mead 2002 [1932]: 52).

REFERENCES

Anderson, R. J. (1994), "Representations and Requirements: The Value of Ethnography in System Design," *Journal of Human-Computer Interaction*, 9(3): 151–182.

Appadurai, A. (1986), *The Social Life of Things*, Cambridge: Cambridge University Press.

Baba, M. (1986), *Business and Industrial Anthropology: An Overview*, Washington, DC: National Association for the Practice of Applied Anthropology.

Baba, M. (2006), "Anthropology and Business," in H. J. Birx (ed.), *Encyclopedia of Anthropology*, Thousand Oaks, CA: Sage Publications, 83–117.

Balsamo, A. (2011), *Designing Culture: The Technological Imagination at Work*, Durham, NC and London: Duke University Press.

Bannon, L. J. (2005), "A Human-centred Perspective on Interaction Design," in A. Pirhonen, H. Isomaki, C. Roast, and P. Saariluoma (eds.), *Future Interaction Design*, London: Springer.

Bansler, J. (1989), "System Development in Scandinavia: Three Theoretical Schools," *Scandinavian Journal of Information Systems*, 1: 3–20.

Barnett, H. G. (1953), *Innovation: The Basis of Cultural Change*, New York: McGraw-Hill.

Beck, E. (2002), "P for Political: Participation Is Not Enough," *Scandinavian Journal of Information Systems*, 14(1): 25–44.

Bentley, R., Hughes, J., Rodden, T., Sawyer, P., Shapiro, D., and Sommerville, I. (1992), "Ethnographically-informed Systems Design for Air Traffic Control," in *Proceedings of the CSCW '92 Conference on Computer-Supported Cooperative Work*, New York: ACM Press, 123–129.

Binder, T., De Michelis, G., Ehn, P., Jacucci, G., Linde, P., and Wagner, I. (2011), *Design Things*, Cambridge, MA: MIT Press.

Bjerknes, G., Ehn, P., and Kyng, M. (eds.) (1987), *Computers and Democracy: A Scandinavian Challenge*, Aldershot, England: Avebury.

Björgvinsson, E., Ehn, P., and Hillgren, P. A. (2010), "Participatory Design and 'Democratizing Innovation,'" in *PDC '10: Proceedings of the 11th Biennial Participatory Design Conference*, New York: ACM Press, 41–50.

Blomberg, J., Burrell, M., and Guest, G. (2003), "An Ethnographic Approach to Design," in J. Jacko and A. Sears (eds.), *Human Computer Interaction Handbook: Fundamentals, Evolving Technologies and Emerging Applications*, Hillsdale, NJ: Lawrence Erlbaum Associates, 964–986.

Blomberg, J., Giacomi, J., Mosher, A., and Swenton-Wall, P. (1993), "Ethnographic Field Methods and Their Relation to Design," in D. Schuler and A. Namioka (eds.), *Participatory Design: Principles and Practices*, Hillsdale, NJ: Lawrence Erlbaum Associates, 123–155.

Blomberg, J., Suchman, L., and Trigg, R. (1997), "Back to Work: Renewing Old Agenda for Corporative Design," in M. Kyng and L. Mathiassen (eds.), *Computers and Design in Context*, Cambridge, MA: MIT Press.

Bødker, S. (1991), "Cooperative Prototyping: Users and Designers in Mutual Activity," *International Journal of Man-Machine Studies*, 34(3): 453–478.

Bourdieu, P. (1979), *Distinction: A Social Critique of the Judgement of Taste*, London: Routledge and Kegan Paul.

Brown, T. (2009), *Change by Design*, New York: HarperCollins Publishers.

Brown, T., with Katz, B. (2011), "Change by Design," *Journal of Product Innovation Management*, 28(3): 381–383.

Buchanan, R. (1992), "Wicked Problems in Design Thinking," *Design Issues*, 8(2): 5–21.

Button, G. (2000), "The Ethnographic Tradition and Design," *Design Studies*, 21(4): 319–332.

Cefkin, M. (ed.) (2010), *Ethnography and the Corporate Encounter: Reflections on Research in and of Corporations*, New York and Oxford: Berghahn Books.

Cefkin, M. (2012), "Close Encounters: Anthropologists in the Corporate Arena," *Journal of Business Anthropology*, 1(1): 91–117.

Clark, B. (2007), "Design as Sociopolitical Navigation: A Performative Framework for Action-orientated Design," PhD dissertation, Mads Clausen Institute, University of Southern Denmark.

Clarke, A. (ed.) (2011), *Design Anthropology: Object Culture in the 21st Century*, Wien and New York: Springer.

Crombie, A. C. (1988), "Designed in the Mind: Western Visions of Science, Nature and Humankind," *History of Science*, 2: 1–12.

Crombie, A. C. (1994), *Styles of Scientific Thinking in the European Tradition: The History of Argument and Explanation Especially in the Mathematical and Biomedical Sciences and Arts*, 3rd edition, London: Duckworth.

Cross, N. (2006), *Designerly Ways of Knowing*, London: Springer.

Dewey, J. (1980 [1934]), *Art as Experience*, New York: Berkeley Publishing Group.

Dilley, R. (ed.) (1999), *The Problem of Context*, New York and Oxford: Berghahn Books.

DiSalvo, C. (2009), "Design and the Construction of Publics," *Design Issues*, 25(1): 48–63.

Dourish, P. (2001), *Where the Action Is: The Foundations of Embodied Interaction*, Cambridge, MA: MIT Press.

Dourish, P. (2006), "Implications for Design," in *CHI'06 Proceedings of the Conference on Human Factors in Computing Systems*, New York: ACM Press, 541–550.

Dourish, P. (2007), "Responsibilities and Implications: Further Thoughts on Ethnography and Design," in *DUX '07 Proceedings of the Conference on Designing for User Experience*, New York: ACM Press, 2–16.

Dourish, P., and Bell, G. (2011), *Divining a Digital Future: Mess and Mythology in Ubiquitous Computing*, Cambridge, MA: MIT Press.

Ehn, P. (1988), *Work-oriented Design of Computer Artifacts*, Stockholm: Arbet-slivscentrum.

Ehn, P. (1993), "Scandinavian Design: On Participation and Skill," in D. Schuler and A. Namioka (eds.), *Participatory Design: Principles and Practices*, Hillsdale, NJ: Lawrence Erlbaum Associates, 41–77.

Faubion, J. D., and Marcus, G. E. (eds.) (2009), *Fieldwork Is Not What It Used to Be: Learning Anthropology's Method in a Time of Transition*, Ithaca, NY and London: Cornell University Press.

Flyvbjerg, B. (2001), *Making Social Science Matter: Why Social Inquiry Fails and How It Can Succeed Again*, Cambridge: Cambridge University Press.

Forsythe, D. E. (1999), "It Is Just a Matter of Common Sense: Ethnography as Invisible Work," *Computer Supported Cooperative Work*, 8: 127–145.

Friedman, K. (2002), "Conclusion: Towards an Integrative Design Discipline," in S. Squires and B. Byrne (eds.), *Creating Breakthrough Ideas: The Collaboration of Anthropologists and Designers in the Product Development Industry*, Westport, CT and London: Bergin and Garvey, 199–214.

Friedman, K. (2012), "Models of Design: Envisioning a Future Design Education," *Visible Language*, 46(1/2): 132–153.

Fry, T. (2009), *Design Futuring: Sustainability, Ethics and New Practice*, Oxford: Berg.

Fry, T. (2011), *Design as Politics*, New York: Berg.

Gardner, K., and Lewis, D. (1996), *Anthropology, Development and the Post-Modern Challenge*, London: Pluto Press.

Garfinkel, H. (1967), *Studies in Ethnomethodology*, Englewood Cliffs, NJ: Prentice-Hall Inc.

Garfinkel, H. (2002), *Ethnomethodology's Program: Working Out Durkheim's Aphorism*, Lanham, MD: Rowman and Littlefield.

Gaver, W. (2012), "What Should We Expect from Research through Design," in *CHI '12 Proceedings of the Conference on Human Factors in Computing Systems*, New York: ACM Press, 937–946.

Geertz, C. (1973), *The Interpretation of Cultures*, New York: Harper Collins.

Gell, A. (1998), *Art and Agency: An Anthropological Theory*, Oxford and New York: Oxford University Press.

Gellner, D., and Hirsch, E. (eds.) (2001), *Inside Organizations: Anthropologists at Work*, Oxford: Berg.

Glowczewski, A., Henry, R., and Otto, T. (2013), "Relations and Products: Dilemmas of Reciprocity in Fieldwork," *The Asia Pacific Journal of Anthropology*, 14(2): 113–125.

Gray, P. (2010), "Business Anthropology and the Culture of Product Managers," AIPMM, Association of International Product Marketing and Management, Newsletter, August 10, 2010. Available at: www.aipmm.com/html/newsletter/archives/BusinessAnthroAndProductManagers.pdf. Accessed October 23, 2012.

Greenbaum, J., and Kyng, M. (eds.) (1991), *Design at Work: Cooperative Design of Computer Systems*, Hillsdale, NJ: Lawrence Erlbaum Associates.

Gunn, W., and Donovan, J. (eds.) (2012), *Design and Anthropology*, Farnham: Ashgate.

Hacking, I. (1992), " 'Style' for Historians and Philosophers," *Stud. Hist. Phil. Sci.*, 23(1): 1–20.

Hallam, E., and Ingold, T. (eds.) (2007), *Creativity and Cultural Improvisation*, Oxford: Berg.

Halse, J. (2008), "Design Anthropology: Borderline Experiments with Participation, Performance and Situated Intervention," PhD dissertation, IT University Copenhagen.

Harper, R. H. (2000), "The Organisation in Ethnography: A Discussion of Ethnographic Fieldwork Programs in CSCW," *Computer Supported Cooperative Work*, 9: 239–264.

Harrison, F. (2010), "Anthropology as an Agent of Transformation," in F. Harrison (ed.), *Decolonizing Anthropology: Moving Further toward an Anthropology for Liberation*, 3rd edition, Arlington, VA: Association of Black Anthropologists, American Anthropological Association, 1–14.

Heath, C., and Luff, P. (1992), "Collaboration and Control: Crisis Management and Multimedia Technology in London Underground Control Rooms," *Computer Supported Cooperative Work*, 1: 69–94.

Helander, M. G. (1997), "The Human Factors Profession," in G. Salvendy (ed.), *Handbook of Human Factors and Ergonomics*, New York: John Wiley and Sons, 1637–1688.

Henare, A., Holbraad, M., and Wastell, S. (2007), *Thinking through Things: Theorizing Artefacts Ethnographically*, London and New York: Routledge.

Holy, L. (1984), "Theory, Methodology and the Research Process," in R. Ellen (ed.), *Ethnographic Research: A Guide to General Conduct*, London: Academic Press, 13–43.

Huizer, G. (1979), "Research-through-Action: Some Practical Experiences with Peasant Organisations," in G. Huizer and B. Mannheim (eds.), *The Politics of Anthropology: From Colonialism and Sexism toward a View from Below*, The Hague: Mouton, 395–420.

Hunt, J. (2011), "Prototyping the Social: Temporality and Speculative Futures at the Intersection of Design and Culture," in A. Clarke (ed.), *Design Anthropology: Object Culture in the 21st Century*, Wien and New York: Springer, 33–44.

Ingold, T. (2001), "Beyond Art and Technology: The Anthropology of Skill," in B. Schiffer (ed.), *Anthropological Perspectives on Technology*, Albuquerque: University of New Mexico Press, 17–31.

Ingold, T. (2007), "Materials against Materiality," *Archaeological Dialogues*, 14(1): 1–16.

Ingold, T. (2011), *Being Alive: Essays on Movement, Knowledge and Description*, London: Routledge.

Ingold, T. (2012), "Introduction: The Perception of the User-producer," in W. Gunn and J. Donovan (eds.), *Design and Anthropology*, Farnham: Ashgate, 1–17.

Iversen, O. S., and Smith, R. C. (2012), "Scandinavian Participatory Design: Dialogic Curation with Teenagers," in *IDC'12 Proceedings of the 11th International Conference on Interaction Design and Children,* New York: ACM Press, 106–115.

Jiménez, A. (ed.) (2007), *The Anthropology of Organizations*, Aldershot: Ashgate.

Jordan, A. (2003), *Business Anthropology*, Long Grove, IL: Waveland Press.

Kensing, F., and Blomberg, J. (1998), "Participatory Design: Issues and Concerns," *Computer Supported Cooperative Work*, 7(3/4): 167–185.

Kilbourn, K. (2010), "The Patient as Skilled Practitioner," PhD dissertation, Mads Clausen Institute, University of Southern Denmark.

Kjærsgaard, M. (2011), "Between the Actual and the Potential: The Challenges of Design Anthropology," PhD dissertation, Department of Culture and Society, Aarhus University.

Kwa, C. (2011), *Styles of Knowing: A New History of Science from Ancient Times to the Present*, Pittsburgh, PA: University of Pittsburgh Press.

Kyng, M. (2010), "Bridging the Gap between Politics and Techniques," *Scandinavian Journal of Information Systems*, 22(1): 49–68.

Latour, B. (1999), *Pandora's Hope, An Essay on the Reality of Science Studies*, Cambridge, MA: Harvard University Press.

Latour, B. (2008), "A Cautious Prometheus? A Few Steps toward a Philosophy of Design (with special attention to Peter Sloterdijk)," Keynote lecture for the Networks of Design meeting of the Design History Society (UK), Falmouth, Cornwall, September 3, 2008. Available at: www.bruno-latour.fr/sites/default/files/112-DESIGN-CORNWALL-GB.pdf. Accessed November 17, 2012.

Liep, J. (ed.) (2001), *Locating Cultural Creativity*, London: Pluto Press.

Malinowski, B. (1922), *Argonauts of the Western Pacific*, London: George Routledge & Sons.

Marcus, G. E. (1998), *Ethnography through Thick and Thin*, Princeton, NJ: Princeton University Press.

McCarthy, J., and Wright, P. (2004), *Technology as Experience*, Cambridge, MA and London: MIT Press.

Mead, G. H. (2002 [1932]), *The Philosophy of the Present*, Amherst, NY: Prometheus Books.

Miller, D., (ed.) (2005), *Materiality*, Durham, NC and London: Duke University Press.

Muller, M. J. (2002), "Participatory Design: The Third Space in HCI," in J. A. Jacko and A. Sears (eds.), *The Human Computer Interaction Handbook*, Mahwah, NJ: Lawrence Erlbaum Associates, 1051–1068.

Nafus, D., and Anderson, K. (2006), "The Real Problem: Rhetorics of Knowing in Corporate Ethnographic Research," *in EPIC 2006, Proceedings of the Ethnographic Praxis in Industry Conference,* 244–258.

Nelson, H. G., and Stolterman, E. (2003), *The Design Way: Intentional Change in an Unpredictable World*, Englewood Cliffs, NJ: Educational Technology Publications.

Nelson, H. G., and Stolterman, E. (2012), *The Design Way: Intentional Change in an Unpredictable World*, 2nd edition, Cambridge, MA: MIT Press.

Orr, J. (1996), *An Ethnography of a Modern Job*, Ithaca, NY: Cornell University Press.

Ortner, S. (2006), *Anthropology and Social Theory: Culture, Power, and the Acting Subject*, Durham, NC and London: Duke University Press.

Otto, T., and Bubandt, N. (eds.) (2010), *Experiments in Holism: Theory and Practice in Contemporary Anthropology*, Oxford: Wiley-Blackwell.

Pedersen, J. (2007), "Protocols of Research and Design: Reflections on a Participatory Design Project (Sort Of)," PhD dissertation, IT University Copenhagen.

Rabinow, P., and Marcus, G. E., with Faubion, J. D., and Rees, T. (2008), *Designs for an Anthropology of the Contemporary*, Durham, NC: Duke University Press.

Redström, J. (2012), "Introduction: Defining Moments," in W. Gunn and J. Donovan (eds.), *Design and Anthropology*, Farnham: Ashgate, 83–99.

Reese, W. (2002), "Behavioral Scientists Enter Design: Seven Critical Histories," in S. Squires and B. Byrne (eds.), *Creating Breakthrough Ideas: The Collaboration of Anthropologists and Designers in the Product Development Industry*, Westport, CT and London: Bergin and Garvey, 17–44.

Sanders, L. (2008), "An Evolving Map of Design Practice and Design Research," *Interactions*, 15(6): 13–17.

Schön, D. A. (1987), *Educating the Reflective Practitioner: Toward a New Design for Teaching and Learning in the Professions*, San Francisco, CA: Jossey-Bass Publishers.

Schön, D. A (1991 [1983]), *The Reflective Practitioner: How Professionals Think in Action*, New York: Basic Books.

Schuler, D., and Namioka, A. (1993), *Participatory Design: Principles and Practices*, Hillsdale, NJ: Lawrence Erlbaum Associates.

Schwartzman, H. (1993), *Ethnography in Organizations*, London: Sage Publications.

Sellen, A., Rogers, Y., Harper, R., and Rodden, T. (2009), "Reflecting Human Values in the Digital Age," *Communications of the ACM*, 52(3): 58–66.

Sengers, P., Boehner, K., David, S., and Kaye, J. (2005), "Reflective Design," in *CC '05, Proceedings of the 4th Conference on Critical Computing*, New York: ACM Press, 49–58.

Sennett, R. (2008), *The Craftsman,* New Haven, CT: Yale University Press.

Shapiro, D. (1994), "The Limits of Ethnography: Combining Social Sciences for CSCW," in *CSCW' 94, Proceedings of the Conference on Computer Supported Cooperative Work*, Chapel Hill, NC: ACM Press, 417–428.

Simonsen, J., and Robertson, T. (eds.) (2012), *Routledge International Handbook of Participatory Design*, London: Routledge.

Squires, S., and Byrne, B. (eds.) (2002), *Creating Breakthrough Ideas: The Collaboration of Anthropologists and Designers in the Product Development Industry*, Westport, CT and London: Bergin and Garvey.

Star, S. L. (1999), "The Ethnography of Infrastructure," *American Behavioral Scientist*, 43(3): 377–391.

Stocking, G. W. (1983), "The Ethnographer's Magic: Fieldwork in British Anthropology from Tylor to Malinowski," in G. W. Stocking (ed.), *Observers Observed: Essays on Ethnographic Fieldwork*, History of Anthropology Series, Madison: University of Wisconsin Press, 1: 70–120.

Stocking, G. W. (ed.) (1991), *Colonial Situations: Essays on the Contextualization of Ethnographic Knowledge*, History of Anthropology Series, Vol. 7. Madison: University of Wisconsin Press.

Stolterman, E. (2008), "The Nature of Design Practice and Implications for Interaction Design Research," *International Journal of Design*, 2(1): 55–65.

Suchman, L. (1987), *Plans and Situated Actions*, Cambridge: Cambridge University Press.

Suchman, L. (2007), *Human-machine Reconfigurations: Plans and Situated Actions*, 2nd edition, New York: Cambridge University Press.

Suchman, L. (2011), "Anthropological Relocations and the Limits of Design," *Annual Review of Anthropology*, 40: 1–18.

Suchman, L., Trigg, R., and Blomberg, J. (2002), "Working Artefacts: Ethnomethods of the Prototype," *British Journal of Sociology*, 53(2): 163–179.

Suri, J. F. (2011), "Poetic Observation: What Designers Make of What They See," in A. Clarke (ed.), *Design Anthropology: Object Culture in the 21st Century*, Vienna and New York: Springer.

Tax, S. (1952), "Action Anthropology," *America Indigenia*, 12: 103–109.

Van den Hoonaard, W. C. (1997), *Working with Sensitizing Concepts: Analytical Field Research*, Qualitative Research Methods Series, Vol. 41, Thousand Oaks, CA: Sage Publications.

Vangkilde, K. T. (2012), "Branding HUGO BOSS: An Anthropology of Creativity in Fashion," PhD dissertation, Faculty of Social Sciences, Department of Anthropology, University of Copenhagen.

Van Veggel, R. (2005), "Where the Two Sides of Ethnography Collide," *Design Issues*, 21(3): 3–16.

Van Willigen, J., Rylko-Bauer, B., and McElroy, A. (eds.) (1989), *Making Our Research Useful: Case Studies in the Utilization of Anthropological Knowledge*, Boulder, CO: Westview Press.

Verbeek, P.-P. (2005), *What Things Do: Philosophical Reflections on Technology, Agency and Design*, University Park: Pennsylvania State University Press.

Verbeek, P.-P. (2012), "Introduction: Humanity in Design," in W. Gunn and J. Donovan (eds.), *Design and Anthropology*, Farnham: Ashgate, 163–176.

Vygotsky, L. S. (1978), *Mind and Society*, Cambridge, MA: Harvard University Press.

Wallman, S. (ed.) (1979), *Social Anthropology of Work*, London: Academic Press.

Wasson, C. (2000), "Ethnography in the Field of Design," *Human Organization*, 59(4): 377–388.

Wasson, C. (2002), "Collaborative Work: Integrating the Roles of Ethnographers and Designers," in S. Squires and B. Byrne (eds.), *Creating Breakthrough Ideas: The Collaboration of Anthropologists and Designers in the Product Development Industry*, Westport, CT and London: Bergin and Garvey, 71–90.

Wright, S. (ed.) (1994), *Anthropology of Organizations*, London and New York: Routledge.

Ybema, S., Yanow, D., Wels, H., and Kamsteeg, F. (eds.) (2009), *Organizational Ethnography: Studying the Complexity of Everyday Life*, London: Sage Publications.

Zimmerman, J. (2009), "Designing for the Self: Making Products that Help People Become the Person They Desire to Be," in *CHI'09, Proceedings of the Conference on Human Factors in Computing Systems,* New York: ACM Press, 395–400.

SECTION I

CONCEPTS, METHODS, AND PRACTICES

2

The Social Life of Concepts in Design Anthropology

Adam Drazin

Anthropology's turn to the material in recent decades has problematized notions of knowledge as abstract, and engagements with design (which can imply progress) are confronting a reticence in anthropological understandings to engage with causality by adopting agendas over the material world. I elaborate on the material culture of design concepts, and rituals of creativity, in an EU-funded design program at TU/e Eindhoven, HP Labs, and Intel Digital Health Group. An exaggerated interest with artifactuality characterizes the treatment of ethnographic knowledge. *Concept* is here the name given to knowledge at the interface of the material and immaterial, existing as a flux whose social life is given momentum by an iterative oscillation between research group and field site in which each alternately assumes the role of critical subject. Such processes can lead to different understandings of social practice from traditional ethnographic processes. I advocate a renewed attention to using iterative design processes for the anthropological process and, independently of research praxis, theoretical attention to critical materialist approaches (Coole and Frost 2010; Tilley 2000).

SPACES FOR DOING DESIGN ETHNOGRAPHY

"Do you have a room?" a design anthropologist in a multinational company asked me recently. We were discussing what were the key elements in a design ethnography course.[1] I talked about our negotiations with the university for some work space where people could conduct research on design and culture. "No," he said, "a room—with whiteboards and all that." The kind of room meant in this simple phrase "a room" will be familiar to any reader who has worked in a corporate or public sector environment where some kind of participatory creative work is involved. From Hong Kong to New York, one can find oneself entering these distinctive spaces located in the bowels of office buildings. Usually the room is oblong. At the center is a table or set of tables. At the periphery are whiteboards, flip charts, and supplies of assorted stationary. Various colors of markers are available, as well as Post-it notes. There are ways of sticking paper to the walls—sticky pads or magnets or white-tack. There is often some way of projecting computer images on the wall, although this is less important. All of this is encompassed somehow in a separate space, so that a group can close the door behind itself. Outside are small offices or open-plan areas where people work individually, together; inside, groups work together away from other people.

Having a room is not just useful, but about recognition and corporate approval of both the group and of its work, which is collaborative. Professional design is constituted as a site through such signifiers: distinctive practices, places, and material culture, which remind us how creativity can be cultural more than actual (Hallam and Ingold 2007). The idea of this field as *a design culture*, one among many, is the conceit upon which this chapter is based. I consider that design is relevant because of its social and cultural engagements first, and secondarily because of its technical achievements. So we should begin with exploring the cultures of professional collaborative design in order to think about the wider cultural fields of design and its paradigmatic ramifications in the world.

Of course, design practices vary a great deal, and these observations are based on my own limited experience from 2000 to 2011, but they represent a recognizable thread within design practice, particularly those areas that overlap with human-computer interaction (HCI) and often deploy ethnographic methods and anthropological traditions of thinking. By *anthropological thinking*, I mean only that an element of the work is aimed at sociocultural understanding or interpretation, and in some instances at theorizing culture, but the actual approaches can vary tremendously from, for example, the United States to Scandinavia to Japan. Importantly, this research does not just move from social research to designing a product or service, but is iterative, moving back and forth between field site and design studio. As I am an anthropologist, by definition the projects I have been involved in have been collaborations between design and anthropological skill sets and are, in this sense of a meeting or recombination of skills, design anthropology.[2] I have written elsewhere about the emergence of this term, the way its work can be characterized, and some of its effects (Drazin 2012). This chapter, however, is not about disciplinary labels, which are of less concern in many research environments than pragmatic considerations of what pools of skills are available to address research issues as they unfold. Rather, I am focusing on *concepts* as a cultural phenomenon in specific instances of design in order to reflect on whether professional design culture may have ramifications in a broader, global, everyday cultural field of design.

I am not at this stage going to define what a concept is in explicit terms, or what sorts of concepts exist. I am concerned with the generalizable ways concepts work, within cultures of knowledge, through exploring the particular aspects of design concepts within design culture (within which, as a rule, many people talk about *concepts* as shorthand for *design concepts*). One of the characteristics of concepts in this instance is that people frequently try to define concepts and subtypes of concepts (design concepts, anthropological concepts, philosophical concepts, etc.), and deny that things that do not fit their own definitions are concepts. Hence the kinds of design concepts found in a more artistic approach such as critical design (Dunne 2008) may be unrecognizable to those with a more scientific or engineering-based notion of design concepts (Imaz and Benyon 2006). Many different design groups have very specific definitions of what they consider design concepts—notable would be the SPIRE group, which specifically defines design concepts and anthropological concepts—but other design groups work with different, equally specific definitions. Considering the cultural construction of concepts, the debates and contestations around concepts, the unfolding and changing act of definition, and the qualities of recognizability or discoverability of concepts are of more interest than any individual definition. Concepts in effect participate in a meta-field of cultures of knowledge, negotiating not only what is known, but ways of knowing, how, and by whom.

I am taking a descriptive approach here, not a prescriptive or definitive one, such that in effect, we can recognize design concepts and concepts in terms of how they occur as a part of what designers do, even if at times there is contradiction within design culture about concepts. The virtue of a descriptive approach is that we can treat the terms we use as emergent more than predefined, and avoid the very real risk of tautology. An authoritative account of concepts aspires to inquire into thought, but it is not possible to absolutely know *how* people think internally: and *what* is easier than *how*. As anthropology and design overlap, they change (Ingold 2011, for example, argues convincingly for anthropology becoming an experimental science). Processes of thinking and interpretation become increasingly collaborative and artifactual, such that to define what concepts are in relation to predefined notions of thinking (design thinking or anthropological thinking) would pre-suggest a cerebral ontological model of a particular kind. A descriptive exploration into the material culture of design anthropology work is, I suggest, a useful approach given this risk of tautology.

One of the common characteristics of work around design concepts is the drive to make and deploy material objects, a process in which the object is not a representation of thought but is a manifest thought. Objects are here material artifacts—paper, Post-Its, slides, white boards. Insofar as the design concept is also a thought and has social properties, it can also be treated as *a thing* (Henare, Holbraad, and Wastell 2007)—a thing may also be immaterial, while an object is normally a material kind of thing. Concepts may also have some of the characteristics of *design things* (Binder et al. 2011), which is a more specific use of the term, as well as describing a design agenda. In sum, I argue that design concepts are culturally specific constructs that have particular material and temporal properties, and that the cultural variability of concepts merits wider exploration because concepts have a much broader potential impact in the global world than just design studios.

DESIGN WORK AS A SITE OF CULTURAL PRODUCTION

Design has been receiving increasing attention in recent years as a cultural site. Much of this takes the form of cultural studies commentaries (see Julier 2007). Contemporary rubrics of "knowledge economies" or the need for "innovation" show how design work is often seen as emblematic of social progress. In economic and political terms, especially in recessions, design has a redeeming quality. Moles (2002) asks what this means for design and materiality: Do people working in design *do* design in a materially creative process, or transact abstract design concepts more? Undoubtedly, immaterial things are given a privileged value of a very real and economically transactable kind.

Because of the prevalence of discourses of the knowledge economy, and debates about what "national innovation systems" (Brøgger 2009) comprise, it is of prime importance to pay close attention to what a design concept is in cultural terms. Design is not a politically or socially neutral space. Concepts are increasingly phenomena that mediate what kinds of relationships individual people, citizens, consumers, and users have with governments, corporations, and international bodies. An interest in the production sites of concepts (such as design studios) is potentially as significant now as the study of scientific laboratories and the production of scientific facts was for critical studies of modernism, and the study of art practice has been for art (Jacob and Grabner 2010). Groundbreaking laboratory studies in science and technology studies have included Latour and Woolgar (1979), Knorr Cetina (1981), and Pinch (1986) among others. Doing (2007) is critical of some of the claims made for work on laboratories, arguing that major claims were made about *facts* based on relatively few studies. The social study of art, meanwhile, has not looked as much at production as on artifacts and their interrelationship with thought (Gell 1998). Morphy (2010) moves away from the rootedly "material" approaches to art, arguing for seeing it as "a form of intentional human action." Compared with labs, art studios, and craft workshops, the design studio has remained relatively obscure as a site of cultural production. Architectural studios have been studied by a range of researchers (Schaffer 2003; Yaneva 2009). Current doctoral research concerning architectural design process and practice, such as that carried out by Hagen (2011) in Oslo, is being conducted in a number of universities. Other design workplaces have been discussed by Coles (2012); Luff, Heath, and Hindmarsh (2000); Hughes and colleagues (1994); and Schön (1985).

Anthropologists in corporate design environments, meanwhile, have been writing highly self-reflexively and critically about their own practices, purposes, and vocations (Blomberg, Burrell, and Guest 2002; Cefkin 2009; Dourish and Bell 2011; Salvador, Bell, and Anderson 1999; Simonsen and Robertson 2012; Squires and Byrne 2002), and arguably more reflexively than anthropologists in academia (Blomberg 2009). Nafus and Anderson (2009) reflect on the significance of design room usage. They outline a project at Intel where a wall collage of a British street moved internationally from one Intel office to another, acquiring more and more post-it notes, commentaries, and evidence of "thinking." This reminds us of the advice from Kelley that "the space remembers" (2001: 59).

Elsewhere (Drazin and Garvey 2009), I have argued that design merits attention as a cultural field in itself, not only as a kind of overlap between art and science or technology. At a popular level, the idea of design provides one way everyone may think about and negotiate subject-object relationships in everyday life, and has particular social effects in the world. Many designed objects act like invitations to belong, offering the possibility of social inclusion or exclusion.

In this chapter, I consider cultures of *knowledge* in design. The design concept is one of the significant compass points of this type of design work, that is an iterative design process aiming toward products or services and drawing on what is called *contextual work*. Teams can emerge from their rooms with newly created design concepts, or, alternatively, enter rooms with concepts to demolish. Design concepts are one measure of the work, and they vary and are continually assessed and debated. I ask how and why the *concept* is an appropriate way of packaging knowledge within design arenas, rather than alternatives such as facts or ideas. Second, can the design concept inform our understandings of *material culture*? Third, can concepts be useful for *anthropological* work and practice?

Observations expressed here are based on my own experience of working as a design anthropologist with three major high-tech multinationals and three major European design schools. This informal, partial, and subjective experience is supplemented by ethnographic research conducted as part of the EU-funded FP6 CHIL project,[3] where I conducted participant observation in projects by industrial design students and in collaborative meetings in various departments of the Dutch government.

During iterative, user-centered design work, concepts are talked about at particular moments—by which I mean there are particular times and places when knowledge, in its various forms, is explicitly considered a concept or concepts. Very often, work begins with exploring a space where design is supposed to have an impact—this is usually linked to the context, the market, or the user for the design, and so a group outlines what I as an anthropologist would call a field site to conduct social research. The field site could be in one place or be distributed across interconnecting sites, according to what makes sense for the project. Information about the field site, however, is not referred to as concepts. For example, a profile of a person, a video clip, or a collage of photographs of a hospital ward is not a concept, it is just information. At a later stage in the design process, a prototype of a product or service may be produced—again, this is not necessarily a concept. Typically, in between these stages is a phase when people sketch out ideas, group their observations, interpretations, and thoughts thematically, and work with representations of possibility. The term *concept* is useful during this phase.

A concept could be a clustering of observations arising from ethnography, which seem somehow related, but for which there is no actual design. The concept is here a space of possibility, not a proposal. A concept could also be a clearly planned drawing of a device that sets out a very specific situation of use, but a device that has not (yet) been prototyped. As the design work continues, it moves further away from the language of the concept. For example, you might have a sketch of a mobile phone that is talked of as the concept— then a model of the phone in polystyrene that, although not a working prototype, is referred to not as the concept but as "demonstrating the concept."

There is often a crucial preparatory phase for any design meeting, involving creating a spatial, physical, and informational void. Any evidence of previous work or activity is cleared away. This means charts, models, coffee cups, packets—traces of previous collaborative efforts. If the markers or post-its are spread across the desk, they are reordered or put back into a cup. Space should be made on the whiteboards, and decisions are made about what to erase or keep. Whiteboards are cleaned with elbow grease and effort, not just erasing writing but even the most minute traces, ticks, and ghostly shapes of prior work. Ideally, a whiteboard should appear as new, whiter than white, and fresh. This voiding is about present physical artifacts, but it is also temporal. A new group work horizon is established. The starting moment to a design meeting should be made or created, and recognizable.

What is being done in the meeting space is simultaneously being done by individuals in their own private work materials. Although no one is actively checking on colleagues, if you look around the room, clutter is gone, books are open, pages are blank, laptop screens show new documents opened. Sometimes, the caps are removed from pens and the pens placed enticingly beside a blank book. Individuals signify their expectation of the commencement of work through spaces about to be filled.

The axis of movement of artifacts in preparation is from inside to outside. The design space is constructed as a space of equals, with no head of the table. At times, the group members are all facing outward, directing their work toward walls; at other times, they are focused on the center, at a model or chart in the middle. There is democracy of a symbolic kind in which different people (except senior managers) play a part in taking notes. You are likely to find administrative staff such as group secretaries at design brainstorms, because everyone's ideas are equally valid; secretaries seem to make good "everybodies," but office cleaners rarely do.

Having *created* a space, an immense effort is then made to mess it all up as much as possible. This is the storming bit in brainstorming, which on occasion involves more storming than brain. Brainstorming alternates between calls to act from rational expertise and subconscious instinct. There is also limited time: in most projects the pressure is on to continuously produce results as soon as possible, quantity first and subsequently quality. There is no perfect product or concept, there is no right answer, the group just has to *do* something to work to the deadline specified.

Design work generally involves a celebration of a sense of freedom of personal choices over the kinds of artifacts produced, through continual declarations that there are no rules. The kinds of objects the group decides to produce are works in progress: spider diagrams, charts, categories, collages, PowerPoint presentations (see Plate 1). Lists are drawn up—variously titled "themes," "observations," "insights." These sorts of artifacts occupy the middle ground in an iterative design process. On one side is research information, sometimes organized into data: field notes, texts, quotes, audio clips, video clips, photographs, and so on. At the other end are finished products of various kinds: reports, concepts, product simulations, patent applications, and so forth. In the middle are various distinctive kinds of material objects suitable to be worked on, reshaped, categorized, defined, sorted, prioritized, and regrouped (see Kjærsgaard, Chapter 3, this volume). These are largely informational, involving paper, whiteboards, post-its, posters, sketches, PowerPoint slides, other presentational aids, and so forth.

The work considered most *creative* in large organizations happens in groups more than individually. The point of the artifactual focus of the work, continually exteriorizing and manifesting knowledge in nugget-sized forms, is that artifacts can be worked on by groups. Text, audio, and video forms of information have a fixed temporal thread, a stream of consciousness that lends itself to individual, not group work, unless properly treated. Groups instead are making associations and divisions between particles of knowledge, and so in this instance an individual must divide up his or her video into clips suitable for group work. Photographs already exist in a particle-like form, and so are often brought en masse into the process, or sometimes selected. Quotations are pulled out in a suitable form from the longer conversations in which they were embedded.

Group work creates objects either in the center or at the periphery of a room, generally alternately. People cluster around a sheet of paper laid flat on the table or in a circle, one or two people typing away on laptops. Then the work may shift toward the walls, drawing on whiteboards, flipcharts, or posters. Post-it notes may be used to record thoughts, to flag up the notable, the bizarre, and the banal, perhaps using different colors for different types or stages of the work. Karen Holtzblatt, for example, has advocated post-its, then blue, pink, and green labels, in that order (Holtzblatt et al. 2005).

As well as the interior-exterior dimension of the group work, which is embodied in the concept of the *room*, there is an articulation of horizontal and vertical ways of working that makes real the possibility of executing informational transformations. Displays and representations on the wall that appear like manifestations of *thoughts* (not only indices of interiorized cerebral processes but materializations of thoughts), for transmission to audiences, become artifacts that are works in progress when taken down and put on the table. While the horizontal dimension does not need to privilege any dimension over another, when on the wall there is a privileging of up and down. This micro-transformation between information that is fit-for-working and fit-to-be-seen is on a small scale an exercise in the kind of transformations of the overall work process, which moves toward a final product or service, and illustrates the mutability of information made material. The material environment enables ways to fix and to liberate collaborative thoughts.

Information *matters* in this process. Working on and around concepts is a social activity. The work that happens around a concept or concepts is represented as moments of unique creativity, but is conducted by routines and ritualization. It pays particular attention to material forms—the paper, its shape and color, is at least as important as what is written on it. Methodologically, in this situation, it is almost impossible to recognize a *unique* moment of creativity. But this is not strange, rather it is a common methodological problem in social science: social meaning must to a certain extent be repeatable if it is to be identifiable and have meaning at all.

In general terms, the concept can be understood as a principle of classification, such that behind any particular thing lies a concept of what *kind* of thing it is. A design concept would then generally be an idea for a sort of product or service, which could be wholly new or could be a redesign. In practice, some design teams or groups have relatively explicit ways of recognizing a concept, while most are more pragmatic. In a social and economic environment that sees its own currency as knowledge, the concept is one way knowledge is defined, packaged, processed, and handled. This happens in actual, material environments with contingent purposes, relationships, identities, and politics. The way concepts happen, are produced, and are transacted is quite particular. We can illustrate this more clearly by comparing concepts with facts and with ideas.

Shanks and Tilley (1992) developed a strong critique of the more scientific tendencies in the field of archaeology through exploring facts. Seeing facts as a form of reification, and also commoditization, of knowledge, they argued that the notion of archaeologists producing facts had particular social and political consequences. The act of materializing knowledge-as-objects had for them an affinity with notions of scientific objectivity. The most important so-cial implication was the assumption that the knowledge might be free from social values. Facts might be circulated and passed from one archaeologist to another, independently of the originator of the fact. Many facts thus are not supposed to be made, so much as discovered. In sum, facts fit particular cul-tural and social requirements. They represent themselves as knowledge with-out social biography, moving without footprints nor lasting associations. But in fact, Shanks and Tilley argued, they do have social lives, and to say otherwise is a pretense. Archaeological facts purport to be descriptive of society when actually being prescriptive.

In design and design anthropology work, the design concept has particu-lar characteristics. It is for a start material, with physical form, in spite of the apparent dictionary definition of the term, which implies a pure thought. As a rule, thoughts in design work are referred to as ideas. If someone has some-thing in mind, it is an idea, not a concept, until that moment when he or she begins to try to sketch it out, to do it, to make it count within the group, and at this moment the term *concept* may begin to be used. In this sense, design concepts are immanent concepts in philosophical terms (Price 1954; see also Deleuze 2001).

Design concepts happen at particular borderline moments in work, and may be described as processes or a flux. They happen at the border between the interiorized thought and the exteriorized object, a moment when, strictly speaking, neither the thought nor the eventual designed product or service actually exists in a coherent form. Design concepts are material in the sense that they consist of matter—they are PowerPoint slides, paper, diagrams—but they are often not objects.

This means that there is a sense of temporal liminality as well. A design concept can be talked about as an aim, the achievement of a possible future product or service. Concepts are soaked with anticipation. Alternatively, it is a term used retrospectively, such that a prototype or simulation on a screen is referred to as demonstrating the concept. The former use of the term implies material pertinence and existence for concepts; the latter use of the term implies that the concept is an abstract that has indications or echoes in the material world, but that is itself immaterial. Design concepts are thus, when considered as part of a design process or workflow, fleeting ways in which one may talk about temporal and material thresholds. Having properties of mate-riality and a degree of discreteness, design concepts are things, and yet are looked back upon, or looked forward to, as much as they are considered in their own terms. Since most design work is not straightforward, but iterative and re-petitive, the work moves back and forth, through preconcept and postconcept moments, as it moves forward, rarely settling on the concept horizon for long.

What design concepts do share with the classical philosophical definition of concepts is categorization. Concepts produce boundaries and enable the grouping of elements in different ways. Frequently, concepts are merged or are separated, but the question is always asked of individual elements: Is this the same concept, or a different one? Is the concept of a hospital service for nurses actually the same concept as a home-care service for patients? They do not have inviolable, bounded discreteness like facts. Rather, they may be molded and disputed, having just enough resistance to gain purchase on them. Concepts are questioned and pummeled continuously in an effort to find out if they will simply fall apart ridiculously, or, through continuous testing, presentation, and handling around, prove to have some kind of integrity.

This means that concepts are rarely individual, but almost invariably social, manifestations of relationships as much as minds (in the Gellian sense—Gell 1998) and actions. Like facts, concepts must have a degree of transactability. Yet they must also retain a certain amount of reference. Concepts simply make no sense if they move too far away from their origination. They have contexts of use and are often connected with particular technologies, manufacturers, or service providers. The implicit purpose in a concept is not necessarily to be moved as far as possible, across the globe if necessary. Rather, in a world of design that is increasingly user centered, concepts are intended to return, not to their specific originators or people who helped create them, but at least to people who are *like* them. They are rather like domesticated facts, allowed to wander to a certain extent but always kept on a leash.

In short, the way concepts are developed, produced, and communicated always has reference to constructions of context (see Dilley 2000). Classical understandings of concepts for an anthropologist would suggest that they are like meanings, ideas, or facts in that they move somehow beyond representation to explain or interpret contextualized referents. This depends on the exact position an individual anthropologist may take on what Herzfeld calls "empirically grounded forms of knowledge" (2001: 4), in which the term *grounded* expresses a connection or reference, which may take a range of forms. Design concepts by contrast are explicated and given meaning by contextual data such as narratives, user studies, interviews, photographs, and so on. In practice, contexts are deployed to explain concepts rather than the other way around.

It is very difficult to identify the moment of development of a concept—the essential story is how knowledge moves through a series of material forms and tweaks. Often the artifactual chain from ethnography to design concept can amount to a chain of smaller steps or a social life (see Kopytoff 1986: 66–67): from encounters with people, to ethnographic data, to representations of contexts, to objects like user profiles and storyboards, to things like design spaces, opportunities, or concepts (see Plate 2). These concepts may travel back into the field repeatedly, in what is called an *iterative* process.

The rural transport research was a piece of work conducted in 2007–2008 by Intel Health Research and Innovation in Europe (previously Intel Digital Health Group). The initial aims were multiple, combining anthropological (to understand the role of isolation and mobility in the lives of older people across rural Ireland) and design aims (turning ethnographic information into credible concepts). Hopefully in the longer-term services, products or other outputs would benefit people like our informants. The gatekeeper was the Irish Rural Transport network, which comprises a raft of organizations across the counties of Ireland. Rural transport organizations vary, but many run minibuses once a week around particular routes. The buses go from door to door in the countryside, picking up mostly elderly passengers at home and bringing them to a central location—a local town or a community center.

In an initial stage of the project, three anthropologists (Adam Drazin, Simon Roberts, and Tina Basi) spent a week in each of five different rural transport organizations, generally on the buses, in the offices, and with assorted passengers at home or visiting shops or at community events. We explored diversity: of size, organizational structure, and geography. We met a wide range of stakeholders: passengers, both on the bus and at home, passengers' relatives, coordinators in the office, drivers, community workers, district nurses, shopkeepers, publicans, and priests. This experience was overwhelming, a celebration of jokes and joyfulness on the buses. It could be intimidating to enter such close-knit groups, and emotional to hear how the advent of the buses had transformed lives. We looked at the rhythm of rural life, how rural inequality can result from mobility rather than wealth, and how a weekly bus ride can open up social networks, possibilities, and aspirations.

The information from the ethnography was collated together in group sessions at Intel, working with video clips, cluster diagrams on whiteboards around particular thematic issues, quotations, and still photographs. We produced a report and convened a two-day meeting with rural transport organizers for their feedback on our observations. Over subsequent months, the group began to build the themes into *concepts*. It was not clear whether these were products, services, or policies at first, nor did we use abstract user profiles or storyboards to present. We worked with the ethnographic data within the team, the members of which were all highly familiar with the material.

A professional designer drafted product concepts as still images or representations; they were critiqued and several were scrapped. Four that remained were developed into interactive screen-based simulations using Flash software. These simulations were often called *demos*, meaning demonstrations, but in conversation we might refer to the four *concepts* as well. It seemed that these simulations had probably already passed a conceptual stage, being more demonstrations of concepts. Yet at the same time, this did not mean that we clearly had four discrete concepts, as the ideas evidently overlapped a great deal, and at times we might refer to having one concept, rather than several. At their root was the use of interfaces and new communication technologies to support the integration of social events and transport, to place mobility at the heart of the social rhythms and initiatives we had witnessed.

The three of us brought four of these demos back to the rural transport projects and, for a couple of days in each place, we showed them to the office staff and the passengers to get their reactions. Through this process, we began to evaluate which concepts had more potential and also envisage specific elements about them—where might these interfaces be located? A home? A church? A rural transport office? A village bus stop? Who uses them, and who has legitimate responsibility for transport? An individual? Their relatives? A community worker? Hospital staff? The publican? Comments were made on the specific forms they took—split screens, maps, or colors.

Discussion of the concepts began to illuminate and problematize particular aspects of the core theme of isolation and mobility. The moment when we presented the concepts also implicated us as anthropologists within the communities and contexts where we worked, and implicated our informants themselves in the concepts and in the particulars of the material forms they took.

The treatment of design concepts, in which ethnographers and anthropologists often participate, indicates an exaggerated concern with the artifactuality of knowledge. This means there is an elective affinity between processes of reification and shifts in the social relationships around the artifactual knowledge. The concepts in question only exist within biographies or work flows that articulate them with notions of context, and only make sense when seen in those terms. This situation suggests that anthropologists and ethnographers working in this area need to think through notions of material things in their own work and understanding. In a sense, every anthropologist who works in or with design has subscribed to materialism, through recognizing the material world as a force for making a difference. This does not mean historical materialism, nor that innovation, products, or technological change are necessarily progressive. Change can be retrogressive, and design anthropology should evidently argue critically against some design. What I mean is that, for better or worse, design is an important fulcrum where potential exists for anthropological engagement with sociocultural issues.

On a broader stage, the material turn in anthropology can be witnessed in sets of ideas such as objectification, embodiment, and phenomenology. Knowledge is increasingly recognized as necessarily embodied or materialized, such that artifacts are not seen as *indices* of immaterial meanings, but *manifestations*. As Bourdieu (1990) writes, anthropological knowledge is itself artifactual, a form of model existing as text. Thus, metaphorical meaning exists in the interrelationships between material objects and forms, not only between material form and immaterial meaning (Tilley 1999). Ingold (2007), in a different way, points out the irony of how the notion of materiality can risk drawing attention away from actually researching material properties. One implication of contemporary materialist thinking is that meanings are much more strongly contested, contestable, and multivariate (Tilley 2000). Design anthropology here begins to explore the move from artifactual meaning to artifactual critique (Lenskjold 2011).

Henare and colleagues (2007) explicitly address the problem of how objects and concepts intersect, proposing that anthropology should focus not less but more on material things, and consider objects in many cases as themselves thoughts. Their argument recognizes an ontological turn in anthropology away from epistemology. They thus recognize that a *thing* itself implies categorization, or a recognition of difference, because the thing is a concept. Their notion of a thing as object-concept contrasts with Ehn's notion of "design things" as gatherings or "socio-material assemblies" (Ehn 2011: 40; Binder et al. 2011). The idea of design things favors design engagements with social practices, and design by doing, more than design by individual thinking or things as thoughts.

There are, then, many tensions implicit within the consideration of design concepts as *things*. How we conceive of these things has much wider implications for how we perceive the contemporary direction of anthropological knowledge, for what practice is, and for design. For these reasons, it is important to direct attention back to the design studio and locales of group work using ethnographic material. I cannot necessarily resolve the debates outlined in this chapter, but I can assert the relevance of my observations about design concepts. Observing studio work tells us we should privilege concepts' temporal qualities and biographies (Kopytoff 1986). As somewhat fleeting objects, they make no sense except in considering that they are as a rule anticipated or viewed retrospectively, the object cotemporaneous with the moment of conception. Iterations of group and individual research work, of studios and field sites, can also be important such that the artifactualized knowledge is cast in different perspectives, in different contexts, and through different ways of knowing. *When* is as important as *what* for design concepts.

PROBLEMS AND POSSIBILITIES OF CONCEPTS

I argue that to talk in terms of concepts is in itself to express particular kinds of processual relationship between yourself and the material world. Concepts facilitate a step away from universals toward specifics and enable mechanisms of measured spatial and temporal distancing. In many ethnographically informed design projects, it is possible to witness the gradual transformation of peoples' experiences into proposals for change, and this is not only justified but demonstrated with quotations or photographs. This happens within the broader patterns and structures of design culture that help people make sense of design socially and culturally, beyond professional circles.

In design culture, concepts are characterized by a compulsion toward the material (not immaterial); are the product of groups (not individual minds);

have reference to particular places (not de-territorialized); and are the product of strongly routinized, even ritualized work. Design concepts are material forms, however transient, without necessarily being objects. Projected Power-Point slides may be ephemeral, but they are as material and physically sensed as a speech, a piece of paper, or a car. It is their material transience that characterizes them. What is important is the temporal dimension and the shifting relations that occur around the concept. In the plethora of stuff, knowledge, and information that pervades design and ethnographic processes, none of it could strictly be pointed out as *self-evidently* a design concept. The state of incipience means that it may be deceptive to attempt to see these entities as objects with some kind of fixity. While they are undoubtedly the focus of fascination, of what one might call fetishism, it is essential to see change as one of their characteristics. Design concepts exist as a kind of *flux*.

This is troubling for anthropology to deal with, partly because it concerns material change. Anthropology lacks terms such as *wavelength* or *frequency* that might describe a flux, or in design language an *iterative* kind of a thing. Rather, most anthropologists' work moves toward fixity in texts, leading Ingold to criticize the perception of anthropological "truth" lying on "the library shelf, groaning under the weight of scholarly books" (2011: 15). Anthropological thinking frequently reflects on the tensions, movements, and transformations between binarisms of potentially fixed states, such as singularization and genericization in social lives (Kopytoff 1986), more than expressing rhythmic forms. This is one area where design and anthropology share a challenge.

Iterative design methodologies can here prove useful in anthropology, in spite of their disenchanting effects (Attfield 1999). It is not the case that concepts are necessarily prescriptive for a context, a predetermining ontology in the same way that Shanks and Tilley (1992) argued about "facts." Concepts are in practice much more malleable, and may be useful when a piece of anthropological work is looking for a process or a way of thinking that is malleable. Concepts and iteration engage a process of knowledge building that involves not so much acts of translation, nor simple drawing of conclusions, but repetitive acts of testing of knowledge to find their fitness. As anthropologists increasingly involve themselves in design work, the question remains whether design concepts are useful for anthropologists to think with. Never mind whether anthropological work can help further design; the point is whether developing concepts can assist in the understanding of social and cultural phenomena. Because of the ways they work, concepts can be helpful in negotiating and contesting not only what we know but how we know. Their advantage in anthropology is their invitation to contextualize thought, incorporating partiality and perspectivality, but accompanying this temporal and contextual referencing comes the inevitability of contestation.

Anthropologists are increasingly carrying out research *of*, *for*, and *with* design and within design studios. I would suggest that this is not only about professional interests and work life but also about the growing significance of the idea of design in everyday life in many parts of the world. As this anthropological work develops, I suggest there is a need to learn from social studies of science and technology, especially work on the production of *facts* in laboratories (Doing 2007), which has led toward considerations of the material world wholly through facticity. Latour's (2005) assertions that matter is itself a politics of causality, and that materialism is another idealism, are both claims which cannot be disputed.

An anthropology *of* design should, therefore, avoid making similar grand claims: the design concept could, if we chose, be understood as one of the cornerstones of a global political order around innovation (Sunley et al. 2008). Companies pursue them. Governments legislate to support them. Ideas of property come to mean intellectual property. Companies' and governments' relationships with their populations come to be signified more through concepts. Yet neither design, nor science, nor art, nor any specific way of characterizing knowledge actually rules above any other in the longer term. My proposal for the way concepts mediate relations with the material world is contingent upon the relevance of design as a cultural field, and on how far we are prepared to admit to the influence of design in the contemporary world beyond the rooms and spaces where people work to make a material difference.

NOTES

1. The course mentioned develops ethnographic methodologies for design engagements and is based in a computer science department, rather than in a design or anthropology department. Emphasis is placed upon applying social science research methods as opposed to design methods or anthropological modes of interpretation. This means that "design ethnography" is how it presents itself, rather than "design anthropology" (see Ingold 2008).
2. *Design anthropology* as a term emerges from the intersection of two disciplinary skill sets that are essentially heuristic and open-ended. Ethnographic skills are traditionally taught in anthropology by leaving the lone researcher to find his or her own feet in a largely alien environment. I would not trust an ethnographer trained by being told what to do at every step. Similar heuristic principles apply in design. Designers or anthropologists are implicitly understood to be formed through experience, developing their own characteristic ways of working and finding the applicability of their tool set themselves. This heuristic quality of skills applies doubly when attempting to define work that alternates between and interweaves design and anthropological practices. There are many ways and reasons

why these two areas are combining and hybridizing productively: the use of *concepts* is one reason, and the one I discuss in this chapter.

3. Computers in the Human Interaction Loop (CHIL) was a project involving a range of university and commercial partners across Europe and the United States that aimed to use embedded computing systems to support work interactions (for example, in meeting rooms) while minimizing the need for physical computers, screens, and interfaces, which often obstruct direct human communication more than they assist it.

REFERENCES

Attfield, J. (1999), *Wild Things*, Oxford: Berg.

Binder, T., De Michelis, G., Ehn, P., Jacucci, G., Linde, P., and Wagner, I. (2011), *Design Things*, Cambridge, MA: MIT Press.

Blomberg, J. (2009), "Insider Trading: Engaging and Valuing Corporate Ethnography," in M. Cefkin (ed.), *Ethnography and the Corporate Encounter*, London: Berghahn, 213–226.

Blomberg, J., Burrell, M., and Guest, G. (2002), "An Ethnographic Approach to Design," in J. Jacko and A. Sears (eds.), *The Human-Computer Interaction Handbook*, Hillsdale, NJ: Lawrence Erlbaum Associates, 964–986.

Bourdieu, P. (1990), "Objectification Objectified," in *The Logic of Practice*, Cambridge: Polity Press, 30–42.

Brøgger, B. (2009), "Economic Anthropology, Trade and Innovation," *Social Anthropology*, 17(3): 318–333.

Cefkin, M. (ed.) (2009), *Ethnography and the Corporate Encounter*, London: Berghahn.

Coles, A. (2012), *The Transdisciplinary Studio*, Berlin: Sternberg Press.

Coole, D., and Frost, S. (2010), "Introducing the New Materialisms," in D. Coole and S. Frost (eds.), *New Materialisms: Ontology, Agency, and Politics*, Durham, NC: Duke University Press, 1–46.

Deleuze, G. (2001), *Pure Immanence: Essays on a Life*, New York: Zone Books.

Dilley, R. (ed.) (2000), *The Problem of Context*, Oxford: Berghahn.

Doing, P. (2007), "Give Me a Laboratory and I Will Raise a Discipline," in E. Hackett, O. Amsterdamska, M. Lynch, and J. Wajcman (eds.), *The Handbook of Science and Technology Studies*, 3rd edition, London: MIT Press, 279–297.

Dourish, P., and Bell, G. (2011), *Divining a Digital Future: Mess and Mythology in Ubiquitous Computing*, London: MIT Press.

Drazin, A. (2012), "Design Anthropology: Working on, with and for Digital Technologies," in H. Horst and D. Miller (eds.), *Digital Anthropology*, Oxford: Berg, 243–265.

Drazin, A., and Garvey, P. (2009), "Design and the Having of Designs in Ireland," *Anthropology in Action*, 16(1): 4–17.

Dunne, A. (2008), *Hertzian Tales: Electronic Products, Aesthetic Experience and Critical Design*, Cambridge, MA: MIT Press.

Ehn, P. (2011), "Design Things: Drawing Things Together and Making Things Public," *Tecnoscienza*, 2(1): 31–52.

Gell, A. (1998), *Art and Agency*, Gloucestershire: Clarendon Press.

Hagen, A.L. (2011), "Striking a Nerve that Opens the Why," in J. Dutton and A. Carlsen (eds.), *Research Alive: Exploring Generative Moments in Doing Qualitative Research*, Copenhagen: Copenhagen Business School Press, 67–70.

Hallam, E., and Ingold, T. (eds.) (2007), *Creativity and Cultural Improvisation*, Oxford: Berg.

Henare, A., Holbraad, M., and Wastell, S. (eds.) (2007), *Thinking through Things: Theorizing Artefacts Ethnographically*, London: Routledge.

Herzfeld, M. (2001), *Anthropology: Theoretical Practice in Culture and Society*, Oxford: Blackwell.

Holtzblatt, K., Burns Wendell, J., and Wood, S. (2005), *Rapid Contextual Design*, London: Elsevier.

Hughes, J., King, V., Rodden, T., and Andersen, H. (1994), "Out of the Control Room: The Use of Ethnography in Systems Design," in *Proceedings of CSCW '94*, Chapel Hill, NC: ACM Press.

Imaz, M., and Benyon, D. (2006), *Designing with Blends: Conceptual Foundations of Human-Computer Interaction and Software Engineering*, London: MIT Press.

Ingold, T. (2007), "Materials against Materiality," *Archaeological Dialogues*, 14(1): 1–16.

Ingold, T. (2008), "Anthropology Is Not Ethnography," *Proceedings of the British Academy*, 154: 69–92.

Ingold, T. (2011), *Being Alive: Essays on Movement, Knowledge and Description*, London: Routledge.

Jacob, M., and Grabner, M. (eds.) (2010), *The Studio Reader*, Chicago, IL: University of Chicago Press.

Julier, G. (2007), *The Culture of Design*, London: Sage Publications.

Kelley, T. (2001), *The Art of Innovation*, London: Profile Books.

Knorr Cetina, K. (1981), *The Manufacture of Knowledge: An Essay on the Constructivist and Contextual Nature of Science*, Oxford: Pergamon Press.

Kopytoff, I. (1986), "The Cultural Biography of Things: Commoditization as Process," in A. Appadurai (ed.), *The Social Life of Things*, Cambridge: Cambridge University Press, 64–93.

Latour, B. (2004), "Why Has Critique Run out of Steam?: From Matters of Fact to Matters of Concern," *Critical Inquiry*, 30(2): 225–248.

Latour, B. (2005), *Reassembling the Social*, Oxford: Oxford University Press.

Latour, B., and Woolgar, S. (1979), *Laboratory Life: The Social Construction of Laboratory Facts*, London: Sage Publications.

Lenskjold, T. U. (2011), "Accounts of a Critical Artefacts Approach to Design Anthropology," paper presented at Nordic Design Research Conference: Making Design Matter, Aalto, May.

Luff, P., Heath, C., and Hindmarsh, J. (2000), *Workplace Studies: Recovering Work Practice and Informing System Design*, Cambridge: Cambridge University Press.

Moles, A. (2002), "Design and Immateriality: What of It in a Post-industrial Society?" in V. Margolin and R. Buchanan (eds.), *The Idea of Design*, London: MIT Press, 268–274.

Morphy, H. (2010), "Art as Action, Art as Evidence," in D. Hicks and M. Beaudry (eds.), *The Oxford Handbook of Material Culture Studies*, Oxford: Oxford University Press, 265–290.

Nafus, D., and Anderson, K. (2009), "Writing on Walls: The Materiality of Social Memory in Corporate Research," in M. Cefkin (ed.), *Ethnography and the Corporate Encounter*, London: Berghahn, 137–157.

Pinch, T. (1986), *Confronting Nature: The Sociology of Solar Neutrino Detection*, Dordrecht: D. Reidel.

Price, H. H. (1954), *Thinking and Experience*, Harvard, MA: Harvard University Press.

Salvador, T., Bell, G., and Anderson, K. (1999), "Design Ethnography," *Design Management Journal*, 10(4): 35–41.

Schaffer, D. (2003), "Portrait of the Oxford Design Studio: An Ethnography of Design Pedagogy," Wisconsin Center for Educational Research (WCER) Working Paper No. 2003–11, Madison.

Schön, D. (1985), *The Design Studio: An Exploration of Its Traditions and Potentials*, London: RIBA Publications.

Shanks, M., and Tilley, C. (1992), *Re-constructing Archaeology: Theory and Practice*, London: Routledge.

Simonsen, J., and Robertson, T. (eds.) (2012), *Routledge Handbook of Participatory Design*, Oxford: Routledge.

Squires, S., and Byrne, B. (eds.) (2002), *Creating Breakthrough Ideas: The Collaboration of Anthropologists and Designers in the Product Development Industry*, London: Bergin and Garvey.

Sunley, P., Pinch, S., Reimer, S., and Macmillen, J. (2008), "Innovation in a Creative Production System: The Case of Design," *Journal of Economic Geography*, 8(5): 675–698.

Tilley, C. (1999), *Metaphor and Material Culture*, Oxford: Blackwell.

Tilley, C. (2000), "Materialism and an Archaeology of Dissonance," in J. Thomas (ed.), *Interpretive Archaeology: A Reader*, Leicester: Leicester University Press, 71–80.

Yaneva, A. (2009), *Made by the Office for Metropolitan Architecture: An Ethnography of Design*, Rotterdam: 010 Publishers.

3

(Trans)forming Knowledge and Design Concepts in the Design Workshop

Mette Gislev Kjærsgaard

This chapter is concerned with the transition from research to design within the Body Games project—an interdisciplinary design project focused on the development of a digital playground for children. In the chapter I describe how various forms of knowledge and field material are turned into design concepts at a particular workshop through the creation, circulation, combination, and transformation of *knowledge pieces*. As a kind of montage this design workshop juxtaposes incoherent research material, perspectives, and knowledge traditions within a dynamic composition, where design possibilities are not disclosed through a piecemeal gathering of facts about the world, but emerge in the friction between various more or less tangible and fragmented images of it. I argue that the anthropological contribution to design (as montage) depends less on detailed accounts from the field, and more on a continuous involvement with and a reframing of field and design practices throughout the design process.

THE BODY GAMES PROJECT

Between 2003 and 2005, I spent nearly a year working as a researcher *for* as well as a researcher *of* the Body Games project. As a researcher *for* the project, I provided data and analyses on children's play based on field studies of and design activities with children. As a researcher *of* the project, I studied the design process itself with a particular interest in the way knowledge of children's play was created, exchanged, transformed, and applied within this design project. My dual role as a participant in and an observer of the project differed from that of a more traditional participant observer in terms of the extent to which I deliberately influenced the practices I had set out to study. This was a difficult role to have, but also a privileged one that allowed (as well as forced) me to experiment with methods and concepts at the intersection between design and anthropology, and which has led me to understand my position in the field as that of a participant interventionist (Karasti 2001) as much as a participant observer.

One Playground—Many Players

The Body Games project was a combined research and product development project funded by the Danish Ministry of Science, Technology and Development. The research context involved a playground company, a theme park, and three university-based research groups with expertise in computer science, children's digitally mediated play, and user-centered design (at the time my affiliation was with the latter). Body Games was from the outset promoted as a kind of health care project aimed at decreasing obesity among children through the development of a digital playground that would encourage children and young people to be more physically active. As a representative from the playground company explained in an interview with a magazine: "Our goal is to outmatch computer games [and] pull the fat boys away from the PC" (Larsen 2003).

However, the design team was not simply on a joint mission to save children from obesity. In fact, everyone had his or her own agendas and reasons to participate in the project. The playground company, for instance, had been losing customers for some time, as older children had stopped playing at its playgrounds and turned to computer games and sports instead. By introducing elements from computer games and sports into its physical playgrounds, the playground company hoped to attract these older children again. The obesity issue seemed the perfect angle for such a project, as it positioned the company in opposition to the computer games industry while simultaneously using elements from it to win back its "lost" children. Project researchers also had their individual and disciplinary research agendas to promote through the project. For the computer scientists, it was ambient and three-dimensional (3D) positioning technology; for the researchers interested in digitally mediated play (from now on called the *play researchers*), it was a particular theoretical perspective on play (Jessen and Barslev Nielsen 2003; Mouritsen 1996); for the design researchers, it was tangible interaction; and for me, it was design anthropology. So it is fair to say that children were not the only *users* of the outcomes of this project.

THE OBESITY FRAMEWORK

The obesity framework served to combine different research, funding, and business interests within a single framework, and was thus as much an instrument in the service of the Body Games project as the other way around. Questioning this framework was, therefore, not only an academic issue but also a political one with possibly fatal consequences for the delicately orchestrated project setup. The way obesity and playground design was initially linked within the Body Games project was based on a very particular understanding of play held by the play researchers (who originally initiated the project together with the playground company and the computer scientists). In the project proposal (Body Games Konsortiet 2002), they describe play as a form of cultural heritage passed from older to younger children in the form of basic rules and formulas, arguing that changes in children's upbringing such as a more institutionalized life and fewer places for free and unsupervised play had limited the possibility for children to pass on these play formulas. According to the play researchers, this had led to a decrease in children's know-how of play, and thus in their ability to create their own games. Children had therefore turned toward the ready-made sedentary computer games with increased obesity as a result. By transferring gaming elements from computer games to the physical playground, the Body Games project wanted to lure these children away from their inactive life in front of the screen. The intention was to make a playground with embedded formulas for play, which could make up for the loss of play mentors and restore children's ability to play physical games. What was needed—it seemed—was to find the right kind of play *formula*—which once embedded in the right kind of technology within a physical playground would captivate children of all ages, sizes, and capabilities in physically challenging body games, producing sweat and healthy bodies in the process.

From Research to Design

In search of appropriate formulas, games, and technology for the Body Games playground, play researchers, designers, and I initially carried out research on children's play through field studies at playgrounds, schools, and after-school centers, while engineers and computer scientists did background research on technologies of possible interest to the project.

KNOWLEDGE IN PIECES

In the following, I focus on a particular design workshop that took place approximately four months into the project and marked the transition from this initial research phase to the actual design phase. At this workshop the entire Body Games team gathered to share knowledge and generate design ideas. Knowledge and material resulting from the research phase was presented at this workshop. Each presentation was captured on an A4 poster with a headline, some drawings, pictures, or keywords and pinned to a moveable pin-up board as references to what the workshop facilitator called "pieces of knowledge." In subsequent design exercises, these posters were combined to form design concepts. The idea, as presented by the workshop facilitator, seemed to be that by assembling pieces of knowledge from different disciplinary fields—likened to assembling pieces in a jigsaw puzzle—the intertwined contours of the current state of affairs and its latent design possibilities would emerge (as illustrated in Plate 3).

In the workshop, posters were treated as repositories for the collection of neutral and disembodied pieces of knowledge, even if they were perhaps better understood as tools that transformed heterogeneous inputs of very different origin, form, complexity, and content into similar and homogeneous design material (paper with images and words) that could be physically handled and manipulated in the design process. The material presented at the workshop was in fact very different in style and content as well as in theoretical and epistemological orientation, and did not come in predefined neutral and compatible pieces ready to be shared and combined. But through the creation of posters it was turned into these (somewhat) shareable and compatible pieces, which I shall refer to as *knowledge pieces*.

The workshop schedule distinguished between two types of knowledge to be presented and combined at the workshop: "knowledge about children's play" and "knowledge about technology." In the following, I give examples of the various forms of knowledge and material presented at the workshop, and describe how this material was appropriated, combined, and transformed through the practices and technologies of the workshop.

KNOWLEDGE OF CHILDREN'S PLAY

The kind of research on children's play presented at the workshop encompassed a variety of research approaches, data, and theoretical perspectives. The presentations might be divided into two types. One type was mainly concerned with play formulas and the mechanics of children's games, aiming to *inform* the design practice while embracing the project's design agenda. The other type was of a more explorative nature, attempting to *reframe* the design practice by challenging established perspectives on children, play, and playground design within the project (Kjærsgaard 2011; Kjærsgaard and Otto 2012). As we shall see, very different insights and perspectives on children's play were all turned into what seemed like compatible and combinable knowledge pieces from which design concepts could be built.

Games and Play Formulas

One example of what was presented under the headline "knowledge of children's play" was a couple of old village games called the bull and the maze (both variations of tag). They were introduced as examples of the kind of play formulas the play researchers saw as essential for the survival of children's play culture and for the success of our playground design. At the workshop, the project team was taught how to play the games, but the possible uses of these games and their formulas in the Body Games project was not discussed at this point. The names of the games—"The Bull" and "The Maze"—were simply printed on separate pieces of paper and pinned to our boards as two separate pieces of knowledge on children's play.

Another example of "knowledge of children's play" presented at the workshop consisted of videos of different games that one of the designers had encountered during field studies at an after-school center. Here too the focus was on the formulas and mechanics of the games and how the design team might learn from (or copy) these. During the presentation, the designer extracted what he called *design values* from the videos. These design values were captured on cards in the form of sentences—such as "children are constantly measuring themselves against each other while playing," or playground equipment should be "continuously challenging"—and the cards were finally pinned to a poster on a board as a piece of knowledge of children's play.

A final example was a presentation of the results of a design experiment called *dogma play* conducted by one of the play researchers. Here a group of children had been given very simple props such as ropes or sticks and asked to design a game. The children had a hard time inventing new games using these tools, which the play researcher interpreted as a sign of their lack of play culture. Based on the experiment, he concluded: "this shows that children need help figuring out how to play," and that as a consequence the design team would have to embed predesigned games or formulas within the Body Games playground. His conclusions sparked a lively discussion in the group about children's ability to invent their own games and the implications of this for our design task. Here the presenter did not simply hand over a piece of knowledge to the group, but the team critically and actively appropriated the material and conclusions presented. Still, what ended up on the board was merely a piece of paper with the title "dogma play," which did not in any visible or physical way capture the points made in the presentation nor the discussion it had raised.

Alternative Perspectives

My own presentation of material from field studies conducted at a summer camp is an example of a different type of material. Like the designer, I showed videos of children's games, but as an anthropologist I was more preoccupied with the relations between activities and the context within which they took place than with the mechanics of the games themselves. With the video "girls in a tent," for instance, I attempted to show that there was more to understanding play—and its possible implications for design—than what could be derived from looking at the mechanics of a single game. The activities portrayed in the video were not distinct and clearly identifiable games, but an incoherent mesh of activities conducted in the playful and intimate atmosphere of a tent accommodating a group of eleven-year-old girls at a summer camp. In the video we see some girls climbing and dancing around the tent pole in what they call a strip show—although they remain fully clothed—while others are laughing at a girl who pretends to vomit with a very loud and disgusting noise. This is juxtaposed with a clip where the girls talk about a story or game that they have collaboratively developed; an absurd tale set in what they call "the sympathetic veterinary hospital" where the girls play themselves reemerged from the dead in the form of fantasy creatures with animal characteristics and silly names. Although the formulas and aesthetics around which the story evolved were an important part of the fun, it was not simply the storyline that made it compelling, but also the role it played within the group. Not all the girls in the tent were included in the story, and its content was kept secret from the outsiders. The story was not simply a fun game, but also a way for some of the girls to form their own exclusive tribe within the wider group of girls. The universe and context within which these girls lived and played therefore turned out to be as relevant for understanding this particular game as the structures and the rules of the game itself. The images of these girls dancing, composing, and acting with a grotesque sense of humor while engaging in something that might or might not be called play did not fit easily within the predominant frameworks of the Body Games project. These girls were not unable to create their own games, and the key to understanding their play did not seem to be located within the structures of a single game. Moreover, their universe far from resembled the stereotypical pink and innocent Barbie land we had often turned toward in the project when trying to design something for the girls. With the video I wanted to give the design team an impression of and a feel for children's worlds and games and to spark discussions about our understandings and assumptions of play and its relation to playground design.

This was also the case with another of my summer camp videos showing a group of children playing tag. Here the focus was on the emergent and somehow accidental character of this particular game, and on how the landscape played an important part in eliciting and shaping the activity. By showing children as creative agents capable of constructing their own playground out of elements at hand, constantly changing the game to fit the situation and the setting, I wanted to offer alternative perspectives on play and to initiate reflections in the design team about the relationship between the game and the environment in which it took place, and hence about the relationship between playground designs, play activities, and the physical context. What these presentations amounted to on the pin-up board, however, was a poster with the headline "Summer Camp," some pictures, and a short descriptive text summing up the contents of each video. As such the exploratory and somewhat elusive content of these videos was turned into solid knowledge pieces, which as a form of design material could be compared and combined with other knowledge pieces regardless of their seemingly incompatible origins.

PIECES OF TECHNOLOGY

The computer scientists presented two different types of technologies at the workshop, which they—as the result of their background research—saw as possible ingredients in a future playground. One option was 3D positioning technology, an advanced GPS system making it possible to identify and trace the movement of children and objects in the playground, and thus to tailor the playground's responses to the individual child. The other option was "smart-its"—small computer processing units that could be built into different pieces of equipment to produce various forms of output. In the workshop, smart-its were illustrated through a physical model called the dancing pad, a rubber tile that worked somewhat like a joystick. By stepping on the tile one could make different sounds. These rather simple smart-its could be combined in various ways to form an intelligent network controlling various inputs and outputs in the playground. As one of the computer scientists explained:

> [O]f course it is not just about controlling sound because you could control any kind of actuation with a system like that . . . we could imagine the surface of the playground being hundreds of these rubber things. And as the child, or the children run around we can probably create different kinds of games.

The form in which these technology options were presented carried with it particular interpretations of possible uses. These presentations resulted in two headlines for the pin-up boards, one simply referring to the technology: "3D positioning." The other headline, "smart-its and soft rocks," referred not just to a particular technology, but also to that technology in the particular shape of soft rocks like the dance pad. As such, an example of possible uses of this technology became synonymous with that technology. What ended up on the boards was therefore not neutral pieces on technology, but references to particular interpretations of the possible forms and uses of this technology.

KNOWLEDGE AS DESIGN MATERIAL

In this first round of presentations, knowledge was treated as if it was context-free and without knowers (Barth 2002: 2)—simply a matter of fact to be easily shared, compared, and combined. However, the examples cited earlier suggest that this was not the case. The knowledge and material presented embodied particular perspectives, interests, and agendas. It was partial, not only in the sense of being incomplete (as the puzzle-solving metaphor suggests), but also in the sense of being situated, embodied, and biased. What happened at the workshop was not a presentation and an accumulation of pieces of knowledge as much as a transformation of material in the attempt to *detach* knowledge from the physical, social, and academic contexts of its origin, in order to render it sharable and combinable with other forms of knowledge embedded in other traditions and contexts. Through the presentations and their representations on the pin-up boards, a complex intangible web of contextualized embodied knowledge, material, and agendas was transformed into discrete and tangible knowledge pieces that could be shared and handled in the design process, like pieces of a jigsaw puzzle at first, but increasingly more like pieces in a game.

By calling them *knowledge pieces*, I want to emphasize the ambiguous status of these pieces, which were treated as pieces of knowledge, but were perhaps better understood as transitional objects facilitating the move from individual—and predominantly intangible—research knowledge to tangible and collective design material. Knowledge pieces were not knowledge, not yet design, and yet both. As such they were like liminal objects mediating between knowledge and design, present and future, as well as between different knowledge traditions. Like "split entities" (Latour and Woolgar 1986 [1979]: 176) representing individual knowledge and localized material, but at the same time taking on a life of their own, knowledge pieces were meant to facilitate interaction between seemingly incompatible types of material, knowledge, and perspectives. It seemed that only through their simultaneous association and disassociation with the knowledge and material they were to represent were they able to work their magic.

Through presentations and their representations on posters, heterogeneous knowledge and material of different origin, form, complexity, content, and scope had gradually been decontextualized, disembodied, and transformed into homogeneous and tangible pieces. It was these homogeneous and tangible knowledge pieces rather than the heterogeneous material originally presented that became the building blocks, or the design material, from which design concepts and strategies were constructed within the project.

BRINGING THE BITS TOGETHER

Having presented the material and accumulated the pieces, it was time for the design work to begin. In groups the project participants were given two posters, one with "knowledge of children's play" and another referring to "a piece of technology." The task was then to combine these to produce a design idea that pooled elements from both. This design idea was then represented on yet another poster with a headline, a drawing, and keywords. The new poster went through a similar group work session where it was combined with other ideas resulting in other posters with more refined design ideas purportedly encompassing more of the insights presented in the first round. In this way the workshop worked toward a design concept using previous posters as fuel for new ideas and new posters, embedding the original material in layers upon layers of interpretation and representation.

The process of combining the pieces was presented as a rather straightforward procedure, but in most cases the attempt to combine different knowledge pieces created friction and raised discussions in the groups, as different perceptions of play, children, and technology collided in our interpretations and combinations of these pieces. In the process, implicit agendas and different understandings were brought into light and challenged in our attempts to stretch our ideas of the design possibilities each piece might offer. Reflection, creativity, and design ideas thus arose from the gaps and frictions that occurred when juxtaposing and combining these knowledge pieces, not unlike the way meaning is constructed in a montage, through the combination and juxtaposing of perspectives (Eisenstein 1949; MacDougall 1998; Marcus 1994). Knowledge pieces afforded, encouraged, restricted, influenced, or elicited certain interpretations and uses more than others, but did not prescribe them. The meaning and possible uses of the pieces were not embedded within them, but emanated from their situated translations, combinations, and juxtapositions. The workshop thus served as a form of interdisciplinary tinkering with skills, knowledge, material, and concepts in a tangible form of montage, where the interpretation of knowledge pieces as well as their design potentials depended not only on their form and content, but just as much on their dynamic composition and framing within the design process—how they were juxtaposed and combined with other types of material in the process and by whom.

COMBINING PIECES—AN EXAMPLE

In the final round of group work, participants were asked to choose a board with knowledge pieces and design concepts from the previous rounds to bring with them to the session. This was a way of forming an attachment to and alliance with the material, forcing us to take a stand and make some kind of commitment to our shared pool of knowledge and ideas. In groups of four, contents of the boards were combined into presumably more complete and coherent design concepts. Here the boards themselves became agentive knowledge pieces in the design process, to some extent acting on behalf of the people whose knowledge and ideas they were seen to contain. At the same time, they were appropriated by the people who chose to bring them into the group work and who may or may not have participated in creating the ideas they contained, but nevertheless felt a connection and therefore chose to serve as their advocate in the session. As such, board and advocate formed a pair and it was these *pairs* that were combined in the session, rather than simply the boards with detached pieces of knowledge and ideas. Thus this session was just as much about combining different people's perspectives, agendas, and skills as it was about combining contents of the boards. The boards became vehicles for the combination of skills, agendas, perspectives, and "corpuses of knowledge" (Barth 2002).

Having chosen a board, everyone proceeded to the adjoining room for the creative work to begin. Here the boards were arranged so that they formed a wall outlining both physically and symbolically the work space of each group. In my group, we started the session by inspecting our collective catch of boards to decide whether they constituted a good match. The group consisted of a playground designer, a computer scientist, a play researcher, and me. We represented quite different agendas, perspectives, skills, and corpuses of knowledge within the project, as our choice of boards and our interpretations of their potentials indicated. The computer scientist, for instance, had chosen a board that contained ideas for a 3D computer game implemented as a virtual layer on top of the traditional playground. Using 3D positioning technology in combination with hand-held devices—like PDAs, mobile phones, or tags—the playground envisioned on this board would be able to track the movements of each player and provide a platform for various kinds of pre-designed games. In his choice of board, the primary focus had been the possibilities 3D positioning technology had to offer, which was his particular agenda in the project. The play researcher had chosen a board that contained somewhat similar ideas about a playground with embedded games, but this time based on smart-its technology. His board contained ideas for playgrounds with embedded storylines or formulas that might serve as play mentors for children, which was a particular concern to him and matched his research interests. The designer's choice of board included ideas for a particular digitalized version of tag set in a rather elaborate playground landscape. This board shared with the previous boards the idea of a predefined and built-in game, but was more focused on the materials and the physical environment—which happened to be this designer's field of expertise—and less specific about the technology behind it. My board, on the other hand, contained ideas for augmenting a traditional playground area by embedding smart-its within surfaces and equipment to elicit different responses—for example sound or light—when used or stepped upon. The children could then incorporate these responses into different kinds of games and activities as they pleased. From my perspective, the ideas on this board differed from the previous ones because they did not prescribe the games played in the playground, but offered more open-ended feedback that could support children's own development of games, which was my particular concern at this point in the project.

The computer scientist made the first move by introducing his board as well as his reasons for choosing it. This started a discussion about the possibilities of designing a three-dimensional computer game and evolved into a more general discussion about the overall design task. The disagreement revolved around the question of whether to design the playground as a game or not, and to what extent the rules of such a game should be designed in advance by us or during play by the children themselves. This discussion, which started as a discussion about 3D role play as presented on the board, eventually became a discussion about our understandings of play, playgrounds, and children, revealing differences in our interpretations of the material presented on the boards as well as in our perspectives on children, play, and design more generally, as is apparent in the following excerpt from our design dialogue:

Computer scientist: So it is really about taking the Harry Potter [universe] or another kind of role play and embedding it in a physical game with the help of technologies that may offer such possibilities.

Me: But I still think that it is important that we do not design the games, but that there are different possibilities [for use] within them . . .

Play researcher: There are two options, as I see it. One is to make a platform for constructing stories, which should be flexible enough to allow us to make many different stories. The other option is to find things that may inspire them [the children] to produce their own games. The last one is not that easy, I don't think. The first one is easy, though it requires that we hire someone to create the stories . . . so the second option is the difficult one; to make something that inspires them [the children] to actually keep the game going [by themselves].

Me: I think it's risky if it becomes too game-like . . . [because] if you look at the way children play, they play many different games within one place, and if it doesn't allow for that, I don't think it will work.

Computer scientist: I also think that it would be good if the elements—that could be the bombs here [points to a drawing] or the dots here [points to another drawing]—if they could be something that children themselves could move and reconfigure, so that we [the design team] could make the building blocks, and they [the children] place them in the playground . . .

Play researcher: But . . . if we simply say, okay here you have all the bombs [elements in the game], now it is up to you to figure out what to do with them, then nothing would happen.

Designer: Are you inferring that the game would need to be initiated [by us]?

Play researcher: It needs to have a form, some kind of form.

Designer: That they [the children] could build on, that would be ideal, right?

Me: I guess it must have [a form] . . . but that seems to imply that there is only one game, if *the* game needs to be initiated.

Play researcher: But play comes with formulas; it rarely occurs as what we might call spontaneous play . . . games are usually based on formulas that the children might be more or less aware of. So when we play games like the bull we are aware of what we're doing, but there are other games, like tag, where we are less aware of the rules and the formulas, but they are there nevertheless. They are almost indispensable.

Me: Even if you're simply climbing the climbing frame, I mean, the more bodily games?

Play researcher: No, not then . . .

Me: But that is Body Games, isn't it?

Play researcher: That's true, if that's all you are after, simply making them [the children] move. But if they really have to sweat . . . that is when a game triggers something through the way it works [the formulas] . . . it can keep them going.

Me: But then we simply have to find something that may trigger these different formulas?

Play researcher: Yeah that's it. . .

Me: But still, I guess, you cannot really decide in advance what [actions] something might trigger, that is really the difficult part.

At some point during the subsequent design activities, I try to change the conversation and the focus away from predefined storylines and games by playing my piece: the augmented playground. Turning the focus to another piece of design material set the group discussion off on another track. Now it was the drawings on my board that were looked to for inspiration. The idea of an interactive surface with built in smart-its gained momentum, as it seemed to combine various interests in the project. The designer saw it as good business for the playground company, because: "The customers complain about the playground mats being far too expensive, but if we could add some cheap technology to them, then . . . " The computer scientist imagined a surface of soft-rock-like tiles with embedded smart-its working as a gaming console and a horizontal computer screen on which children could be their own avatars in a physical computer game. As he put it:

> Then it would simply be a horizontal computer screen, and this [the tiles] would be the pixels, and then you have the x and the y coordinates on this guy here, so you know where he is, and then instead of computer avatars, it's the children moving about [in the game].

Combined with 3D positioning technology, this could be developed into something resembling the 3D computer game on the computer scientist's board. To him it was an expansion of the design concept on my board, because the technology and the physical design remained the same. To me it was a completely different concept that afforded different kinds of activities in the playground and embodied a different view on children and play. This developed into a discussion about whether to understand the children as game consumers or game designers.

Searching for a solution that each member of the project team could be happy with led us to explore design ideas, which allowed for some degree of electronic control of the game as in computer games, but also some degree of freedom for the children to construct and reconfigure their own games. We wrote this down as a shared design principle, "Partly electronically controlled computer games & partly construction of own universes/worlds," and posted it on our board as a new and shared piece in this design game. Based on this principle we developed ideas that allowed the children to reconfigure, program, or shape the playground by, for instance, moving in particular patterns (codes). This opened up the possibility of a playground in which children themselves could create zones and design responses, simple games, and universes, but which might also have elaborate and predefined games as an option. It was not simply a games console, but a platform for the performance and development of different kinds of games and activities.

In the clashes occurring when juxtaposing and combining the material on the boards, implicit assumptions and dormant differences were elicited and negotiated both explicitly and implicitly through our design moves. The friction between perspectives embedded in the ideas and material posted on the boards as well as in our interpretations of them forced us to keep stretching and transforming this design material—and to some extent our own perspectives on it—in the attempt to create design concepts that made some kind of sense to everyone if for different reasons. With the design principle, we had established some degree of temporary common ground, even if the discrepancies in our understandings of children, play, and design were not dissolved.

At the very end of the design workshop we were left with a single design vision or strategy, fixed in a single drawing (see Plate 4). With this final piece, it seemed we had successfully managed to transform the heterogeneous material we started out with into a coherent design strategy, and that a new shared order had been established. Still, our differences and disagreements remained latent even within this final piece, which was itself a kind of collage or hybrid of different design concepts, agendas, and viewpoints, and (as it turned out) open for reinterpretations and renegotiations at each stage of adjustment and refinement toward becoming a real playground in the real world (Kjærsgaard 2011).

Like Latour's circulating references (Latour 1999: 58), the material presented at the collaborative design workshop went through "a regulated series of transformations, transmutations, and translations, at each stage losing particularity, multiplicity and continuity, but gaining circulation and compatibility" (Latour 1999: 70–71) on its way from individual and situated knowledge to collective design material, and finally shared (interdisciplinary) design concepts. Inspired by Latour, we might depict the process as shown in Plate 5.

As in Latour's description (1999), this transformation happened as a trade-off between what was gained (compatibility, coherence, interdisciplinarity, collaboration) and what was lost (particularity, professional expertise, multiplicity). In retrospect, it might seem like the design process was a battle between predefined and fixed positions, fought through the production and transformation of various forms of material at the workshop, but this was not how we experienced it at the time. No one joined the workshop with a clear mission, but everyone came simply with his or her different input and backgrounds. This obviously predisposed us toward some interpretations and design moves rather than others, but did not mean that our positions were settled from the outset. We were also inquisitive, susceptible to influence, and unsure of what to make of it all. On one hand, the design process was like a strategic game, with everyone trying to position their perspectives and ideas to maximize their influence on the outcome; but on the other, it was simply a struggle to understand and make use of each other's material, knowledge, and skills when interpreting, stretching, bending, and negotiating the material at hand in the process. Although it may seem as if our positions were more or less stable, while the design material was in constant flux, our perspectives and interests were also stretched and bent, if sometimes only slightly and temporarily. Often we would fall back on earlier positions when confronted with new material, and the process would start all over again. New insights, perspectives, or positions had to be continuously reproduced through the transformation and negotiation of the material at hand. Neither design concepts nor our positions were settled once and for all, but only found temporary stability in between sessions in the shared pieces (of paper) pinned to the boards.

THE WORKSHOP AS MONTAGE AND RITUAL

Like a rite of passage the design workshop facilitated the transition from *research* to *design* (Halse and Clark 2008). At the workshop, dissimilar and not necessarily coherent forms of knowledge and material of an actual present were transformed into shared visions for a potential future through a temporary suspension of ordinary life and a detachment of people, knowledge, and material from their usual surroundings.

Inspired by Kapferer (and with him Turner and Deleuze), we might think of this design workshop as a ritualized descent into the virtuality of reality

(Kapferer 2004), a special kind of reality suspended between the *actual* and the *potential*. Within the virtual reality of the workshop, the usual rules, roles, and hierarchies were (temporarily) suspended, and everyone was allowed to tamper with knowledge and material outside their area of expertise while playing with boundaries between the present and the future, the social and the material, at the periphery of their knowledge traditions. At the design workshop, diverse forms of knowledge and material were gradually turned into shared design concepts, visions, and strategies via the creation, circulation, combination, and transformation of knowledge pieces. The dynamic composition of people and material at the workshop did not simply facilitate a *transition* of the project from one predefined fixed stage to the next, but also a *reorientation* and a *transformation* of perspectives and material.

In the analysis presented here, interdisciplinary collaboration was not about assembling pieces of knowledge about a predefined reality out there into a complete picture of design possibilities, but rather a question of negotiating images of and interest in different realities through the construction, composition, and transformation of various kinds of knowledge pieces. Rather than regarding the process as a jigsaw puzzle, we might think of it as a form of montage that combines and juxtaposes various types of data, ideas, insights, technology, people, skills, perspectives, and knowledge traditions. In the design workshop reflection, creativity and design arose from the dynamic composition of and the *gaps and frictions* (Tsing 2005) between these elements, not unlike the way meaning is constructed in a montage. Knowledge, meaning, and design implications did not reside *in* the material presented at the workshop as much as in the dynamic composition and transformation *of* it. It was less about the material itself, and more about the way it was created, transformed, appropriated, combined, and juxtaposed with other types of materials and by whom.

If design collaboration is more like a montage than a jigsaw puzzle, this has implications for our understanding of the material presented at such events as the workshop, as well as for our understanding of the role of anthropology (and other knowledge traditions) within the design process in general. Perceiving design as a form of montage also means recognizing that forming an understanding of the field (of use) is a collective endeavor that happens throughout the project, not simply the work of the anthropologist prior to it. In the design montage, the anthropological contribution therefore depends less on an accurate representation of the world on the basis of research conducted prior to design and more on a continuous involvement with and reframing of practices (in the field as well as in the design studio) throughout the design process in the attempt to stimulate discussions about assumptions and frameworks that were taken for granted within the design team.

REFERENCES

Barth, F. (2002), "An Anthropology of Knowledge," *Current Anthropology*, 43(1): 1–18.

Body Games Konsortiet. (2002), *BodyGames—IT, leg og bevægelse: At udvikle produkter, der udnytter IT teknologi til at skabe interactive legetilbud med udfordrende fysiske lege for alle aldersgrupper*, Projektansøgning til IT-Korridoren, Denmark.

Eisenstein, S. (1949), *Film Form: Essays in Film Theory*, New York: Harcourt Brace.

Halse, J., and Clark, B. (2008), "Design Rituals and Performative Ethnography," in *Proceedings of the 2008 Ethnographic Praxis in Industry Conference*, EPIC 2008, Copenhagen, Denmark, 128–145.

Jessen, C., and Barslev Nielsen, C. (2003), "Børnekultur, Leg, Læring og Interactive Medier" (excerpt from "The Changing Face of Children's Play Culture," Lego Learning Institute). Available at: www.carsten-jessen.dk/LegOgInteraktiveMedier.pdf. Accessed September 27, 2012.

Kapferer, B. (2004), "Ritual Dynamic and Virtual Practice: Beyond Representation and Meaning," *Social Analysis*, 48(2): 35–54.

Karasti, H. (2001), "Increasing Sensitivity towards Everyday Work Practice in System Design," PhD dissertation, Department of Information Processing Science, Oulu, Oulu University Press.

Kjærsgaard, M.G. (2011), "Between the Actual and the Potential: The Challenges of Design Anthropology," PhD dissertation, Department of Culture and Society, Section for Anthropology and Anthropology, University of Aarhus.

Kjærsgaard, M.G., and Otto, T. (2012), "Anthropological Fieldwork and Designing Potentials," in W. Gunn and J. Donovan (eds.), *Design and Anthropology*, Farnham: Ashgate, 177–191.

Larsen, K.H. (2003), "Fremtidens interaktive legeplads—Legeredskaber med kunstig intelligens skal give fysiske udfordringer til fremtidens børn," *Ungdom og Idræt*, 29: 12–15.

Latour, B. (1999), "Circulating Reference: Sampling the Soil in the Amazon Forest," in B. Latour and S. Woolgar (eds.), *Pandora's Hope: Essays on the Reality of Science Studies*, Cambridge, MA: Harvard University Press, 24–80.

Latour, B., and Woolgar, S. (1986 [1979]), *Laboratory Life: The Construction of Scientific Facts*, Princeton, NJ: Princeton University Press.

MacDougall, D. (1998), *Transcultural Cinema*, Princeton, NJ: Princeton University Press.

Marcus, G. (1994), "The Modernist Sensibility in Recent Ethnographic Writing and the Cinematic Metaphor of Montage," in L. Taylor (ed.), *Visualizing*

Theory: Selected Essays from V.A.R. 1990–1994, New York: Routledge, 37–54.

Mouritsen, F. (1996), *Legekultur: Essays om børnekultur, leg og fortælling*, Odense, Denmark: Syddansk Universitetsforlag.

Tsing, A. (2005), *Friction: An Ethnography of Global Connection*, Princeton, NJ: Princeton University Press.

4

Tools and Movements of Engagement: Design Anthropology's Style of Knowing

Kyle Kilbourn

THE AFFINITY OF TWO FIELDS

With the kickoff meeting for a health care innovation project looming, Lars glances at the board (see Plate 6) where I have arranged images from visits to Danish hospital sterile supply wards in an overlapping pattern.

Speaking in a tone of admiration, he says to me, "you are the only one with a sense of aesthetics around this place." This should not be surprising because the institution where I work educates primarily engineers. Yet, Lars, an industrial designer by training, calls me *the scientist* when we discuss upcoming research projects and writing papers as a contribution. There are several tensions in play here: first, what counts as research and, second, research's role in generating knowledge within design and engineering processes. I can see why my practice-based teaching colleagues chose this moniker. There is a clear tension between different styles of knowing, which is itself the result of the increasing interdisciplinary collaboration taking place in the name of innovation. While Hacking (1992) details several "styles of reasoning" in an effort to debunk the idea of a singular science, my colleagues are most familiar with that of the laboratory where controlled experiments, using specifically built equipment, are used to observe and measure. In contrast the current exemplar of magnetic resonance imaging technology to describe which parts of the brain activate when people are shown products, as if measuring will deduce why we buy these objects, seems almost nonsensical when viewed from a perspective of social and cultural science. Holbraad explains that "fieldwork is the exact opposite of lab work: an experiment out of control, fieldwork is by nature orientated not towards planned eventualities but rather toward arbitrary coincidences" (2010: 82). The lab style of knowing parallels the production of knowledge in engineering where piecemeal models are constructed. The premise is that one can break down components into their smallest parts and then subsume them into a system with a particular valuable function. This is familiar to positivist natural sciences, in that the key to understanding life is to reverse engineer it into ever smaller bits and pieces, and it is a shared source of mutually defined objectivity for these styles.

However, this is quite different from either design or anthropology. At the core, design and anthropology embrace holism, an emergence of knowledge through the bringing together of differences in context and critique to lay a foundation for transformation (see Kolko 2011 and Otto and Bubandt 2010 for design and anthropology perspectives, respectively). In reaffirming the bricolage of design and anthropology (Sperschneider, Kjærsgaard, and Petersen 2001), this chapter shows that design anthropology is a particular style of knowing where the tools we think with and the movements of translating knowledge across disciplines and practices is valuable to the collaborative projects where innovation and future-orientated perspectives are paramount to bridging contextual practices with societal forecasts. The affinity of design and anthropology is more than a fleeting infatuation and goes to the core of how we understand.

TOWARD A PARTICULAR STYLE OF KNOWING

Sympathy for a particular style of knowing is crucial to a field with both anthropology and design as part of its identity. Crombie's (1988) six styles of scientific thinking through the methods they employ (simple postulating, laboratory experimenting, hypothetical modeling, taxonomical ordering, statistical analyzing, and genetic deriving) indicate that what is considered knowledge is generated within and through a particular style. Hacking postulates that "every style of reasoning introduces a great many novelties including new types of objects, evidence, sentences (new ways of being a candidate for truth or falsehood), laws (or at any rate modalities), [and] possibilities" (1992: 11; formatting modified). What characterizes design anthropology as a style of knowing? What objects are introduced? What possibilities become available through this style of knowing?

The experience of doing research tends to be left out of accounts of knowledge generation in many of the styles of scientific thinking, especially laboratory and statistical methods. This emphasis might be conceived as a superficial add-on to the core of one's work, yet the magnitude of its importance on the field is worth taking into account as it suggests a deeper value for our way of generating knowledge than only the production of knowledge, namely a growth of human potential. Descola writes of anthropological process as experiential: "It should be seen, rather, as a certain style of knowledge—that is, as a pattern of discovery and a mode of systematisation that are supported by a set of skills progressively acquired through practice, both a turn of mind and a tour de main, a particular knack picked up through experience" (2005: 72).

The embeddedness of the researcher into particular practices and communities permeates the theoretical knowledge, and, rather than see this as an unwanted side effect, take a close look at the benefits of embracing the experiential. This kind of research practice builds a set of skills, experiences, and knowledge that is more than pure application of a technique repeated. It is generative and provocative and facilitates knowledge that reframes the social imaginary. The researcher as a kind of scientific tool, intertwined with the process, implies a set of perspectives and values integral to building and creating knowledge that cannot be ignored. Its impact also extends into other fields where defining human potential is essential. Within the participatory design field, Ehn (1988: 30) echoes the significance of style in the creation of knowledge and argues that designing computer artifacts is as much social and political as it is simply the application of scientific process or principles. If we are to consider design anthropology as a collaborative endeavor *with* others, the approach we take in the generation of knowledge, without alienating our partners, requires empathy and sensitivity to support and sustain emerging, wavering, and ephemeral values that differ from our previous experiences. The discovery process is fractal in that the particular path to knowledge scales beyond the instance to encompass larger social practices and systems. Similar to how prototyping in design is a way of trying out design moves, the experiential style of knowing in design anthropology validates particular choices contextually and collaboratively.

Within the design research community, a passionate debate about styles of knowing still dominates as the field struggles to free itself from the shackles of other disciplines and strives to be taken seriously on its own merits through a research process that takes to heart the contribution of design (Koskinen et al. 2012). If, as a field, design anthropology desires an impact on future practices, it also has to develop a way to nurture and support this creative and experiential approach to generating knowledge. But to grasp what this means, one must consider the medium in which we work as having both spatial and temporal properties that shape what kinds of tools and methods we choose when engaging in practices.

DIRECTIONALITY REQUIRES EMBRACING INTERVENTION

To consider design anthropology as collaboration, a study *with* rather than *of*, is to resituate the work undertaken from a neatly demarcated space and place in time to a critical stance with directionality toward future practices and relations. Shifting from a fixed frame to an emerging assembly is to frame a study "as practices of construction through (preplanned or opportunistic) movement" (Marcus 1995: 106). While anthropology traditionally draws upon the field as the site of research, Sperschnieder, Kjærsgaard, and Petersen (2001) have pushed the discipline to discard terms like *fieldwork* and *ethnography* to pursue phenomena in a contemporary positioning rather than studying people as if they were abstract from time. Marcus conceives of this as the milieu in which the anthropologist works: "The course or map of fieldwork has to be found within its confines. Such a found imaginary is not the end of research or its descriptive-analytic object, but its medium" (Rabinow et al. 2008: 66). Bridging the vernacular of *field* with the *imaginary*, the authors extend the territory to also include an *event*. Through this conceptual arc they have explicitly incorporated the realm of design as an environment in which to work. The medium of design anthropology extends from the spatially oriented field to the performance-oriented event (Brandt 2001) and becomes a hybrid place or third space (Muller 2008). As we consider the fundamental properties of our medium, we will find that it simply "affords movement and perception" (Ingold 2007: S25), crucial to what characterizes a style of knowledge.

Expansion of the territory of work suggests that the role of the researcher will not only include seeing (observation) as a form of engagement, but also making (design). This redefines the *participant-observer* role to a *facilitating-provoker* or an active and reflexive reengagement with the context of analysis. The role of perception has been central to both design research and anthropology. In anthropology, Grasseni's (2006) edited volume on skilled perception showcases various practices in which kinds of seeing play a critical social role. Schön explored the notion of *seeing-as* from a range of disciplines, which has heavily influenced design research through reflection-in-action:

> [T]he inquirer arrives at a new description of the phenomena before him by reflecting-in-action on an earlier perception of similarity . . . But the idea of reflection on seeing-as suggests a direction of inquiry into processes which tend otherwise to be mystified and dismissed with the terms "intuition" or "creativity," and it suggests how these processes might be placed within the framework of reflective conversation with the situation. (1983: 186)

Fulton Suri highlights several cases in which designers turn their detailed observations of the world into design opportunities: "rather than observing it to describe what they see (which would involve seeing literally and objectively), their purpose is a generative and strategic one" (Fulton Suri 2011: 31). This then questions the role of anthropologists if designers learn to appreciate the world through observation. What is left for them? While there may be a role to play, Hunt (2011) emphasizes the tepidness of engagement on the part of anthropologists, especially given the discipline's history. To value movement as well as perception requires that design anthropologists address detachment in the fundamental approaches to working. Through these events of inter-vention, the tools of inquiry become crucial to producing knowledge. Drawing upon design tools as "things-to-think-with" (Gunn 2008) provides a reflective aspect of possibilities, creating the materials necessary to conduct design ex-periments for future practices. Design experiments help concretize the possi-bilities of human ways of working by producing concepts, which help to trigger associations between theoretical insights and the empirical material. But this has an effect on the researcher in that being in the world shapes our percep-tion and how we come to know, as Ingold points out:

> It rather educates our perception of the world, and opens our eyes and minds to other possibilities of being. The questions we address are philosophical ones . . . But it is the fact that we address these questions in the world, and not from the armchair—that this world is not just what we think about but what we think with, and that in its thinking the mind wanders along pathways extending far beyond the envelope of the skin—that makes the enterprise anthropological, and by the same token, radically different from positivist science. (2008: 82–83; original emphasis)

It is here the opening for a kind of design anthropology appears. *What we think with* is the crucial element that distinguishes it from the larger discipline of (take your pick) design or anthropology. I argue that it is the tools we as design anthropologists bring to the situations we engage that differentiate us from other fields. It is our style of knowledge, the environments of thinking, and ways of working, weaving observation, interpretation, and inspiration that distinguish the field of design anthropology.

EXPLORING METHODS OF INQUIRY IN DESIGN ANTHROPOLOGY

Fetishizing methods and their appropriate use can occur in any discipline, yet methods remain one of the main ways a practice meets the world outside of scholarly literature. This *packaging* of research into bundles of tools often fo-cuses on the *terminology* and, therefore, places emphasis on written commu-nication and what to name things and phenomena. While documentation and reportage play roles in the spread of knowledge, in some ways it is an end point where method becomes immutable in form and approach, ultimately becoming the standard process rather than a tool kit of options. Design an-thropology tends toward the emergent. Important to note is a shift away from purely analyzing and preserving practices toward facilitating and crafting na-scent human potentials. Clark (2007), as an example, creates the *tangible analysis kit* as a way to ensure social interaction becomes a resource as part of the design process when straddling ethnography and design. The tool kit for crafting potentials will build upon conversation and observation to include the staging of collaborative workshops that span knowledge traditions in the spirit of generating instances of multi-sited fieldwork. Written documentation will merge and be enhanced with video annotation in a synthesis of meaning through design moves.

The spillover, crossover, or gray zones between anthropology (focusing on ethnography) and design has been described as a bow tie (Wasson 2002) that quickly morphs into a matrix stringing together designers and researchers. It also has been envisioned as a horseshoe (Jones 2006), which pushes research toward design concepts. However appropriate (and useful) these metaphors are, more intriguing is the tension created in approaches that embody the desire to understand the present while simultaneously intervening in the future; being both critical yet generative as seen in Plate 7.

Halse "explores the possible in the existing" and proposes "understanding and intervening can be done in one movement" (2008: 32). So while acknowledging the limitations of espousing yet more methods, there is great value in looking at the tools we use as a way of crafting potentials to scaffold the creation of meaningful human experiences. Tools in design anthropology must have several qualities in common. They *guide* a process in eliciting possibilities and potentials. Effectively, there is a directionality and future orientation. Often they are embodied in a *tangible* way, reminiscent of practices rather than staying wrapped up textually. Perhaps most important, they maintain a kind of *duality* or hybridity among a set of elements. Tools allow for an unfolding relation to grow, whether that means between a current and future practice, stickiness around observation and provocation, or even bridging participation with control. The following tools show how the values of a practice are embedded within a seemingly benign tool.

ROBOTS TAKE OVER? TOOLS FOR QUESTIONING FUTURES

On a Danish island, perhaps most famous as the birthplace of Hans Christian Andersen, a new generation of tales is being told. Situated between mainland Europe and the Danish capital of Copenhagen, Funen (Fyn in Danish) is the epicenter for a confluence of thinking to implement automation technology into the health care and social sectors. While administratively it is known as the region of southern Denmark, the Welfare Tech Region has the goal to acquire resources, skills, and influence to become a generator of jobs, infrastructure, and knowledge. One of several projects initiated through regional development funding, The Sterilcentral Project brings together local hospital sterile supply departments, technology providers (robotics and information technology), and other knowledge partners (network clusters and university departments) to negotiate a future that includes multiple kinds of automation technology to help complete the work of resterilization of medical devices for operations. But what if we begin to unravel this ideal future narrative? Will robots take over the sterilization ward to fully automate the process? What kinds of tools allow for an unpacking of assumptions yet also orientate toward a reweaving of the tale through more collaborative efforts? Through sketching this project, I will introduce three tools to get a sense of how design anthropology might undertake such an endeavor.

While the process of synthesizing and creating meaning from our experiences is present in both anthropology and design, it is the latter that draws more often upon other approaches than textual ones to communicate the resulting synthesis. It is odd that we experience the world with a range of perceptual systems and then, when trying to make sense of it, we resort to squeezing it into words. Designers have used mood boards, targeted collections of imagery, as a way of absorbing the material and visual surroundings at a particular moment and as a way of pointing toward a possible trajectory; a way of making sense of the present while also carving out a space for exploring the future. The first design anthropological tool I call *perceptual synthesis* as it explores ways of understanding based upon visual, embodied, and nontextual frameworks rather than starting with linguistic encoding.

In preparing for the Sterilcentral Project kickoff workshop, where all of the partners met for the first time as part of the three-year journey of working together, an immersion toolkit was created to help everyone find a way to experience a part of the hospital workplace and, through negotiation and discussion, to frame an issue to explore through designing. The components included a foam floor plan of a hospital sterile supply ward, which had photographs we had taken from observations pinned to different areas. These photographs were indexed to short video clips that showed a particular action or conversation in preliminary fieldwork (inspired by the video card game in Buur and Soendergaard 2000). Each group chose several clips to watch and annotated its own observations. Relying on the photo representation and the video content, each group brought together clips (represented by the paper cards) that could share common characteristics. This transforming of concrete instances by simultaneously stringing together and pulling into a higher level of abstraction gives this *perceptual synthesis* a hybridity of form and content. The way of working is both very tangible (the cards are physically manipulated) and ephemeral (the actions recorded quickly fade unless annotated and described). It is also an individual and collaborative effort at the same time in that the insights come from each actor's perceptual observations while themes are generated in the group. The approach begins from visual roots and only the final step enters into written language. This hesitancy or slowing down of the final outcome allows others to join the process. What would happen if as a discipline we started to incorporate and embody nontextual synthesis as a part of our repertoire? One hopes that a practice that embraced and collaborated with more knowledge traditions would be the result.

The second category of tool for design anthropology that I suggest is *experience juxtaposing*. The purpose of such a tool is to explore potential experiences while firmly present in the here and now. Imagining such a possibility is, of course, not the same as having the experience, but the strength comes from comparison. As part of the preliminary engagement with the hospitals in the Sterilcentral Project, we created a series of cards depicting *superpowers* that our participants could select such as *super strength*, *shape shifting*, and *microscopic vision*. While it might seem silly or childish with cards and illustrations that looked as if they came from a comic book, the participants took them quite seriously when asked which three they would choose and why. We took this approach to understand what the role of robot technology would be in the worker's practice. While visions of technology often turn out much more mundane than anticipated, by pushing the hospital worker into the central role with the choice to wield technology as a power we could get closer to what it would feel like if technological solutions were implemented. Through the conversations mediated by the superpower cards, several themes emerged, including that of *distinguishing details*. The sterilization technician explains, "a robot cannot see if there is dirt or which instrument needs to be greased. So you are not quite unemployed, anyways." While we had introduced our purpose as an initial exploration of robotic technology in the hospital, workers had already carved out a niche that would preserve a specific role for people in the fully automatic sterilization ward. The "microscopic vision" superpower card served both as the prompt and as support for articulating this position. The tool helped turn a forecast of robotic technology into a collaborative foretelling of what value technicians bring to their work. The juxtaposition of the immediate workplace with the future gave a creative space to envision the appropriateness of potential technology.

The third kind of design anthropological tool, *potential relationing*, is concerned with ways to experience the embeddedness of future practices. Often, concepts are great for addressing one particular aspect of a problem, but they tend to leave behind the interconnected nature of social life. Drama and acting can be used to great effect in exposing the seams of practices. These performances are rich with explicit understandings of our current relationships and how we wish them to change. In another workshop for the Sterilcentral Project, four groups of participants generated scenarios of completed solutions as a way of understanding conflicting visions for the project and how workers would relate to the likely new robotic coworkers. Through the performances, we hoped conflicting visions of technology would emerge. To ensure robotics were part of the solution space, we advised the teams that at least one person in every group should play the role of the robot. However, everyone volunteered! The technological vision of the fully automated ward came to life through the play. The scenario most sympathetic to a human role in the work had robots sorting simple instruments from complex ones, with the latter worked on by people.

These embodied performances, while effective at seeing a system in use, struggled to illustrate the tensions in introducing new technology. As a result of its performative aspects, *potential relationing* highlights the socialness of the event, meaning that in collaborating the performers run the risk of playing to the audience to weave a cohesive narrative. The strength of working with a tool such as this is that the social web (including people and their environment) quickly gets laid out to allow for a space to critique, question, and reflect before full-scale implementation and its inherent danger of failure (Kilbourn and Bay 2011). Inconsistencies and conflicts push to the surface much more quickly than in the usual process of building the technology first and asking questions of appropriateness and social integration later. One anthropological contribution was in the questioning of assumptions and establishing meaningful frameworks beforehand, rather than post-project.

How do these kinds of tools relate to building a research practice in design anthropology? How do researchers engage with theory? If design anthropology is a collaborative rather than a solitary process, how do we reposition our own research practices in a similar manner? One running approach I have trialed with other researchers involves making theory tangible as part of an embodied practice. Drawing upon design processes, I sought to make a more direct relationship between theory and empirical data. Often the hidden aspect of the research craft is how experiences, theory, and empirical material collaborate. Through this design process, I wished to expose how theoretical perspectives change ways of working with the empirical material. As part of an inquiry into theory and practice, I created a workshop format called the Research Game in which condensed theoretical perspectives (in the form of key quotes on cards) were used as a starting point for developing research questions and subsequently used as a way to analyze a set of video clips. There have been three variations of the game, the first in the context of a PhD seminar to delve into one specific field site from multiple perspectives, the second was a workshop at an international design conference using many different field contexts (Sitorus and Kilbourn 2007), and the third was part of a strategic department planning session to envision types of research and how they relate to the educational profile. Each variation pushed the boundary of collaborative research practice in that theory became more than literature because it was embodied throughout the process, from framing to reflecting. In the conference workshop it was interesting to see how theory guided the design process. There were difficulties in transitioning from large theoretical concepts to specific empirical materials, and some participants suggested it would be more fruitful to end with theoretical concepts rather than begin with them, which makes sense for design anthropology rather than anthropological design.

The game provided a slightly more transparent and tangible approach to incorporating theoretical concepts in design research. The workshops were a microcosm of representations that find their way in design practice. The ethics of rearranging people's skills explores the role of empirical material in framing the dialogue. Should we preserve or enhance a particular practice? What role should theory play? Will a certain kind of theory overpower practice? As the field of design anthropology straddles a strong practice-based tradition with a rich theory-generating field, comparative tools for collaboration should be a key component of such a discipline, forming one of several modes of engagement of this research practice.

SKETCHING DIFFERING TRAJECTORIES OF ENGAGEMENT

In preparing the ground for new kinds of research in design anthropology, its scholars will have to grapple with the traditional practices of ethnography such as observation, description, and interpretation in a way that acknowledges local knowledge practices but also introduces artifacts to facilitate learning as part of an innovative research field. Through my work, I distinguish three overlapping modes with a particular style, medium, and tools, which underlies the shift at the core of a design anthropology discipline: *moving in*, *moving along*, and *moving out*. These modes are not separate components that can be delineated and parceled out to experts, but integral to the researcher to engage in all three iteratively.

Moving in is concerned with the collaborative approach of understanding *with* other people as part of our research. In many ways it is not enough to document and archive: it is critical to reflect *with* and *through* practice to introduce change. To do this requires helping to articulate embodied practices while also bringing together design and use practice. Mogensen (1992) investigated how "provotyping" could critique everyday practice in systems development as way of rising above the dilemma between tradition and transcendence in participatory design. Rather than having to choose either to support the current practice or to ignore skills and knowledge and push for a future-orientated agenda, provotyping suggests a dialectical tension that manages to relate the familiar and the new through reflection-in-practice. In educational action research, McNiff describes the fundamental tenet of the approach as "research WITH rather than research ON" (1988: 4; original emphasis). For a successful *moving in*, research tools are developed for collaborations among knowledge practitioners. In the Sterilcentral Project, an immersion tool kit of photos, floor plans, and video worked to tie together separate knowledge traditions toward a common purpose. To characterize this mode of movement as intimate points to the level of engagement familiar to anthropological fieldwork, yet also different in the deliberate dialogue generated through an intermediary artifact. While these types of movements are essential for any anthropological pursuit, design anthropology should aim to go beyond an ethnographic encounter within a field site.

Moving along frames the research beyond the specific contexts we find ourselves in and approaches the project as one with larger boundaries than anticipated. As Hines says, "moving around gives us ways to suspend judgment
about the appropriate places to study experience and make interventions and
the appropriate ways to reproduce methodologies" (2007: 669). One way of
smoothing and shading the complexity is to explore how the research might
temporarily span contexts. The Sterilcentral Project cast my role as the expert
in understanding work practices for design. I chose to embrace the role before the project kickoff meeting and then hand off aspects of expertise to others as appropriate to flexibly situate myself in reframing the relevant issues.
While within the project boundaries, other participants were invited to share
the expert role of engaging in fieldwork at the hospital sites through a field
guide that served as a team-building exercise as more people collaborated in
fieldwork. The unbundling of the anthropologist as the observer expert helped
balance competing interests while building empathy among all participants.
This movement relates the project site with the field site, but I also wished
to bring student learning to the forefront of the Sterilcentral Project. Many of
the workshops were an active collaboration with students as agendas, goals,
and methods were developed as part of learning the research craft of design
anthropology. The seepage along multiple contexts helps not only to scaffold
knowledge building but makes the research dynamic and, in a sense, action
orientated.

Movements between research projects show not only an understanding
within one particular place or configuration, but also an interrelationship in
how materials and knowledge are mediated through various actions in multiple contexts. This allows for an emergent dimension to the research. The
boundaries between the projects are not fixed, but instead are threaded by
the research. The comparison needs to extend along projects to avoid the closure that Bezaitis and Robinson point out results from a focus on outcomes:
"the arcs of research came to tiny ends with each project finish rather than
building and accumulating across instances, clients, and careers" (2011:
191). Finally, I propose *moving out* as the more experimental movement that
leaves a zone of mutual understanding. Rather than close down lines of inquiry in fine-grained analysis, it is about bringing forth intriguing ways of being.
It is about the "what ifs" and inspired by probing the edges of the known. Mc-
Niff points to the trajectories created by such an approach:

> [t]he need for a theory of generative capacity, that is, that could communicate
> the potential of one theory to create new theories. Rather than stopping at the
> traditional notion of a theory arising out of a specific set of circumstances and
> having relevance only to that setting, a generative approach views a theory as
> an organic device to create other theories that may be applied in other settings.
> (1988: 43)

Moving out from a particular practice toward opportunity sounds risky, even a loss of entanglement that is sought for in generating contextual knowledge. But Anderson sees this as exposing the frame of rationality at work in a context to bring "deep design possibilities to light" (1994: 179). These might seem to be speculative potentials, but Fulton Suri underscores the relationship between empathy and imagination: "By definition, as soon as we start to think ahead to future experiences and how people might respond, we begin to draw upon our intuitive and interpretive abilities. We begin to imagine and empathize" (2008: 54). The alternative is to leave it to the engineers and technologists to figure out the future so we can get on with producing descriptions informants can agree upon as accurate. But if we opt for this exploring of potential practices, it allows us to make explicit inherent, yet unnoticed influences as a form of critique. Another name for these potential practices could be *theory* as Bagnara and Crampton Smith conceptualize discourse: "But 'theory' is also commonly used to mean the constantly evolving configuration of epistemological assumptions, conceptual constructs, methodologies, and critical values that flow around and through individual practices and fields of study, contributing to their wisdom and power" (2006: xxi).

To recognize the styles of knowledge within practices, even research practices, is to come to terms with their trajectories. Design and anthropology, like many fields, has problematized the relation between theory and practice as one between practitioners in the field and those building conceptual walls, as it fights for a place and funding in a crowded university. The question is how can a field like design anthropology move beyond this characterization and consider theory a form of practice? For design, Erickson (2006) proposes the need to draw upon theories in multiple fields, but being free to partake in conceptual pruning when required, leaving behind disciplinary arguments and baggage while retaining a certain amount of complexity to be helpful. For design anthropology to be a merger of equals rather than a takeover by design or anthropology requires forward-leaning practices to become recognized as a particular style of knowledge of embodied theory. Or more simply, design anthropologists need to engage in designing! The tool kit of the anthropologist magnifies as it takes on new roles of imagining news ways of being, rather than describing the previous ways. The distance between design and anthropology collapses as the style of knowledge generates its own collaborative notion of accountability in its modes of (dis)engagement.

CRAFTING POTENTIALS TOGETHER

Proposing a move toward a crafting of potentials, as I suggest here, means that our theoretical processes and products take a generative turn and shift directionally toward future ways of being. This is not the same as finding design opportunities or creating design concepts. Crafting potentials is not about presenting tactical options to a particular client. The focus is of much larger import to the realm of humanity; it concerns how to frame future ways of experiencing while challenging the current infrastructure of thought. To appreciate the value of the design anthropological style of knowledge, we need to consider the medium through which we work as not only being about *seeing* but also *making*. Staying critical yet also experimental in creating the tools for emerging events will shift trajectories toward multiple modes of engagement with the world. Through this design *with* anthropology (Gunn 2008; Ingold 2008), researchers aim to achieve a more intimate understanding through the movement of knowledge among differing practices by engaging and collaborating. Rather than breaking human experiences down into factors and components for analysis, design anthropology scaffolds knowledge that allows for emergent relations, interconnections, and associations—theories generated through practice with potential for change. Tackling the difficult and value-laden domain of change and intervention is a worthy cause for design anthropology to move knowledge beyond its own discipline. In the beginning, this new field will contribute and support design's own blossoming critical positioning of its endless production mode. In the case of the Sterilcentral Project, robots may not be taking over but they surely are finding a place in the ecosystem of welfare and health care work. For anthropology, it suggests and envisions a reengagement through new movements and tools as a way of embracing a collaborative theoretical undertaking that breathes new life with each material reworking of previous concepts. Objects introduced in this style of knowing will be framed around facilitating and provoking rather than participant observing. Teasing together, instead of apart, is the movement of knowledge that characterizes design anthropology in contrast with an ethnography of design.

REFERENCES

Anderson, R. J. (1994), "Representations and Requirements: The Value of Ethnography in System Design," *Journal of Human-Computer Interaction*, 9(3): 151–182.

Bagnara, S., and Crampton Smith, G. (2006), *Theories and Practice in Interaction Design*, Mahwah, NJ: Lawrence Erlbaum Associates.

Bezaitis, M., and Robinson, R. E. (2011), "Valuable to Values: How 'User Research' Ought to Change," in A. J. Clarke (ed.), *Design Anthropology: Object Culture in the 21st Century*, Vienna and New York: Springer, 184–201.

Brandt, E. (2001), "Event-driven Product Development: Collaboration and Learning," PhD dissertation, Department of Manufacturing Engineering and Management, Technical University of Denmark, Lyngby, Denmark.

Buur, J., and Soendergaard, A. (2000), "Video Card Game: An Augmented Environment for User Centred Design Discussions," in *Proceedings of DARE 2000 on Designing Augmented Reality Environments*, Elsinore, Denmark: ACM, 63–69.

Clark, B. (2007), "Design as Sociopolitical Navigation: A Performative Framework for Action-oriented Design," PhD dissertation, Mads Clausen Institute, University of Southern Denmark.

Crombie, A. (1988), "Designed in the Mind: Western Visions of Science, Nature and Humankind," *History of Science*, 24(1): 1–12.

Descola, P. (2005), "On Anthropological Knowledge," *Social Anthropology*, 13(1): 65–73.

Ehn, P. (1988), *Work-oriented Design of Computer Artifacts*, Stockholm Arbetslivscentrum.

Erickson, T. (2006), "Five Lenses: Towards a Toolkit for Interaction Design," in S. Bagnara, G. Crampton Smith, and G. Salvendy (eds.), *Theories and Practice in Interaction Design*, Mahwah, NJ: Lawrence Erlbaum Associates, 301–310.

Fulton Suri, J. (2008), "Informing Our Intuition: Design Research for Radical Innovation," *Rotman Magazine*, Winter 2008: 53–57.

Fulton Suri, J. (2011), "Poetic Observation: What Designers Make of What They See," in A. J. Clarke (ed.), *Design Anthropology: Object Culture in the 21st Century*, Vienna and New York: Springer, 16–32.

Grasseni, C. (2006), *Skilled Visions: Between Apprenticeship and Standards*, New York: Berghahn Books.

Gunn, W. (2008), "Learning to Ask Naive Questions with IT Product Design Students," *Arts and Humanities in Higher Education*, 7(3): 323–336.

Hacking, I. (1992), " 'Style' for Historians and Philosophers," *Studies in History and Philosophy of Science*, 23(1): 1–20.

Halse, J. (2008), "Design Anthropology: Borderland Experiments with Participation, Performance and Situated Intervention," PhD dissertation, IT University of Copenhagen.

Hines, C. (2007), "Multi-sited Ethnography as a Middle Range Methodology for Contemporary STS," *Science, Technology & Human Values*, 32(6): 652–671.

Holbraad, M. (2010), "The Whole beyond Holism: Gambling, Divination, and Ethnography in Cuba," in T. Otto and N. Bubandt (eds.), *Experiments in Holism: Theory and Practice in Contemporary Anthropology*, Oxford: Wiley-Blackwell, 67–85.

Hunt, J. (2011), "Prototyping the Social: Temporality and Speculative Futures at the Intersection of Design and Culture," in A. J. Clarke (ed.), *Design Anthropology: Object Culture in the 21st Century*, Vienna and New York: Springer, 33–44.

Ingold, T. (2007), "Earth, Sky, Wind, and Weather," *Journal of the Royal Anthropological Institute (NS)*, 13: S19–S38.

Ingold, T. (2008), "Anthropology Is Not Ethnography," in *Proceedings of the British Academy*, 154, Radcliffe-Brown Lecture in Social Anthropology, 69–92.

Jones, R. (2006), "Experience Models: Where Ethnography and Design Meet," in *Proceedings of the Ethnographic Praxis in Industry Conference*, Portland, Oregon, 82–93.

Kilbourn, K., and Bay, M. (2011), "Exploring the Role of Robots: Participatory Performances to Ground and Inspire Innovation," in *Proceedings of the Participatory Innovation Conference*, Sønderborg, Denmark, 168–172.

Kolko, J. (2011), *Exposing the Magic of Design: A Practitioner's Guide to the Methods and Theory of Synthesis*, New York: Oxford University Press.

Koskinen, I., Zimmerman, J., Binder, T., Redström, J., and Wensveen, S. (2012), *Design Research through Practice: From the Lab, Field, and Showroom*, Boston, MA: Morgan Kaufmann.

Marcus, G. E. (1995), "Ethnography in/of the World System: The Emergence of Multi-sited Ethnography," *Annual Review of Anthropology*, 24: 95–117.

McNiff, J. (1988), *Action Research: Principles and Practice*, Houndsmills and London: Macmillan.

Mogensen, P. (1992), "Towards a Provotyping Approach in Systems Development," *Scandinavian Journal of Information Systems*, 4(1): 31–53.

Muller, M. J. (2008), "Participatory Design: The Third Space in HCI," in A. Sears and J. A. Jacko (eds.), *The Human-Computer Interaction Handbook: Fundamentals, Evolving Technologies, and Emerging Applications*, 2nd edition, New York: Lawrence Erlbaum Associates, 1061–1081.

Otto, T. and Bubandt, N. (2010), *Experiments in Holism: Theory and Practice in Contemporary Anthropology*, Oxford: Wiley-Blackwell.

Rabinow, P., and Marcus, G. E., with Faubion, J. D., and Rees, T. (2008), *Designs for an Anthropology of the Contemporary*, Durham, NC and London: Duke University Press.

Schön, D. A. (1983), *The Reflective Practitioner: How Professionals Think in Action*, New York: Basic Books.

Sitorus, L., and Kilbourn, K. (2007), *Talking and Thinking about Skilled Interaction in Design*, Workshop Proposal at Designing Products and Pleasurable Interfaces Conference, Helsinki, Finland.

Sperschnieder, W., Kjærsgaard, M., and Petersen, G. (2001), "Design Anthropology—When Opposites Attract," First Danish HCI Research Symposium, PB-555, University of Aarhus: SIGCHI Denmark and Human Machine Interaction. Available at: www.daimi.au.dk/PB/555/PB-555.pdf. Accessed October 6, 2012.

Wasson, C. (2002), "Collaborative Work: Integrating the Roles of Ethnographers and Designers," in S. Squires and B. Byrne (eds.), *Creating Breakthrough Ideas: The Collaboration of Anthropologists and Designers in the Product Development Industry*, Westport, CT: Bergin and Garvey, 71–90.

SECTION II

THE MATERIALITY OF DESIGN

–5–

Designing by Doing: Building Bridges in the Highlands of Borneo

Ian J. Ewart

SITUATING PRODUCTION

My intention in this chapter is to champion the role of the producer as de-signer. As an engineer turned anthropologist, it seems to me to be something of a folly to attempt to isolate the process of design from that of production, as much as it is to separate out and valorize consumption (Miller 1995) over the creative activity that necessarily precedes it. An ongoing fascination in anthropology with design and consumption makes it difficult to position pro-duction, especially of the sort in focus here, namely what we might call *an anthropology of engineering*. Engineering is a specific form of activity, which I suggest can be defined as the communal production of large-scale or complex objects. This generic definition removes engineering from its popular percep-tion as somehow uniquely Western and industrialized, and, as I show in this chapter, allows us to reconsider what constitutes production, and what, by unhelpful contrast, often separately constitutes design or consumption. My broader aim is to envisage engineering (communal, technical production) as a mainstream activity neither dependent on nor excluding some of those con-texts of the West, industrialization, science, modernity, and progress, to thus become more common in anthropology generally.

Different approaches to production avoid or confront the separation of de-signing from making and consuming, of which a few deserve mention here.[1] Engineering sociology takes the view that groups of engineers negotiate a settlement in a rather businesslike way (Bucciarelli 1994, 2002), resulting in an adequate compromise instead of an ideal solution. Engineering design is commonly described as part of a complex sociotechnical system, involving, for example, the need to comply with a wider scheme (Petroski 1996), or the economic realities of a large project and its inherent potentials for misunder-standing and abuse (Petroski 2012). Engineering comes across as a practice of subverting an ideal design into a practical reality through a production pro-cess that is slowed by specifications and compromises and dragged along by deadlines and economics. A second approach, promoted by scholars of industrial design, assumes a close reading of the needs of the consumer and consequently ignores production as a delay between conception and use. A successful design, they argue, can predict and preempt the use of this type of object (Cross 2011; Norman 2004), usually what we would call a commodity. These same objects form the foundation of consumption anthropology, whose students reject such determinism and contend that creative use is a valid extension of design activity (e.g., Hebdige 1988; Miller 1991, 2009). Whereas for sociologists of engineering the relationship between design and production is one of friction and compromise, for scholars of design it is largely irrelevant since there is an overt emphasis (in common with consumption anthropology) on the use of objects and not on their production.

If these first two approaches start from the assumption that production is a hapless consequence of design, or subservient to use, then what of the practice of actually making something? Certain strands of anthropology have over the years made efforts to think about production, especially a French tradition of the anthropology of technology (see Lemonnier 1992), but a more explicit consideration of the relationship between conception and production has come from Tim Ingold. As a prominent advocate of skilled production, Ingold has emphasized the continual formation of relations between maker and materials, questioning the influence of a preconceived plan and the implicit reduction of the environment to a mere backdrop for action (2000). In contrast to Cross and Norman, Ingold argues that to separate out the act of designing from life generally is reductionist and unrealistic, and specific to the culture of Western industrialism. To illustrate these themes, he draws on examples of craftsmanship and skill, emphasizing the importance of the relationships between people and their continually developing environment.

Setting aside criticisms of nostalgia and overemphasis on traditional materials and skills (see Ingold 2007a,b; Miller 2007), Ingold demonstrates the significance of production in a way largely ignored in many other accounts. For the engineering sociologists and the various students of commodities, the physical act of production is given no more than a secondary role in the creation of an object. It is true to say that an object is created socially as well as physically, and there are interesting processes at play that deserve our attention. For anthropologists of design, of course these are essential, but in examining those processes it is important not to lose sight of the fact that somewhere along the line, people are actually making things.

To demonstrate the potential for an engineering approach, I present a brief ethnography of the design and construction of two bridges. The first is traditional in the sense that it remains the same as described by early visitors three or four generations ago (Harrisson 1959), while the second was built to a more formal design using recently introduced materials, and was essentially innovative and unfamiliar. This allows us to consider whether a design, as a preconceived and formally inscribed concept, is able to dominate and direct the production process, in contrast to an intuitive or informal idea that suggests weaker mechanisms of control, which might lead to greater variety. The traditional and familiar bridge was produced with very little discussion or trouble, while the new and unfamiliar design required a more detailed plan that remained incomplete. This lack of familiarity provoked substantial uncertainty in production, requiring a series of improvised solutions to complete the project. As well as relative familiarity, a further axis of comparison comes from the fact that one of these bridges is made from traditional local materials, whereas the other is built with modern materials including wire rope and concrete. This raises questions about readily accepted concepts of industrial production and craftsmanship, and the usefulness of that distinction. Ultimately, the relationship between designing and making is a complex entanglement, and whether it is useful or even possible to separate them is at the heart of this chapter.

The ethnographic data presented here come from fieldwork with the Kelabit people in the mountainous north of Malaysian Borneo (see Janowski 2003 for greater detail).[2] The Kelabit are a small ethnic group living on a highland plateau in a rural territory that has historically straddled the international border between Malaysia and Indonesia. Surrounded by the Tama Abu mountain range to the west and north, and the Apad Uat range to the east, access is difficult. A small airstrip serves the largest town, Bario, and in the last five years or so commercial logging has reached the brink of the area, pushing a system of rough roads through the forest so that the highlands are now directly connected to the rest of Borneo. Most important, this includes the coastal town of Miri, a jarring ten-hour drive away, which has attracted many rural Kelabits into paid employment and a place to load up a Toyota 4WD with half a ton of whatever the world has to offer. Access to industrial resources is now possible, but still severely limited by the terrain, the weather, and the cost of transport. Access to ideas is more straightforward, as television and Internet connections are spreading to even the most remote villages. One such place is the village of Pa' Dalih—home to around 150 people, many of whom live an agricultural life, growing rice in irrigated padi fields and hunting for meat in the surrounding forest. This relative remoteness means the villagers remain proudly self-reliant, resourceful, and practical, always willing to try their hand at something new. It was in and around Pa' Dalih that I watched construction of the two bridges between 2008 and 2010.

A QUESTION OF DESIGN

Ganang cocked his head to one side, his good eye peering intently at the piece of paper he had pushed in front of me. It was a piece of A5 from my notebook, now covered with a rough scribble in black biro (Plate 8). This was August

2008, and the villagers of Pa' Dalih had for some time been planning to build a new bridge over the river Kelapang to replace the traditional bamboo bridge washed away several years before. On the other side of the Kelapang, some of the villagers had fruit trees, padi fields, forest farms, and, most important, relatives. Without the bridge, getting to the village meant a long detour and wading across the river: not difficult when shallow, but in the rainy season the river became angry and unpredictable, and access grew much more hazardous. So plans had been hatched to build a new bridge, but not the traditional bamboo variety, something much more substantial and permanent—the Apir Long Da'an (bridge by the junction of the Da'an river), as it was named.

Ganang had been involved with many of the larger projects in the village and was nominally the village engineer, responsible for drawing up plans. He had, for example, shown me a rather professional-looking plan of a proposed new house for the pastor, which he kept pinned to his wall in a clear plastic envelope. What he had pushed in front of me was his idea for the new bridge; it was no more than a sketch, but became the basis of the formal design. Subsequently he drew something more detailed, which was the plan ultimately used on site during construction (see Plate 9). The four main components are the tall support towers, large concrete anchor blocks with anchor posts, wire ropes, and wooden walkway. Ganang's drawing bore a remarkable resemblance to a suspension bridge, something the Kelabit had never built themselves, although a similar bridge had been built in 2002 in nearby Remudu by a British charity, bringing in materials and volunteer labor.

The novelty of this design lies in its differences to a typical hanging bridge. Introduced in the 1960s by British troops stationed in the area, a hanging bridge is the standard design for a more or less permanent bridge. These are usually made of a pair of wire ropes strung between trees or posts on each bank, onto which planks are fixed to form a walkway. More wire rope is strung across as a handrail, and the whole thing is supported by tying it to overhanging trees with rattan or electrical wire. Fixed at one side and pulled tight, this type of bridge requires progressively more tension to pull the base cables level, to the extent that it is theoretically impossible to make its base flat. In practice, the best you can achieve is a characteristic droop, which increases over time as the various components stretch and loosen.

A suspension bridge is based on a different concept, which is to support (or suspend) the weight of the base on overhead cables anchored at each end and raised on towers. The base is connected to these overhead cables with suspending wires every meter or so, whose lengths can be altered to make the base level, avoiding the steep entry and exit slopes of a hanging bridge. For Ganang and the other Kelabit, the principles of a suspension bridge were at best fuzzily understood, gleaned from their observations of the Remudu bridge and colored by their knowledge of hanging bridges. This lack of detail in the plan meant that decisions, mistakes, and new discoveries were made during construction.

I knew from early descriptions (Harrisson 1949, 1959) and my travels to various villages that the form and construction of the traditional bamboo bridge remained remarkably consistent. My host, Anderias (the Headman of Pa' Dalih), is, like most Kelabit, a very practical man and proudly able to turn his hand to any task. I saw him fix his car's suspension with a belt, repair an electrical grinder, and make all kinds of things from bamboo—cups, containers, shelters, spatulas, and so on—as well as build his house. When I asked him to draw a bamboo bridge, he replied derisively, "Why should I draw one when we can just make one?" Then he put both elbows on the table and interlocked his fingers: "There, like that!" He was mimicking the principle of interlocking bamboo poles stretching from each side of the river and meeting in the middle (see Plate 10).

The Kelabit bamboo bridge is essentially a series of poles anchored on each bank and raised slightly to meet over the center of the river, where they are bound with rattan to form a shallow arch. The idea is that the poles flex and bounce as you walk on them, so that when you reach the center, the arch has flattened out somewhat. Along the sides, more bamboo poles are fixed as handrails and, like the hanging bridges, the whole structure is strengthened with rattan stringers tied to overhead trees. These materials are all perishable, so the whole thing needs to be rebuilt after a year or two, and often the rattan bindings will be replaced once or twice in the meantime.

So, do the two bridges have a *design*? The suspension bridge had never been made before, but had in some way been preconceived by the Kelabit engineers. The basic concept was committed to paper in two significant forms: first as a shape, an outline, a basic layout of major components; and second as a list of parts, a breakdown of the bits and pieces to be acquired and brought together into one place to form the object. If the drawing is conspicuously lacking in detail, logistical requirements and the contents of the list are evidence that this had been carefully planned: prepared *belian* (a type of very resistant hardwood) posts, 2.6 kg of 9-inch bolts, 5.4 kg of 6-inch bolts, sixteen 20-mm shackles, four 12-mm shackles, wire netting, and so on. Transporting all the materials to site was no easy matter, requiring truckloads from Miri, *belian* from a village 40 kilometers away, sand and stones from the river, boats to move things, and several strong men to drag it all up the bank. Arrangements for assembling the thinly dispersed tools and skills were equally complex: petrol for the generator, power tools, plastic tubing, canoes, tin sheets to make a shelter, experienced house builders, young men to watch and learn, and so on. Plans for the bamboo bridge, on the other hand, were far less detailed or carefully considered. In fact, there was not really much consideration at all. In the same spirit as Anderias's reaction to my request for a drawing, a spur-of-the-moment decision prompted a group of men to set off, taking nothing more than they had on them at the time, including the concept of a bridge made of bamboo.

While the suspension bridge design depends on a drawing and a list of parts, as well as numerous discussions, the bamboo bridge depends on experience and memories of previous practice, everyday tools, and readily available materials. It may be that in the future the suspension bridge or its descendant becomes a part of Kelabit technological tradition so that the components, tools, and skills required become similarly everyday and widely accessible. But for now, if we ask whether they know exactly how to make these two bridges, for the planned object the response has to be no, or at least not exactly, whereas for the unplanned object the answer is yes. It is the validity and nature of this link between preconception and production that needs further investigation.

An engineered object does not come about purely by chance; there has to be some amount of determination in bringing together the rag-tag assemblage of ideas, tools, skills, components, and materials to become a coherent whole. Ingold has criticized the concept of design as a predetermining and final plan of action by suggesting that objects come about through a more organic mechanism akin to growth.[3] He describes a "field of forces" responsible for generating an artifact, including the maker as part of the environmental conditions that come together in the process. "These are truly creative engagements, in the sense that they actually *give rise* to the real-world artefactual and organic forms that we encounter, rather than serving— as the standard view would claim—to transcribe pre-existent form onto raw material" (2000: 345; emphasis in original). His argument is that organisms and artifacts can be seen as being created through similar processes, such that it is impossible to specify a *complete* design, either through the DNA of the former or blueprint of the latter. Hence, for Ingold, to consider a preconceived plan of activity as the basis for an artifactual outcome is to ignore the ecological truth of man's existence in the world at large. Raw materials exist in a relationship with their environment, into which the maker steps and changes the potential form of some of the parts. In other words, and germane to this discussion, it is the relational environment that is responsible for the process of making, and not just the intentional person. The person and his actions are directed and formed by the materials as well as directing and forming them.

Ingold's ecologically framed relational thinking can contribute to an anthropology of engineering in a number of ways: the notion of the mutual influence of materials and environment on a process of making; the understanding that the conceptual design is never going to be complete; and the point that skilled production is an active part of life that includes responding to circumstances. This needs to be tempered by accepting that groups of people who undertake such large-scale projects do set out with an objective in mind and make a conscious effort to manipulate materials into desired forms with the aim of overcoming the obstacles that hinder and divert them.

Contrary to the relational approach, with its emphasis on patterns of coordination rather than inherent properties, scholars of industrial design adopt a view that designers are able to empathize with their consumers and take into account their numerous desires and responses. Don Norman (1998, 2004) has written of the need for designers to understand not only aesthetics, materials, and production techniques but also, for example, psychology and biology. For Norman, there is very little that cannot be accounted for in designing an object. A well-designed object will allow for the users' various proclivities and inherently guide appropriate use—the scope for subversion or inappropriate use is limited. Mass production of industrially designed objects weakens the link to the environment and thus for Norman the producer is not (as per Ingold) part of a creative engagement; in fact, the production process is in many ways completely independent of humanity and ecology. This provides the platform for a consumer uprising: reinserting the human into the material world by appropriating the object and enculturing it through personalization and redefinition (Hebdige 1988; Miller 1991). Consumption studies have done a good job of bringing in the users' perspective and critiquing the idea that objects are imposed onto society, but still neglect the importance of the actual production of the object before it comes into people's hands. Both approaches, with their respective focus on commodities or craft objects, also seem unsuitable for describing an engineered object, understood as a large or complex object that is communally produced. The first overemphasizes the designer, and the second, the influence of materials and environment. Production is more ad hoc and fluid than the predetermined and anonymous activity Norman suggests, while engineers act in a more mechanical and forceful way than Ingold's artisans and craftsmen.

They are nonetheless a collection of creative agents engaged with their environment, and as a group share a common goal. For a large and/or complex object, the scope for misunderstanding and mistakes is magnified, and an exact plan is unlikely to be comprehensive enough to cope with the inevitable surprises of the production process. Bucciarelli is prominent in analyzing processes of engineering design, and uses the concept of *object worlds* to illustrate the fact that these are communal projects requiring a mix of skills, responsibilities, interests (1994), and languages (2002). His approach is based on the project being driven by corporate goals, using a business or management perspective as its starting point. The team is made up of specialized individuals who need to be brought together as a team to operate efficiently. As Bucciarelli says, "Different participants work in different domains on different features of the system; they have different responsibilities and more often than not, the creations, findings, claims and proposals of one individual will conflict with those of another" (2002: 220). This is true of engineering in the industrialized world, but is not exactly true of Kelabit engineering. Bucciarelli's object worlds consist of unique tools, texts, suppliers, codes, and unwritten rules. Their language is deceptive because although it is English it is still foreign and needs to be learned. However, the Kelabit object world is less problematic and more coherent because the same people who are doing the engineering are also farming, hunting, and relaxing together in a small-scale community. Still, Bucciarelli's point is clear: the design process, even in the controlled environment of computers and industrialized production, does not always work.

It seems that an anthropology of engineering can draw on each of these approaches, but rely entirely on none. The Kelabit are certainly more akin to craftsmen than they are industrialists, but building a suspension bridge is undoubtedly an engineering project and uses industrial materials. Their relations with the environment are key to their success, but we need to acknowledge the radical changes that have expanded the scope of their environment beyond their highland plateau to other parts of Borneo, and ultimately much of the world. Dynamic and expanding environmental relations and historic social traditions provide the context for their design practices, which can now be illustrated with a description of the bridge building projects.

A TALE OF TWO BRIDGES

Construction of the suspension bridge was done through the Kelabit system of voluntary communal labor, *kerja sama*, in which groups of villagers gather to help each other in labor-intensive tasks. For work on the bridge, this meant that on the appointed day, a group of about ten men would turn up, deposit their tools, and light a fire. Most prominent of these were Ganang, the nominal designer; Robert, an experienced house builder; Anderias, the headman; and Jolly, his brother, who along with Anderias had accumulated most of the materials. All Kelabit men are likely to have some experience in building and repairing houses and, through regular trips into the forest, a practical ability to improvise with whatever materials are at hand. In the case of the new bridge, these materials consisted of coils of wire, piles of fixings, wood, and tools put under a temporary tin roof by the construction site. Work began according to discussions based around Ganang's drawing, with individuals largely left to do what they thought was best. Very soon, however, the drawing was left crumpled and ignored as the group began to see how components and materials could be used and what problems needed to be resolved. Referring to the four main bridge components mentioned earlier, I now briefly describe the construction sequence.

The concrete anchor blocks were made by digging large holes and filling them with concrete made with imported cement from Miri, river sand, and stones from the roadside. Concrete is still a relatively new material, although rapidly becoming popular, so the mixing was left largely to Robert, who had worked in the building trade in Miri and was acknowledged as the most skilled builder. He effortlessly scooped up a shovelful of sand and cement, then with a flick of his wrist mixed them in a mid-air swirl. This mixture was then layered with stones to form a large solid block into which pairs of 100mm square hardwood *belian* anchor posts were set.

Before the main wooden towers could be raised, a datum level had to be set across the river to make sure the walkway remained flat and to even out the strain. In house building, to set a level the trick is to use a clear pipe filled with water and mark the naturally equal height at each end of the pipe. As there was no pipe long enough to reach across the river, brief discussions led to a simple solution: a level was set between a tree and a stake about three meters apart on one bank, in line with the opposite bank. Two nails, one in the tree and one in the stake, were leveled with a short tube of water. Looking through one eye along the line of the two nails toward the opposite bank meant that with a bit of shouting, the same level could be marked with a cut on a tree on the other side.

The support towers were eight meters in height, made up of two four-meter lengths of *belian*, then set two meters into the ground. This was much higher than any other bridge, and the joint connecting the two four-meter lengths was the cause of much discussion. House supports are made with a lower portion of *belian* set into the ground, jointed onto a more readily available local wood with a bolted angled lap joint. The same joint was proposed here, but many felt the stresses would be far higher and ultimately too great. Ganang organized thick metal reinforcing plates, one to be bolted on each side of the joint, but it was discovered that the nine-inch bolts were too short to pass through the two metal plates and the five-inch wooden posts. No longer bolts were readily available, so a compromise was reached by using extra bolts and discarding the plates.

Once the towers were raised, two pairs of thick wire ropes were strung across the river. One pair went over the top of the tower as the main support cables, and the second pair went near the base of the tower to take the wooden walkway. Then came the tricky task of connecting the lower cables to the upper pair three meters overhead with a series of wire stringers. Different people had privately suggested several ways of doing this, including using a makeshift platform on the upper rails or fixing the stringers before the ropes were pulled taut. No one knew exactly what to do. In the end, the solution was clumsy and not particularly effective. The four main ropes were pulled taut; each connecting stringer had a loop put in one end that was thrown over the upper cable, the loose end threaded through its loop and pulled as tight as possible. Even after much effort, the wires could not be pulled tight enough to prevent them slipping, and the whole procedure became mighty precarious toward the center of the bridge where there was nothing to stand on except a few planks balanced on the lower ropes. Ultimately, many of the connecting wires slipped down and offered no tensioning support at all.

I describe some of the tribulations of construction, not to highlight them in particular or to imply that the Kelabit struggled to cope with the size or complexity of the project. On the contrary, these and a myriad of other minor hiccups were all dealt with in good humor and the usual Kelabit resourcefulness. The Apir Long Da'an was eventually completed in late 2009, after about six months of work. The villagers of Pa' Dalih are rightly proud of their achievement, describing it as "the best Kelabit bridge ever," and in many ways it is. It is probably the largest they had built, using the best materials available, and as several of the builders said to me, it looked at home in its forest setting (see Plate 11).

Crossing the river Kelapang via the new suspension bridge and walking along the path a few hundred meters, you come to a tributary, the Da'an River. The Da'an was crossed by scrambling over a pile of flood-deposited logs, and it was agreed that a new, relatively small, bamboo bridge would be built here. The span was about ten meters, nowhere near as long as the forty meters of the suspension bridge just upstream, and seen as a relatively simple task. Before the new bridge was constructed, a forty-meter bamboo bridge would have been made across the Kelapang in the same place.

A notably skilled forest man, Isi Berawan (Robert's father), along with Robert, Ganang, and Lian, a young bull of a man, set off one morning to do the job, with me keenly tagging along. The two main materials—rattan and bamboo—were both readily available: bamboo is especially prolific in the area, including right next to the site of our bridge over the Da'an. Bamboo is not deliberately planted, but poles are carefully chosen so as to leave enough growth for future use, resulting in extensive stands rising up an impressive twenty or thirty meters. Having seen the size and number of poles in several bamboo bridges in the area, I expected this new bridge to be a fairly major job requiring considerable planning and coordination. And so we set off, a homemade cigarette hanging from the corner of Isi's mouth, Robert poling his canoe upriver to meet us, Ganang loping along at his own steady pace, and Lian crashing off into the forest without a word. No sooner had we reached the site than everyone seemed to spring into action at once. Isi selected and chopped down several of the huge bamboos, pushing them into the river where Robert collected them and, along with Ganang, hauled them up onto the bank. As they did this, Isi fixed one bamboo horizontally across two trees on the opposite bank at about the same height as the bank where I was standing (setting levels was not an issue here). They slung three poles between this one and my bank and began lashing them beautifully together with rattan to form a walkway. Meanwhile Lian reappeared noisily, carrying what looked like several enormous trees on one shoulder, trimmed the ends to stake points with his *parang*, and hammered them into the ground. I found out later that these were a particular species of tree, known to root enthusiastically when planted like this. Before I knew it, a handrail was fitted, an exit ramp constructed, and Isi was clambering about high in the trees, tying up the rattan, now woven into ropes, to support the center. After three hours, including a break for lunch, the bridge was complete and Isi's attentions were taken up with his next cigarette.

DESIGNING BY DOING

The contrast between the two projects was immediately obvious. On one hand, the Apir Long Da'an suspension bridge had been progressing slowly, beginning with that rough sketch drawn by Ganang. On the other, the *apir bulu'* (bamboo bridge) was thrown up without fuss and with very little discussion, each person knowing what needed to be done and apparently able to turn his hand to it. The traditional bridge lacked the uncertainties of the new; its principles had been honed by generations of Kelabit, each overlapping with the next in a continual flow of bridge-building expertise. By contrast the new bridge was still something of a trickle, various drips of approximate knowledge coalescing to form an emerging flow of experience and understanding.

With the introduction of new materials and tools, the uncertainties in production required a more formal design for the suspension bridge. This in turn defined certain actions, such as the acquisition of suitable materials and identifying and gathering useful skills, specialized tools, and so on. Unlike the traditional bridge, in the initial phases there was a distinct separation between design and production: acts of production were imagined as future activities in the abstract, rather than grounded in experiential knowledge. In the course of production, these abstract uncertainties came to the fore and became focal points for the generation of new techniques and experiences. In effect the distance between design and production was progressively reduced to the extent that the Kelabit engineers, in their designing-by-doing, merged the two activities into a single performance. Although the design phase of the project could be likened to Norman or Petroski's industrial view of engineering, in practice it played out as an act of craftsmanship. The constant need for adjustments was driven by a nuanced understanding of the potentials of materials and environment. The design acted as a resource rather than a blueprint for action (Suchman 1987), a point of departure rather than a final destination.

Conversely the traditional bridge crafted from local materials was in some ways more industrialized. The mass production of bamboo bridges is a routinized activity for the Kelabit with quite rigid guidelines, in the same way as other industrial commodities might be mass produced. The scope for flexibility in design and construction techniques is limited by cultural and historic factors, largely removing any uncertainties from the process. The mutual effect of materials and skilled maker, framed by specific environmental circumstances (Ingold 2000), the craftsman's perspective, which we might have assumed applies to the bamboo bridge, does not fit this situation any more closely than the industrial engineering perspective of the new bridge. Craftsmanship and industrialization were not distinctly separate.

The act of *doing* contributes significantly to any design, as can be seen in these two different projects. An unfamiliar object begins as an imagined concept, but in the course of production, as solutions to unforeseen problems are devised, the original idea is diluted or diverted. The design is effectively post-conceived, the idea of the bridge and the process by which it is made coming about in tandem with, and subsequent to, the practices of production. On the other hand, building the familiar traditional bridge is a repeat of previous designs and activities. The basic idea is fixed in the minds and bodies of Kelabit engineers; there is still a design, but it is a materially different form of design. Bamboo bridges as a tradition remain remarkably resilient, even in the face of new materials and techniques. No chainsaws were used in the making of this bridge, for example, and rattan tends to be used by default, only occasionally or later on replaced with wire. Continually "doing" the same design makes it increasingly habitual and less likely to change. Designing does not therefore require a special "designerly way of knowing" (Cross 2011), but depends instead on a designerly way of doing: design on-the-job, rather than in the mind.

TOWARD AN ANTHROPOLOGY OF ENGINEERING

The space between design and production has been considered from various academic positions, including industrial design and commodity production (Norman), ecological responsiveness (Ingold), and a sociology of engineering (Bucciarelli). Each provides insights that are useful to understanding the ethnographic examples given here, but they are equally problematic in focusing on particular means and materials of production. As an anthropology of engineering, the Kelabit bridges blur easily accepted distinctions between nonindustrial craftsmanship and industrial design and production, as well as illustrate the differences between habitual and novel production.

Considering engineering as an anthropological topic allows us to adopt a position of cultural neutrality when investigating production practices. Engineering is a particular form of production, one often seen as synonymous with industrialism and mass-produced commodities rather than, more broadly, the communal construction of large-scale or complex objects. Such a close association of engineering with industrialization brings with it a number of consequences that need to be critically examined. The most significant is multiple acts of separation: specialization of roles; corporate motivations remote from production activity; the natural from cultural environments; technology from the common man, and so on. Production generally and engineering specifically is seen in many different ways as separate from everyday cultural life, and yet that same everyday life is full of the work of the engineer and producer.

Industrial design and production as described by Norman (2004), for example, actively distinguishes between designer, producer, and user. The designer is seen as separate from the engineer, and hence the process of design is separate from that of production. Over time this has become something of a truism, such that the act of designing is considered a separate activity to production, requiring different, even special, skills (Cross 2011). However, extending this idea to nonindustrial contexts opens it up to question. In the Kelabit highlands, for example, the location and activities of engineering projects are integral to the life of the community. There is no translation or appropriation between designer, producer, or user.

The industrial concept of engineering resolves the differences between these separate actors and activities through negotiated compromise (Bucciarelli 1994; Petroski 1996), bringing together experiences, processed materials, and mechanical equipment in a controlled collaboration. This was also the basis of the Kelabit suspension bridge as a product of industrial materials, tools, and techniques. But rather than a negotiated plan or carefully controlled chain of actions, it depended on skill and innovation to overcome the many unpredicted complications. In effect it was an act of craftsmanship. It may be that the same could be said of all industrial engineering, but skilled practices are obscured by the proliferation of devices and systems, particularly in Western cultural circumstances.

By way of contrast, an object handmade of *natural* materials, is often seen (see Ingold 2000) as governed by the materials as much as the design. The craftsman depends on an empathetic understanding and a feeling for the raw materials to create his object, which, from an industrial perspective, is an activity more akin to artistry than engineering. As can be seen from the example of the bamboo bridge, this is not necessarily the case. That object, handmade from natural materials, was seen by the builders as prosaic and necessary, lacking the cachet of the modern bridge, and in some ways much closer to the concept of an industrial production.

For the Kelabit, building a bamboo bridge is a familiar performance and a regular part of life, something that happens at relatively frequent intervals. This is a mainstream activity, well established in social and technical terms. Groups of men will make this type of bridge from familiar materials in known ways, maintaining routines and traditions through repetition. This is an intuitive, embodied form of knowledge, where the design is quite firmly fixed through repeated acts of making, and not the result of an abstract preconception. Their standard way of making is detailed and yet flexible enough to cope with differences in site conditions or unforeseen problems. The new suspension bridge is a more uncertain concept, whose planned outcome is much less familiar and thus in the course of its construction encounters greater degrees of uncertainty. The design in this case emerges during construction, beginning as a vision and a formal plan of action that is then discarded in the wake of uncertainty as the producers grapple with new problems. Not only is the design incomplete and unable to anticipate the object, but more fundamentally it is inseparable from the performance of production.

As an alternative to the industrial perspective or production-as-craftsmanship, an anthropology of engineering can use examples such as the construction of these two bridges to offer useful insights into the relationship between design and production. Dominant concepts of production, such as industry or craft, include specific notions that are not necessarily universal, as demonstrated by the mass-produced bamboo bridges and the craftsmanship inherent in the new suspension bridge. Despite the material differences between these bridges, seen in the planning, components, tools, and techniques, both demonstrate that production incorporates aspects of designing *and* making. Design and production are not separate activities, nor is design an act of preconception; instead it would be more accurate to say that designing happens on the go and in the hand: Design, in other words, does not exist per se, but only as part of the performance of making.

NOTES

1. These are of course by no means the only examples of the social sciences' involvement with engineering. There is extensive literature in the history of technology, of which Petroski is a part (for example, 2012), and in science and technology studies, of which two more anthropological authors are Downey (1998) and Suchman (1987). Penny Harvey has also produced a number of ethnographic papers documenting road building in Peru (for example, see Harvey and Knox 2010), which foreground the cultural perception of civil engineering projects.
2. Fieldwork was carried out during an ESRC doctoral studentship at the University of Oxford, and as part of a wider AHRC-funded project—The Cultured Rainforest.
3. Suchman (1987) also questions the idea of a predetermined and complete plan, describing it more as a starting point from which subsequent actions take their cue.

REFERENCES

Bucciarelli, L. L. (1994), *Designing Engineers*, Cambridge, MA: MIT Press.
Bucciarelli, L. L. (2002), "Between Thought and Object in Engineering Design," *Design Studies*, 23: 219–231.
Cross, N. (2011), *Design Thinking: Understanding How Designers Think and Work*, Oxford: Berg.

Downey, G. L. (1998), *The Machine in Me: An Anthropologist Sits among Computer Engineers*, London: Routledge.

Harrisson, T. (1949), "Explorations in Central Borneo," *The Geographical Journal*, 64: 129–149.

Harrisson, T. (1959), *World Within: A Borneo Story*, London: Cresset Press.

Harvey, P., and Knox, H. (2010), "Abstraction, Materiality and the 'Science of the Concrete' in Engineering Practice," in T. Bennett and P. Joyce (eds.), *Material Powers: Cultural Studies, Histories and the Material Turn*, London: Routledge, 124–141.

Hebdige, D. (1988), *Hiding in the Light*, London: Routledge.

Ingold, T. (2000), *The Perception of the Environment: Essays in Livelihood, Dwelling and Skill*, London and New York: Routledge.

Ingold, T. (2007a), "Materials against Materiality," *Archaeological Dialogues*, 14: 1–16.

Ingold, T. (2007b), "A Response to My Critics," *Archaeological Dialogues*, 14: 31–36.

Janowski, M. (2003), *The Forest, Source of Life: The Kelabit of Sarawak*, London: British Museum Occasional Paper no. 143.

Lawson, B. (2004), *What Designers Know*, Oxford: Elsevier.

Lemonnier, P. (1992), *Elements for an Anthropology of Technology*, Ann Arbor: Museum of Anthropology, University of Michigan, Anthropological Papers no. 88.

Miller, D. (1991), *Material Culture and Mass Consumption*, Oxford: Blackwell.

Miller, D. (1995), "Consumption as the Vanguard of History: A Polemic by Way of an Introduction," in D. Miller (ed.), *Acknowledging Consumption: A Review of New Studies*, London: Routledge, 1–52.

Miller, D. (2007), "Stone Age or Plastic Age?" *Archaeological Dialogues*, 14: 24–27.

Miller, D. (2009), *Stuff*, Cambridge: Polity Press.

Norman, D. A. (1998), *The Design of Everyday Things*, London: MIT Press.

Norman, D. A. (2004), *Emotional Design: Why We Love (or Hate) Everyday Things*, New York: Basic Books.

Petroski, H. (1996), *Invention by Design: How Engineers Get from Thought to Thing*, Cambridge, MA and London: Harvard University Press.

Petroski, H. (2012), *To Forgive Design: Understanding Failure*, Cambridge, MA and London: Harvard University Press.

Suchman, L. A. (1987), *Plans and Situated Action: The Problem of Human-Machine Communication*, Cambridge: Cambridge University Press.

6

Anatomical Design: Making and Using Three-dimensional Models of the Human Body

Elizabeth Hallam

MODELS IN ANTHROPOLOGICAL PERSPECTIVE

The study of anatomy yields challenging and captivating ways of visualizing the human form. This chapter explores three-dimensional (3D) models of anatomy, focusing on processes of design, making, and use in contemporary contexts where models are mobilized to generate and communicate anatomical knowledge. Key questions regarding this knowledge are widely debated among anatomists and their associates in university medical schools throughout Britain: How is the anatomy of living, growing, moving bodies best taught, and which methods and equipment are necessary in this task? This teaching—in which design practices are embedded—is important because what students learn of anatomy at the start of their medical careers is perceived to have serious implications for their later work. According to experts, "Anatomy underpins clinical practice. Doctors call on anatomical knowledge to perform examinations, formulate diagnoses, undertake interventions, and communicate findings to patients and other medical professionals" (Kerby, Shukur, and Shalhoub 2011: 489). So where design is integral to the teaching and learning of anatomy it ultimately feeds into the biomedical management of life and death.

Here I analyze *designs* as necessarily interrelated material and mental constructs and *designing* as a social process. This approach is informed by anthropological work on the significance of materials, embodied practice, and social interaction in the formation and transformation of knowledge (see Grasseni 2007; Marchand 2010). Hence, I attend to embodied sensory and imaginative engagements with materials in sites of learning. As a contribution to the emerging field of design anthropology (see Gunn and Donovan 2012), the examination of anatomical design brings a new perspective to bear on several intersecting concerns in anthropological studies of the body, material culture, and biomedical science: how perceptions and experiences of human bodies are socially and culturally constituted, how material qualities of things shape persons and their relationships, and how science is (creatively) practiced (see Edwards, Harvey, and Wade 2007; Ingold 2007; Lock and Farquhar 2007). Examining the materialization of designs and the enactment of designing as an embodied, dialogic, and imaginative process provides insight into relations both between persons and material entities, and between the conceptual and the physical in the formation of knowledge. These relations are socially and materially negotiated through design(s) in practice. While the roles of design in the making of science, and of designers in publicly displaying science in museums, have received some scholarly attention (de Chadarevian and Hopwood 2004; Macdonald 2002), I address aspects of design in medical—specifically anatomical—training, which have so far remained unexamined in anthropological works (for example, Good 1994; Prentice 2013; Sinclair 1997). This design focus is timely, given anatomists' recent interest in "cooperative interactions" with professionals, for example, architects, employed in the design of anatomy teaching facilities and equipment—for design has effects on how anatomy is conducted in its designated workplaces (Trelease 2006: 241).

To examine anatomical design, this chapter pays detailed attention to one ethnographic setting in northeast Scotland: the University of Aberdeen's Anatomy Facility (previously the Anatomy Department), housed until 2009 at Marischal College and now located in the Suttie Centre at Foresterhill Campus as part of the School of Medicine and Dentistry. Here a senior lecturer, teaching fellow, and technician, working with students, have been active in designing a still developing set of related anatomical models, made as part of their routine educational activities.[1] Their working practices differentiate several types of model: purpose-made models that they produce on site and regard as collectively constructed rather than attributable to a single person; "historical models" considered valuable artifacts from the past; and "modern plastic models" purchased from a commercial manufacturer during the last two decades for regular use in teaching. Despite these distinctions, all models are related as they are ranked in "generations," with more recent versions seen as descendents of previous ones. This chapter touches on one aspect of this kinship among models—their (re)production, which occurs when existing models either undergo modifications that expand and enhance their functionality, or when interactions with them give rise to the design of new ones. Here (re)modeling takes place through dialogic teaching and learning encounters in which the limits of extant models become apparent.

In this process, distinctions between design and use often break down (see Redström 2008): only when models are used are their limitations recognized and designs to overcome such limitations initiated. And it is only in use that some models actually come to be realized as models. Design and making are similarly entwined as it is in the making that an anatomical model's design more fully materializes. Thus models develop in time—through conception and construction, through users' engagement with them, and through retrospective reflection upon this engagement, which proceeds into future modeling. If, as Nicholas Thomas argues, "objects are not what they were made to be but what they become" (1991: 4), analysis of these objects has to take place over time. The set of models with which this chapter is concerned has been developing since approximately 2002, a relatively short period, which is enmeshed in longer-term developments in anatomical modeling. In the following sections, I briefly situate models as pedagogical aids in analytical and historical context, indicating their roles in current medical school education in Britain. I then discuss how models are used to constitute and disseminate knowledge of the body at the University of Aberdeen's Anatomy Facility, exploring designs and designing in terms of the materials and social interactions that motivate, propel, and shape them. Teachers here see on-site model design as integral to their teaching (rather than as a specially marked design activity), arising both from ideas, which are collectively generated, and through their work with materials. These materials include commercial models and other products not originally designed for anatomical purposes, and my discussion of models improvised with a specific type of wire indicates how the material and visual properties of such elements shape designs in practice. This improvisation is a social and creative materially grounded productive process (Hallam and Ingold 2007). Last, I consider the dynamics of anatomical design in relation to the dialogic interaction that successful communication in learning necessitates.

This account draws on fieldwork, including museum and archive-based research, begun in 1999 at sites for medical education in Scotland and England (Hallam 2006, forthcoming). Although an analysis *of* design processes positions anatomists and students as subjects of study, these subjects are also situated as coproducers of this account because their actions, descriptions, and explanations are crucial in its composition. Research participants will also read and possibly act in relation to the account. Such anthropological works are not, therefore, simply descriptive of social life, but constitutive and potentially formative of it; they can be consumed and have effects within the fields of practice they analyze, opening out to unanticipated future deployments (see Harvey 2009). For design anthropology, this indicates the capacity of anthropological accounts to feed back into processes of design, depending on how those accounts are disseminated among design practitioners by collaborating anthropologists.

ANATOMICAL MODELS: ISSUES OF DESIGN

Historical studies of science highlight the changing significance of 3D models in knowledge formation (de Chadarevian and Hopwood 2004). Not only do models vary and transform—their perceived validity and efficacy being subject to reevaluation and contestation—but understandings of the very term *model* shift according to historical and social context, as recent anthropological work suggests (Isaac 2011). Whether regarded as replicas of that which is already materially present or as tools for transforming the world (Harvey 2009), models take shape, find purpose, and exercise effects in the social environments of their production and use. Within these processes practices of design and perceptions of designs emerge and alter.

Eighteenth- and nineteenth-century anatomical models made in Continental Europe often featured high degrees of compelling detail shown in wax, plaster, and papier mâché (see Maerker 2011). Many of these, and later variants of them, were acquired by anatomists in Britain for medical school teaching, especially during the second half of the 1800s and into the early twentieth century (see Plate 12). By the 1950s, the advantages of "modern materials," especially plastics, which could withstand frequent handling, were recognized among practitioners involved in teaching anatomy (Blaine 1951: 338). Continental European manufacturers—in particular, SOMSO° in Germany, founded in 1876—produced plastic models from around the mid-twentieth century onward, each model comprising several parts for repeated dismantling and reassembly by teachers and students. These gained ground as major teaching resources in British medical schools.

Although commercial model manufacturing has not developed to the same extent in Britain, model making has, nevertheless, been significant—not in established studios and factories, as in Continental Europe, but in the less prominent workshops and other spaces of medical schools. Characterized by the use of eclectic methods and heterogeneous materials, this medical school modeling has created, for specific purposes, models as one-offs or in small numbers for local on-site consumption, rather than in high numbers for international distribution. Unlike the celebrated eighteenth-century plaster models of William Hunter and Joseph Towne's accomplished nineteenth-century waxes (Alberti 2009), fashioned in London, purpose-made models improvised in mixed media (sometimes recycling products) by a multitude of anatomists, technicians, and medical students have remained, to date, largely unresearched. Yet these practices—consistent with and often closely related to other modes of anatomical making, for example, the dissection of embalmed bodies and preparation of preserved specimens, which appropriate techniques, tools, and materials from other domains of work and activity (Hallam 2010)—have often been crucial in facilitating and deepening anatomical understandings of the body. Products from napkins to newspapers were enlisted in improvised modeling during the 1800s (for example Pettigrew 1901), and in the mid-twentieth century anatomists continued to emphasize the importance of model making. Although imported commercial models were deemed useful, they had drawbacks in that they were "rarely designed as an integral part of a particular system of instruction" (Hamlyn and Thilesen

1953: 472). By contrast, models designed *within* a medical school arose out of and were fully integrated into specific teaching practices.

Purpose-made anatomical models have, therefore, taken shape as material entities enmeshed in changing educational contexts. Their design has been influenced, since the 1970s, by the reduction in time allocated to the study of anatomy within the medical curriculum, and by developments in other teaching methods and equipment. So that while students' opportunities to dissect human bodies have decreased, there has been a rise in students' study of prosections (preserved body parts dissected in advance by teaching staff), computer-based anatomy software (with, for example, interactive databases of anatomical images and video clips), and commercially produced plastic models (Collins 2008; Fitzgerald 1979). Local assemblages of this anatomical "material," as it is termed, help form environments (described in the next section) in which purpose-made models are designed and deployed (*Guide* 2009: 16). Within these, no models—whether commercial or made on site—are treated as substitutes for (what are regarded as) "real" human bodies. Rather, they operate as "adjuncts" to those bodies, living and deceased, which are utilized in learning (*Guide* 2009: 17). And, given the time available to students for anatomy, models are not required to possess high degrees of convincing anatomical detail, which is considered too time-consuming or irrelevant to learn. Instead, models—which, when purpose-made, can become quite minimal and abstract in form—act as devices for managing the absolute detail or complexity of "real" bodies. While aiding clarification in learning, models are crucial in mediating, as the following analysis suggests, not only between expert and novice but also between the physical and the conceptual. Design in action is here a material mode of social mediation.

LEARNING ANATOMY IN PRACTICE

Designing at the University of Aberdeen's Anatomy Facility has the primary aim not of producing tangible products, but of enabling anatomical knowledge to be appropriately and effectively taught and learned within a community of experts and students. This involves critical evaluations of existing commercial anatomical models, leading to their on-site remodeling, as well as the local crystallization of new models. But these material entities are not regarded as ends in themselves, for they are designed to be put into practice as anatomical material with which to learn.

Learning anatomy in this setting is intended to "provide students with a framework of basic knowledge and practical skills relating to the human body that form a vital part of understanding how human beings function in health and disease." References to *the* body here embrace *all* human bodies, while physical differences, especially those relating to sex and age, are highlighted as is the "spectrum of usual variation of normal human structure and function" beyond which is "abnormality" (*Guide* 2009: 7, 9). Anatomical practices thus participate in the very definition of the (normal) human body; indeed they are influential in constituting this body, even as they purport to simply reveal it. *Anatomy*, as defined by contemporary teachers and students, is both a domain of already existing factual knowledge and a (changing) field of disciplined practice in which learners must actively participate to properly understand the body. So anatomical knowledge is both communicated *and* generated through learning (which can only take place in authorized, legally regulated institutions).

This learning is a tactile as well as a visual process, as "anatomical skills" are developed through "practical experience." First-year medical students must become demonstrably skilled in "being able to visualise in the mind's eye and feel with an examining hand the body structures as they lie beneath the skin" (*Guide* 2009: 8). The "mind's eye" is understood as that part of the person's memory that assimilates and stores sensory impressions, be they visual, tactile, aural, or olfactory (Morgan and Boumans 2004), and in this anatomical context the notion is used to describe the learning process as one that engages not just the learner's mind but also his or her body. The importance of learning by participating in (directed) practical activity, by "doing Anatomy" (*Guide* 2009: 10), has itself to be learned by students who are often initially unfamiliar with this approach, especially as it tends to destabilize entrenched assumptions that oppose, and hierarchically order, mental and manual work, theory, and practice (see Roberts, Shaffer, and Dear 2007).

Training students' eyes and hands is meant to enhance their capacity to visualize and remember "how parts of the body are put together and how these components work" (*Guide* 2009: 8). To visualize is to accurately imagine and understand spatial relationships between anatomical parts or structures, and this skill is honed through extended periods of close visual and manual investigation. From this perspective, learning anatomy "build[s] up a complete 3D image in your mind," mentally assembling and integrating "components" of the body into a single functioning unit (*Guide* 2009: 16). Envisaged as dynamic, not fixed or finished, this image—which is valued as the core of anatomical knowledge—is expected to be augmented over time as students engage with anatomical material during their training, and in the future when, as medical practitioners, they conduct clinical examinations of and provide treatment for patients. So, anatomy teachers, with years of experience, possess "expert 3D conceptualizations" compared with those of students, which are still to properly form (Patten 2007: 14).

As a visual education conducted by means of disciplined bodily action, learning anatomy also exercises the students' imagination. To build the necessary 3D mental image, students take external visual and tactile impressions from anatomical material, and they internalize or incorporate these impressions to compose an image of a moving bodily interior that is neither entirely derived from that material, nor entirely imagined, but that emerges somewhere in between. Students must develop the capacity to retain and continuously refine a mental anatomical image from which they can extrapolate and visualize from different angles for different medical purposes over time. To achieve the required command of anatomical knowledge is here a matter of developing an enduring mental image, one that relies on the immediacy of ongoing embodied practice for its maintenance and modification, but also one that is expected to have longevity, to be remembered, built upon, and refined, rather than constantly generated afresh.

Building students' 3D mental image of the body requires tactile visualization through interaction with anatomical material in designated teaching rooms. This material comprises preserved, dissected, or prosected bodies; museum specimens; 3D models; illustrated textbooks; diagrams; medical images such as X-rays and scans from magnetic resonance imaging (MRI) and computed tomography (CT); computer-assisted learning packages; and also students' own bodies when they are taught to observe anatomical aspects of themselves and of others acting as models (appropriately clothed) in surface anatomy classes. No single teaching material and method alone is regarded as sufficient. Rather, it is in the movement among multiple and different renderings of anatomy in two and three dimensions—that is, in the tracing of relations between anatomical material—that knowledge is generated and transmitted as an intermedial process (Hallam 2006, 2009).

Students' movement within this field of interrelated material is guided by teachers' evaluation of the different anatomical renderings employed. Commercially produced plastic models are deemed "not as good as the real thing," that is, the deceased or living body (*Guide* 2009: 17). By comparison with the "real," these plastic models are limited in not showing the variation apparent in actual human bodies (because each plastic model of a specific anatomical part appears identical to another, rather than varying as in life). Nevertheless, teachers define them as "valuable stepping stone[s] towards understanding" anatomy (*Guide* 2009: 17), providing a route to rather than a direct source of knowledge. As plastic models simplify rather than simulate the complex anatomical interior, they are used not as primary points of reference (as are actual human bodies) but as anatomical material that students can mobilize when, for instance, navigating between the detail of a prosected body part and a schematized diagram of the same. Providing an intermediate level of detail, plastic models mediate; they facilitate observational and tactile movement as learning. Also utilized as mediators are purpose-made models, designed and constructed on site as discussed in the rest of this chapter, which assist in clarifying and communicating anatomy

MODEL MATERIALS

Models can be particularly useful, teachers at the University of Aberdeen's Anatomy Facility point out, for helping students to visualize aspects of the human body difficult to see in dissections and prosections—especially fine structures such as nerves, blood vessels, and lymphatic vessels. To enable a clearer grasp of these structures, teachers and a technician, in dialogue with students, have engaged in designing models by reworking existing ones and by drawing upon other readily available materials to create new ones. The main principles of their approach are that materials should be to hand or otherwise easy to obtain, inexpensive, and good to work with speedily. So difficult aspects of anatomy are modeled from the mundane and the familiar. Raw materials, for example, wood, are sometimes called upon, but many model materials are commonly used products originally designed for other purposes but that have recognizable potential for adaptation in modeling tasks.

This anatomical redesign/use of available products is consistent with curator Nicolas Bourriaud's notion of postproduction, which identifies a tendency in contemporary art practice to create works on the basis of preexisting works: "The material they [artists] manipulate is no longer *primary*. It is no longer a matter of elaborating form on the basis of raw material but working with objects already in circulation on the cultural market, which is to say, objects already *informed* by other objects" (2002: 13). Such artwork, argues Bourriaud, "does not position itself as the termination point of the 'creative process' (a 'finished product' to be contemplated) but as a site of navigation, a portal, a generator of activities" (2002: 19). Similarly, the on-site design and making of anatomical models is enacted through the selection, combining, tailoring, and recontextualizing of products, and this form of postproduction creates models that prompt action, that facilitate learning.

In 2007, for instance, the senior anatomy lecturer initiated a model of the lymphatics of the breast. As students were struggling to understand this aspect of the breast, and he could find no commercially available models of it, he set up a project for a third-year medical student to make one, providing all of the materials as well as outline instructions and advice. Using an existing plastic model as the basis—a model already deployed in teaching the anatomy of the thorax and upper limb—the student modeled the relevant anatomical parts over it (see Plate 13), guided by diagrams in current anatomy textbooks. The breast was made from a tennis ball bought at a sports shop and cut in half, the lymph nodes from wooden beads from a local haberdashery, and the lymphatic vessels themselves from colored (green) wire, which was by now basic equipment used by the technician in the Anatomy Department's workshop. The model is used to help students learn how fluid (lymph) is drained from the breast through lymphatic vessels, in particular how the flow of lymph can contribute to the spread of cancer from the breast to other parts of the body. To activate the model in anatomy classes, students are asked to place a glass-headed pin (usually employed in sewing) into the breast—the pin represents a tumor, which can block lymph vessels—and then to imagine alternative routes that the lymph, possibly carrying cancer cells, might take.

There are two central issues to note here. First, the design emerged out of interactions between anatomy teachers and students and then developed through a collaborative making process—it was, therefore, generated through the social relations and practices of anatomy teaching. Second, existing commercial products, especially the plastic model and wire, were reworked through use. The plastic model, like the Anatomy Facility's 200 or so other models of this type, was manufactured by a leading company SOMSO®, based in Coburg, which highlights the accuracy, craft, and skill involved in its produc-tion processes.[2] SOMSO's® models have been distributed to medical schools in Britain since the late 1920s by the company Adam,Rouilly, which also man-ufactures medical training models in Sittingbourne, England. Although com-mercial model designs change, or morph as Adam,Rouilly's directors term it, with modifications arising partly from users' feedback, gaps become apparent between those designs and anatomy teachers' specific needs. Teachers ad-dress these gaps when they initiate and coordinate the adaptation and build-ing of models on site. In Aberdeen, the Anatomy Facility's teachers consider their models to be "made from experience" for particular local uses, unlike commercial models with generalized designs manufactured for wide consump-tion. In the case of the lymphatics model, teachers, working with students, initiated the modification of a plastic model's generalized design so that it was tailored or particularized to promote learning. Moving from the general to the particular entailed improvisation, and this was carried out through the ma-nipulation of materials, especially a specific kind of wire. Next I focus on this wire, and the purpose-made models—of nerves—that it has composed, to ex-amine the significance of materials in suggesting design possibilities and the social interactions through which anatomical models are designed.

HOOK-UP WIRE

This wire travels a long way: it moves from a world of electrical cables—like those that disappear into computers and walls in university teaching rooms—into anatomical practices that aid students in visualizing human anatomy. In 2002, the Anatomy Department's technician ordered a stock of wire (about eight 100-meter reels) for modeling. The reels were supplied by RS Com-ponents, a firm in Northamptonshire, England that distributes cables, con-necting devices, tubes, aerials, switches, tools, and so forth—an enormous array of products for maintaining our electrical and mechanical lives. The hook-up wire, made of tinned copper insulated by a plastic (PVC) wall and with a 1mm diameter, is designed and marketed for "internal wiring applications in electrical and electronic equipment."[3] Its current manufacturer, supplying RS Components, is RG Wire and Cable Ltd in Fife, Scotland, which designs and sources products for the telecommunications, electronics, automation, and medical equipment industries.[4]

The wire selected by the technician thus came out of this extensive design and manufacturing domain, lending itself nicely to anatomical uses, where it has been seen as particularly apt for modeling parts of the nervous system. Indeed, nerves are often likened in anatomical discourse to insulated wires that conduct electricity and to telephone cables (for example, Moore and Agur 2002). The use of these metaphors strengthens descriptions of nerves such as those given to students at the Anatomy Facility: "nerves are bundles of fibres that carry the impulses that produce movement and sensations" (*Guide* 2009: 15). Not only is hook-up wire in tune with anatomical turns of phrase, but its linear form is well suited to modeling elongated fibers. This cheap and easily obtainable product is also available in a range of colors, its colored insulation rendering it especially useful in modeling—where there is a need to distinguish different nerves by color. The deployment of hook-up wire in anatomy teaching capitalizes especially on its flexibility and capacity to hold shape when manipulated. Pliability—malleable handleability—and color become valued material and visual qualities that assist students in enhancing their knowledge of nerves.

MODELING NERVES

Brachial Plexus

During 2002/03, teachers in the Anatomy Department found that first-year students were experiencing difficulties in understanding a particular part of the nervous system—the brachial plexus, a "network" of nerves running from the spine, through the neck, and into the arm (Moore and Agur 2002: 436). In embalmed, dissected bodies, whose preserved interiors appear a uniform brown/grey, nerves are difficult to see and can be too fine to feel. In addition, the available commercial plastic models were not helping. The SOMSO® model showing the brachial plexus—represented by colored plastic strands (see Plate 13)— was found insufficient: its design did not adequately demonstrate how different nerves branch out and run along their pathways. So students were struggling to visualize this anatomical structure. To address this, the senior anatomy lecturer arranged for a second-year student to make a series of four enlarged models of the brachial plexus, with assistance from the technician.

Making the models involved consulting diagrams and other models and mapping out the nerves in sketches and summary tables. Plastic tubing was used for the spinal cord, multiple strands of hook-up wire for the nerves (held together with fishing wire), and large wooden beads removed from a dismantled abacus represented the ganglia, or nerve centers. Initial plans for the model were modified when the student and technician grappled with their materials: a rib cage was too difficult to assemble and an artery made from a transparent hose too awkward. When constructed, the student's model displayed the distribution—the branching and merging—of the different nerves (shown by wire in six colors) (see Plate 14, left). Over the following year, the technician made a set of seven second-generation models, simplifying the initial design and making it less "clumsy and floppy," according to the senior anatomy lecturer, with shorter strands of wire nerves and a section of a broom handle recycled as a spinal cord (see Plate 14, right). The second-generation models were seen as more robust and "compact," and better able to "hold themselves together." To activate one of the technician's models in teaching, it was exhibited with a diagram of the same anatomical part. Students could then compare the 3D model and the simplified 2D diagram, a movement between anatomical material that drew students into a more concentrated visual exploration of both renderings.

Following the development of the brachial plexus, the usefulness and aptness of hook-up wire for modeling nerves seemed to grow as it found its way into further constructions. The wire has an absorbing flexibility when handled, it can be guided and turned in different directions, undone and shaped again, qualities considered (in this context) unusually suited to helping students imagine anatomy.

Nerve Pathways

In subsequent years, students used more of this wire to better understand particular nerve pathways. Compared with the brachial plexus, the models designed for this purpose are minimal in form, each comprising a six-inch piece of wire. Rather than enabling students to visualize complicated structures, these models are intended to help them focus on—to see and feel—pathways or routes taken by nerves. Wire pieces can be used to represent any nerve, depending on the anatomical region being studied, but they are especially useful where a nerve's pathway is long and convoluted and therefore difficult to clearly visualize.

Numerous pieces of wire are cut from reels by the technician, but these pieces do not become models until they are used. To operationalize the models, in small classes of around twelve students, teachers demonstrate how to wind and push the wire into the correct positions on commercial plastic models of the relevant anatomical part. Each student then takes up a piece of wire and performs this movement himself or herself. For example, on the underside of a white-ish plastic model of the skull, colored wire is pushed through one of the openings (foramina) to model where a certain nerve travels through that part of the body. As each student manipulates a piece of wire, bending and twisting it along its channel, the wire comes into place and is visualized as a nerve, the bright color of the wire contrasting starkly with the pale plastic skull. In the interaction between the student, the plastic skull, and the wire the nerve's pathway is modeled—the wire taking direction and shape and thereby enabling the student to clearly visualize the nerve's route in three dimensions.

In this case, anatomy teachers have designed a modeling technique through which pieces of wire are temporarily mobilized as models by students. Teachers demonstrate the technique, highlighting the wire's potential and how to use it. But it is the wire user's actions that realize that potential—the model is formed through its use and lasts only for the duration of that use. Afterward the wire pieces are smoothed out ready for subsequent modeling.

Pterygopalatine Ganglion

Just as the purpose-made models of the brachial plexus developed out of perceived limitations in a commercial model's design, so a further model—that of the pterygopalatine ganglion (or nerve center) (see Plate 15)—took one of its points of departure from a SOMSO® model of the skull. In 2008, an anatomy teaching fellow needed a model of this ganglion for students, especially as her verbal descriptions of this part were not fully communicating it. On the commercial plastic skull, only the ganglion's spatial location could be observed—in a pyramid-shaped recess under the cheekbone, described in anatomy textbooks as a "small pyramidal space" (Moore and Agur 2002: 568). And in prosections students could barely see this ganglion, except as what appeared to be a yellow dot in which the different interconnected nerves were indistinguishable.

To help students visualize these nerves, especially their spatial relationships and passage through openings in the skull, the teaching fellow began designing a model of the ganglion. This was made by the technician according to the teaching fellow's requirements, using materials already available in the workshop, with modifications that emerged during the making process. Part of the skull, greatly enlarged, was constructed in transparent Perspex as an inverted pyramid through which a wooden ganglion and wire nerves could be seen. Wire, in different gauges and color coded to show different nerves, was arranged and twisted together to convey a clear sense of the nerves' positioning, orientation, and relations. To use the model effectively, students currently examine it in relation to their own modelings. In classes, they each handle a plastic skull and use a piece of wire to trace the pathways of the relevant nerves (as described earlier). Then they view their own wire models alongside the enlarged ganglion model, repeatedly moving their anatomical observations between the two to enhance their visualization of this nerve anatomy.

ANATOMICAL DESIGN

In 2010, the senior anatomy lecturer referred to designing as a matter of making certain kinds of decisions—deciding which materials for modeling best represent which anatomical parts, as in the choice of wire for nerves, for instance. These decisions are necessarily contextual. They are made in particular social situations in which anatomists, technicians, and students enter into dialogues, along with coordinated, creative interactions with materials, in dedicated educational sites. Analyzing anatomical design, from an anthropological perspective, brings into focus the interactive and imaginative dimensions as well as the embodied and material aspects of knowledge formation as a social and cultural process. It also highlights the dynamic interrelation of design and use, as the practices of making explored in this chapter manifestly entail both.

An initial idea for a design emerges out of teaching situations in which students have difficulties visualizing an anatomical part and its relations—that is, when their visual and tactile exploration of existing anatomical material, including commercial models, does not produce the required and demonstrable clarity and depth of understanding. Such difficulties interrupt the 3D mental image of the bodily interior students are building (or incorporating), and teachers decide to trial alternative solutions to address this. Thus interruptions or gaps that become apparent in students' conceptual and imaginative work prompt teachers to reflect on and collaboratively devise material methods for alleviating them. Here critical reflection and action are interrelated, as conceptual processes develop through embodied practices (see Portisch 2009; Schön 1991). Designing is enacted so that anatomical teaching and learning can (re)gain momentum.

At the Anatomy Facility, as in other medical schools in Britain, designing purpose-made anatomical models attuned to particular local needs is conducted with various mundane materials (contrasting with high-tech anatomy learning aids, for example, the Visible Human Project and the commercial company Anatomage's Virtual Dissection Table, which feature 3D digital images). This ordinariness is integral to the efficacy of these models because for teachers to swiftly respond to emergent conceptual gaps in teaching situations—which become apparent through ongoing dialogues and so are not possible to entirely anticipate in advance—solutions that utilize readily available, inexpensive materials are necessary. With properties conducive to rapid shaping, sculpting, and assemblage, these materials become models that enhance time-efficient communication, and indeed mutual learning, between teachers and students.

Hook-up wire, originally designed to connect electrical components, has proved especially productive in modeling human anatomy, where the body is conceived as a functioning assemblage of parts. Appropriated within anatomical design, this wire helps to compose models to convey anatomical knowledge, thereby connecting teacher and student. In this context wire is adapted through socially situated practices of design so that it mediates the teacher's expert 3D mental image or conceptualization of the anatomical body and the student's novice, yet improving, 3D mental image. And furthermore, this view of social connectivity, as a traversing of gaps, parallels anatomical accounts of living nerves where impulses travel via points of contact or synapses between neurons (Moore and Agur 2002); such conceptions of the anatomical body appear to inform perceptions of the functioning social body of teachers and students.

The interactive manipulation of wire, in concert with other anatomical material, is both physical and conceptual work. Like the string in Susanne Küchler's anthropological analysis, wire is "good to think with," where thinking is an embodied process (2007: 129). Looping, twisting, and bending, hook-up wire has material capacities that motivate anatomical design, especially the modeling of elongated and convoluted bodily fibers and vessels. Flexible and attachable, it is also readily combinable with other material elements in improvised modeling: wire is integrative in a sort of anatomical bricolage (see Lévi-Strauss 1996 [1962]). Designing is thus propelled by embodied exploration and deployment of materials; emergent material properties, in this case of wire, inform design practices just as those practices produce form.

Purpose-made models are not designed as completed, stand-alone, or discrete objects but as open entities that operate within a field of related anatomical material with which students learn. These models must be activated in order to facilitate what is deemed to be successful learning, and so they rely on students' visual, tactile, and imaginative engagement with them to be fully realized. As both teachers and students are involved in making and using such models, anatomical design is distributed among participants within this working and learning environment (see Turnbull 2007). Anatomical models are thus socially as well as materially generated through processes of design, which are always embedded in social relationships.

Hook-up wire has taken grip in the context analyzed here. Initially purchased for one series of models (of the brachial plexus) in 2002, this wire has since offered further possibilities for modeling anatomical structures through which fluids and impulses move. Over time, a growing set or network of models—related through dialogic improvisation with wire—has developed.

This ongoing set comprises a distributed material entity with spatially and temporally separated parts that are nevertheless connected in terms of their composition and form as well as the social relations of their creation, modification, and use (see Gell 1998). Produced through social and material interactions in the field of anatomy teaching and learning, this distributed nervous system, each part with its own micro-history, relies upon the dynamics of design that bring it into material being and ensure that it works its way into the imaginative processes necessary in the continued generation of anatomical knowledge. These modeling practices are constitutive in helping to form knowledge necessary for students' future work as medical practitioners, but they are also transformative as they contribute to each student's lengthy transition from novice to professional expert. This chapter's exploration of anatomical design thus highlights, for design anthropology, the significance not only of the interrelation of making and using, and of the material and the mental, but also of the temporal dimensions of embodied socially and spatially situated designing that produces dialogically generated designs *and* persons with expertise.

NOTES

1. As participants in my research, they prefer anonymity and to be referred to by their professional roles in my published work.
2. See www.somso.de/. Accessed April 2012.
3. See http://uk.rs-online.com/web/. Accessed April 2012.
4. See www.rgcable.com/. Accessed April 2012.

REFERENCES

Alberti, S.J.M.M. (2009), "Wax Bodies: Art and Anatomy in Victorian Medical Museums," *Museum History Journal*, 2(1): 7–36.

Blaine, G. (1951), "Biological Teaching Models and Specimens," *The Lancet*, 258(6678): 337–340.

Bourriaud, N. (2002), *Postproduction*, New York: Lukas and Sternberg.

Collins, J. (2008), "Modern Approaches to Teaching and Learning Anatomy," *British Medical Journal*, 337(7671): 665–667.

de Chadarevian, S., and Hopwood, N. (eds.) (2004), *Models: The Third Dimension of Science*, Stanford, CA: Stanford University Press.

Edwards, J., Harvey, P., and Wade, P. (eds.) (2007), *Anthropology and Science: Epistemologies in Practice*, Oxford: Berg.

Fitzgerald, M.J.T. (1979), "Purpose-made Models in Anatomical Teaching," *Journal of Audiovisual Communication in Medicine*, 2(2): 71–73.

Gell, A. (1998), *Art and Agency: An Anthropological Theory*, Oxford: Oxford University Press.

Good, B. (1994), *Medicine, Rationality and Experience: An Anthropological Perspective*, Cambridge: Cambridge University Press.

Grasseni, C. (ed.) (2007), *Skilled Visions: Between Apprenticeship and Standards*, Oxford: Berghahn Books.

Guide to Anatomy Facility and Anatomy Learning (2009–2010), unpublished report, Anatomy Facility, University of Aberdeen.

Gunn, W., and Donovan, J. (eds.) (2012), *Design and Anthropology*, Farnham: Ashgate.

Hallam, E. (2006), "Anatomy Display: Contemporary Debates and Collections in Scotland," in A. Patrizio and D. Kemp (eds.), *Anatomy Acts: How We Come to Know Ourselves*, Edinburgh: Birlinn, 119–135.

Hallam, E. (2009), "Anatomists' Ways of Seeing and Knowing," in W. Gunn (ed.), *Fieldnotes and Sketchbooks: Challenging the Boundaries between Descriptions and Processes of Describing*, Frankfurt: Peter Lang, 69–107.

Hallam, E. (2010), "Articulating Bones: An Epilogue," *Journal of Material Culture*, 15(4): 465–492.

Hallam, E. (forthcoming), *Anatomy Museum: Death and the Body Displayed*, London: Reaktion Books.

Hallam, E., and Ingold, T. (eds.) (2007), *Creativity and Cultural Improvisation*, ASA Monographs 44, Oxford: Berg.

Hamlyn, L. H., and Thilesen, P. (1953), "Models in Medical Teaching with a Note on the Use of a New Plastic," *The Lancet*, 262(6784): 472–475.

Harvey, P. (2009), "Between Narrative and Number: The Case of ARUP's 3D Digital City Model," *Cultural Sociology*, 3(2): 257–275.

Ingold, T. (2007), "Materials against Materiality," *Archaeological Dialogues*, 14(1): 1–16.

Isaac, G. (2011), "Whose Idea Was This? Replicas, Museums and the Reproduction of Knowledge," *Current Anthropology*, 52(2): 211–233.

Kerby, J., Shukur, Z. N., and Shalhoub, J. (2011), "The Relationships between Learning Outcomes and Methods of Teaching Anatomy as Perceived by Medical Students," *Clinical Anatomy*, 24(4): 489–497.

Küchler, S. (2007), "The String in Art and Science: Rediscovering the Material Mind," *Textile*, 5(2): 124–138.

Lévi-Strauss, C. (1996 [1962]), *The Savage Mind*, Oxford: Oxford University Press.

Lock, M., and Farquhar, J. (eds.) (2007), *Beyond the Body Proper: Reading the Anthropology of Material Life*, Durham, NC: Duke University Press.

Macdonald, S. (2002), *Behind the Scenes at the Science Museum*, Oxford: Berg.

Maerker, A. (2011), *Model Experts: Wax Anatomies and Enlightenment in Florence and Vienna, 1775–1815*, Manchester: Manchester University Press.

Marchand, T.H.J. (2010), "Making Knowledge: Explorations of the Indissoluable Relation between Minds, Bodies, and Environment," *Journal of the Royal Anthropological Institute*, 16(s1): S1–S21.

Moore, K.L., and Agur, A.M.R. (2002), *Essential Clinical Anatomy*, second edition, Philadelphia, PA: Lippincott, Williams, and Wilkins.

Morgan, M.S., and Boumans, M. (2004), "Secrets Hidden by Two-dimensionality: The Economy as a Hydraulic Machine," in N. Hopwood and S. de Chadarevian (eds.), *Models: The Third Dimension of Science*, Stanford, CA: Stanford University Press, 369–401.

Patten, D. (2007), "What Lies Beneath: The Use of Three-dimensional Projection in Living Anatomy Teaching," *The Clinical Teacher*, 4(1): 10–14.

Pettigrew, J.B. (1901), "Anatomical Preparation-making," *The Lancet*, 158(4082): 1399–1403.

Portisch, A.O. (2009), "Techniques as a Window onto Learning: Kazakh Women's Domestic Textile Production in Western Mongolia," *Journal of Material Culture*, 14(4): 471–493.

Prentice, R. (2013), *Bodies in Formation: An Ethnography of Anatomy and Surgery Education*, Durham, NC: Duke University Press.

Redström, J. (2008), "Re-definitions of Use," *Design Studies*, 29(4): 410–423.

Roberts, L., Schaffer, S., and Dear, P. (eds.) (2007), *The Mindful Hand: Inquiry and Invention from the Late Renaissance to Early Industrialization*, Amsterdam: Koninklijke Nederlandse Akademie van Wetenschappen.

Schön, D.A. (1991), *Educating the Reflective Practitioner: Toward a New Design for Teaching and Learning in the Professions*, San Francisco, CA: Jossey-Bass Publishers.

Sinclair, S. (1997), *Making Doctors: An Institutional Apprenticeship*, Oxford: Berg.

Thomas, N. (1991), *Entangled Objects: Exchange, Material Culture and Colonialism in the Pacific*, Cambridge, MA: Harvard University Press.

Trelease, R.B. (2006), "Anatomy Meets Architecture: Designing New Laboratories for New Anatomists," *The Anatomical Record Part B: The New Anatomist*, 289B(6): 241–251.

Turnbull, D. (2007), "Maps and Plans in 'Learning to See': The London Underground and Chartres Cathedral as Examples of Performing Design," in C. Grasseni (ed.), *Skilled Visions: Between Apprenticeship and Standards*, Oxford: Berghahn Books, 125–141.

7

Designing Heritage for a Digital Culture

Rachel Charlotte Smith

Emerging landscapes of digital media and technologies provide an opportunity for museums to involve audiences as active coproducers of expressions and experiences of cultural heritage. Often, however, the focus for the cultural institutions remains on the technologies themselves, and how to apply these to already existing knowledge and exhibition plans. In the following, I argue that the real challenge of integrating technologies into museum practice is to understand how digital cultures of communication affect the emergence, creation, and conceptualization of cultural heritage itself. I present experiences from a design anthropological research and exhibition experiment, Digital Natives. The project worked to create possible futures and understandings of contemporary heritage, digital cultures, and media technologies and involved the collaboration between a group of teenagers, anthropologists, and interaction designers in the process of designing an interactive exhibition. The case demonstrates alternative ways of designing anthropological research through a dialogic design process. Findings generated through the research show how understandings and creations of the digital emerged through the project and provide insights into the cocreated and dialogic qualities of cultural heritage that challenge the traditional museum focus on material and historical matters.

EXHIBITIONS FOR THE DIGITAL ERA

Contemporary museums and heritage institutions are under pressure in terms of attracting and engaging audiences. Facing a decrease in visitors and funding opportunities, many museums are exploring how digital technologies and media can capture the younger audiences in particular and engage them in art, culture, and heritage experiences. Development of digital technologies for museums has taken two main directions. First, museums are using the technologies to convey existing knowledge related to collections and design of exhibition spaces to visitors inside the museum. Such approaches to involving digital technology have emphasized visitor participation, learning, and social interaction inside the exhibition space (Heath and Lehn 2008; Pierroux et al. 2007). Second, substantial efforts have been made to create technologies for extending the bandwidth to and accessibility of audiences, utilizing mobile and online platforms, digital archives, and virtual galleries (Deshpande, Geber, and Timpson 2007; Galani and Chalmers 2010). Although cultural projects are emerging focused on networked social content and living heritage (Giaccardi and Palen 2008; Lui 2012), few have actively used technologies in the development of museum exhibitions to achieve participation and engagement of audiences in creating the exhibition itself (see, for example, Ciolfi 2012; Iversen and Smith 2012a).

Museum projects tend to lack involvement, not just with the technologies and audiences, but also with the *digital* as a cultural and social phenomenon. With this I refer to everyday digital practices, new participatory cultures and grassroots activities, and extensions of space and place characteristic of the information era (Castells 2000, 2010) that are part of shaping meaningful experiences for people in their everyday lives. Cultural institutions exist in a world of technology, social media, and instantaneous digital communication. These institutions must understand how digital technologies are made meaningful in the culture around them and how shifting paradigms of communication effect conceptions and expressions of heritage—both inside and outside the museum.

Giaccardi argues that the impact of social media is to reframe our "understanding and experiences of heritage by opening up more participatory ways of interacting with heritage objects and concerns" (2012: 1). Here the traditional focus on materiality and historical objects, and oppositions between the digital and material, no longer holds (Witcomb 2007). Moreover, "[T]he impact on heritage discourse and practice is significant, as new digital technologies alter and transform the complex set of social practices that interweave memories, material traces, and performative enactments to give meaning and significance in the present to the lived realities of our past" (Giaccardi 2012: 5). The age of information and communication technologies (Castells 2000) challenges our understanding of and approach to cultural heritage as something materialized from the past; as preserved historical objects and sites; and as privileged, authoritative knowledge communicated from museums to audiences. Rather, as Fairclough (2012) comments, while building on constructions of the past, heritage becomes as much a dialogue between the present and the future—something constructed and negotiated here and now—that everyone is engaged in producing. Digital technologies and social media forge participatory forms of communications and engagement and can play an essential role in transforming museums into places of dialogue and interaction, enabling institutions and audiences to connect in new ways.

A design anthropological approach can be a means to exploring alternative forms of digital cultural communication, not by describing what is already there, but through actively experimenting with possible futures (Halse, Chapter 10, this volume). Through a human-centered and critically reflective approach to anthropology and design (Hunt 2011; Binder et al. 2011), the *conditions* for creating and designing heritage can be established with audiences and communities through collaborative processes of design and curation. This approach involves intervention into social and cultural practices that actively challenge existing assumptions of heritage, museums, and exhibitions. Such interventions can recast the focus from technological issues, linear communication, and obsolete distinctions of material, intangible, and virtual forms of heritage to exploring how contemporary hybrid experiences and meanings of culture can be cocreated *in* and *through* dialogue with its audiences. In the following sections, I present experiences from the Digital Natives project, whereby a research team worked through practices of anthropology and design to explore digital cultures and experiences of heritage.

A DESIGN-BASED EXHIBITION PROJECT

Digital Natives was an exhibition project exploring possible futures of cultural heritage communication. The project involved collaboration between a group of seven teenagers, two anthropologists, and twelve interaction designers. During the project, I acted as the lead anthropologist and project manager.[1] Utilizing the academic concept of "digital natives" (Prensky 2001), the project focused on the contemporary culture and practices of young people raised in the digital era, surrounded by new media and information technologies. The exhibition explored young people's everyday relation to digital technologies and experimented with new ways of representing and interacting with their life worlds. The project aimed to create dialogical spaces of engagement between exhibition installations and audiences. We worked from the premise that a dialogical museum exhibition demanded a dialogical design process in which young stakeholders were included as genuine cocreators (Iversen and Smith 2012b). Narratives, arguments, or characteristics concerning the local digital natives had to emerge *through*, not *prior to*, the collaborative process of designing. Hence, a main concern was to integrate the voices and perspectives of the differently positioned stakeholders in the project from the inception of ideas to the final exhibition. The project became a *heritage-making* project in the sense that we actively explored and created issues of heritage that were not there from the outset. Four interactive installations were designed for the exhibition through the project, all focusing on the everyday lives and social practices of the seven young "natives" involved in the project.

The design process was set up as a loosely structured framework drawing upon concepts, tools, and methodologies from social anthropology and Scandinavian participatory design (Bjerknes, Ehn, and Kyng 1987; Ehn 1993). There was no predetermined exhibition concept, only a "Digital Natives" headline and a design space formed by the collaboration of the design partners. We made a timeline indicating major design events and milestones (workshops for matchmaking, scenarios, mock-ups and prototyping, and the final exhibition) and a set of nine dogmas, or design principles, created from our initial research into the challenges of contemporary museums and their use of digital technologies. The principles were formulated by the two main designers and me to articulate our interests in the dialogic paradigm we wished to pursue, but without predefining the potential outcomes of the project.[2] The purpose was that the exhibition concept itself develop as part of the collaborative process while challenging existing curatorial practices and preconceived ideas of heritage. This approach to design reflects Löwgren and Stolterman's (2004) definition of a *vision*. As they argue, a vision is not a solution or a specification of *how to* work, but rather an organizing principle or a preliminary idea that can help the designer structure his or her work and response to the situation as it unfolds over time.

We did not endorse Prensky's (2001) definition of digital natives that included everyone born after 1980, assuming that their brains had been mentally and socially rewired by the impact of digital technologies. However, the concept was a central driving idea for the project and a framework for exploring local youngsters' relation to the digital media. Moreover, in our critical understanding, the headline both claimed that the natives existed and worked as a frame for challenging and negotiating whether they existed at all. The title also suggested a reference to the history of ethnographic exhibitions in which natives have traditionally been represented as less privileged "Others" (Fabian 1991). Simultaneously, the concept granted a focus on contemporary digital practices and technologies not normally affiliated with heritage or exhibitions anywhere. On the level of participatory design, focusing on the digital natives placed the teenagers in a triple role. They were subjects *in* and cocreators *of* the design process and exhibition. They were also the potential audience for it. They were subjects in the sense that their worlds were exhibited, with them as active participants. Creating an exhibition *about*, *with*, and *for* these people was to carve out a central position for them throughout the project. In this way, the title encompassed multiple meanings and challenges, and functioned both as a boundary object (Bowker and Star 1999) and a vision for the project.

EXPLORING THE NATIVES

I commenced the project with a two-month period of research and recruitment. A series of small-scale anthropological field studies were carried out among teenagers in Aarhus, focusing on their everyday use and ideas about digital technologies. Meetings ranged from informal conversations in cafés and observations in schools to semi-structured interviews and photo journeys in home environments. The research was structured and facilitated by me and analyzed collaboratively in iterative workshop sessions involving anthropology students who carried out part of the field studies. Through the research, I recruited a group of seven teenagers aged between sixteen and nineteen for the project from various schools, creative clubs, cultural organizations, and online gaming sites. All were recruited individually, based on their interests and engagement with digital media, as well as their personal interests in, for example, film, photography, painting, sports, and politics, that could help them to work creatively in the project. This age group emerged as particularly interesting as they identified strongly with various digital media and were creative and reflective about their identities. Also, museums generally deemed this group of teenagers out of reach and only accessible through educational institutions. Through a series of five workshops and an online project blog, the research team consisting of the teenagers, a museum anthropologist, and me carried out research collaboratively with the teenagers, focusing on everyday practices and relations to digital technologies. Throughout this process, the youngsters did not only participate, but became critically engaged with their own role as well as the design project as a whole.

Hybrid Virtual Possessions

The research demonstrated how effortlessly the teenagers moved among various media platforms and social networks. They spent many hours every day chatting on Facebook, texting their friends, gaming, fashion blogging, reading online manga comics, and updating digital music libraries. One young girl, Lil, was very passionate about her digital devices: "I just looooove my iPhone," she exclaimed when asked in the first session about her personal digital objects. She was also desperately fond of her shiny white iMac computer that accompanied her everywhere. Observing and discussing Lil's everyday interactions with digital objects, it was obvious to her and the team that she spent most of her time switching between digital devices, listening to music, texting, checking Facebook, and chatting online with friends and classmates in a continuous mash-up of digital and online activities.

The devices played a vital role for the teenagers. They were not mere technological objects affording them access to online networks and virtual spaces. They were precious *belongings*, and virtual and inalienable *possessions* (Odom, Zimmerman, and Forlizzi 2011; Weiner 1992). They represented material and immaterial parts of their identities; relations to friends; personal collections of images, music, games, and social events; and long traces of private communication. Anne, who had bought into the iPhone frenzy six months previously, found eight thousand text messages accumulated in her mobile.

One evening she was cut off from her mobile network at home, just to find a forest of messages waiting for her the next morning. "Hello, Anne, are you there?" "Where are you, Anne?" "Anne?????" "?????". Her friends wanted help with their mathematics assignments and were getting desperate. She blogged: "It's strange, its only really today I realize exactly *how* addicted you get to the Internet and mobile . . . It's funny, it's not just me who's dependent on my mobile, it's all of my friends who are dependent on *my* mobile." Johan often spent four to five hours a day gaming online with his usual team or random online players. Sometimes he spent days creating video sequences of his best "kills" from the game, carefully overlaying them with music before releasing them on YouTube and Facebook to stir up maximum attention among his friends. Martin would post mobile updates on Facebook at least six times a day, especially on the long train ride to and from school, and continuously collect inspiration and images online and in shops for broadcasting on his newly established fashion blog. The devices were like hybrid connectors of time and space, in Castells's (2010) sense. Moreover, they were hybrids of material, digital, and virtual possessions, deeply engrained in everyday life. They carried and traced personal narratives and social networks and were used incessantly to create, access, and distribute experiences, meanings, and identities.

Heritage or ?

Prompted by the inquiry of the project, the teenagers were surprised and often shocked upon realizing their own level of involvement with the digital media and devices. This oblivion was also apparent from the diverse responses to the question: "Do you consider yourself to be a Digital Native?" Philip (aged sixteen), who had three to four computers, received 600 Facebook updates an hour, claimed to be lost without Google, and spent £150 a month on mobile communication, said promptly: "No, I'm not a digital native. I'm too old. I still remember when I didn't have a computer and mobile. They're much younger, the natives, those who grew up with the media. Like my little brother who's eleven and plays Counter Strike four hours every day." Others replied: "I guess you could say that's someone like us, who use media technologies all the time," or "My dad would be a digital native. He grew up with each of the new technological devices; a television, a telephone and a computer." None of the teenagers were familiar with the concept of digital natives, veven if it only took them a split second to respond, always spurring enthusiasm and engaged conversation. Something was at stake, although it had never been consciously reflected. It was experiences of common practices and relations, shared networks, and constructions of narratives and personal identities. These were cultures, not of virtual realities, but of *"real virtuality"*

(Castells 2010: 428), as real as any experiences and expressions of their cultural life worlds, with no distinctions between real and virtual realms of meaning. In their daily practices, the teenagers were developing a sense of self and identity that was heavily dependent on the modern media they were using, and in that process they were producing the traces of a cultural heritage of the future. The effect of the digital native project was to make this process more explicit by articulating the youngsters' identities as part of an exhibition, which was a public digital-material rendering of the emerging intangible cultural heritage.

CREATING DIGITAL INSTALLATIONS THROUGH PARTICIPATORY DESIGN

After six weeks of collaboratively exploring and developing ideas about themselves as natives, the teenagers had created a series of design ideas that they expressed in a mock-up exhibition. The interaction designers, representing the project's three design partners, were invited into the teenagers' exhibition and introduced to their materials. The ideas were created as expressions of the youngsters' visions, as design materials suggesting directions for design and contributions to creating the exhibition concept. Drawing the designers into the design process at this later stage was an intentional move to weaken the customary roles and power relations of *users* and *professionals* and to forge more genuine user involvement (Bødker 1999; Iversen and Smith 2012b). Facilitating the process in this way allowed the teenagers to gain presence and commitment in the project and provided them with a language and authority to collaborate on more equal terms with the designers.

Working in Dialogue

The designers and youngsters partnered in groups toward developing ideas for their digital installations. Here my role as design anthropologist changed and I acted as a mediator between the teenagers as cultural agents, the designers as professional creators, and the curation of the exhibition as a whole. I functioned as the glue connecting the individual groups, and continuously worked on a micro level inside the groups, as well as on a macro level managing the overall project. I attempted to fill various roles as design anthropologist, project manager, coordinator, exhibition curator, friend, and liaison in a discursive creative process of dialogue and intervention. A main concern was to support the youngsters as cocreators, mediating between the multiple voices of the project. A central issue was also an active interweaving of the different perspectives during the design process: digital cultures (heritage issues); technologies (means of expression); and audience experiences (modes of engagement). A balanced integration of these aspects was essential for creating a whole exhibition, with dialogic spaces intersecting the boundaries of material/digital and museum/audience.

It was exactly at the center of these issues that challenges between teenagers and designers arose, also creating a productive tension from which each installation emerged. The designers were drawn toward the digital as a fascination with technology. Many imagined themselves as "related natives," claiming validity to their own ideas because of their familiarity and involvement with designing technologies. Some saw the teenagers as mere content providers and found it inhibiting to work from the teenagers' ideas, as well as the critical nature of the anthropological research perspectives, as it seemed to impede on their professional creativity as designers. Thus their own assumptions about design, users, and technology prevented them from actually engaging with the worlds of the teenagers, *with* and *for whom* they were designing. For the youngsters, it was an enormous process to externalize their identities, being creative experts representing a generation while being mere teenagers in their own particular lives.

Designing from Experiences or Technologies

Many of the team discussions came to center on issues of *categories*. What cultural categories from the lives of the digital natives were suitable for expressing their everyday experience? One prominent example was the Portraits installation, cocreated by two young girls, Lil and Ida. Their idea was to make an artistic video installation based upon a series of portraits about people they knew. It focused on passions, which all youngsters had, for example, books, photography, film, and fashion. Through a couple of workshops, the two designers working with them explored their fascination with visual media and aesthetics. But when the designers attempted to use these insights as information for creating systemic categories for the audiences' interaction, the girls reacted promptly. They refused to have their lives reduced to a series of simple choices or random buttons to be selected by the audience. They also rejected the designers' ideas of mixing their images with thousands of arbitrary videos from YouTube to express the endless networked options of the digital age. These solutions diminished their artistic expressions as creators and tampered with their sense of integrity, identity, and privacy. It was tricky for the designers to grasp that, even though the youngsters were continuously occupied with digital activities, their focus was never on the technologies as *such*. In fact, the teenagers consistently pulled away from a focus on technologies and especially on interaction per se. They defied generalized concepts or categories of "their generation" and continued to stress their personal values and experiences. It was here the interests and focus of the designers and teenagers clearly diverged, and the assumptions of the designers sometimes overruled their interests in the youngsters.

Lil's Digital World

Later in the design process, based upon discussions about the central concept of the exhibition, Lil and I created a three-meter-long poster illustrating Lil's digital world. It was covered with tiny printouts of collected digital images, Facebook updates, text messages, and photographs from events in her past year, meticulously combined into digital traces of personal narratives (see Plate 16). For example, the concert with her favorite band, Kashmir, a photo of her with the lead singer, a printout of her featuring in one of their music videos, and strings of Facebook comments and text messages by her and others linking the fragments. Or the episode when she was celebrating her completion of high school with all her friends and mourning the loss of her grandfather who died at the same time. People in the project who saw the poster were excited about its ability to represent particular personal experiences weaving in and through the technologies. It was a material expression of an intangible digital world allowing the research team to "move reflection beyond a superficial intellectual awareness to new lived experiences" (Sengers et al. 2005: 50). The poster helped bring about the reflective collaborative design space we aimed for, a third position from which common understandings could emerge. It helped the designers appreciate the rich particularities of the youngsters' lives, and me in attempts of catalyzing the people-centered aspects of their digital lives into the design process. In this way *materializing the digital* contributed to the emergence of the central idea of the exhibition that no stakeholders could have envisioned singlehandedly. In Schön's (1991 [1983]) sense of creating a reflective conversation with the materials of design, the iterative design process allowed us to oscillate between the digital, intangible, and material to explore and understand our materials and to create possibilities for a cultural heritage pointing to the future.

THE DIGITAL NATIVES EXHIBITION

The Digital Natives exhibition was built up around four digital installations: Digital Sea, Portraits, Google My Head, and DJ Station. Each of them experimented with modes of visual and aesthetic communication allowing audiences to explore and interact with the lives of the natives.

Digital Sea

At the center of the exhibition was Digital Sea, a visually striking floor projection allowing audiences to explore digital materials from various media and mobile platforms of the seven young natives (see Plate 17). Facebook updates, photos, text messages, and videos floated randomly on the floor, and people could activate fragments according to their interest by physically standing on them. Audience movements were tracked with ceiling-mounted cameras, and chosen materials were enlarged on the floor while related images from the "sea" surfaced and surrounded the visitor. With its blue graphical shades, swivels, and well effects, the five-by-three-meter Digital Sea was aesthetically prominent and functioned as the physical and virtual center of the exhibition. The installation was connected to the other installations so that activities in other parts of the exhibition influenced what appeared in the sea. Digital Sea represented fragmented everyday narratives and the infinite grid of digital connections constructed across various media platforms in the daily lives of the teenagers.

Google My Head

Joined to Digital Sea was Google My Head, an interactive tabletop installation with a large multi-touch display (see Plate 18). Audiences were encouraged to browse in the repository of digital natives' online and mobile updates, pictures, and videos posted on the interface. While browsing through the digital traces, audiences were confronted with the task of completing the sentence "Digital Natives are: . . . " They could select four digital fragments or pictures to support their argument and use an onscreen keyboard to create statements such as "Digital Natives are 'creative,'" "Digital Natives are 'egocentric and spoiled,'" and "Digital Natives are 'no different than others.'" Audiences could browse the materials following their personal interests and create new connections and statements about digital natives, stored and displayed as part of the exhibition. Thus using the form and language of social media, audiences were invited to explore the everyday life and cultures of digital natives and to contribute to their emerging understanding through engaging with the exhibition.

Portraits

Portraits was an artistic interactive video installation projected onto a large two-by-three-meter semitransparent screen. The installation invited people to explore the worlds of a girl and a boy and their passion for books and photography. The films were personal and aesthetic accounts giving an intimate glimpse of the dreams and self-representations of the young digital generation. The visuals were fragmented clips, not a linear film, with which audiences could interact. Infrared cameras tracked the audience, and the intensity of the audience's movements influenced the timing and selection of clips, playback speed, and coloring of the visuals. Dancing or jumping made the visuals more frantic and cold in color, building up to a climax where pages from the book rained over the girl while she was dancing, facing the audience. Slower movements made warm-colored sequences appear of her calmly reading her book. Being a direct visual representation made by and of the teenagers themselves, the installation opened for novel personal experiences and subjective interpretations by the audience.

DJ Station

DJ Station was an interactive audiovisual installation using a tangible user interface based on fiducial tracking.[3] The installation contained a series of musical cubes and effects cubes for audiences to engage with. Each cube represented one digital native's musical taste, and each side of the cube contained a unique loop coproduced with the teenager in question. By placing more musical cubes on the table and applying effects to them, people could combine and alter loops and create complex mash-ups (see Plate 19). Visual images of the youngsters gathered around their respective musical cubes and interacted with images from other cubes on the interface. The live activities on the tabletop were projected onto a wall, while tracks created by the audience were streamed on the exhibitions website. In this way, DJ Station allowed audiences to interact with the musical universe of the seven youngsters, while getting firsthand experience with the remix and mash-up cultures that characterized their approach to the digital media.

ENGAGING WITH THE AUDIENCE

The exhibition attracted visitors from primary and high school classes and teenagers, to university students, teachers, parents, and middle-aged couples. Observations, qualitative interviews, and walk-throughs suggested that, despite the highly saturated media space, the installations invited people to spend much time exploring and engaging with them. The installations spurred individual reflection, conversation, and creative interaction between audiences about the key themes: What did it mean to be a digital native? Did they exist at all? Were they just like the rest of us?

The Portraits installation seemed to challenge the audiences' personal boundaries and their relationship with the two characters represented. The subtle interactions confused some audiences and made them experience the technology as a barrier for engagement. For others it created a range of emotional and reflective experiences and a feeling of connecting directly with the characters and the artistically striking universe in the installation. One woman commented: "it touched me in one way or the other . . . of course because you influence what happens, and therefore it creates, in that moment, a sense that you just reach out and touch that person, or establish a contact with that human being sitting there." In contrast to the secluded space of Portraits, Digital Sea and DJ Station were more inclusive and visibly explorative. Audiences were attracted by the aesthetics and playfulness of both installations, and returned to them between exploring other parts of the exhibition. People walked, jumped, and danced on the floor and related to their own tracking of the visual materials, as well as to the movements of other audiences surrounding them. At the same time, the connections of Digital Sea to the other installations gave a subtle sense of repetition and coherence in the exhibition. At DJ Station, people would spend more than thirty minutes exploring and creating tracks and music singlehandedly or in groups. Again, the language, layout, and physicality of the installations transformed the exhibition into a social arena and allowed the audience to become an expressive part of the exhibition.

A considerable number of audiences saw the installations and materials as an expression of the youngsters' worlds that opened up and invited them to engage with their digital universes. Several noted a braveness and sincerity in the youngsters' way of presenting themselves through the exhibition, which prompted audiences to reflect on the practices and behaviors of the teenagers as well as their own digitalness, and relations to the technologies. Two girls in their mid-twenties said, "It was a bit difficult to get behind the Facebook image. It's my impression that digital natives are very conscious of the image they create, and that sometimes provokes me. So I thought by seeing this exhibition I would get behind that image and get a sense of the things that concern them. But that was missing, I thought." The differences in audiences' reactions were less determined by age or acquaintance to the digital technologies than by their own expectations as visitors. There seemed to be a correlation between people who were regular museum visitors and had certain assumptions about their own role as audiences and those who found it challenging to engage with the exhibitions' interactive and explorative approach.

Most people appreciated the interaction and the empowerment the technologies afforded them, connecting them to the subjects of the exhibition. They were engaged reflectively, creatively, and physically with the exhibition space, and used the technologies to actively explore and interact with the natives as well as each other. One woman expressed her experience in the following way: "It doesn't come naturally to me to get caught by it [the technology]. But I think spending that extra time, some things appear that

I'm completely surprised about getting through the media. It's that the technology gets something more drawn in . . . that it gets the human drawn into it. I think that's the essence of it: the sense that there is a *human presence* there." Likewise, the exhibitions' explorative approach was generally valued also for its ability to create a whole range of individualized experiences. One man commented, "It means that the work is experienced in many many different ways. That's no different than ordinary artwork, but here you can really influence it." Experiencing the audiences' engagement and reactions through the exhibition also gave the teenagers participating in the project a deeper understanding of the interactive aspects the designers had pushed through the design process. The shift from design process to exhibition meant they were temporarily *defamiliarized* with their own digital materials and narratives, and experienced them in new ways through the audiences' engagements with the installations. As such the materialization and engagement with the digital opened up new experiences and understandings of digitalness and heritage.

THE DESIGN OF CULTURAL HERITAGE

Was the Digital Natives project a successful demonstration, or design, of cultural heritage? What difference did the digital make in the project? And what was the effect of the design anthropological process through which it was created?

The Digital Museum

The audiences' experiences stress the presence or absence of the young natives in the exhibition. Some experienced the technology as a barrier to their engagement; however, most people felt that new forms of fragmented narratives and stories *emerged* through the intertwining of digital elements and experiences. There was no separation between the exhibition content and the technologies. The installations demanded active engagement of the audiences, which in turn became cocreators of their experiences. In this way, various dialogic spaces emerged connecting the audiences to the lives of the natives while confronting them with their own practices and assumptions about technologies, young people, and contemporary heritage. The project shaped a new language and "virtual materiality" inherent to the exhibition, demonstrating that objects can be digital and new information technologies can be material (Witcomb 2007). The installations were objects in their own right, not merely interpretations of objects, apart from the exhibition. And they forged multiple layers of subjective engagement by, with, and between the audiences. There was no singular voice speaking in the exhibition, but a myriad of fragmented perspectives and cocreated narratives. The exhibition demonstrated that both youngsters and audience were attracted to the technologies used in the installations as a means of exploration, rather than a focal point in themselves. Rather, the focus was on human-centered issues of self-expression, establishment of relationships, and identities in which they were continuously engaged. And as in the lives of the so-called natives, sometimes *reality* became even more alive and present when reframed, transformed, and augmented in and through digital representations.

Designing Heritage

Through the design process and the oscillation between the digital and material, we created an alternative understanding and experience of cultural heritage. But we did this by involving people into dialogical spaces, negotiating intangible meanings and expressions of contemporary heritage that were continuously produced and recreated through everyday life. This was the same fluidity and dialectic of cultural formation and transformation stressed by anthropologists, in which cultures and identities exist only through—not apart from—representation and consumption. And how people experience these cultures and identities cannot be separated from the situated dialogical acts in and through which they are performed and negotiated (Ashcroft 2001). During the exhibition, the teenagers *became* the natives, *our* natives, temporarily, and a sense of shared culture emerged that did not exist prior to the project. Through the exhibition the teenagers experienced themselves as cocreators of the exhibition. They acted as hosts for school classes and audiences, invited bloggers to review the exhibition, wrote on the Digital Natives Facebook page, and were presented through the press as: The Digital Natives! This was an unintended and essentializing outcome, but it became part of the exhibition's momentum, as yet another dialectic layer and iteration of cultural transformation and cocreation.

Digital Natives was an ongoing performance through which we actively created heritage with the natives and audiences inside the exhibition. But rather than claiming authenticity, history, or expert knowledge, we experimented with the present, situated, and fluctuating. The project was successful in the shift it created from an emphasis on individuals acting in the moment to individuals, communities, and museums participating in the social and cultural production of heritage. The "natives" were not studied in their own environment, but rather expressions of them were negotiated, transformed, and created through the design process and exhibition, just as they were in their everyday engagements with the digital media and technologies. The project produced a view on heritage as a present concern. And in this sense of heritage *making* and *design*, using the digital technologies to frame, explore, and express, the exhibition created alternative possible futures.

Participatory Design and Social Anthropology

The participatory design process allowed us to merge research and design in various ways by working closely with both users and audiences. The explorative and dialogical design space was extended into the exhibition, creating continuity between process and product and allowing the exhibition concept to emerge as a shared creation. Working with the youngsters as cocreators in the project, exploring and negotiating with them what was meaningful, engendered a focus on the youngsters as subjective individuals rather than generalized objects of representation. The design anthropological process meant that we could work with observed practices, outspoken reflections, and ideas created and materially expressed. This extended triangulation, between what was said, done, *and* created, gave new insights into the values and assumptions of both youngsters and designers and their nuanced perspectives on the digital.

While the common focus in the Digital Natives project was on the development of an exhibition, the overall aim was academic, to inform anthropology as much as design. As the design anthropologist in a collaborative project, I played a central role in laying the conditions for the research and the fundamental framing of an explorative project that challenged existing ways of curation and design in museums. Through my anthropological approach, I continuously attempted to push and ingrain the human dimension into the research and exhibition as I worked to understand and include the perspectives and roles of the teenagers as genuine cocreators. The loosely structured design process, and the large number of stakeholders in the project, was highly demanding, especially when collaboration broke down, and often personal interests and agendas of teenagers, designers, and museum partners did not align with my anthropological insights or concerns. This aspect of the collaboration was challenging and demanded continuous negotiation. But it forced us constantly to alternate between a focus on the individual and collective, the personal and the externalizable, as well as the digital and material to create unforeseen forms of heritage expressions and experiences. It was through this process of dialogic curation and heritage *design* that perspectives coalesced into the exhibition as the medium.

TOWARD A DESIGN ANTHROPOLOGY

If museums and cultural heritage institutions wish to engage audiences in new ways using the opportunities digital media and technologies afford, they need to look more carefully at how these media provide meaning to people through their everyday lives. As the Digital Natives project showed, technologies are ingrained and intertwined with various meanings and expressions of contemporary digital cultures outside the museums. We need to learn to create experiences of heritage that connect to, challenge, and negotiate such contemporary issues and allow participation and dialogue. This can be done not merely with material objects, but a whole range of contextual layers at once; social, affective, reflective, and so forth. If exhibitions have conventionally been about materiality and learning, they are as much about coming together to intervene, create, or augment intangible aspects of human life, for a period, relating to digital, virtual, and material worlds.

Design anthropology can be a reflective and creative way of approaching such challenges, enabling conversations between present and future worlds without losing sight of the past. This approach to exploring opportunities does not necessarily provide stable solutions or concise design requirements. But through collaborative processes, iterative work flows, and the production of design opportunities, design anthropology can create insights, merge differing perspectives, and work against preconceived assumptions. Anthropologists can play a vital role in such projects, in scaffolding the infrastructures for research and intervention, compiling the theoretical visions and human-centered methodological approaches in collaboration with multiple stakeholders. The work is unpredictable and loaded with contest and uncertainties, but offers possibilities for experimental ways of designing anthropological fieldwork, or "refunctioning" ethnography (Holmes and Marcus 2005), that can enrich the field and practices of design anthropology.

ACKNOWLEDGMENT

I wish to thank everyone involved in Digital Natives, especially the seven young participants in the project. Digital Natives was created as a collaborative research and exhibition project, and could not have been realized without the dedicated efforts of the teenagers, colleagues, and design partners whom I was lucky enough to work alongside.

NOTES

1. Digital Natives was carried out at the Center for Digital Urban Living, Aarhus University, Denmark, between October 2009 and January 2011 in collaboration with a number of external partners: Center for Advanced Visualization and Interaction (CAVI), The Alexandra Institute, Innovation Lab, and Moesgaard Museum. The exhibition was held at Kunsthal Aarhus in December 2010. Our research is carried on in the Center for

Participatory IT and the program for Contemporary Ethnography, Aarhus University.

2. The dogmas included such principles as the following: 1. The audience has a central role in creating content and experiences in the exhibition; 2. The museum experience should be a socially engaging experience; 3. Communication in the exhibition must be dialogic, but not necessarily true.

3. Fiducial markers are manually applied to objects to enable tracking in a particular scene or installation.

REFERENCES

Ashcroft, B. (2001), *Post-colonial Transformation*, London: Routledge.

Binder, T., De Michelis, G., Ehn, P., Jacucci, G., Linde, P., and Wagner, I. (2011), *Design Things*, Cambridge, MA: MIT Press.

Bjerknes, G., Ehn, P., and Kyng, M. (eds.) (1987), *Computer and Democracy: A Scandinavian Challenge*, Aldershot: Avebury.

Bødker, S. (1999), "Computer Applications as Mediators of Design and Use: A Developmental Perspective," Doctoral dissertation, University of Aarhus.

Bowker, G.C., and Star, S.L. (1999), *Sorting Things Out: Classification and Its Consequences*, Cambridge, MA: MIT Press.

Castells, M. (2000), *The Rise of the Network Society*, Oxford: Oxford University Press.

Castells, M. (2010), "Museums in the Information Era: Cultural Connectors of Time and Space," in R. Parry (ed.), *Museums in a Digital Age*, London and New York: Routledge, 427–434.

Ciolfi, L. (2012), "Social Traces, Participation and the Creation of Shared Heritage," in E. Giaccardi (ed.), *Heritage and Social Media*, London and New York: Routledge, 69–86.

Deshpande, S., Geber, K., and Timpson, C. (2007), "Engaged Dialogism in Virtual Space: An Exploration of Research Strategies for Virtual Museums," in F. Cameron and S. Kenderdine (eds.), *Theorizing Digital Cultural Heritage*, Cambridge, MA and London: MIT Press, 261–280.

Ehn, P. (1993), "Scandinavian Design: On Participation and Skill," in D. Schuler and A. Namioka (eds.), *Participatory Design: Principles and Practices*, Hillsdale, NJ: Lawrence Erlbaum Associates, 44–77.

Fabian, J. (1991), *Time and the Work of Anthropology: Critical Essays 1971–1991*, Amsterdam: Harwood Academic Publishers GmbH.

Fairclough, G. (2012), "A Prologue," in E. Giaccardi (ed.), *Heritage and Social Media*, London and New York: Routledge.

Galani, A., and Chalmers, M. (2010), "Empowering the Remote Visitor: Supporting Social Museum Experiences among Local and Remote Visitors," in R. Parry (ed.), *Museums in a Digital Age*, London and New York: Routledge, 159–169.

Giaccardi, E. (ed.) (2012), *Heritage and Social Media: Understanding Heritage in a Participatory Culture*, London and New York: Routledge.

Giaccardi, E., and Palen, L. (2008), "The Social Production of Heritage through Cross-media Interaction: Making Place for Place-making," *International Journal of Heritage Studies*, 14(3): 281–297.

Heath, C., and Lehn, D. (2008), "Configuring 'Interactivity': Enhancing Engagement in Science Centres and Museums," *Social Studies of Science*, 38(1): 63–91.

Holmes, D., and Marcus, G. (2005), "Refunctioning Ethnography," in N. Denzin and Y. Lincoln (eds.), *Handbook of Qualitative Research*, London: Sage Publications, 1099–1113.

Hunt, J. (2011), "Prototyping the Social: Temporality and Speculative Futures at the Intersection of Design and Culture," in A. Clarke (ed.), *Design Anthropology: Object Culture in the 21st Century*, Vienna and New York: Springer, 33–44.

Iversen, O. S., and Smith, R. C. (2012a), "Connecting to Everyday Practices. Experiences from the Digital Natives Exhibition," in E. Giaccardi (ed.), *Heritage and Social Media*, London and New York: Routledge, 126–144.

Iversen, O. S., and Smith, R. C. (2012b), "Scandinavian Participatory Design: Dialogic Curation with Teenagers," in *Proceedings from IDC 2012*, Bremen, Germany, 106–115.

Löwgren, J., and Stolterman, E. (2004), *Thoughtful Interaction Design*, Cambridge, MA: MIT Press.

Lui, S. B. (2012), "Socially Distributed Curation of the Bhopal Disaster: A Case of Grassroots Heritage in the Crisis Context," in E. Giaccardi (ed.), *Heritage and Social Media*, London and New York: Routledge, 30–55.

Odom, W., Zimmerman, J., and Forlizzi, J. (2011), "Teenagers and the Virtual Possessions: Design Opportunities and Issues," in *Proceedings from HCI 2011*, Vancouver, BC, Canada, 1491–1500.

Pierroux, P., Kaptelinin, V., Hall, T., Walker, K., Bannon, L., and Stuedahl, D. (2007), "MUSTEL: Framing the Design of Technology-enhanced Learning Activities for Museum Visitors," in J. Trant and D. Bearman (eds.), *Proceedings of International Cultural Heritage Informatics Meeting (ICHIM07)*, Toronto: Archives and Museum Informatics, October 24, 2007. Available at: www.archimuse.com/ichim07/papers/pierroux/pierroux.html. Accessed October 16, 2012.

Prensky, M. (2001), "Digital Natives, Digital Immigrants," *On the Horizon*, 9(5): 1–6.

Schön, D.A. (1991 [1983]), *The Reflective Practitioner: How Professionals Think in Action*, Farnham: Ashgate.

Sengers, P., Boehner, K., David, S., and Kaye, J. (2005), "Reflective Design," in O. Bertelsen, N. Bouvin, P. Krogh, and M. Kyng (eds.), *Proceedings of the 4th Decennial Conference on Critical Computing: Between Sense and Sensibility (CC '05)*, New York: ACM, 49–58.

Weiner, A. (1992), *Inalienable Possessions: The Paradox of Keeping-While-Giving*, Berkeley: University of California Press.

Witcomb, A. (2007), "The Materiality of Virtual Technologies: A New Approach to Thinking about the Impact of Multimedia in Museums," in F. Cameron and S. Kenderdine (eds.), *Theorizing Digital Cultural Heritage*, Cambridge, MA and London: MIT Press, 35–48.

SECTION III

THE TEMPORALITY OF DESIGN

–8–

From Description to Correspondence: Anthropology in Real Time

Caroline Gatt and Tim Ingold

AS, OF, AND BY MEANS OF DESIGN

Anthropology comes to design from two ends. From one end, it approaches design in the spirit of the universal, in the same way that it might approach, for example, language or symbolic thought, as a human capacity to propose, to set ends in mind in advance of their material realization. From the other end, however, it approaches design in the particularizing mode of ethnographic description, as the study of the knowledge, values, practices, and institutional arrangements of people in contemporary Western societies who identify themselves professionally as designers. And if there is a connection between the two ends, it lies only in this: that the assumptions that provide a kind of founding charter for the design profession and that underwrite its legitimacy are much the same—and indeed issue from the same source—as those that have long driven the anthropological search for universals of human cognition. They go back to the definition of man as a maker, as *Homo Faber*, who distinguishes himself (and in this discourse, it usually is a "he") from beings of all other kinds that merely use what nature has to offer. For what lifts making from using, according to this definition, is *design*. Friedrich Engels was typical of many when, back in 1875, he declared that the works of humans differ fundamentally from those of other animals insofar as they are driven by an "aim laid down in advance" (Engels 1934: 34). Humans produce, animals merely collect, and it is design—the conception that precedes and guides the task—that distinguishes even the most inept of human makers from the most accomplished of animals. Here, the capacity to design—what Nigel Cross (2006) calls "design ability"—is taken to be constitutive of our very humanity.

The assumption is that every act of making has two components: an intellectual component of design and a mechanical or bodily component of execution. Thus the very notion of design is linked to a pervasive dualism between the mind that projects and the body that executes. In some European languages, the word for *design* is the same as the word for *drawing*: in French *dessin*, in Italian *disegno*, in Spanish *dibujar*. But this is drawing understood not as the trace of a movement or gesture but as the geometric projection of a mental image (Maynard 2005: 66–67). As long ago as 1568, Giorgio Vasari wrote, in this vein, that "design is nothing but a visual expression and clarification of that concept which one has in the intellect, and that which one imagines in the mind and builds up in the idea" (cited in Panofsky 1968: 62). Four centuries later, much the same view was reiterated in a work widely heralded as a manifesto for a truly scientific approach to design, namely Herbert Simon's *The Sciences of the Artificial* (1969). Closely linked to contemporaneous developments in artificial intelligence, computer technology, management, and organizational theory, this "design science" emerged, as Lucy Suchman (2011: 16) notes, during the very same period in which the discipline of anthropology was about to embark on its own internal self-examination. As it did so, and as old certainties about cognitive universals and cultural particulars were progressively deconstructed or exposed as fallacies of modernism, anthropology and design, once joined at the hip, became increasingly at odds. Anthropology's critical examination of its own founding conception of the human—as a being that, by its own nature, transcends nature—inevitably entailed a parallel critique of the cognitivist underpinnings of design science, according to which the very mechanisms of thought render thought capable of the intelligent design of mechanisms.

In this spirit, Suchman urges us not to reinvent anthropology *as* (or for) design but rather to adopt a critical anthropology *of* design as part of a wider anthropology of the contemporary. Such an anthropology, she argues, would require "ethnographic projects that articulate the cultural imaginaries and micropolitics that delineate design's promises and practices" (2011: 3). It would take us, in effect, from one end of the spectrum to the other: from a cognitive anthropology that incorporates the very idea of design into its founding axioms to an anthropology-as-ethnography that sets out to situate these same axioms, and the professions that espouse them, in their cultural, political, and economic contexts. Our argument in this chapter, however, is that an anthropology *of* design, of the kind Suchman proposes, is too limiting, insofar as it narrows the scope of anthropology, in relation to design, to an essentially ethnographic project, and one, moreover, that in its focus on the emergence of design science—specifically in the United States in the second half of the twentieth century—is of an exceedingly constricted historical and geographical reach. The trouble with the "anthropology *of*" formula, whether applied to design or to any other human activity, is that it turns the activity in question into an *object* of analysis. Our aim, to the contrary, is to restore design to the heart of anthropology's disciplinary practice. This is not to advocate a return to cognitivism. But it is to suggest that there are other ways of thinking about design than in terms of setting determinate ends in advance, and other ways of thinking about anthropology than as the description and analysis of what has already come to pass. More particularly, we argue for an open-ended concept of design that makes allowance for hopes and dreams and for the improvisatory dynamic of the everyday, and for a discipline of anthropology conceived as a speculative inquiry into the conditions and possibilities of human life.

Combining the two, we propose an anthropology not *of*, *as*, or *for* design, but an anthropology *by means of* design. Such a design anthropology would adopt what Hirokazu Miyazaki (2004) has called the "method of hope." Like the lives it follows, it would be inherently experimental and improvisatory, and its aim would be to both enrich these lives and render them more sustainable. In its temporal orientation, it would be the precise reverse of conventional anthropology-by-means-of-ethnography, moving forward with people in tandem with their desires and aspirations rather than looking back over times past. We could draw a parallel, perhaps, from anthropology's relation with theology. This might seem an unlikely place from which to start thinking about the discipline's relations with design. However, a recent article on the former by Joel Robbins offers the closest equivalent we have found to what we are attempting here. Robbins distinguishes three approaches to the anthropological engagement with theology. The first is to expose and critique the way Christian theology has underwritten such universalizing concepts of anthropology as religion and culture. The second is to treat the works of theologians themselves as data for ethnographic analysis. In the third approach, however, anthropology might open up to theology as a potent source of inspiration for its own projects, acknowledging that we have much to learn from the faith, commitment, and wisdom that give hope and commitment to others' lives (Robbins 2006: 285). Our "third way" approach to design mirrors Robbins's to theology. This is not to render the other two approaches inadmissible. There can still be a critical design anthropology alert to the intellectual currents that have shaped our modern understandings of the human condition. And there can still be an anthropology of design committed to placing the activities of designers in their social and cultural context. But our aim is different.

The key to both the rethinking of design and the rethinking of anthropology for which we call is the concept of *correspondence*. We therefore begin by introducing this concept. We then go on to consider what this means for the design of everyday life. This leads to a reconsideration of the central role of participant observation in an anthropology-by-means-of-design. We illustrate what this entails in experimental practice by drawing on the recent fieldwork of one of us (Caroline Gatt) with the environmentalist organization Friends of the Earth International (FoEI). We conclude with some reflections on the implications of our argument for the reflexive turn in anthropology.[1]

ON CORRESPONDENCE

In his 1925 *Essay on the Gift*, Marcel Mauss repeatedly insisted that in gift exchange, the thing given is indissolubly bound to the person of the giver. Therefore the bond created in the exchange "is in fact a bond between persons, since the thing itself is a person or pertains to a person. Hence it follows that to give something is to give part of oneself" (Mauss 1954: 10). Note this well: the persons who give and receive, according to Mauss, are not mere *dramatis personae*, nor is their exchange the role play of actors who, in the performance of their parts, themselves remain confined behind their masks and closed to one another. What Mauss established, and what made his essay so revolutionary at the time of its first publication, was the possibility for selves to interpenetrate, to mingle, for each to participate in the ongoing life of the other, without thereby sacrificing their identities to a higher-order entity of the kind Emile Durkheim had previously posited under the rubric of "society." In social life, Mauss wrote, we see people and groups and their behaviors "as we observe octopuses and anemones in the sea" (1954: 78). Quite unlike Durkheim's society, this is a fluid reality in which nothing is the same from one moment to the next and nothing ever repeats. In this oceanic world, every being has to find a place for itself and avoid being swept away in the current by sending out tendrils or lifelines that can bind it to others. In their interweaving, these lifelines comprise a boundless and ever-extending meshwork.

Critically, the weaving of the meshwork involves the passage of time. In the exchange of gifts one does not make immediate recompense but always allows a certain period to elapse, else the relationship with the original donor is deemed terminated. "The period interposed," as Pierre Bourdieu observes, "is quite the opposite of the inert gap of time," which, being incidental to the realization of a preconceived project, could in principle be extended indefinitely or compressed into an instant (1977: 6). Persons and relations can only carry on or *perdure* in the current of real time. As the material embodiment of a generative process, the gift is also imbued with duration, carrying with it a history of relations among those through whose hands it has passed, and propelling these relations into the future. The spirit of the gift, its vital force or impulse, is precisely equivalent to this durational content. Divorced from the flux of real time, the gift would revert to the status of an inert object, and persons to individuals, fixed points in the social fabric between which only a reciprocal, back-and-forth exchange would be possible. Gifts, however, do not travel back and forth but *along*, passing from hand to hand where lifelines overlap and wrap around one another, as on a relay. Like a line uttered in conversation, a particular transaction picks up the flow of social life and conveys it forward, and its meaning can only be comprehended in the context of a history of previous exchanges of which it is but a singular moment.

Alfred Schutz, phenomenologist of the social world, hit on much the same idea in his characterization of social life as a process of "growing older together." Sharing a community of time, Schutz maintained, every consociate participates in the on-rolling life of every other (1962: 16–17). In a celebrated paper, he compared this participation to making music. The players in a string quartet, for example, are not exchanging musical ideas—they are not *inter*-acting, in that sense—but are rather moving along together, listening as they play, and playing as they listen, at every moment sharing in each other's vivid present (Schutz 1951). In a study of everyday walking, my colleague Jo Lee and I came to a very similar conclusion (Lee and Ingold 2006). We found that walking abreast was generally experienced as a particularly companionable form of activity. Even while conversing, as they often did, companions would rarely make immediate eye-to-eye contact, at most inclining their heads slightly toward one another while coordinating their gait and pace by means of peripheral vision, which is especially sensitive to movement. Direct face-to-face interaction, by contrast, was found to be far less sociable. A key difference is that in walking along together, companions share virtually the same visual field, whereas in face-to-face interaction, each can see what is behind the other's back, opening up possibilities for deceit and subterfuge. As they turn to face one another, stopped in their tracks, each blocking the other's path and eyeing each other up, conversants appear locked in a contest in which views are no longer shared but batted back and forth.

In a classic essay on "visual interaction" dating from 1921, Georg Simmel argued that eye-to-eye contact "represents the most perfect reciprocity in the entire field of human relationships," inducing a kind of union between the persons involved. This union, he surmised, "can only be maintained by the shortest and straightest line between the eyes" (1969: 146). However, a straight line drawn between two points, as Simmel describes eye-to-eye contact, leaves each point motionless and unfeeling. Such contact may be rational, but it cannot be vital. Like walkers who have turned in discord to square up to one another, there is no way forward. The implication of the prefix *inter-* in *interaction* is that the interacting parties are closed to one another, as if they could only be connected through some kind of bridging operation. Any such operation is inherently detemporalizing, cutting across the paths of movement and becoming rather than joining along with them. In the kind of relation we propose to call *correspondence*, by contrast, points are set in motion to describe lines that wrap around one another like melodies in counterpoint. Think, for example, of the entwined melodic lines of the string quartet. Though the players may be seated opposite each other with their bodies fixed in place, their movements and the ensuing sounds correspond. So too, do the movements of pedestrians in walking along together. Likewise, the exchange of gifts or of words in conversation sets up a correspondence in which each line is continually answerable to the others. To correspond with the world, in short, is not to describe it, or to represent it, but to *answer* to it.

With this established, we can proceed to our principal aim in this chapter. It is to propose a kind of design anthropology that seeks to correspond with, rather than to describe, the lives it follows. Our contention, in short, is that *whereas anthropology-by-means-of-ethnography is a practice of description, anthropology-by-means-of-design is a practice of correspondence.*

DESIGNING ENVIRONMENTS FOR LIFE

Design is about shaping the future of the world we live in. Yet in many ways it seems a hopeless endeavor predicated upon the failure of our predecessors. Had they succeeded in shaping a future for us, then we would have nothing left to do save to fall in line with their imperatives. Likewise, were we to succeed in shaping the future of our successors, then they in turn would become mere users, confined to the implementation of designs already made for them. Designs, it seems, *must* fail, if every generation is to be afforded the opportunity to look forward to a future that it can call its own. Indeed the very history of design could be understood as the cumulative record of concerted human attempts to put an end to it: an interminable series of final answers, none of which turns out, in retrospect, to be final after all. Or to adapt a maxim from architectural writer Stewart Brand: all designs are predictions; all predictions are wrong (1994: 75). This does not sound like a formula for sustainable living. Sustainability is not about projections and targets, or about the achievement of a steady state; it is about keeping life going. Yet design seems bent on bringing it to a stop by specifying moments of completion when the forms of things fall into line with what was initially intended for them. "Form is the end, death," insisted artist Paul Klee in his notebooks, "form-giving is movement, action. Form-giving is life" (1973: 269).

By setting ends to things, do we not, as Klee intimates, kill them off? If design brings predictability and foreclosure to a life process that is open-ended and improvisatory, then is not design the very antithesis of life? How, following Klee's example, might we shift the emphasis in design from form to form giving? How, in other words, can we think of design as an aspect of a process of life whose primary characteristic is not that it is heading to a predetermined target but that it *perdures*?[2] Here we call for such rethinking. We want to argue that design, far from being the exclusive preserve of a class of professional experts tasked with the production of futures for the rest of us to consume, is an aspect of everything we do, insofar as our actions are guided by hopes, dreams, and promises. That is to say, rather than setting the parameters for our habitation of the earth, design is part and parcel of the very process of dwelling (Ingold 2000). And it is, by the same token, about the ongoing creation of the kinds of environments in which dwelling can occur. What, then, can it mean to design things in a world that is perpetually under construction by way of the activities of its inhabitants, who are tasked above all with keeping life going rather than with bringing to completion projects already specified at the outset? The answer, we suggest, is that design is not so much about *innovation* as about *improvisation*.

This is to recognize that the creativity of design is found not in the novelty of prefigured solutions to perceived environmental problems but in the capacity of inhabitants to respond with precision to the ever-changing circumstances of their lives. To equate creativity with innovation is to read it backward, in terms of its outcomes, rather than forward in terms of the movements that gave rise to them (Ingold and Hallam 2007: 3). You start from a result in the form of a novel object and trace it through a sequence of antecedent conditions to an unprecedented idea in the mind of an agent. The idea is then taken to be the design for the object. To equate creativity with improvisation, by contrast, is to read it forward, following the ways of the world as they unfold rather than seeking to recover a chain of connections from an end point to a starting point on a route already traveled (Ingold 2011: 216). Such creative improvisation calls for both flexibility and foresight. The element of flexibility lies not only in finding the grain of the world's becoming—the way it wants to go—but also in bending it to an evolving purpose. It is not, then, merely a matter of going with the flow, for one can give it direction as well. Designing for life is about giving direction rather than specifying end points. It is in this regard that it also involves foresight.

There is a critical distinction to be made here between foresight and prediction. It has long been the conceit of planners and policy makers to suppose that to imagine the future is to predict: that is, to conjecture a novel state of affairs as yet unrealized and to specify in advance the steps that need to be taken to get there. To foresee, however, is to run ahead of things and to pull them along behind you, rather than to project by an extrapolation from the present. Seeking not to speculate *about* but to see *into* the future, it is to improvise a passage rather than to innovate with representations of the unprecedented. It is to tell how things will go in a world where everything is not preordained but incipient, forever on the verge of the actual (Ingold 2011: 69). And it is about opening up pathways rather than setting targets; about anticipation, not predetermination. Most important, foresight involves the exercise of imagination. This is to think of imagination, however, not as the capacity to conjure up images, or to represent things in their absence, but as the perception of a world in becoming. We have already noted that in some European languages, the words for *designing* and *drawing* are one and the same. Suppose that we retain the synonymy but consider drawing not as the geometric projection of a mental image but as the trace of an evolving perception. What would design look like then?

Klee famously described drawing as taking a line for a walk (1961: 105). The line that goes for a walk does not project or prefigure anything. It simply carries on, tracing a path as it goes. Traveling light, unencumbered by the weight of heavy materials, the line of the draughtsman-designer gives chase to the phantasms of a fugitive imagination and reins them in before they can get away, setting them down as signposts in the field of practice that builders or makers can track at their own more labored and ponderous pace. The designer, let us say, is a dream catcher. If there is a distinction between design and making, it is not between projects and their implementation but between the pull of hopes and dreams and the drag of material constraint. It is here, where the reach of the imagination meets the friction of materials, or where the forces of ambition rub up against the hard edges of the world, that human life is lived. The difference between plans and projects on one hand, and hopes and dreams on the other, is that the former anticipate final outcomes whereas the latter do not. The verbs *to hope* and *to dream* are not transitive—like *to make* or *to build*—but intransitive—like *to dwell* and *to grow*. They denote processes that do not begin here and end there but *carry on through*. We suggest that in designing environments for life, *to design*, too, should be treated as an intransitive verb.

It is in this sense that design can be open-ended. Recall Klee's contention that form is death but form giving is life. In his celebrated *Creative Credo* of 1920, Klee declared that "art does not reproduce the visible but makes visible" (1961: 76). By this he meant that it does not seek to replicate forms that are already settled, whether as images in the mind or as objects in the world. It rather seeks to join with those very forces that bring form into being. Thus the drawn line grows from a point set in motion, as the plant grows from its seed. Thinking of drawing along these lines, and returning to the synonymy between drawing and design, we can see how designing, too, can be a process of growth. Like the growing plant, it would unfold within constantly transforming life conditions. Design, in this sense, does not transform the world. It is rather part of the world's transforming itself. This process of self-transformation, however, unfolds along not one but many paths. It is, in essence, a *correspondence*. As such, it has no particular beginning point or end point, and no one knows what will come of it. As architect Juhani Pallasmaa writes, "design is always a search for something that is unknown in advance" (2009: 110–111). It is precisely this inner uncertainty, according to Pallasmaa, expressed in the hesitancy of his drawing, that drives the creative process.

Let us, in short, think of the process of designing environments for life as a correspondence: one that embraces not only human beings but all the other constituents of the life world—from nonhuman animals of all sorts to things like trees, rivers, mountains, and the earth. This is a correspondence that is not only processual and open-ended but also fundamentally inclusive.

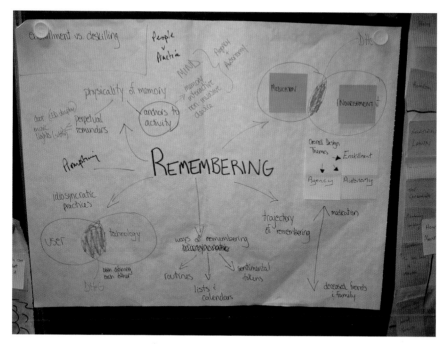

Plate 1. Working from ethnographic observations thematically towards concepts, using a collage on paper.

Source: Intel Health Research and Innovation. Photograph by Adam Drazin.

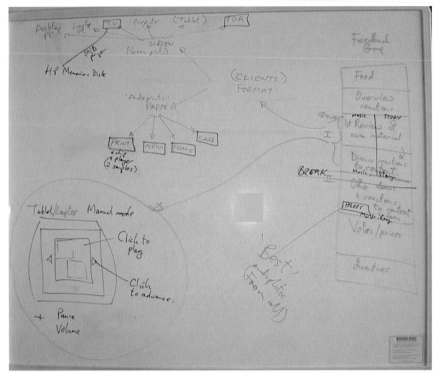

Plate 2. A concept emerges on a whiteboard (encircled bottom left, with arrows leading help-fully from ethnographic observations).
Source: Photograph by Adam Drazin.

Plate 3.   The workshop as black box through which different pieces of knowledge about the present may be assembled to form design concepts for the future.
Source: Diagram by the author © Mette Gislev Kjærsgaard 2011.

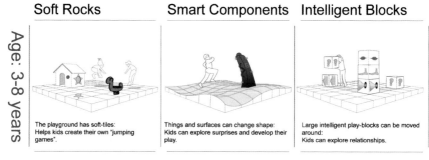

Body Games - Design Strategy

Sønderborg 19.08.03

Age: 3-8 years

Soft Rocks

The playground has soft-tiles:
Helps kids create their own "jumping games".

Smart Components

Things and surfaces can change shape:
Kids can explore surprises and develop their play.

Intelligent Blocks

Large intelligent play-blocks can be moved around:
Kids can explore relationships.

Age: 6-12 years

Soft Rocks/Rotators

An interaction between different play tools and surfaces:
Can stimulate the kids' experiments.

Smart Components

Smart components and climbing structures:
Encourage new tag-games.

3D Positioning

The playground can recognise who is who:
Gives kids richer possibilities to play-out stories.

Søren Bolvig - Mads Clausen Institute at the University of Southern Denmark

Plate 4. The final piece.
Source: Diagram by the author © Mette Gislev Kjærsgaard 2011.

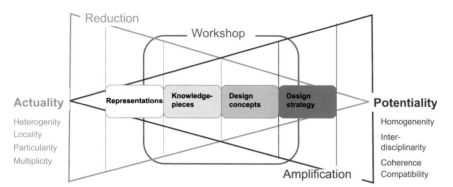

Plate 5. Transformation of localized knowledge and material of the present into shared design concepts and strategies for the future.

Source: Diagram by the author © Mette Gislev Kjærsgaard 2011.

Plate 6. Fieldwork collage made from photos gathered during preliminary visits to hospital sterilization centers as inspiration for a project's kickoff meeting.
Source: Kyle Kilbourn.

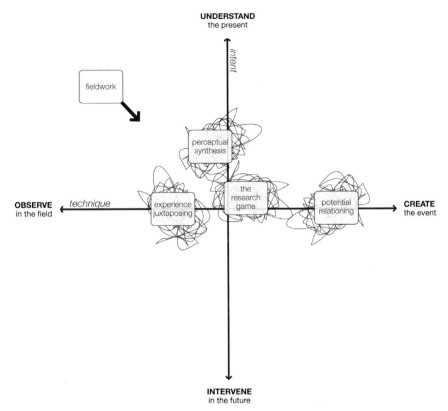

Plate 7. Tensions in design anthropology. Mapping my approaches to design anthropology that rely on tools weaving together the field and the event, while also understanding the present to intervene in the future.
Source: Kyle Kilbourn.

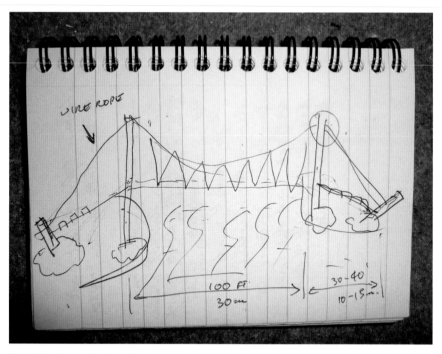

Plate 8. Ganang's plans 1.
Source: Photograph by Ian Ewart.

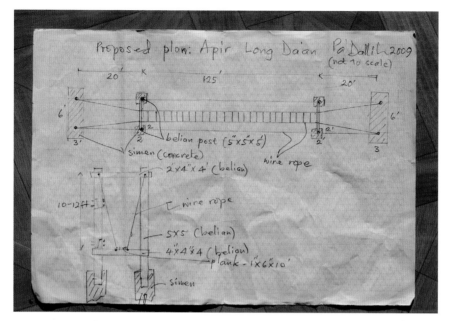

Plate 9. Ganang's plans 2.
Source: Photograph by Ian Ewart.

Plate 10. Typical Kelabit bamboo bridge near the village of Pa' Mada.
Source: Photograph by Ian Ewart.

Plate 11. The completed Apir Long Da'an suspension bridge.
Source: Photograph by Ian Ewart.

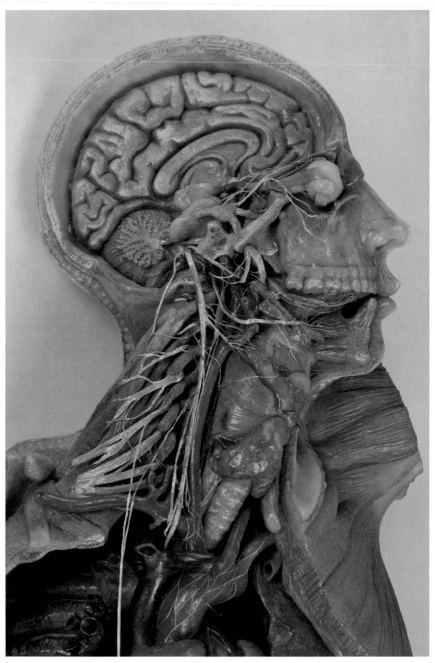

Plate 12. Human anatomy in wax: model of the head and torso (male) by Dr. Rudolf Weisker, Leipzig, 1879. This is held in the historical model collection of the Anatomy Facility, School of Medicine and Dentistry, University of Aberdeen. The photograph shows the detailed nerves of the head and neck, modeled in wax-covered thread.
Source: Photograph by John McIntosh, 2005.

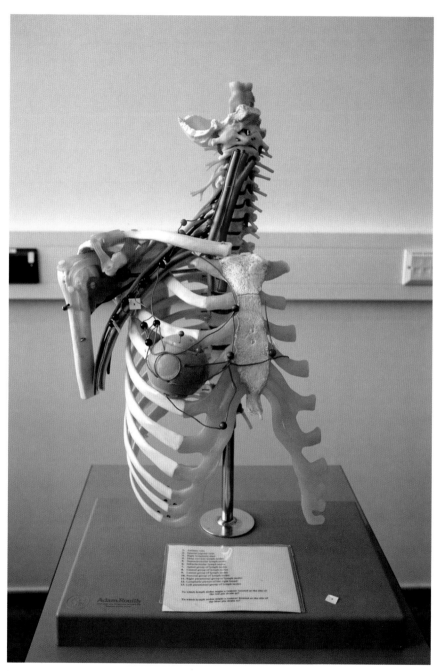

Plate 13. Wire model of the lymphatics of the breast at the Anatomy Facility, School of Medicine and Dentistry, University of Aberdeen. The purpose-made model is modeled onto the surface of the "PO81 Cervical Vertebral Column with Shoulder Girdle" (which includes the brachial plexus in colored plastic strands), a commercial SOMSO® model from Adam Rouilly. *Source*: SOMSO® model from Adam Rouilly. Photograph by Elizabeth Hallam, 2010.

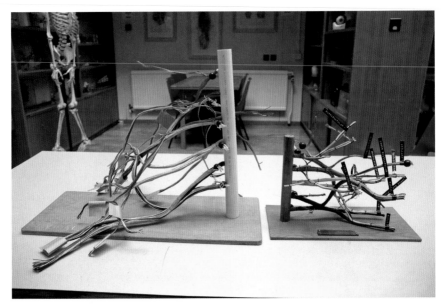

Plate 14. Purpose-made models of the brachial plexus in the Anatomy Museum, Marischal College, University of Aberdeen (prior to the relocation of the Anatomy Facility to the Suttie Centre). The photograph shows a first-generation model (left) and a second-generation model (right).

Source: Photograph by Elizabeth Hallam, 2008.

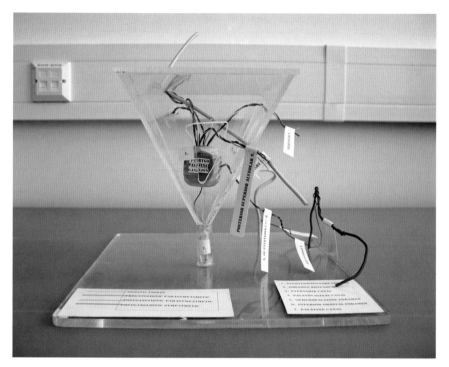

Plate 15. Purpose-made model of the pterygopalatine ganglion at the Anatomy Facility, School of Medicine and Dentistry, University of Aberdeen.
Source: Photograph by Elizabeth Hallam, 2010.

Plate 16. Lil's digital poster.
Source: Photograph by Rachel Charlotte Smith © Digital Urban Living / Centre for Participatory IT, Aarhus University.

Plate 17. The Digital Sea installation, Kunsthal Aarhus, Denmark.
Source: Photograph by Stine Nørgaard Andersen © Digital Urban Living / Centre for Participatory IT, Aarhus University.

Plate 18. The Google My Head installation, Kunsthal Aarhus, Denmark.
Source: Photograph by Stine Nørgaard Andersen © Digital Urban Living / Centre for Participatory IT, Aarhus University.

Plate 19. Audiences at the DJ Station, Kunsthal Aarhus, Denmark.
Source: Photograph by Matthew Charnock © Digital Urban Living / Centre for Participatory IT, Aarhus University.

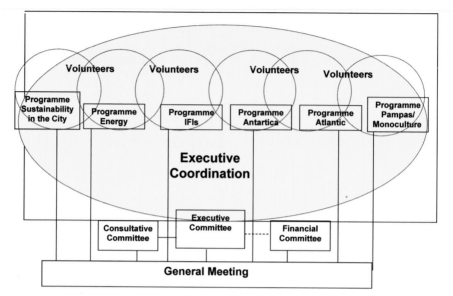

Plate 20. The organogramma.

Source: Diagram by Caroline Gatt.

Plate 21. Materials for designing across sites.
Source: © SPIRE. Photographs by Jacob Buur.

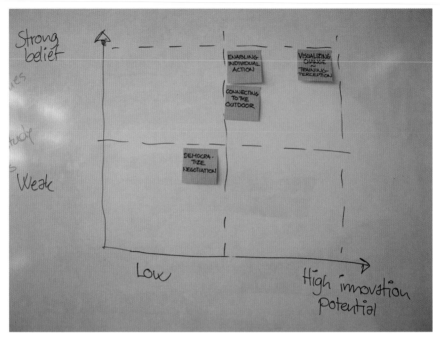

Plate 22. How much do you believe things will actually become true?
Source: Photograph by Jacob Buur.

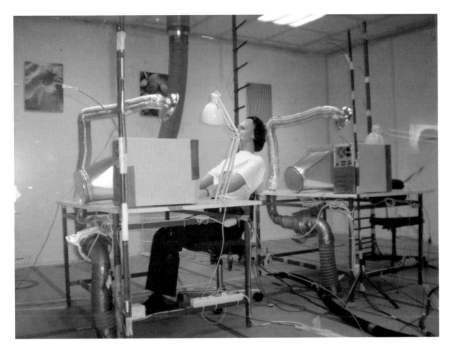

Plate 23. Indoor climate chamber.
Source: Danish Technical University Indoor Climate Research Unit.

Plate 24. Collaborative workshop in the town hall of Herlev.
Source: T. Binder, The Royal Danish Academy of Fine Arts–School of Design.

Plate 25. Materials to instigate collaborative reflection and imagining.
Source: T. Binder, The Royal Danish Academy of Fine Arts–School of Design.

Plate 26. A shop owner demonstrates how to swipe an ID card to register for the full benefits of having returned used batteries.

Source: T. Binder, The Royal Danish Academy of Fine Arts–School of Design.

Plate 27. An improvised use of shopping baskets with paper labels allowed the participants to bodily explore modes of imagined interaction.
Source: T. Binder, The Royal Danish Academy of Fine Arts–School of Design.

Plate 28. Participants are drawn together not because they agree, but because they disagree.

Source: T. Binder, The Royal Danish Academy of Fine Arts–School of Design.

Plate 29. The paper and cardboard mock-up of the Beacon concept.
Source: Photograph by Brendon Clark.

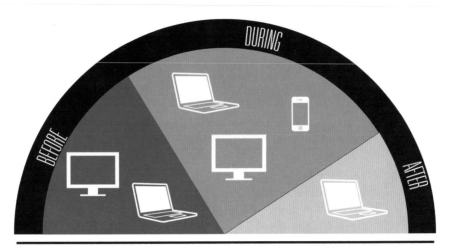

MICHAEL'S OMELET TRAJECTORY

BEFORE
- **Television**
  - Cooking shows
- **Laptop**
  - AllRecipes.com

DURING
- **Television**
  - Good Eats
- **Laptop**
  - AllRecipes.com
- **Smart Phone**
  - Stopwatch for Timer

AFTER
- **Laptop**
  - Future Ideas

Plate 30. Michael's omelet trajectory.
Source: © Christina Wasson and Crysta Metcalf.

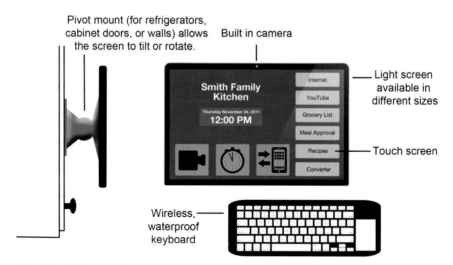

Plate 31. Kitchen media device to support sociality.
Source: © Christina Wasson and Crysta Metcalf.

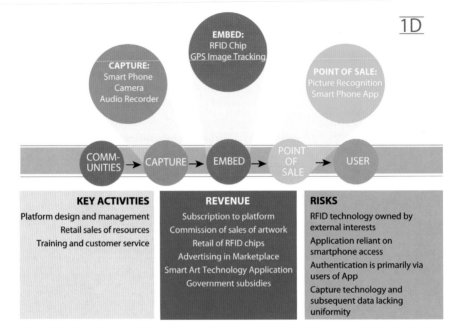

Plate 32. Experience model of Aboriginal Smart Art Process with concept of ID technologies. *Source*: Experience model by Elizabeth (Dori) Tunstall and the Smart Art student team.

REPOSITIONING PARTICIPANT OBSERVATION

Anthropology, in our view, is a generous, open-ended, holistic, comparative, and yet critical inquiry into the conditions and potentials for human life in the one world we all inhabit. It is generous because it is founded in a willingness to both listen and respond—that is, to *correspond*—to what others have to tell us. It is open-ended because its aim is not to arrive at final solutions that would bring social life to a close but rather to reveal the paths along which it can keep on going. Thus the holism to which anthropology aspires is the very opposite of totalization (Otto and Bubandt 2010: 11; Willerslev and Pedersen 2010: 263). Far from piecing all the parts together into a single whole in which everything is joined up, it seeks to show how within every significant event of social life is enfolded an entire history of relations of which it is the momentary outcome. As Mauss wrote of the gift, to place it in the context of the whole is *"to catch the fleeting moment* when the society and its members take emotional stock of themselves and their situation as regards others" (1954: 77–78; our emphasis). Anthropology is comparative because it acknowledges that no way of being is the only possible one, and that for every way we find, or resolve to take, alternative ways could be taken that would lead in different directions. Thus even as we follow a particular way, the question of "why this way rather than that?" is always at the forefront of our minds. And it is critical because we cannot be content with things as they are. By general consent, the organizations of production, distribution, governance, and knowledge that have dominated the modern era have brought the world to the brink of catastrophe. In finding ways to carry on, we need all the help we can get. But no one—no indigenous group, no specialist science, no doctrine or philosophy—holds the key to the future, if only we could find it. We have to make the future for ourselves, but that can only be done through dialogue. Anthropology's role is to expand the scope of this dialogue: to make a conversation of human life itself.

Now anthropologists have a way of working of which they are justly proud. They call it *participant observation*. It is, in essence, a practice of correspondence in which the anthropological observer joins with the lives of those whom he or she follows, coupling his or her movements of awareness or attention with theirs. What we might call *research* or even *fieldwork* is in truth a protracted master class in which—by way of this correspondence—the novice researcher gradually learns to see things, and to hear and feel them too, in the ways his or her mentors do. It is, in short, to undergo an *education of attention* (see Gibson 1979: 254; Ingold 2001). This education is transformational in its effects upon the learner. It shapes the way you think and feel and makes you a different person. In this respect, we contend, learning through participant observation differs fundamentally from ethnography (Hockey and Forsey 2012: 72–74). For the objective of ethnography is not transformational but documentary. This is not to deny that the practice of ethnography may have transformational effects. The very act of ethnographic writing, for example, is a movement in real time, which, in the attention and concentration it demands, transforms the writer. Reading an ethnographic monograph, too, can be transformative. But this effect is ancillary to ethnography's descriptive purpose and is distant, especially in the case of reading, from the situations in which its descriptions were formed. In terms of their respective temporal orientations, description is retrospective, transformation prospective. In proposing an anthropology-by-means-of-design as an alternative to the conventional anthropology-by-means-of-ethnography, our aim is to locate design in the transformational effects of participant observation, in the real-time prospective correspondences with the people among whom we work. Design, in this sense, comes before ethnography rather than after it. It forces us to turn once again toward the world for what it has to teach us. And it restores the participant observer to where he or she belongs, in the midst of things.

This leaves us, however, with the question of whether, or in what way, an anthropology-by-means-of-design calls for practices of participant observation different from those to which ethnographer-anthropologists are accustomed. Does it require of us to reevaluate the position of participant observation within the projects of *both* ethnography and anthropology? We believe it does. In anthropology-by-means-of-design, the active participation of the anthropologist in building relationships and making things—that is, in contributing to the unfolding happenings in fieldwork—necessarily becomes more deliberate and more experimental. At the same time, it is important to recognize that what is produced *during* fieldwork, in the anthropological task of correspondence by means of design, is of a value equal to, if not greater than, what is produced *after* fieldwork in the documentary form of written ethnography. Anthropologists who, in their fieldwork, have engaged with people in a particular area over an extended period of time already recognise the value of the relationships thus formed for their own lives (Kleinman, cited in Das 2011). Veena Das is one such anthropologist. Thanks to her experiences, she is also searching for a way to reposition the value of relationships built during fieldwork within the academy of anthropology.[3]

Over a period of eleven years, Das (2011) has carried out research in poor neighborhoods on the outskirts of Delhi that she has visited every year. During these years she also participated in setting up a nongovernmental organization (NGO) called the Institute of Socio-Economic Research on Development and Democracy (ISERDD). ISERDD is a research organization that offers medical and educational assistance to the poor in the areas that the organization surveys. Many of the fieldworkers recruited and trained by ISERDD come from areas similar to the ones in which the organization carries out research. During her visits, Das not only undertakes her own fieldwork but also helps with the work of ISERDD. She has, for instance, helped train the staff in fieldwork skills; she participates in their meetings and follows the cases of those people whom the NGO assists. The small projects of assistance that ISERDD, with its limited resources, is able to provide, as well as Das's exchanges with ISERDD staff, feed into her own inquiries about urban poverty and the everyday.

In reflecting upon her many years of work in this area, Das (2011) comments that she is committed to the idea of life as flux and she regrets that as a form of writing, ethnography is not conducive to this fluidity. "We inevitably end up," she writes, "by using the discrete moments when something becomes clear rather than the continuous time in which problems of what events mean emerge." Miyazaki proposes his method of hope, to which we have already alluded, specifically as a counter against which to highlight the inherently retrospective character of ethnographic description. Such description prevents anthropologists from perceiving the effects of people's visions and hopes for the future, the not yet, on their current activities. A method of hope, Miyazaki argues, would take into account the effects of future-oriented practices. He claims, however, that it is impossible for anthropologists in their writing to remain temporally coeval with the subjects of fieldwork, and therefore *not* to be retrospective (2004: 11). For Miyazaki, the only way to understand hope is to enact hope and, in scholarly writing, the only way to enact that hope is to highlight the unsatisfied hope in the present. In writing, as in life, "acts of delegation produce an effect of indeterminacy" (2004: 84); they postpone closure. However, the reason Miyazaki gives up on synchronicity, or in our terms on correspondence, is because he considers anthropological practice to hinge on the production of *texts*. In order to prioritize the ongoing strivings of daily life, Das (2010) notes, the relationships we build during fieldwork may be *more* important, as products of our work as anthropologists, than the texts we subsequently write. These relationships of correspondence pertain to the processual; they perdure and so retain the qualities of the ongoing, the not-yet that Das finds missing from ethnographic texts.

In the relationships formed during her prolonged fieldwork in Delhi, Das's contribution is recognizable: in the principles of providing assistance to those who furnish research data, in training people from similar backgrounds to carry out the research, and especially in providing ongoing support for fieldworkers when she is there and by telephone when she is in the United States (Das 2010). These relationships are as much products of Das's fieldwork as are her texts. In the same way that anthropological knowledge is now widely considered intersubjectively created (Coleman and Collins 2006), we can also recognize fieldwork relationships or engagements such as Das's as dialogically constituted anthropological products. This recognition calls for a repositioning of participant observation in anthropology, from a data-gathering exercise that feeds the production of academic texts to the locus and focus of anthropological productivity. We agree with Das that these anthropological products in fieldwork are as important as, if not more important than, ethnographic texts. Thinking of participant observation as correspondence, these relationships in fieldwork—these dialogic products—exemplify how design can reveal paths for carrying on as opposed to defining end points. In what follows, Gatt relates an experiment in anthropology-by-means-of-design in her fieldwork with Friends of the Earth International.

AN EXPERIMENT IN ANTHROPOLOGY-BY-MEANS-OF-DESIGN

Unlike Das's eleven years, my fieldwork was confined to a shorter period of doctoral study. In this experiment, my anthropology-by-means-of-design work was elicited because of the research I was carrying out, specifically because of how the people I was working with came to understand what anthropologists could offer. A characteristic of anthropology-by-means-of-design is the deliberate and reflexive interweaving of research and artifact production during fieldwork.

My doctoral fieldwork explored whether, and if so how, the transnational environmentalist federation called Friends of the Earth International (FoEI) "hangs together" (Hannerz 1996: 64). I sought to understand how such an organization, spread over seventy-six countries, was constituted and maintained. As part of this research, I carried out six months of fieldwork with the Brazilian FoEI group called Núcleo Amigos da Terra (NAT).[4] In organizing my fieldwork, I had been in touch by e-mail with the coordinator of the group. I explained in a few detailed e-mails and subsequent e-mail exchanges what my fieldwork would focus on and what I expected to do while I was spending time in the office and with the Brazilian activists.

When I arrived in Brazil, it turned out that the activists were already very familiar with visitors, as volunteers would often come to spend six months working with them. They were also familiar with the interests of social scientists in their work and in their history. Porto Alegre is considered the birthplace or pioneer state for environmentalism in Brazil, and NAT is one of the pioneering NGOs of this movement (Urban 2001). For this reason a number of doctoral students have interviewed NAT activists. In addition, two of the activists had followed anthropology courses at university and were therefore familiar with the notion of participant observation. One of the activists shared with me what she considered key books on environmentalism in Brazil. It became clear early on that my own research questions were "shared puzzles" (Marcus and Fischer 1999: xvii) among the people with whom I worked. Marcus and Fischer (1999) foresee that much anthropological fieldwork of the contemporary will revolve around such shared puzzles, where anthropologists and "informants" will have intellectual interests in common. Annelise Riles (2000) offers one example. In her research with women's NGOs in Fiji, Riles found that the forms of social relationships anthropologists have classically explored were already being questioned, analyzed, and represented by her informants through the use of organizational diagrams and maps.

Similarly, in my fieldwork with NAT, I shared with the activists an interest in understanding the forms of relationships within the organization. One difference, compared with Riles's experience, was that I was both asked by NAT activists and volunteered to make organizational diagrams myself. This required an analysis of the ongoing relationships that constituted the organization at the time. A second and key difference was that I was asked to create these diagrams not simply as documentation, as depictions of the existing state of affairs, but with a view to incorporating the aspirations of activists for how the organization should develop over the next couple of years. I was asked to compose procedural regulations, and organizational diagrams to illustrate them, that would guide the organization's future actions according to apparently conflicting ideals of management and leadership. The decision to ask me to propose these regulations was based on activists' knowledge that I had drafted procedural regulations for a number of NGOs before. In addition, and more important, I was asked to do this task because I had been talking at length to all of them, especially the different factions in the discussion on leadership, as part of my anthropological research. Their impression that as an anthropologist I was primarily interested in understanding activists' experience, and the fact that I had managed to build trust across the different members of the group, meant that my proposals could be relied upon not to be partisan or to be aligned a priori with one or other side of the argument.

The argument concerned leadership styles. One of the activists, Veronica, was not particularly influential within NAT, but did have a certain degree of influence on the opinions of the founding members of the organization, who are still greatly respected by current activists, and on other NGOs in Brazil. She wanted the group to be led by "clear and strong leadership." On several occasions, she complained to me that the current coordinator of NAT, Andrea, did not provide such leadership. The activities of NAT seemed to Veronica to be mired in endless internal discussions of "process." As a result, NAT was achieving much less than it did when one of the founding ladies was coordinator. On the other hand, Andrea, supported by most of the current NAT activists, believed that leadership should not mean the imposition of one person's will. Rather, leadership lies in the ability to harmonize activists' varying interests and abilities. This understanding of leadership, in Andrea's view, is also best suited to the realities faced by NGOs such as NAT. The reality Andrea refers to is the ongoing challenge NAT activists face in funding their activities. Most activists work on very small salaries, which they have to secure themselves, year on year, by winning funding for projects they propose. This means that at the end of each year, a number of activists will likely be unable to carry on working for NAT. The implication is that activists have to be motivated enough to propose projects to find their own funding, which reduces the possibility for a leader to impose her own priorities without alienating her staff. It also means that NAT needs to be flexible enough organizationally to survive changing priorities and staff turnover, as well as to adapt to the changing requirements for environmental activism to which NAT aims to respond.

The procedural regulations I was asked to draw up for NAT had to accommodate these different positions. The documents I then produced arose from FoE Brazil's need and desire for a guide that could incorporate enough structure to facilitate continuity and productivity and enough flexibility to incorporate the principles of diversity and inclusion as well as the demands of rapid staff turnover. These documents are an example of a dialogically designed anthropological artifact that arose from and through the collaborative learning process of fieldwork. The anthropological artifact, in this case, was a tangible trace of the workings of correspondence. This trace, rather than referring only at some remove—whether temporal or geographic—from its source, participated directly in the ongoing correspondence that followed.

The task of producing these regulations influenced aspects of my fieldwork. Together with individual activists, I made maps of the work they carried out in order to understand the sorts of endeavors the procedures would need to cover. These work maps also informed my understanding of environmentalist practice, which then fed into my doctoral research. I explicitly incorporated what I had learned from life history interviews and the five months of participant observation I had carried out by that time into the procedural regulations. This provided an empirical foundation on which to build a discussion about the documents based on mutual trust between the parties in the different factions and myself as document proposer. Had Andrea, or anyone known to support Andrea, proposed the document, the discussion would have started out in confrontational terms, as it would had the proposals been advanced by Veronica.

The thrust of my proposal was that those activists who have to find their own funding should become project managers empowered to manage their own projects. As project managers, however, they would become more accountable for their work by reporting not only to the Executive Committee (*Conselho Diretor*), but also to the Annual General Meeting (*Assembléia Geral*). In practice this meant that, although on a day-to-day basis the project managers had more freedom, they had to convince the General Meeting every year to support their planned projects, and to be accountable to them at the end of the year. In effect, this proposal reduced the need for an overall coordinator, but expected project managers to become stronger leaders or coordinators for their own projects, and to be personally responsible for the quality of their own project management. Plate 20 shows the *organogramma*, or the organizational structure map, I drew up as a result of my empirical observations, coupled with my proposals based on what the different members of NAT were hoping for at the time.

THE NEXT TWIST OF THE REFLEXIVE TURN

The documents Gatt produced during fieldwork were not adopted unchanged: that was not the goal. They provided a concrete starting point grounded in activists' concerns and experiences. The work that went into producing and proposing these procedural regulations informed her doctoral research. Conversely, the activists knew that Gatt's research interests coincided with what she would need to explore in order to produce the documents. She was asked to do this specifically because of her presence, her specific interests, and her neutral position in office politics as an anthropologist interested in understanding activists' experiences.

Anthropologists have long been alert to the implications of their presence in the situations in which they carry out fieldwork. Indeed as we have already shown, the method of participant observation is enshrined in, and depends upon, the anthropologist's personal commitment to others (Okely 1996). In the case described previously, for example, Gatt's position as an anthropologist was pivotal. The acknowledgment that the anthropologist is necessarily implicated in the field of study came to the fore in the 1980s in the so-called reflexive turn. This was the period when anthropology commenced its self-examination. In the years that followed, reflexive sensitivity tended to imply that anthropologists would include in their writing details of the contexts in which their particular researches were carried out—including the political and economic preconditions that led to some projects but not others being financially supported—as well as spelling out potential sources of bias (Whitaker 1996). Reflexivity was also honed into a tool within participant observation to yield further insights. The position of the anthropologist within social situations was reflexively analyzed to understand the cultural specificities elicited by their presence (see Kenna 1992, for a pointed example). The reflexive turn has made the notion that anthropological knowledge is intersubjectively generated more or less mainstream. Anthropologists are widely considered coauthors of the knowledge that results from the personal relationships of fieldwork; in this the creativity of the anthropologist is recognized (Amit 2000; Coleman and Collins 2006). But this creativity, at least for the purposes of academic evaluation, remains restricted to the production of texts (or if it extends beyond text, it is taken only as far as the production of ethnographic films).

Though the reflexive turn brought the creative role of the anthropologist to the fore, for various reasons this new paradigm did not encourage anthropologists to engage in public debate or to collaborate with their informants (see Eriksen 2006; Gatt 2010; MacClancy 1996; Whitaker 1996). This was contrary to the hopes of Marcus and Fischer, who had taken center stage in the reflexive turn when in 1986 they published the first edition of *Anthropology as Cultural Critique* (Marcus and Fischer 1999). We suggest that the anthropologist's deliberate and reflexive participation in the production of artifacts (such as personal relations, documents, or even texts) during fieldwork—in other words anthropology-by-means-of-design—is the next step to be taken in the discipline of anthropology, following from the reflexive turn. In this regard, anthropology-by-means-of-design carries forward a long-standing disciplinary concern with reflexivity.

In the example presented earlier, as an anthropologist carrying out participant observation Gatt was not only learning how to learn; she was also contributing her own experiences and skills to the ongoing, unfolding paths of the people with whom she worked in the field. Although any participant observation is a practice of correspondence, anthropology-by-means-of-design takes participant observation one step further: it becomes *observant participation*. Doing anthropology-by-means-of-design neither leaves fieldworkers as eternal cultural apprentices (Agar 1996) who have nothing to contribute beyond critical questioning, nor does it turn them into managers of development projects in an all-too-familiar top-down regime (Croll and Parkin 1992; Hobart 1993). In creating the draft procedural regulations, Gatt participated from a unique position—as unique as for every other activist—and with unique skills. It was her role to elicit the understandings of others and to present her own proposals based on these observations, including observations accrued from previous experiences, the NAT activists' hopes, and her imaginative contribution. The procedural regulations were a form of dialogically constituted artifact, identical to an ethnographic text insofar as it resulted from the cocreative contributions of fieldwork participants and the anthropologist. Unlike an ethnographic text, however, the form and audience for this anthropological product participated in the ongoing happenings in situ.

In anthropology-by-means-of-design, anthropologists turn away from the broad public discussion envisaged by Marcus and Fischer as *cultural critique*, and that most others call *engaged anthropology* (Eriksen 2006; MacClancy 1996; Scheper-Hughes 1995), toward correspondence with the everyday lives of the people among whom they do fieldwork. In so doing, they become participants in among, rather than above and beyond, the ongoing life situations with which they deal, where they and their designs play out on the same level field as everyone else.

NOTES

1. Though we have collaborated in writing this chapter, all the sections barring this introduction and the concluding section on "the next twist of the reflexive turn" have been single authored. The first two sections "on correspondence" and "designing environments for life" are by Tim Ingold; the following two sections on "repositioning participant observation" and

"experiments in anthropology-by-means-of-design" are by Caroline Gatt. In our respective uses of the first person singular in these sections, each of us is referring to ourselves.

2. We do not deny, of course, that for many practitioners, designs can never reach completion, and that they see their practice as an ongoing correspondence between ideas and material form. Our question, which is one for practitioners too, is: What can design *mean* if this is so?

3. We recognize the parallels with action research, especially its notion of "living inquiry" (Reason and Bradbury 2008). However, disciplinary gatekeeping and what qualifies as "good ethnography" remain adjudicated by academic audiences (Kelty 2009) and not by the people with whom anthropologists correspond during fieldwork. Indeed anthropologists working outside universities are not always considered "properly anthropological." Nancy Scheper-Hughes (2009) goes so far as to caution anthropologists against mixing advocacy with academic work. Ironically, Scheper-Hughes is considered a champion of engaged anthropology (see Scheper-Hughes 1995). We are discussing here theoretical questions— on process and the everyday—that would drive conventional academic practice toward such living inquiry, not only for the ethical implications it holds, but also for the theoretical insights it promises.

4. The fieldwork for Gatt's doctoral research included six months of participant observation with FoE Brazil, five months with the FoE International Secretariat in Amsterdam, and six months with FoE Malta, as well as the three years between 2003 and 2006 during which Gatt was engaged with FoE Malta as an activist. It also included attendance at nine international meetings between 2003 and 2007 and continuous participant observation by e-mail throughout the period from February 2003 to December 2007. Gatt gratefully acknowledges the University of Aberdeen's Sixth Century Studentship award, which funded her research.

REFERENCES

Agar, M. (1996), *The Professional Stranger*, London: Academic Press.

Amit, V. (ed.) (2000), *Constructing the Field*, London: Routledge.

Bourdieu, P. (1977), *Outline of a Theory of Practice*, trans. R. Nice, Cambridge: Cambridge University Press.

Brand, S. (1994), *How Buildings Learn: What Happens to Them after They're Built*, New York: Penguin.

Coleman, S., and Collins, P. (2006), "Introduction: 'Being. . .where?' Performing Fields on Shifting Grounds," in S. Coleman and P. Collins (eds.), *Locating the Field: Space, Place and Context in Anthropology*, ASA Monographs 42, Oxford: Berg, 1–21.

Croll, E., and Parkin, D. (eds.) (1992), *Bush Base: Forest Farm. Culture, Environment and Development*, London: Routledge.

Cross, N. (2006), *Designerly Ways of Knowing*, London: Springer Verlag.

Das, V. (2010), "Reversing the Image of Time: Technologies of the Self and the Task of Detachment," Unpublished paper presented at the conference Reconsidering Detachment: The Ethics and Analytics of Disconnection, Cambridge, UK, June 30–July 3.

Das, V. (2011), "Poverty, Suffering and the Moral Life." Unpublished paper presented at the American Anthropological Association conference, Montreal, Canada, November 19.

Engels, F. (1934), *Dialectics of Nature*, trans. C. Dutt, Moscow: Progress.

Eriksen, T. H. (2006), *Engaging Anthropology: The Case for a Public Presence*, Oxford: Berg.

Gatt, C. (2010), "Serial Closure: Generative Reflexivity and Restoring Confidence in/of Anthropologists," in S. Koerner and I. Russell (eds.), *Unquiet Pasts: Risk Society, Lived Cultural Heritage and Re-designing Reflexivity*, Farnham: Ashgate, 343–360.

Gibson, J. J. (1979), *The Ecological Approach to Visual Perception*, Boston, MA: Houghton Mifflin.

Hannerz, U. (1996), *Transnational Connections: Culture, People and Places*, London: Routledge.

Hobart, M. (1993), "Introduction: The Growth of Ignorance?" in M. Hobart (ed.), *An Anthropological Critique of Development: The Growth of Ignorance*, London: Routledge, 1–32.

Hockey, J., and Forsey, M. (2012), "Ethnography Is Not Participant Observation: Reflections on the Interview as Participatory Qualitative Research," in J. Skinner (ed.), *The Interview: An Ethnographic Approach*, London: Berg, 69–87.

Ingold, T. (2000), *The Perception of the Environment: Essays on Livelihood, Dwelling and Skill*, London: Routledge.

Ingold, T. (2001), "From the Transmission of Representations to the Education of Attention," in H. Whitehouse (ed.), *The Debated Mind: Evolutionary Psychology Versus Ethnography*, Oxford: Berg, 113–153.

Ingold, T. (2011), *Being Alive: Essays on Movement, Knowledge and Description*, London: Routledge.

Ingold, T., and Hallam, E. (2007), "Creativity and Cultural Improvisation: An Introduction," in E. Hallam and T. Ingold (eds.), *Creativity and Cultural Improvisation*, Oxford: Berg, 1–24.

Kelty, C. (2009), "Collaboration, Coordination, and Composition: Fieldwork after the Internet," in J. Faubion and G. Marcus (eds.), *Fieldwork Is Not What It Used To Be: Learning Anthropology's Method in a Time of Transition*, New York: Cornell University Press, 184–206.

Kenna, M. (1992), "Changing Places and Altered Perspectives: Research on a Greek Island in the 1960s and the 1980s," in J. Okely and H. Callaway (eds.), *Anthropology and Autobiography*, London: Routledge, 147–162.

Klee, P. (1961), *Notebooks, Volume 1: The Thinking Eye*, ed. J. Spiller, London: Lund Humphries.

Klee, P. (1973), *Notebooks, Volume 2: The Nature of Nature*, trans. H. Norden, ed. J. Spiller, London: Lund Humphries.

Lee, J., and Ingold, T. (2006), "Fieldwork on Foot: Perceiving, Routing, Socialising," in S. Coleman and P. Collins (eds.), *Locating the Field: Space, Place and Context in Anthropology*, Oxford: Berg, 67–85.

MacClancy, J. (1996), "Popularizing Anthropology," in J. MacClancy and C. McDonaugh (eds.), *Popularizing Anthropology*, London: Routledge, 1–57.

Marcus, G., and Fischer, M. (1999), *Anthropology as Cultural Critique: An Experimental Moment in the Human Sciences*, Chicago, IL: University of Chicago Press.

Mauss, M. (1954), *The Gift*, trans. I. Cunnison, London: Routledge and Kegan Paul.

Maynard, P. (2005), *Drawing Distinctions: The Varieties of Graphic Expression*, Ithaca, NY: Cornell University Press.

Miyazaki, H. (2004), *The Method of Hope: Anthropology, Philosophy and Fijian Knowledge*, Stanford, CA: Stanford University Press.

Okely, J. (1996), *Own or Other Culture*, London: Routledge.

Otto, T., and Bubandt, N. (2010), "Anthropology and the Predicaments of Holism," in T. Otto and N. Bubandt (eds.), *Experiments in Holism: Theory and Practice in Contemporary Anthropology*, Chichester: Wiley-Blackwell, 1–16.

Pallasmaa, J. (2009), *The Thinking Hand: Existential and Embodied Wisdom in Architecture*, Chichester: John Wiley.

Panofsky, E. (1968), *Idea: A Concept in Art Theory*, New York: Harper and Row.

Reason, P., and Bradbury, H. (2008), "Introduction," in P. Reason and H. Bradbury (eds.), *The Sage Handbook of Action Research: Participative Inquiry and Practice*, London: Sage Publications, 1–10.

Riles, A. (2000), *The Network Inside Out*, Ann Arbor: University of Michigan Press.

Robbins, J. (2006), "Anthropology and Theology: An Awkward Relationship," *Anthropological Quarterly*, 79(2): 285–294.

Scheper-Hughes, N. (1995), "The Primacy of the Ethical," *Current Anthropology*, 36(3): 409–440.

Scheper-Hughes, N. (2009), "Making Anthropology Public," *Anthropology Today*, 25(4): 1–3.

Schutz, A. (1951), "Making Music Together: A Study in Social Relationship," *Social Research*, 18: 76–97.

Schutz, A. (1962), *The Problem of Social Reality*, collected papers I, ed. M. Nathanson, The Hague: Nijhoff.

Simmel, G. (1969), "Sociology of the Senses: Visual Interaction," in E.W. Burgess and R.E. Park (eds.), *Introduction to the Science of Sociology*, 3rd edition, Chicago, IL: University of Chicago Press, 146–150.

Simon, H. (1969), *The Sciences of the Artificial*, Cambridge, MA: MIT Press.

Suchman, L. (2011), "Anthropological Relocations and the Limits of Design," *Annual Review of Anthropology*, 40: 1–18.

Urban, T. (2001), *Missão (Quase) Impossível: Aventuras e Desaventuras do Movimento Ambientalista no Brasil*, São Paulo: Peirópolis.

Whitaker, M. (1996), "Reflexivity," in A. Barnard and J. Spencer (eds.), *Encyclopedia of Social and Cultural Anthropology*, London: Routledge, 470–473.

Willerslev, R., and Pedersen, A. (2010), "Proportional Holism: Joking the Cosmos into the Right Shape in North Asia," in T. Otto and N. Bubandt (eds.), *Experiments in Holism: Theory and Practice in Contemporary Anthropology*, Chichester: Wiley-Blackwell, 262–278.

Conceptions of Innovation and Practice: Designing Indoor Climate

Wendy Gunn and Christian Clausen

While moving within and between homes, institutions, and offices people come to know indoor climate as lived experience, along the way remembering a history of opening and closing windows and doors; turning thermostats for radiators, air conditioners, towel rails, and under floor heating on and off; putting clothes on and taking them off; coping with breakdowns in heating, ventilation, and water systems; doing something about drafts; and where possible trying to find ways of conserving energy. These "incidents and encounters en route" involve responding to other people and things within continually changing environments (Ingold 2011: 154). Knowing thus comes through movements "in the passage from place to place and the changing horizons along the way" (Ingold 2000: 227, 2011: 154). In this way what people come to know about indoor climate is not about correlating levels of physical factors such as temperature, relative humidity, or carbon dioxide concentration. Rather, "Lying at the confluence of actions and responses, they are identified not by their intrinsic attributes but by the memories they call up. Thus things are not classified like facts or tabulated like data, but narrated like stories" (Ingold 2011: 154). Importantly, these stories do not encode instructions; they describe a rhythmic process. Comfort here has a temporal dimension. People negotiate old sensors and old technological models while at home, in the kindergarten, or in the office, implying both people and technologies have life histories. They become old over time.[1]

WHERE ANTHROPOLOGY MEETS INDUSTRY

The Indoor Climate and Quality of Life project was a three-year (2008–2011) Participatory Innovation Project organized by Sønderborg Participatory Innovation Centre (SPIRE)[2] and funded by the Danish Enterprise Construction Authority (EBST). Five Danish companies and two university partners were invited to participate in the project, including a skylight window manufacturer, a natural ventilation engineering manufacturer, an insulation manufacturer, a mechanical ventilation manufacturer, building project management, researchers from the Indoor Climate Research Unit, Technical University of Denmark (DTU), and SPIRE, University of Southern Denmark. The core idea of the project was to explore how involving a wider group of stakeholders in designing indoor climate products and systems may bring about innovation in the building industry (Buur 2012: 3).

Whereas our project partners working in the field of indoor climate emphasize identifiable, measurable parameters of comfort (temperature, humidity, light, noise, air quality, CO_2) and focus their efforts on engineering products and systems based upon behavioral models, as researchers interested in the idea of participatory innovation, SPIRE researchers aimed toward involving both quantitative and qualitative knowledge in the design of indoor climate products and systems of control. As such, SPIRE researchers attempted to involve a broader group of stakeholders in the design process through engaging with the improvisatory capacity of people involved in the course of their everyday activities of inhabiting indoor climate (Boer and Donovan 2012; Buur and Matthews 2008; Jaffari, Boer, and Buur 2011; Jaffari and Matthews 2009). Specifically, the research team was concerned with the dilemma between two meanings of environment. One stemmed from lived everyday experience of engaging with indoor climate in homes, kindergartens, and offices; the other stemmed from an environment where everyday experience is considered independent of a projected world and numbers and scientific evidence are the basis for legitimate knowledge claims.

Participation in SPIRE workshops with project partners enabled the authors of this chapter (an anthropologist and an engineer) to become familiar with different conceptions of innovation and practice relating to designing indoor climate. Our main research question concerned how differing (and similar) perceptions of indoor climate converge during collaborative practices of designing indoor climate products and systems of control. Seventeen workshops and four telephone meetings involving SPIRE researchers, indoor climate researchers from DTU, and company representatives took place at SPIRE, DTU, and company representative workplaces (2008–2011). The workshops focused on exploring possibilities for involving nursery teachers and children, family members, and office workers who lived experiences of indoor climate. Importantly, we asked: Could qualitative knowledge gained through field studies[3] of everyday practices of negotiating indoor climate products and systems of control be a resource for innovation potential in the building industry? As researchers our role was to explore the uptake of user knowledge in project partners' organizations (Gunn and Clausen 2012b). Working with an analytical framework grounded upon ethnographic inquiry gained through ongoing participation in The Indoor Climate Project, SPIRE workshops, research seminars, and interviews with workshop participants, we made the following claims to guide further research based upon our project partners' responses to involving end user knowledge in their design processes:

- Claim 1: There is nothing the user can give us in terms of innovation potential.
- Claim 2: User knowledge only results in small movements (if any) within existing frameworks of innovation.
- Claim 3: Through dialogue involving material traces of different forms of knowledge you do not reproduce existing ways of doing innovation.

PRACTICE(S)

SPIRE Workshops

Field studies engaging with nursery children and teachers, families, and office workers in Denmark showed that people often use indoor climate products and systems in ways far beyond what designers of these products and systems imagine. For example, controlling fresh air in a nursery, family home, or office is not only related to opening and closing windows, but also intertwined with social relations. Our research also suggested that people actively intervene in configuring products and systems through ongoing use. People are constantly improvising in their negotiations with design judgments of indoor climate between the tension in what is given and what is left open to response. Project partners were surprised by SPIRE researchers' observations of people's everyday practices of negotiating indoor climate products and systems of control: "I was surprised to see that users often do not know how to work the systems . . . I was also surprised to see that users were not able to control their indoor climate and to translate this into a new configuration practice" (Natural Ventilation Engineer).[4]

In contrast to our partners' understanding of people's practices, we argue, during processes and practices of negotiating indoor products and systems, people become skilled practitioners instead of passive consumers (see Kilbourn 2010). To replace the idea of the passive consumer of indoor products and systems with that of a skilled practitioner is to challenge the notion of the consumer and to refocus our attention on local practices of appropriation and enskillment. This requires different ways of thinking about designing that allow for people to develop skills and to create meaningful relations with *things* through use (Gunn and Donovan 2012). We take the position that indoor climate is immediate, experienced, and involves local practices of appropriation. Taking this position within processes of collaborative indoor climate design, we also argue, does not lead to innovation but to a reframing of what innovation could be.

During a series of workshops organized by SPIRE (2008–2011), project participants were encouraged to participate in activities concerned with "reflection-in-action" (Schön 1983). This was done to provoke workshop participants and move end user insights toward innovation potentials with the aim of: a) creating an awareness of implicit assumptions of end users' potential to contribute to innovation in designing indoor climate; b) explore possibilities of involving people's everyday experiences of interacting with indoor climate product and systems within design processes and practices; and c) bring attention to differing perceptions of indoor climate among project partners. In parallel, a series of SPIRE research seminars focused on shifting assumptions of SPIRE researchers themselves in terms of perceptions of project partners' interpretations of users' knowledge.

The workshops were constructed processually throughout the duration of the project. Drawing upon design materials during unfolding events of SPIRE workshops can be considered a form of a design studio practice whereby "the field or the particular story or theme that is emerging takes over the design" (Rees 2008: 116). Influenced by George Herbert Mead's (1934) research on taking the role of the other, ideas were generated through emergent understandings created in ongoing collaborative engagements and led to participants taking up different positions—from a company representative, an end user of indoor climate, to university researcher. During workshop activities, SPIRE researchers wanted to challenge implicit understandings of innovation potential based upon end users' practices, that is, an understanding of end users as potentially active in codesigning indoor climate was something our project partners saw happening far in the future. SPIRE researchers began to ask what mechanisms are required to bring end users closer to being involved in innovating the design of indoor climate. In order to address this question, workshop participants worked with design materials in the form of video clips, provotypes, A-frames, design themes, and sensitizing concepts based upon findings from field investigations in Danish kindergartens, family homes, and offices. A variety of design materials were also placed in family homes, kindergartens, offices, and project workshops to support reflections on a number of levels: a) to understand how people relate to indoor climate over time; and b) to provoke reflection-in-action on lived experience of indoor climate (see Plate 21). During collaborative sense making of field study findings, materials were understood as an active way of bringing attention to people's experiences rather than focusing on statistics associated with indoor climate parameters. Importantly, materials were important *to talk with* in order to have a shared dynamic, were made with the intention of providing workshop participants with something to relate to that resonated with their *way of talking*, and co-analysis of materials was considered a kind of design work (Boer 2012; Donovan and Gunn 2012; Mogensen 1994). Workshop facilitators involved combinations of these different materials with the aim of drawing upon material resources to support participants in co-analysis, collaborative design, and cross-comparison activities. It is important to remember, however; participants were not working directly with people from kindergartens, offices, or homes who use indoor climate. They were also not mobilizing insights gained from field materials presented. Instead, they were engaged with making explicit implicit framings of end user knowledge to prepare them for being introduced to other forms of relations within processes of designing indoor climate. Staging workshops to make things *move* in this direction involves a performer—a workshop facilitator—who (in the SPIRE research group's world) takes the user seriously. Taking the *user* seriously, however, is to problematize the idea of the user itself and to move beyond the idea that a designer involves users to provide the designer with ideas. SPIRE researchers, therefore, were not interested in representing users as such. Rather, we were interested in keeping voices of the people we carried out research with present during workshops as a means of building relations between designing and using.

Tracing relations made during this process presented challenges for the authors of this chapter. Something was happening with how end users' narratives were framed in this journey of building relations. Workshop participants were confronted by analytic understandings of constantly changing objects, and the subject (in this instance the end user of indoor climate) was defined by this temporal thinking. The subject was thus, as Marcus has argued, "alternatively imagined" (2011: 19). The role framing plays in generating knowledge during workshop activities is not easily articulated. The reason was the ongoing temporal nature and emergent qualities of the sense-making, co-analytic, cross-comparative activities involving design materials. To be able to make explicit the implicit framings of end users' knowledge that take place while workshop participants are engaged in generating knowledge is, as discussed previously, to prepare participants to be open to reframing relations between designers and end users.

Engaging with Traces of Narratives

Workshop participants made sense of unfolding events through emergent processes of mapping different and similar ways of understanding indoor climate (Turnbull 2007). Sometimes this led to individuals saying that they could not see how a statement from an end user of indoor climate could be used in their organization. Time was a crucial issue here, especially when nonverbal knowledge translates to verbal, because all participants were involved in doing activities at the same time. An example of a co-analytic activity was to work with a series of comfort themes: "Comfort is what people make; Comfort is bringing feeling and understanding in tune; Comfort is about social relations; Comfort is a political construct; Comfort means becoming healthy;

Indoor comfort connects to the outdoor." Each theme provided a focus for co-analysis of specific narratives originating from video materials across different field sites. This resulted in the development of a series of research questions. Addressing the questions, comfort themes were subsequently modified both within and without the workshop space by SPIRE researchers, external researchers, and workshop participants. The themes were meant as a form of ethnographic provocation and were made collaboratively by SPIRE researchers and workshop participants over a six-month period (Buur and Sitorus 2007). An important aspect of this activity was to give form to otherwise difficult to grasp abstract concepts related to experiencing indoor climate during collaborative sense making.

The lead facilitator organizing workshops was usually a senior researcher skilled at knowing *where* and *when* to bring in the competencies of workshop participants to shift the focus of the discussion. He or she was also skilled at bringing attention to differing perceptions of what it means to inhabit indoor climate to find shared places for "imaginative empathy" through design activities and transformation of materials (Rapport and Harris 2007: 325). In August 2009, one workshop was designed to move the comfort themes toward future innovation projects. During the workshop, the facilitator summarized ideas generated through the day-long collaborative sense-making and co-analytic activities. Participants selected four potential themes to work with: "Democratizing Negotiation," "Enabling Action," "Connection to the Outdoor," and "Visualizing Change." Previous themes generated through workshop activities were formulations of field narratives from people's past and present practices of negotiating indoor systems and products, whereas the four themes overlaid upon the BCG matrix[5] were concerned with the future.

Workshop participants began to tell the facilitator where post-it notes should be placed on the BCG matrix, indicating greater or less innovation potential. The facilitator placed post-it notes with themes onto the matrix according to participants' imaginings of each of the themes' future innovation potential in terms of a) belief in the theme or b) belief the theme will come true. Plate 22 shows the BCG matrix with Post-It notes as decided by three of the workshop participants. Participants also verbally expressed their beliefs concerning individual themes' innovation potential to become true in the future: "Democratizing Negotiation" originated from working with field materials in Danish offices. The theme emerged from a discussion of problems faced by office workers while negotiating temperature control in an open plan office. This theme was difficult to believe in as becoming true by one of the workshop participants: "I think this theme will move the discussion in the office and the kindergarten but I am not sure it will move innovation potential" (Engineer from Insulation Manufacturer). "Enabling Action" originated from users wanting more control of indoor climate products and systems. One engineer recognized greater individual control could have high innovation potential. He did not, however, believe all individuals were capable of utilizing control in the right way: "The way forward therefore could be to create an impression of control" (Engineer from Indoor Climate Research Unit, Technical University of Denmark). The idea of enabling people to better control their indoor climate was problematic for one engineer: "I see more trouble than innovation with that theme because the communication part is enormous" (Engineer from Window Manufacturer). There still, however, remained "huge innovation potential" in doing something with this theme "even if this meant educating the user" (Engineer from Insulation Manufacturer). "Connection to the Outdoor" was a way of thinking about how people relate their perceptions of indoor climate to external environments. Creating an awareness of the relational aspects of internal and external environments suggested an explorative possibility for both the user and the designer. This involved making systems of control "available to people," and that was considered "not so easy" (Engineer and SPIRE Researcher). For the window manufacturer, this theme was top priority and thus "should have innovation potential" (Engineer from Window Manufacturer). However, according to the insulation manufacturer, although the potential was "big . . . no one is doing it." The reason no one was doing it raised the question, "Is innovation missing?" (Engineer from Insulation Manufacturer). "Visualizing Change" was somewhere in between low and high innovation potential. The potential lay with the ability to repeatedly show people that "something is wrong" and they need to rectify the situation immediately (Engineer from Indoor Climate Research Unit, Technical University of Denmark). If visualizing change could help people "control making connections to the outdoor," "then that would have high innovation potential" (Engineer from Window Manufacturer).

These design themes were written on Post-Its and then overlaid on a BCG matrix. Juxtaposing design materials was a way of making a familiar system of engineering representation both strange and familiar. Importantly, juxtaposing here was a means to realize the relation (or not) between design practices and use practices. Here traces of narratives belonging to nursery children, teachers, family members, and office workers were, as Anderson argued, strategically placed to a) "enable designers to question the taken-for-granted assumptions embedded in the conventional problem-solution design framework" (Anderson 1994: 158); and b) offer reflection "on that central plank of design thinking, the problem-solution frame of reference" (Anderson 1994: 159, 161).

Within the process of making implicit framings of innovation potential of end users' knowledge explicit, unfolding concepts were valued more than methods. Such design concepts based upon people's practices of negotiating indoor climate were understood by SPIRE researchers as central for moving beliefs of what kinds of knowledge had (or did not have) innovation potential. The ethnographic approach toward designing offered in the workshops differs from involving *users* for the purposes of generating ideas for the designer. Instead, designerly ways of knowing and doing are discovered through emergent social dynamics and the workshop format is not a constraint on the content.[6]

EXCHANGE AND SHARING OF KNOWLEDGE

Indoor climate models, daylight calculators, and building requirements are based upon generalized systems of knowledge and embedded in indoor climate engineering practices, marketing, and configuration of products, systems, and services. This type of engineering knowledge gives precedence to calculation of a single factor as the basis for engineering design solutions or survey-based research (Jaffari and Matthews 2009). By contrast, qualitative knowledge generated through people's practices of negotiating indoor climate is difficult to involve in mathematical models informing engineering conceptualizations of indoor climate. SPIRE workshops attempted to question engineering models underlying project participants' judgments of what kinds of knowledge were perceived as having or not having innovation potential.

Exchange of knowledge during the workshops did not result in any immediately usable results by project partners in their companies, institutional settings, and sites of reception. But keep in mind the effects of knowledge exchange and sharing in workshops did not mean value equates to utility by project partners when they tried to implement what was learned in the workshops within company or institutional settings (Leach 2011: 90–91). User knowledge of experiencing indoor climate had value in terms of informing models simulating design variables such as temperature and ventilation. Project partners also valued the role scientific institutions can play in producing credibility in their organizations. Co-analysis of 2:1 interviews also showed that project partners were interested in the idea that several knowledge practices may coexist in an organization. These practices were valued in terms of their ability to adapt over time and reflect shifting political concerns and perspectives.

Utilizing dynamic resources available in the moment within workshops was important to navigate in unfamiliar territories but did not always lead toward a process of agreement (Farnell 2000: 410). In an interview with the Indoor Climate and Quality of Life project manager[7] focusing on the differences between university and industrial partners, he said, "Researchers become attached to the moment and try to make use of the openings created to continue the conversation" (2010). He continued, "it is possible to partly take up" what has been generated during these moments. He compared his experiences of participating in the project to taking steps: "when you backtrack or look ahead you learn, but when you know the step it is an angle on the same." What is important here is the ways of knowing and doing are coming together (or not) and the friction that is encountered in being confronted with *both*

similarity and difference (Tsing 2005). Collaboration between SPIRE researchers and their project partners succeeded in part, as Tsing says, "because no
one stopped to realize the depth of their disagreements. Collaboration was
not consensus making but rather an opening for productive confusion" (2005:
247). Agreeing to disagree was a way of working together (Suchman 2011: 15).

TRACES OF MOVEMENT

SPIRE workshops attempted to shape the terms of relationships where knowledge could be shared. As researchers, we were interested in how knowledge
is produced through such activities and is able to move between different communities during transactions (Strathern 2004). Collaborative activities were
central to the design of SPIRE workshops, leaving no time to work with participants on an individual basis. We therefore became interested in working with
individual project participants in their organizational or institutional context.
Our challenge as researchers was to find ways of tracing shifts in conceptions
concerning innovation potential of involving qualitative knowledge from field
studies in their working practices, and how this knowledge was then practiced
in their companies and universities (Lave 2011). Semi-structured 2:1 interviews were carried out in Danish with three engineers from the project's company partners and with three researchers from the Indoor Climate Research
Centre, all active in the participatory innovation workshops at SPIRE.

Our approach was to trace the movement of qualitative knowledge across
sites and analyze how this knowledge was taken up, rejected, or transformed
in workshop participants' organizations and institutions. Questions addressed "tempos of change, and moments in the flow of events" (Marcus
2011: 23). As such, we were concerned with a kind of knowledge that is
"as much modulated in temporal terms as placed in spatial terms" (Marcus 2011: 23). Specifically, we asked project participants to describe the
characteristics of dominant knowledge practices in their organizations and
compare this with the kind of knowledge shared while participating in SPIRE
workshops. As a next step, interviewees were asked to comment on design
themes depicting stills from video clips and excerpts from end user narratives presented in the workshops. During the interviews, interviewees did
not refer so much to the specific design themes as to observations from
the field studies. Through further analyses, we traced associations made by
the engineers. In particular, relations were made between end user narratives, knowledge practices, and knowledge objects of their organizations and
the wider systems they related to in order to pursue innovation potentials.
Interview questions focused on the uptake of end users' knowledge in project partners' organizations and institutions. We also raised questions concerning standardization and the role played by regulations in conceptualizing

innovation potential. In parallel, both authors studied transcriptions and video material from previous workshops and field studies where company and university partners were involved. Co-analysis of 2:1 interviews and workshop documentation led toward developing an analytical framework focusing on how workshop participants formed relations between a) abstract—material; b) social—technoscientific; and c) qualitative—quantitative while negotiating their professional practices. The analytical framework was grounded on ethnographic materials emerging from the conditions of our fieldwork. The reason we developed the framework in this way was linked to repeated evidence through our ongoing workshop participation, video archival footage, and interview transcriptions of distinctions rather than relations made by engineers between these categories.

A recurring challenge for us as researchers in the workshops, presentations, and subsequent writings was keeping all project participants' voices present. This included bringing "the dominant [the strongly "current"], residual ["the thinking and orientations that linger"], and the emergent ["the speculative and planned for"] into fullness and into relation with each other" (Rabinow et al. 2008: 103). As Rabinow says, "This triad seems to structure a set of complex temporalities that we need to make choices about and that we can't forget" (Rabinow et al. 2008: 103). As participants of the workshops and SPIRE researchers, we were confronted with the limitations of our own positioning because as researchers, our positioning was to question others during the research process. To question the form and domains of our knowledge traditions during collaborative activities, as opposed to afterward, was a challenge. What was valued in our day-to-day participation within collaborative design activities was not what was produced afterward, that is, an ethnographic monograph or a critique, a patent or a product idea, but what we did during our engagement with people at a particular *moment* in time (see Gatt and Ingold's discussion of the anthropological task of *correspondence* by means of design, this volume).

Working with the conditions of a participatory innovation project, we questioned the idea that if you just bring different knowledge traditions together this will lead to innovation—it is not that easy. Our ongoing collaboration, our roles within the research team—an engineer and anthropologist—from particular methodological positions led us to ask why a user-oriented approach does not lead immediately to innovation. It is often assumed in ideas of contemporary knowledge production that a combination of different disciplines is the main road to creating innovation potentials (Strathern 2004). We adopted the position that while the combination of different kinds of knowledge is important for research, disciplinary exchange and collaboration between universities and industry do not lead immediately to innovation (Gunn and Clausen 2012a).

WHAT DID WE FIND OUT?

The Engineer from the Skylight Window Manufacturer's Response

The engineer from the skylight window manufacturer expressed a strong aware-ness of the rules for making accounts in his organization, as they were per-ceived as a strong barrier for the dissemination and sharing of knowledge. He appreciated the confrontation with qualitative knowledge generated through SPIRE activities, but as he pointed out, there seems to be limited uptake of this kind of knowledge in the wider organization. Especially when it came to the identification of innovation potential, the engineer had difficulties in point-ing out where innovation could take place in the organization. User narratives were appreciated, as long as they supported the skylight manufacturer's cur-rent marketing strategy, insofar as it underlines the very framing of its prod-uct, that is, "Indoor climate does not stop at the window." He accepted that end users of indoor climate—nursery teachers and children, office workers, and family members—were in fact active in creating their environment. He re-fused, however, to adopt the idea that innovation potential lay within the active use of the environment by users of indoor climate. Rather, the most important aspect of his participation in the project was the discussion of finding different ways of controlling indoor climate. This is where reframing the idea of a win-dow *speaks to him* and the traces of users' narratives presented in the work-shop *speak to him*. He did not expect innovation to come out of a project like the Indoor Climate and Quality of Life project. On the other hand, he welcomed the "magic" SPIRE methods brought to him during the workshop as a partici-pant, and he tried them out in his company with some success. The reason the uptake of the kind of knowledge generated at SPIRE in the wider organiza-tion proved so difficult was connected to the fact that his organization relied on evidence-based technical arguments. Only quantitative-based arguments were recognized as valid by top management and in the sales and marketing departments. This meant evidence needed to be based upon large data sets and/or other kinds of evidence-based measurements informed by science. He experienced this kind of knowledge as a different kind of scientific knowl-edge than that presented in the SPIRE workshops. He deliberately described a meeting between knowledge practices happening during the workshops—he did not discard this. As he said, "it has something to say to us." He then referred to the qualitative knowledge as being related to "a small number . . . we can actually be informed by a few statements and they are actually say-ing something to us . . . But then the organizational structures we work within begin speaking to us. They say something about this kind of knowledge as being difficult to spread in the organisation . . . if I had something written, then it would be easier" (Engineer from the Skylight Window Manufacturer).

The engineer from the skylight window manufacturer was interested in using qualitative knowledge to magnify "small numbers to big numbers." This was important because knowledge must always refer back to the system in his organization. In his world, sales and techno economic reasoning demanded *hard* evidence. He was clear that this kind of evidence counted in his organization and it was difficult for him to say something was interesting in the organization "if it does not count." As he said, "A structure that speaks of the techno economic is the only one that speaks . . . and opens different channels of where knowledge can go." He was aware that other indoor climate product specialists might criticize him and/or his organization because they were only interested in whether people could open and close their windows. Imagining a window could be used for other things beyond opening and closing, for example, having a social function that creates meaning, was difficult for the engineer. The idea of reframing the window in this way appeared to the engineer to be related to the past, or something that architects had no measurement tool for. Importantly, the engineer related to the idea that windows have a social function as having no innovation potential. He also emphasized that SPIRE researchers should forget the idea of innovation happening between project company participants. In terms of the way things work in the building industry, that is unimaginable.

The Engineer from the Insulation Manufacturer's Response

The engineer from the insulation company did not recognize a significant difference between her own understandings and the comfort design themes debated within the workshops. In fact, the other engineers actually expressed that the engineer from the insulation manufacturer was the only participating engineer able to make sense of the qualitative field materials during workshops. She explained how knowledge practices in her department included a close social connection to and learning from marketing channels. Compared to the marketing side, knowledge practices in the laboratories and in product development were highly quantitative, parametric, and oriented toward the improvement of technical performance indicators. Accordingly, she was used to handling rather diverse and coexisting knowledge practices and did not experience difficulties in disseminating observations from workshops to colleagues or in obtaining management support in the organization. By connecting to a wider context of designing sustainable housing, the insulation manufacturer engineer pointed at the need to coordinate indoor climate definitions and product designs across diverse social and engineering worlds. As she said, "I see the workshops as an opportunity to extend our dialogue across the companies and research in order to develop a platform for developing industry solutions." Here, the engineer from the insulation manufacturer expected innovation mainly to occur through relation building and creation of new markets. She also pointed at the common interest across companies in setting up a space for innovation concerned with standard development based on qualitative user insight. Here the end user is not just a variable social component separated from the material world but a competent player innovators may relate to. Still, while the end user is implicated in the innovative process, the end user is not necessarily ascribed an active role, but rather considered a figure to be educated and informed.

LIFE WORLDS AND ENGINEERING WORLDS

Findings from field studies conducted in Danish homes, kindergartens, and offices indicated that end users of indoor climate are interested in developing an awareness of the quality of their indoor climate in relation to otherwise difficult-to-perceive parameters, such as carbon dioxide. Numbers, however, did not always make sense to people, as one co-analyst reminded us: "They seem to be saying these machines have numbers that I cannot see. But in your home, you do not need numbers because you can feel changes in indoor climate" (Designing Environments for Life Participant).[8] As is indicated by claim 1 on page 161, we did in fact find examples of innovation potential based on user accounts, but that was not the dominant view. Our company and university partners' belief in technical arguments based on numbers prevailed, despite recognition that end users of indoor climate do not always understand numbers while trying to negotiate indoor climate products and systems of control. As researchers, we were also aware numbers could be treated in ways that surface qualities in addition to quantities, as Anderson and colleagues have shown (2009: 125). That said, the researchers and engineers we were collaborating with were fixated upon the functional aspects of numbers (Crump 1990: 149). Here numbers move from one context to another with ease and provide the appearance of authority (Crump 1990; Guyer et al. 2010).

As mentioned previously, field study and design materials were perceived by project partners as based upon a different kind of knowledge produced by statistical analysis. Design materials were difficult to interpret for engineers, and research outputs, provotypes and prototypes, for example, were considered incomplete. However, field study materials in the form of user statements were considered useful as hypothesis generators and in developing quantitative survey questions. In the end, these hypotheses needed further testing by quantitative methods. There was, however, an attempt by one of our partners (Engineer from Indoor Climate Research Unit, Technical University of Denmark) to draw upon SPIRE field studies to confront the prevailing distinction between the social and material in designing quantitative questionnaires.

The questionnaires were designed as part of a general survey involving one thousand users of indoor climate products and systems in Denmark. The quantitative questionnaires based upon findings from SPIRE field studies was a move instigated by engineers from our partner university (focused upon the development of indoor climate models in a controlled environment) to an increasing focus on human behavior (real-life surveys). The findings from the quantitative questionnaires were targeted toward informing building regulations and improving engineering practice. The questionnaire's role in the project was to validate qualitative knowledge from field studies and contribute to the generation of research hypotheses tested through quantitative surveys. As with recent experiments in ethno-mining, the engineer from the Indoor Climate Research Unit was unable to develop a "means of bridging between individual and large scale data sets" (Aipperspach et al. 2006: 10).

In the design of the quantitative survey questionnaire there was an attempt in a generalized system of knowledge to extend and potentially reframe research questions. Still, in order to generalize findings, engineers from the Indoor Climate Research Unit maintained that field study findings should be confirmed by quantitative surveys across a high number of respondents. Accordingly, qualitative methods in the end should be confined to generating hypotheses and questions for quantitative surveys.

Dominant Systems of Engineering Knowledge

Through collaborating with indoor climate engineers over a three-year period, we observed a gradual movement away from the current and prevailing generalized understandings of end users' lived experiences of indoor climate. But this movement was vague and constrained by ideas of producing single dimensions and even a single figure as design recommendations, informed by expectations of providing explanations and predictions of user behavior. In this sense, the user is reduced to a variable in the engineering calculation. Dominant systems of engineering knowledge in the building industry dealing with indoor climate have in common a reference to climate models. These models describe general relations between certain indoor climate parameters (often temperature, air quality, light, and noise). In the world of engineering, the role of engineering models and how indoor climate models are constructed is rarely questioned. The Indoor Climate Research Unit, Technical University of Denmark has been an important player in the development of research-based indoor climate models and represents an internationally respected research environment. The first climate models were based on laboratory experiments with dummy models of human bodies or real test persons in an artificial, but controlled environment (see Plate 23). In these models the inhabitant of indoor climate is represented as a generalized human being as made up across the variety of a test sample (Jaffari and Matthews 2009; Shove 2002).

In engineering worlds, examples of theoretically informed reflections of engaging everyday practices of negotiating indoor climate products and systems of control (especially in housing) are limited (Rohracher 2003; Stevenson and Leaman 2010). However, housing occupancy feedback is a critical area of debate emerging in discussions of building performance and evaluation. Researchers are concerned with evaluating users' perceptions and behavior in relation to how housing performs and why (Vischer 2008). Researchers in this area are limited to finding gaps between predicted and actual performance (Stevenson and Leaman 2010). Engineering systems demand a strong technological regime—including systemic knowledge embodying certain ideas of how knowledge flows through a system. This would suggest difficulties in flow of knowledge, and existing knowledge and institutional structures cannot take up just any kind of knowledge.

The difficulty engineers have in understanding what others could take up from practices of inhabiting indoor climate says something about how difficult it is to make radical innovation in such a system. By focusing on the processes and dynamics belonging to the practices of inhabiting indoor climate, SPIRE researchers challenged these established configurations of knowledge (Marchand 2010; Rapport and Harris 2007). In particular, we challenged notions about where exactly designing takes place and by whom.

USER-CUM-PRODUCER

It was difficult for company and university partners to say where innovation could take place in the design of indoor climate products and systems of control. Participants were, however, willing to make *judgments* of what kind of knowledge had innovation potential based on unclear ideas of what innovation is. We did find evidence to suggest the conceptualization of end user knowledge was challenged and moved slightly, despite dominant framings received from engineering modeling practices. There remained a fixation with the *user* providing ideas for designers of indoor climate.

Ingold makes a distinction between professional and inhabitant knowledge as related to the distinction between occupation and inhabitation. Inhabitant knowledge is a way of knowing and is part of the movement through the world. The line of movement goes along instead of cutting across, each movement part of an ongoing activity (2011: 154). Therefore, as opposed to considering inhabitants of indoor climate as potential *users* of designed things, Ingold's concept of *user-cum-producer* posits end users of indoor products and systems of control as designers themselves (2012). Ingold asks us to consider design, inherent to the concept of *user-cum-producer*, as imagining a future that is open-ended. Unlike objects that imbue some form of closure in the relation between using and producing, designing and using, people and things—things are not finished, "but are carried on in their use even as you carry on with your own life" (2010: 5). Things here are considered in the Heideggerian sense. Everyday practices of negotiating indoor climate products and systems of control could then be understood as a way of designing. However, *the way* people negotiate and thus design in the course of their everyday actions is not a matter of determining in advance the final forms of things and all the steps needed to get there, but of "opening up a path and improvising a passage" (Ingold 2012: 27). To foresee, in this sense, "is to see into the future, not to project a future state of affairs in the present; it is to look where you are going, not to fix an end-point" (Ingold 2012: 27). Such foresight is about prophecy and not prediction as found in engineering models or functional numbers. Foresight is what allows people using indoor climate products and systems of control to carry on rather than be hindered by things brought into being through the course of their actions (Ingold 2012: 27). By contrast, engineers' reliance on numbers as a form of prediction reduces people to a variable in an engineering calculation. The aim for certainty in projecting into the future is also in opposition to an open-ended approach to innovation, where processes of uncertainty and continuous reframing are keys to innovation instead of sources of unwanted uncertainty.

Making Innovation Potential Judgments

Continuous innovation with users of indoor climate was perceived by project participants as contradictory to what they do; after all, companies need to freeze concepts in order to produce. If companies acknowledge that radical innovation is required by inviting *user-cum-producers* of indoor climate to work with them then a wider perspective is required than is currently possible within engineering knowledge traditions. This requires contextual and political reflections upon how *judgments* are made of innovation potential within indoor climate engineering design practices.

A number of our project partners asked why SPIRE researchers were interested in scaffolding improvisatory skills. Some interpreted this as a need for flexible systems, while others argued that it was an unnecessary deroute toward obtaining a pleasant indoor climate. Unlike innovation, improvisation in a field of practice is concerned not so much with producing novelty but to find ways of keeping on going. The difference, as Ingold and Hallam have previously argued, between innovation and improvisation is that innovation is linked to a retrospective view of production (2007: 2). That something is considered innovative by comparison to something that has gone before. So as soon as you *judge* something as innovative, it is necessary to return to a prior state from which the innovation arose. Improvisation, by contrast, is concerned with moving forward and is in itself a process that moves concurrently with the flow of people's actions within the world. This is not to say that improvisation and innovation are different activities; they are different kinds of judgments of the same activity. One is a prospective judgment in terms of our involvement in a movement, a forward movement. The other is a retrospective judgment in terms of prior states.[9]

ACKNOWLEDGMENTS

We are grateful to SPIRE for generously supporting our collaborative research. We would also like to thank the Indoor Climate and Quality of Life project partners for allowing us to continue working with them in their organizations.

NOTES

1. Sønderborg Participatory Innovation Centre (SPIRE) conducted a series of three workshops in 2009 for the Scottish Universities Insight Institute's Designing Environments for Life program. Background information on the program is available at: www.scottishinsight.ac.uk. Accessed March 11, 2013. At workshop 3 (November 10, 2009), Symons, Chandler, and Ingold posited the idea that lived experiences of indoor climate are temporal.
2. See SPIRE website. Available at: www.sdu.dk/SPIRE. Accessed May 27, 2012.
3. Field studies were conducted in Danish homes, kindergartens, and offices (2008–2010) by two doctoral students, one with a background in language and communication, the other with a background in interaction design; one postdoctoral researcher in interaction design; the project manager; a mechanical engineer; and master students in IT product design with backgrounds in interaction, industrial design, and engineering.
4. In this instance and hereafter, except where reference is explicitly made to published and bibliographic sources, we acknowledge material gathered from interviews with unnamed project partners. To avoid confusion between primary and secondary sources, references to partners here are italicized. To ensure anonymity of project participants we have not included company names and referred to individuals as professional roles.
5. A BCG matrix is a management tool used widely by engineers to visualize prioritization of product lines for business units of companies.
6. Emilia Ferraro's reflection-in-action of SPIRE's workshop practices, *Designing Environments for Life Workshop 4*, Scottish Universities Insight Institute, Strathclyde University, Glasgow, December 16–17, 2009.

7. In parallel to conducting 2:1 interviews with project partners, we also interviewed the SPIRE project manager.
8. Comment made by participant during *Designing Environments for Life Workshop 3*, Scottish Universities Insight Institute, University of Strathclyde, Glasgow, Scotland, November 10, 2009.
9. Comment by Tim Ingold concerning the institutional division between innovation and improvisation at *Designing Environments For Life Workshop 1*, Scottish Universities Insight Institute, University of Strathclyde, Glasgow, Scotland, September 10, 2009.

REFERENCES

Aipperspach, R., Rattenbury, T. L., Woodruff, A., Anderson, K., Canny, J. F., and Aoki, P. (2006), *Ethno-mining: Integrating Numbers and Words from the Ground Up*, Electrical Engineering and Computer Sciences, University of California at Berkeley, Technical Report No. UCB/EECS-2006–125. Available at: www.eecs.berkeley.edu/Pubs/TechRpts/2006/EECS-2006–125.html. Accessed May 21, 2011.

Anderson, K., Nafus, D., Rattenbury, T. L., and Aipperspach, R. (2009), "Numbers Have Qualities Too: Experiences with Ethno-mining," in *Ethnographic Praxis in Industry Conference Proceedings: The Fifth Annual Ethnographic Praxis in Industry Conference*, Chicago, IL, August 30–September 2, 123–140.

Anderson, R. J. (1994), "Representations and Requirements: The Value of Ethnography in System Design," *Journal of Human-Computer Interaction*, 9(3): 151–182.

Boer, L. (2012), "How Provotypes Challenge Stakeholder Conceptions in Innovation Projects," PhD dissertation, Mads Clausen Institute, University of Southern Denmark.

Boer, L., and Donovan, J. (2012), "Provotypes for Participatory Innovation," in *Proceedings DIS '12 Designing Interactive Systems Conference*, Newcastle Upon Tyne, UK, June 11–15, 388–397.

Buur, J. (ed.), (2012), *Making Indoor Climate: Enabling People's Comfort Practices*, Sonderborg: Mads Clausen Institute, University of Southern Denmark.

Buur, J., and Matthews, B. (2008), "Participatory Innovation," *International Journal of Innovation Management*, 12(3): 255–273.

Buur, J., and Sitorus, L. (2007), "Ethnography as Design Provocation," in *Ethnographic Praxis in Industry Conference Proceedings*, Keystone, CO, 140–150.

Crump, T. (1990), *The Anthropology of Numbers*, Cambridge: Cambridge University Press.

Donovan, J., and Gunn, W. (2012), "Moving from Objects to Possibilities," in W. Gunn and J. Donovan (eds.), *Design and Anthropology*, Farnham: Ashgate, 121–134.

Farnell, B. (2000), "Getting out of the *Habitus*: An Alternative Model of Dynamically Embodied Social Action," *The Journal of the Royal Anthropological Institute*, 6(3): 397–418.

Gunn, W., and Clausen, C. (2012a), "Reframing What Innovation Could Be: Observation, Juxtaposition and Challenging Taken for Granted Assumptions" (abstract), in *Proceedings of International People Environment Studies Conference*, University of Strathclyde, Scotland, June 24–29.

Gunn, W., and Clausen, C. (2012b), "What Does This Mean to Industry?" in J. Buur (ed.), *Making Indoor Climate: Enabling People's Comfort Practices*, Sonderborg: Mads Clausen Institute, University of Southern Denmark, 31–35.

Gunn, W., and Donovan, J. (2012), "Design Anthropology: An Introduction," in W. Gunn and J. Donovan (eds.), *Design and Anthropology*, Farnham: Ashgate, 1–16.

Guyer, J.I., Khan, N., and Obarrio, J., with Bledsoe, C., Chu, J., Diagne, S.B., Hart, K., Kockelman, P., Lave, J., McLoughlin, C., Maurer, B., Neiburg, F., Nelson, D., Stafford, C., and Verron, H. (2010), "Introduction: Number as Inventive Frontier," *Anthropological Theory*, 10(1–2): 36–61.

Ingold, T. (2000), *The Perception of the Environment: Essays in Livelihood, Dwelling and Skill*, London: Routledge.

Ingold, T. (2010), *Bringing Things to Life: Creative Entanglements in a World of Materials*, Realities (Part of the Economic and Social Research Council National Centre for Research Methods Working Papers no. 15). Available at: www.socialsciences.manchester.ac.uk/morgancentre/realities/wps/15–2010–07-realities-bringing-things-to-life.pdf. Accessed November 11, 2012.

Ingold, T. (2011), *Being Alive: Essays on Movement, Knowledge and Description*, London: Routledge.

Ingold, T. (2012), "Part I Introduction: The Perception of the User-producer," in W. Gunn and J. Donovan (eds.), *Design and Anthropology*, Farnham: Ashgate, 19–33.

Ingold, T., and Hallam, E. (2007), "Creativity and Cultural Improvisation: An Introduction," in E. Hallam and T. Ingold (eds.), *Creativity and Cultural Improvisation*, Oxford: Berg, 1–24.

Jaffari, S., Boer, L., and Buur, J. (2011), "Actionable Ethnography in Participatory Innovation: A Case Study," in *Proceedings of The 15th World Multi-Conference on Systemics, Cybernetics and Informatics*, Orlando, FL, July 19–22, 100–106.

Jaffari, S., and Matthews, B. (2009), "From Occupying to Inhabiting: A Change in Conceptualising Comfort," Beyond Kyoto: Addressing the Challenges of

Climate, *IOP Conference Series: Earth and Environmental Science*, 8(1): 1–14.

Kilbourn, K. (2010), "The Patient as Skilled Practitioner," PhD dissertation, Mads Clausen Institute, University of Southern Denmark.

Lave, J. (2011), *Apprenticeship in Critical Ethnographic Practice*, Chicago, IL: University of Chicago Press.

Leach, J. (2011), "'Step Inside: Knowledge Freely Available': The Politics of (Making) Knowledge-objects," in P. Baert and F. Domínguez Rubio (eds.), *The Politics of Knowledge*, London: Routledge, 79–95.

Marchand, T.H.J. (2010), "Making Knowledge: Explorations of the Indissoluble Relation between Minds, Bodies, and Environment," *Journal of the Royal Anthropological Institute*, (N.S.): S1–S21.

Marcus, G.E. (2011), "Multi-sited Ethnography: Five or Six Things I Know about It Now," in S. Coleman and P. von Hellerman (eds.), *Multi-sited Ethnography: Problems and Possibilities in the Translocation of Research Methods*, London: Routledge, 16–34.

Mead, G.H. (1934), *Mind, Self, & Society from the Standpoint of a Social Behaviorist*, Chicago, IL: University of Chicago Press.

Mogensen, P. (1994), "Challenging Practice: An Approach to Cooperative Analysis," PhD dissertation, Computer Science Department, University of Aarhus.

Rabinow, P., and Marcus, G.E., with Faubion, J.D., and Rees, T. (2008), *Designs for an Anthropology of the Contemporary*, Durham, NC and London: Duke University Press.

Rapport, N., and Harris, M. (2007), "A Discussion Concerning Ways of Knowing," in M. Harris (ed.), *Ways of Knowing: New Approaches in the Anthropology of Experience and Learning*, Oxford: Bergahn, 306–330.

Rees, T. (2008), "Afterward 'Design' and 'Design Studio' in Anthropology," in P. Rabinow and G.E. Marcus, with J.D. Faubion and T. Rees (eds.), *Designs for an Anthropology of the Contemporary*, Durham, NC and London: Duke University Press, 115–121.

Rohracher, H. (2003), "The Role of Users in the Social Shaping of Environmental Technologies," *Innovation*, 16(2): 177–192.

Rohracher, H. (2005), "From Passive Consumers to Active Participants: The Diverse Roles of Users in Innovation Processes," in H. Rohracher (ed.), *User Involvement in Innovation Processes: Strategies and Limitations from a Socio-Technical Perspective*, Munich: Profil-Verlag, 9–35.

Shove, E. (2002), "Converging Conventions of Comfort, Cleanliness and Convenience," Department of Sociology, Lancaster University, Lancaster, UK. Available at: www.lancs.ac.uk/fass/sociology/papers/shove-converging-conventions.pdf. Accessed November 11, 2012.

Schön, D. (1983), *The Reflective Practitioner: How Professionals Think in Action*, New York: Basic Books.

Stevenson, F., and Leaman, A. (2010), "Evaluating Housing Performance in Relation to Human Behaviour: New Challenges," *Building Research & Information*, 38(5): 437–441.

Strathern, M. (2004), *Commons and Borderlands: Working Papers on Interdisciplinarity, Accountability and the Flow of Knowledge*, Oxon: Sean Kingston Publishing.

Suchman, L. (2011), "Anthropological Relocations and the Limits of Design," *Annual Review of Anthropology*, 40: 1–18.

Tsing, A. L. (2005), *Friction: An Ethnography of Global Connection*, Princeton, NJ and Oxford: Princeton University Press.

Turnbull, D. (2007), "Maps, Narratives and Trails: Performativity, Hodology and Distributed Knowledges in Complex Adaptive Systems—An Approach to Emergent Mapping," *Geographical Research*, 45(2): 140–149.

Vischer, J.C. (2008), "Towards a User-centred Theory of the Built Environment," *Building Research & Information*, 36(3): 231–240.

–10–

Ethnographies of the Possible

Joachim Halse

ANTHROPOLOGY AND THE IMAGINATIVE

During a recent experimental graduate course at the Royal Danish Academy of Fine Arts School of Design, where students of anthropology and design worked closely together, anthropology student Esther Fritsch expressed her experience of active participation in a design intervention this way:

> We were not just describing a here-and-now. For me, the synergy between the two disciplines emerged through our "interventions" where it was allowed to suggest a distorted here-and-now, or a possible future that gave access to a new type of data. By articulating a hypothetical world we were physically invited into a new universe of peoples' thoughts and reflections. (2011)

This chapter is about inquiring into this kind of possible future as an extension of the ethnographic gaze. But before going into more detail with what is meant by *ethnographies of the possible*, I will first ground the topic of the imaginative in established anthropological discussions.

In *Designs for an Anthropology of the Contemporary*, Rabinow and Marcus, in conversational dialogue with Faubion and Rees (2008), seek to renew and invigorate anthropology. The challenge, as they see it, is to release anthropology from its conventional methodological focus on people out of time and instead better equip anthropologists to deal with the contemporary, understood as an open moment in which the world is potentially changing. To do this, the four interlocutors project the future of anthropology in the image of an architectural design studio. In considering the virtues of the architectural design studio they play with the idea of understanding research as a design process, where the dominant mode of knowledge production is characterized by critical experimentation and collaboration with peers, users, and clients around unfinished concepts (Rabinow et al. 2008: 83–85). I am sympathetic to this goal of enriching anthropological knowledge production by learning from certain aspects of design processes, particularly collaborative and experimental inquiries. With this chapter I wish to contribute to the discussion by suggesting that a design anthropological practice may not only take inspiration from the design studio in its form of inquiry, but also in the object of its inquiry, namely that which does not concretely exist, the imaginative.

In a recent anthology on design anthropology, Jamer Hunt expresses a concern with the leap from the descriptive, similar to the one pursued in this chapter, when he states that "ethnography is rarely projective; it does not speculate on what might happen next" (2011: 35). Ethnographic projects conventionally describe present or past situations through observation, interview, analysis, and interpretation, as is also instructed in disciplinary introductions (see Hammersley and Atkinson 1995). I am concerned that the imagination and speculation about what might be, how people's near futures are consciously shaped and projected, is not discarded by the emerging field of design anthropology as mere reveries of the real, just because it is difficult to scrutinize this realm of creative possibility through conventional ethnographic methods.

This is not to say that anthropology does not deal at all with what might happen next. Certainly Vincent Crapanzano's *Imaginative Horizons* deals with the process of imagination and how people understand possibility. Crapanzano uses the horizon as a metaphor for the imagination: "when a horizon and whatever lies beyond it are given articulate form, they freeze our view of the reality that immediately confronts us—fatally I'd say, were it not for the fact that once that beyond is articulated, a new horizon emerges and with it a new beyond" (2004: 2). The dialectic between openness and closure is central. Through an inspirational style of montage and juxtapositions, Crapanzano demonstrates a keen ethnographic attention to concrete manifestations of processes of imagination. But in inquiring into the hopes, fears, and aspirations of people from around the world, Crapanzano relies on the conventional ethnographic interview, observation, and literary sources. It seems as if there are no ethnographic tools for inquiring into the bodily and material experience of *the possible* or the processes through which it is given articulate yet tentative forms.

The question I am raising here is aiming to expand the range of ethnographic practices: How can ethnography be part of these transformative actions themselves? What does it look like when imaginative issues are actively brought from beyond the horizon to a point where their contours can begin to be articulated and contested? What methodological resources may assist us when we get confronted with their immediate manifestation and people either seek opportunities to celebrate what they see or hurry to dismiss it as unrealistic fantasies or all too realistic threats?

In a similar vein, Sneath, Holbraad, and Pedersen ask: "What would an anthropology that takes the imagination seriously look like?" (2009). Their ambition is to move away from a conceptualization of the imaginary that is overly homogeneous and that glosses over local differences. They specifically criticize Charles Taylor's understanding of the social imaginary as "shared by large groups of people, if not the whole society" (Taylor cited in Sneath et al. 2009: 8). To avoid the all-encompassing connotations of the imaginary and to refine the anthropological characterization of the imagination, Sneath and colleagues suggest to focus instead on technologies of the imagination, that is, "the social and material means by which particular imaginings are generated" (2009: 6). The concept of "technologies of the imagination" is useful for our purposes here to appreciate the heterogeneous processes through which the concrete imaginings of particular visions and concerns are generated in design events.

ETHNOGRAPHIC INQUIRIES INTO POSSIBLE FUTURES

To ethnographically qualify the imaginary, as Sneath and colleagues also pointed out, we must move into the concrete. For an ethnography concerned with the social and material means by which particular imaginings are generated, I suggest a focus on design events understood as lived moments of becoming, particularly those that move out of the design studio into the wild, so to speak. One of the immediately intriguing aspects of design practices is that the object of concern is nonexistent. The very point of designing is a process of bringing into being something that does not yet exist. Sometimes this happens on an abstract level as ideas, visions, or fantasies, sometimes on a more concrete level as drawings, prototypes, or specifications for manufacture. The object of design is not available during the practice of design: it is in the making. In researching this space of possibility as it unfolds within actual design practice, one would be researching something that is not yet available for scrutiny—at least not in the conventional sense of ethnographic fieldwork.

Because the object of exploratory design partly belongs to the realm of imagination and lies beyond the point where it can be fully articulated, it is fairly commonplace to experiment with prototypes in everyday life situations carried out under the name of living labs, design interventions, and field trials. The immediate purpose of these experiments is to establish and explore a credible and meaningful practice around a particular issue and an idea for its resolution in the environment *of* and *by* the people it addresses, before the idea is fully developed. Given the availability of alternative resources (for example, new technologies, processes, or organizations), this kind of design experiment works through a playful mode of trying out how everyday life might play out differently in light of this, and in a way that seeks to be meaningful to the involved participants. The archetypical question of the design prototype, *what happens if we look at it this way?* seeks to give articulate form to a proposal or hypothesis and when it works best, expose the proposal or hypothesis to critical dialogue and reflection.

From a position within the emerging field of design anthropology, I focus on two empirical design events where the imaginary was concretely performed in doll scenarios and in full-scale enactments in order to reflect about what it implies to appropriate an anthropological methodological heritage for an orientation toward possible futures. I wish to point to the potential of extending the ethnographic gaze from practices that are given and more or less historically manifest to practices that are suggested, future-oriented, and facilitated through a more or less temporary design event. The ambition is to arrive at a potential transdisciplinary position for interventionist experiments, which draws on designerly tools and methods for articulating possibilities in corporeal forms while retaining an ethnographic sensitivity to its social and political implications for the people involved.

TRANSFORMATIVE EVENTS

Recently Bruce Kapferer revisited the role of "the event" in ethnographic work and criticized the way events are often chosen for their typicality, as illustrative examples supporting the ethnographic account of general patterns. Instead, Kapferer points to the heritage from situational analysis developed by Max Gluckman of the Manchester School, among others, to see the event as constitutive in and of itself: "it was Turner who realized most of all a key implication of Gluckman's situational analysis—that it is through a focus on events that anthropologists can come to grips with social processes in their creative and generative moments" (Kapferer 2010: 9). Kapferer even ascribes Victor Turner chief credit for an understanding of the event as a locus of creativity and change (2010: 10). One of Turner's central points was that the ritual suspension of normal order was a critical step for enabling reconfigurations of existential realities (Turner 1969). Drawing on Victor Turner's work on rituals and social dramas, Richard Schechner used "actual" to define those nonmimetic and particularly transformative moments when something contestable happens here and now with irrevocable consequences for the participants (1988: 26–65). With the concept of actuals Schechner was very concretely traversing the boundaries between ethnography and performance theory, as he links it with ritual combat and exchange, staged theater performances, and political activism. What is particularly interesting about the concept of the actual is that it locates change, creativity, and future making not in the realm of presumably shared imaginaries nor in the decidedly nonexisting as in the virtual, but as something actualized in the event by concrete articulations of things and processes.

Ethnographic field techniques in support of commercial design processes have been charged with naïve realism when collecting evidence of purportedly *real people who live out there* (Nafus and Anderson 2006). To counter the sim-plified image of ethnographers documenting existing practices and designers inventing future practices, it may be productive to complexify the temporal re-lationship between past, present, and future. In his posthumously published *Philosophy of the Present*, George Herbert Mead (2002 [1932]) laid out an understanding of the present as constitutive of both past and future. Mead states that a present "marks out and in a sense selects what has made its peculiarity possible. It creates with its uniqueness a past and a future. As soon as we view it, it becomes a history and a prophecy." The past and the future, according to Mead, "are the boundaries of what we term the present, and are determined by the conditioning relationships of the event to its situ-ation" (2002 [1932]: 52–53). In this light, that which is prototyped during a design event can be understood as extending the boundaries of the present. The design event is where lived life meets the imagined artifact, be it in the shopping center, the architectural studio, or the unemployment center, where people's bodily comportment, social relations, cultural preferences, and tech-nological ability can be projected onto an artifact that is still in the making.

EXPLORING POSSIBLE WASTE HANDLING FUTURES

Let me introduce two concrete design events that took place in Denmark during 2008. The events were generated through a design and research project about waste handling, from which I have extensive firsthand experience. Because of growing amounts of unsorted waste, the incinerator at Vestforbrænding, a pub-licly owned company located outside of Copenhagen, was reaching its limits. Vestforbrænding invited a team of design researchers from universities and pro-fessional consultancies with varied backgrounds in industrial design, concept development, and anthropology, including me, to explore existing and new waste handling practices. The project was funded in part by the Danish government pro-gram for User Driven Innovation and by the participating partners themselves.

The project's stated objective was to engage citizens and professional stakeholders in design-oriented dialogues to explore and unfold potentials for improving waste handling practices. A two-month challenge was organized by Herlev Municipality and Vestforbrænding to identify possible cross-sector local partnerships between small shops, citizens in housing compounds, and the municipality. Bangs Torv, a medium-sized shopping center combined with residential homes, was chosen as a concrete stage for the dialogues. In the following empirical account, I would like to suggest two attention points as particularly intense occasions for an ethnography of the possible: miniature doll scenarios and 1:1 bodily enactments, both taking place in the present in very corporeal forms, yet extending this moment and these forms by project-ing aspirations and concerns onto a possible future.

In the design research team, we became familiar with the shopping center and its people through short-term participant observation: walking along and video filming the caretaker on his rounds and conducting semi-structured shop floor interviews with shop owners and staff, in-home observations, and semi-structured interviews with residents. In addition to the ethnographic techniques we devised dialogue board games for playing with customers at the shopping square and maintained an online weblog to allow and encourage participants to see what was made of the stories generated by these mixed methods. In parallel we facilitated workshops for members of the professional waste sector and asked them to formulate their versions of future dream projects to gain a sense of what was becoming technologically possible and desirable from a waste expert's perspective.

From the material generated by these methods we could have tried to identify patterns, triangulate hypotheses, and eventually write up a coherent ethnographic account of waste handling practices of Bangs Torv. Instead, we created a stage for those involved to participate in making sense of the data in the form of a workshop in the municipal town hall (see Plate 24). This methodological choice was part of a larger approach developed and practiced by the CoDesign research cluster at the Royal Danish Academy of Fine Arts School of Design, among others. The approach draws on resources from participatory design (e.g., Greenbaum and Kyng 1991), American pragmatism and the formation of publics around issues of concern (Dewey 1988 [1927]), Stengers's cosmopolitical proposal toward critical reflection as a collective practice (2005), as well as recent design theory bringing some of these aspects together with particular creative design practices (Binder et al. 2011).

COLLABORATIVE DOLL SCENARIOS

By bringing together differing horizons of citizens' imaginings, concerns, design ideas, environmental challenges, and business opportunities in very concrete terms, our motive was to synthesize an account of waste handling by all the project participants in collaboration, rather than writing a single authored detailed ethnographic monograph. The stated goal of the workshop was to familiarize the participants with field material from the shopping center, prompt them to discuss issues from the waste experts' dream projects, coproduce synthesized stories of possible future waste handling practices in this specific shopping center, and finally to enact these stories as small video recorded doll scenarios.

To this end the research team organized the documented material from previous inquiries into workshop activities and materials. Photographs, video clips, and stories from Bangs Torv were not presented as ethnographic evidence or representations of the real, but rather as fragmentary snapshots that invited further interpretations, cuttings, and reuse in montages or juxtapositions with design ideas (see Plate 25). As the basis of this selection and organization of the material was not an ethnographic analysis but rather an intuitive estimate of its qualities for participatory sense making, how well could this particular piece of field material lend itself to diverse interpretation by the broad range of participants? The selection process had two ideals: first to lead participants to a general recognition of rhythms and happenings at this particular shopping center, and second to try and make partial connections between the hopes and dreams of all participants in order to offer possibilities of how things could be different.

Workshop participants, comprised of local residents, municipal waste planners, shop staff, the board chair of the shopping center, technical waste specialists, the caretaker and his son, and the design research team, explored and discussed in small groups the meaning of the open-ended selection of field material. The room and the furniture were arranged as a place of participatory creation, rather than one of listen and learn. Instead of smooth-looking visuals, demonstrations of new technologies, or authoritarian statements of what goals to reach, there was a large amount of local photographs and quotations by project participants, rough sketches of design ideas, and materials for tinkering scattered over the tables, along with utensils to transform them. The tables were arranged in small islands, signaling a degree of group autonomy. Municipal officials were the official hosts as workshop activities occurred in the town hall, while I and my colleagues in the design research team planned, introduced, and facilitated the three-hour workshop program.

To structure the process of group familiarization with the open-ended material a design game was employed (for an in-depth treatment of design games, see Brandt, Messeter, and Binder 2008). Game rules instructed participants to choose what they found to be the most interesting material to work with and place it or replace it on a simple game board. Thereafter they were asked to explain to each other what the material and its placement in relation to other materials on the board meant to them. The rules involved turn taking and invited participants, including the researchers, to rely on personal and professional experience in creating an account of Bangs Torv as a landscape of waste-related practices. During this collaborative crafting of the account, the voice of the ethnographer is supplemented by other voices like that of the teenager concerned with the right to smoke cigarettes, the engineer concerned with the cleanliness of the sorted materials, and the resident concerned with the aesthetics of the parking lot, just to name a few.

Halfway through the workshop the populated landscapes of Bangs Torv were turned into concrete stages for possibilities when the event moved into a more playful mode, asking, "What if things were different at Bangs Torv?" In line with the fragmentary status of the empirical snapshots, a number of design suggestions were presented as visual sketches of "what if" situations crafted to evoke further reflection and imaginings rather than to convince about given qualities through stylistically finished aesthetics (see "the evocative sketch" by Foverskov and Dam 2010). The sketches were accompanied by questions derived from waste professionals' dream projects like, "What if there was a waste collection station on the plaza?" and "What if it was fun to hand in used mobile phones?" After a short, intense working session, a retired shop owner working together with a young designer explained the direction they were moving in their imagining of a residential waste area that was active and invited a range of recreational activities where people could meet over coffee: "So that it would be more than just a place to get rid of your stuff and then rush off" (transcribed from video, February 5, 2009).

Using simple materials like the field photos, sketches, and blank paper, the participants created stories of possible futures and eventually enacted them as six short doll scenarios. They were captured on video demonstrating how a group's idea of an attractive future waste practice could play out over time for particular persons. Considered as a technology of the imagination, the doll scenario works to reconnect a somewhat abstract and general product of the imagination with highly concrete constraints of a particular place in a particular time: Where exactly is the furniture for the coffee drinkers placed in relation to the parking lots? If this is a private lot, who is maintaining the public containers? Is it open on Sundays? Based on extensive experience with facilitating creation of doll scenarios beyond the present case, the process often leads to the surfacing of a number of trade-offs between conflicting interests.

One future scenario was developed by Ulla, who has lived at Bangs Torv for more than thirty years, together with the municipal waste planner, Dorte. The latter led a doll looking like the shop owner, Allan, and Ulla led a doll dressed like her close friend Lillian, who also lives at Bangs Torv. The two doll characters meet in Allan's shop:

Allan (led by Dorte): Just leave your used batteries here, then Michael the caretaker will bring them over to our new shared waste sorting station. Have you seen how busy it already is?

Lillian (led by Ulla): Oh, yes. How pretty it is with the beautiful flowers and trees and all. It does look good. It must be Michael who is keeping it so nice. (transcribed from video, February 5, 2009)

This little excerpt from a doll scenario is a coconstructed story of things, relationships, and environments that point *both* to well-known places and relationships *and* to imaginary aspects of these. The participants use dolls and photographs to build a scene that resembles their particular shopping center, but they also use design sketches and improvised props to accomplish their story of a possible future. Dorte, the waste planner, focuses on the benefit of an imaginary waste sorting station while Ulla, the resident, expresses an aesthetic concern for her particular home environment.

While encompassing highly localized and particular concerns ("how can we avoid used batteries in the incinerator?" or "what if we could make the citizens sort better?" or "what if our parking lot was a really nice and clean place to meet?"), the resulting new stories and situations as they were enacted as doll scenarios did in fact link up some of these different voices. Doll scenarios were a promising ending point for the workshop, a concrete coproduced result. But as somewhat idealized future stories based on scale models they also glossed over some concrete conflicts of interest. After the workshop, the research team reviewed video recordings of the workshop discussions and doll scenarios and analyzed them for points of convergence and conflict. We synthesized promising and recurrent features across the material into four more concise and illustrated design proposals. Drawing on performance theory (Schechner 1988) and performance-oriented design methods (Binder 1999; Brandt and Grunnet 2000; Buchenau and Fulton Suri 2000), we then prepared design proposals as open-ended invitations to be concretized through performances in situ no longer with dolls, but by the project participants themselves in full scale.

FULL-SCALE ENACTMENTS

A few weeks after the workshop, the project participants assembled in the basement of Allan's retail shop on Bangs Torv itself. When presented with the roughly sketched idea In and Out of the Shop, the municipal waste planner, Dorte, commented: "It would be new to make something shared for the residents and the shops here. But it would also be new to make something where it was allowed to bring something from elsewhere" (transcribed from video, March 5, 2009). The shop owner, the caretaker, two residents, the municipal waste planner, and the design research team went on to explore how roughly sketched ideas could potentially play out in concrete physical surroundings of the shopping center. The goal was to build a scene as concretely as possible by using foam, cardboard, tape, and other props adapted from the local setting so that participants could subsequently *try out* the imagined arrangement. In other words, Allan the shop owner would now play his part himself, rather than being led by a puppeteer. Two researchers trained in industrial design were taking the lead in arranging the physical materials to support the ideas, I was acting as a kind of stage manager, and local participants were contributing as experts, each in their own domain. When everybody had had a chance to raise their concerns, and it seemed that we might have agreed on an acceptable configuration of an imagined alternative practice and artifact with respect to placement, ownership, size, and functionality, we moved into an explicitly playful performance mode with the question: *What if this was really working?*

Allan, the shop owner, introduced his customer to the partly imagined, partly mocked-up in-shop waste handling system, and Lillian responded with appreciation of the imagined, yet concrete, new possibility (see Plate 26). The performance was located on the shop floor during regular business hours, and other staff members walked in and out of the scenario stage while carrying out their work.

The cardboard and paper mock-up of an imagined battery machine is not merely figuring as an inclusive receptacle for suggestions, but is detailed enough to prompt the shop owner to carefully demonstrate how an ID card is swept correctly in order for the machine to recognize the user. This particular incident gave rise to a lively and important discussion of the trade-off between the potential benefit of earning and registering an individual bonus through good recycling habits vis-à-vis the pressing question of unwarranted surveillance and "why anybody needs to know that I am here doing this." The shop owner and the resident balanced between play acting for the case of the situation and consciously expressing their real and concrete concerns for how this artifact could make sense for them and possibly become part of their life worlds. When it comes to critical moments in the scenario, this play is very serious for the implied participants. For example, the direct question if the shop owner was willing *in the scenario* to offer his customers a discount on purchases when they brought in used batteries forced him to think twice before promising something his business concerns *outside the scenario* would not allow him to. What played out in the scenarios was indeed performative in the sense that even a playful commitment to offer a discount has to be explicitly withdrawn or marked as just pretend to bracket it off from ordinary life and restrict it to a feature of a temporary imaginary world. The fine line between real and imagined was traversed many times in ways that implicated the participants beyond the particular performance, and eventually when the service was implemented for a twelve-month test period the shop owner *did* offer a discount in return for used batteries.

Another idea had taken its point of departure in a workshop discussion with Michael the caretaker about problematic household waste left by the bus stop in front of the shopping center. Project participants hesitantly agreed it could be interesting to pursue an opportunity to accommodate this illegal practice instead of their immediate reaction: trying to stop it by sanctions. However, in preparing for trying it out, Ulla, who was playing her own part as citizen and local resident, exclaimed, "I don't think it could work! I don't believe in it! Why should we take down our trash to this place?" Some of the design researchers tried with an explanation that this was already happening (although illegally), but Ulla persisted: "I don't buy it! Suddenly we will have three big containers here. It will not look nice!" (transcribed from video, March 5, 2009). Subsequently this imagined waste collection point was moved to a less prominent place to the side of the shops and residential homes.

Piling up a handful of shopping baskets and attaching handwritten paper labels to them (see Plate 27) seemed a fairly small effort to achieve the effect of exploring the detailed bodily interactions of a mini recycling station; not in general, but placed right there, right then. Its concrete qualities served to bring out disagreements hidden by the less detailed props in the previous doll scenarios. This particular mock-up evidently held five small fractions of waste, no more, no less. A suggestion of a larger number of fractions necessarily reopened the discussion of size, aesthetics, and inclusion in the home environment for the residents. A suggestion to include medicinal waste immediately raised a concern with the station's sturdiness to prevent desperate drug users breaking into it.

The entire session at Bangs Torv dealt with four main design suggestions for possible waste handling practices and lasted about three hours. One suggestion was rejected by the residents before reaching the point where it was defined enough to act it out. So after having enacted and filmed three scenarios, the session was coming to an end. The participants physically stood back a little and prompted each other to briefly reflect on the experiences with the enactments. It also became an occasion to raise any remaining objections:

Joachim (design researcher): Dorte, do you think it could work?

Dorte (municipal waste planner): I think some of these things could actually work. Of course we would have to find a way to solve the problems of payment and fees. We don't want the citizens to pay for the businesses and vice versa, so there will be some practical issues. But it could be done as a trial period; I think we could try that. (transcribed from video, March 5, 2009)

Exhausted from the intense activities of imagination, discussion, reflection, and enactment, as well as the cold weather, we departed.

Our project on waste practices was set within a more general cultural imaginary of environmental sustainability, waste recycling, and local participation in decision-making processes as three vaguely defined ideals. However, the particular technologies of the imagination employed shifted the focus to a more concrete level of how these grand narratives play out concretely as moments of locally contested possibility and constraint for those involved. Technologies of the imagination thus allow participants to specify details of something otherwise only partially visible on the imaginative horizon, or at least at such a distance that it may have appeared as uncontested goods or the opposite. With this empirical account of two design events, I have presented doll scenarios and full-scale enactments as occasions for articulating features of possible futures that lie partly beyond the known. The specific forms of doll scenarios and enactments render the imaginative directly available for an experiential inquiry, ethnographic or not, as observable phenomena in the present.

The process of repetitive figurations of possible future waste practices with cheap intermediary materials like paper sketches, scenarios, and cardboard mock-ups reflects a widespread design approach to iterative prototyping, whereby misunderstandings and errors in the specification of a proposal are revealed earlier than is the case in more strict phase-divided design processes. From a design anthropological perspective, however, it does more than that. The concrete technologies of the imagination described here allow for the dialectic of openness and closure Crapanzano refers to to be positioned as a focal point of design anthropology. This is so both in terms of providing specific ethnographic encounters with the imaginary and in terms of providing inspiration for anthropological knowledge production processes that are inclusive of multiple stakeholders.

CRITICAL ENGAGEMENTS WITH DESIGN

Anthropologists have often sought a critical position of analysis from where the given order of the world can be challenged. Everything that is ordinarily taken for granted can be rendered exotic and in need of explanation; for example by revealing how dominant assumptions rest on sociohistorical contingencies. The implied conclusion, that the world could be different—at least in principle, can of course be left at that: an anthropological afterthought with no immediate consequences. For people enrolled as informants, however, the conclusion has different immediate implications. They will rarely rest assured that "the world could be different," at least not with the addendum "in principle." Dealing with people's dreams, hopes, and aspirations as well as with their fears and concerns is usually tightly linked with practical struggles to influence the world in ways that comply with these imaginings. Instead of leaving the follow-up question "what if things really *were* different?" for designers, future casters, or innovation strategists to pursue, I suggest that the exploration of how imaginative horizons can be given articulate but tentative form could be a welcome challenge for an anthropology that takes the imagination seriously.

As a former employee at Xerox's Palo Alto Research Center (PARC) pioneering the use of anthropology in commercial design research in the 1980s, anthropologist Lucy Suchman is in a highly qualified position to consider the disciplinary encounter between design and anthropology. Her early work of applying ethnographic competencies in high-profile design processes in what was once one of the world's self proclaimed centers of innovation serves as a backdrop for her recent academic work, where she has developed a more distanced critical stance informed by posthumanist and feminist theories. Given her extensive experiences in the field of design, Suchman takes great measures to establish an analytical distance to it. In "Anthropological Relocations and the Limits of Design," Suchman warns against a naïve celebration of design's ability to solve the world's most pressing problems through wishful thinking, for example about "massive change" that overly simplifies transformation processes (2011: 5). Focusing on the hubris implied by design's self-promoting "future makers," she states that "design and innovation are best positioned as problematic objects for an anthropology of the contemporary" (2011: 3). What Suchman is requesting with this analytical distance between the disciplines is a scholarship that illuminates its own entanglements in the knowledge it makes. I envision a design anthropological practice that, in line with this request, commits to the insistence on our own entanglements in the knowledge we produce. Heidegger famously expressed it as "Being-in-the-World is always already entangled" (2003 [1927]: 180).

For a design anthropology that engages actively with transformation processes, explicit as well as implicit agendas of any of the participants cannot be categorized and treated as problematic features of an empirical field comfortably distinct from analytical resources. These agendas are features of the analytical field as well because they too belong to a research institution's constituency, ultimately judging if the outcome is valid. As there are no free lunches, nor is there free access to ethnographic fields. As anthropologists or as design researchers, we are rarely if ever free to enter settings of prototyping solely based on a generalized scholarly curiosity. We are as much recruited for, and have to continuously consider our role for, those particular interests that initiate the projects we become part of. From a phenomenological perspective these project-entangled agendas are all there is, and inescapably they are also the conditions of possibility for the kinds of knowledge produced. There is undoubtedly more room for conducting a critical review of unquestioned assumptions and problematic consequences of a given design event after the fact, than during. But with that approach we are left with the all too common division of labor between designers who intervene and anthropologists who object with belated critical commentary.

A distinct contribution of design anthropology could be to develop particular technologies of the imagination that enable and encourage critical reflection *during* future-making processes. The use of doll scenarios, open-ended mock-ups, and enactments presented here attempts to iteratively connect projective and reflective modes of future making. These technologies of the imagination are carefully designed and facilitated by a design research team to allow all participants to playfully shift perspective by stepping in and out of imagined story worlds, shifting between immersion and commentary. The participants on Bangs Torv did not simply play roles or pretend to like any particular idea, but continuously refused to step into its story world unless their concerns had been articulated or the idea remodeled. They did not enroll as scenic performers of pre-given ideas, but rather acted as themselves under slightly altered conditions invoked by the magic *what if*.

There is nothing innocent about the interventionist research process outlined in this chapter—the games and performance techniques have been carefully designed by my colleagues and me to nurture a dialogue around the formation of a new public that cuts across conventional organizational borders of municipal officials, technical experts, citizens, and business people (cf. Clark, this volume). Research and design participants clearly did not agree on what makes up an attractive future waste handling practice. But everybody joined in this kind of project for *something* and all share aspirations for improvement (albeit) from their point of view (see Plate 28). For some, aspirations have to do with increased efficiency of operations; for others, it is about an increased experience of a provided service. For still others, aspirations were directly based in environmental concerns. For me, aspiring to both anthropological and designerly ways of knowing, the project was an occasion to follow an interest in participatory change processes committed to democratic ideals of respectful disagreements. Demonstrating that this kind of dialogical and relatively open-ended future-oriented encounter is even possible was an important driver for my engagement.

During the 2010 Prototyping Cultures: Social Experimentation, Do-it-Yourself Science and Beta-knowledge conference in Madrid, Jiménez and Estalella raised the critical question of what gets detached or disappears when particular possibilities are proposed: "What is going on when we allow prototypes to hold a sociological imagination in suspension for us, regardless of it turning on hopeful / liberating / communitarian abeyance?" (Jiménez and Estalella 2010). Well, in this particular project illegal waste practices were silenced, as they seemed too difficult to handle on this kind of exposed project stage in a short period of time. Suggestions of technological quick fixes to sorting problems were largely ignored because they tend to exclude one of the project's shared priorities: the social as a resource in design processes. The list of guilty ommitments could be continued ad infinitum, but serves here merely to allude to the trivial fact that collaborative research spaces are as contested as any other.

CONTESTED FUTURE MAKING

There is an established anthropological discussion of the contemporary as an open moment. Rabinow and colleagues suggested that collaborative and experimental design methods can be helpful in anthropological inquiries into the contemporary (2008), Crapanzano demonstrated how empirical imaginative horizons can be conceptualized anthropologically (2004), Sneath and colleagues suggested focusing on concrete technologies of the imagination (2009), and Kapferer underlined the transformative character of events (2010). Drawing on these anthropological resources, I have proposed the design event as an important occasion for inquiring into the possible—not in the abstract, but through concrete tools and practices whereby the possible appears partly available for embodied experience and reflection. To inquire into design events as moments of becoming, the projection of concerns and aspirations onto an artifact in the making, constitutes an expansion of the conventional ethnographic gaze on the present and on past presents. As Mead argued, the future is also constituted through interactions in the present (2002 [1932]). Anthropology could leave contemporary future making to those privileged enough to claim directions for attractive futures on behalf of everyone, or we can begin to employ the anthropological sensitivity to differences and particularities as an active driving force of establishing design events as more open-ended dialogues about what constitutes attractive from various viewpoints.

Ethnographies of the possible are a way of materializing ideas, concerns, and speculations through committed ethnographic attention to the people potentially affected by them. It is about crafting accounts that link the imagination to its material forms. And it is about creating artifacts that allow participants to revitalize their pasts, reflect upon the present, and extrapolate into possible futures. These ambitions lie in the borderland between design and anthropology. For designers involved in this type of process, it is a new challenge to craft not beautiful and convincing artifacts, but evocative and open-ended materials for further experimentation in collaboration with non-designers. For anthropologists, on the other hand, it is a new challenge to creatively set the scene for a distorted here and now with a particular direction as a first, but important step toward exploring particular imaginative horizons in concrete ways.

REFERENCES

Binder, T. (1999), "Setting the Stage for Improvised Video Scenarios," in *CHI '99 Extended Abstracts on Human Factors in Computing Systems*, Pittsburgh, PA: ACM Press, 230–231.

Binder, T., de Michelis, G., Ehn, P., Jacucci, G., Linde, P., and Wagner, I. (2011), *Design Things*, Cambridge, MA: MIT Press.

Brandt, E., and Grunnet, C. (2000), "Evoking the Future: Drama and Props in User Centered Design," in *Proceedings of Participatory Design Conference 2000*, New York: CPSR, 1–10.

Brandt, E., Messeter, J., and Binder, T. (2008), "Formatting Design Dialogues: Games and Participation," *CoDesign*, 4(1): 51–64.

Buchenau, M., and Fulton Suri, J. (2000), "Experience Prototyping," in D. Boyarski and W. A. Kellogg (eds.), *DIS '00 Proceedings of the 3rd Conference on Designing Interactive Systems: Processes, Practices, Methods, and Techniques*, New York: ACM Press, 424–433.

Crapanzano, V. (2004), *Imaginative Horizons*, London: University of Chicago Press.

Dewey, J. (1988 [1927]), *The Public and Its Problems*, Athens: Ohio University Press.

Foverskov, M., and Dam, K. (2010), "The Evocative Sketch," in J. Halse, E. Brandt, B. Clark, and T. Binder (eds.), *Rehearsing the Future*, Copenhagen: Danish Design School Press, 44–49.

Fritsch, E. (2011), "Designantropologi: Hvad er og kan denne sammensmeltede disciplin?" Royal Danish Academy of Fine Arts School of Design, Copenhagen.

Greenbaum, J., and Kyng, M. (eds.) (1991), *Design at Work: Cooperative Design of Computer Systems*, Hillsdale, NJ: Lawrence Erlbaum Associates.

Hammersley, M., and Atkinson, P. (1995), *Ethnography: Principles in Practice*, London, New York: Routledge.

Heidegger, M. (2003 [1927]), "Care as the Being of Da-sein," trans. J. Stambaugh, in M. Stassen (ed.), *Martin Heidegger: Philosophical and Political Writings*, London: The Continuum International Publishing Group, 180–198.

Hunt, J. (2011), "Prototyping the Social: Temporality and Speculative Futures at the Intersection of Design and Culture," in A. Clarke (ed.), *Design Anthropology: Object Culture in the 21st Century*, Wien: Springer, 33–44.

Jiménez, A. C., and Estalella, A. (2010), "The Prototype: A Sociology in Abeyance." Available at: http://anthropos-lab.net/studio/episode/03. Accessed May 15, 2012.

Kapferer, B. (2010), "Introduction: In the Event—Toward an Anthropology of Generic Moments," *Social Analysis*, 54(3): 1–27.

Mead, G. H. (2002 [1932]), *The Philosophy of the Present*, New York: Prometheus Books.

Nafus, D., and Anderson, K. (2006), "The Real Problem: Rhetorics of Knowing in Corporate Ethnographic Research," in *Proceedings of the Ethnographic Praxis in Industry Conference* (EPIC 2006), Portland, OR, 244–258.

Rabinow, P., and Marcus, G. E., with Faubion, J., and Rees, T. (2008), *Designs for an Anthropology of the Contemporary*, Durham, NC: Duke University Press.

Schechner, R. (1988), *Performance Theory*, New York: Routledge.

Sneath, D., Holbraad, M., and Pedersen, M. A. (2009), "Technologies of the Imagination: An Introduction," *Ethnos*, 74(1): 5–30.

Stengers, I. (2005), "The Cosmopolitical Proposal," in B. Latour and P. Weibel (eds.), *Making Things Public: Atmospheres of Democracy*, Cambridge, MA: MIT Press, 994–1003.

Suchman, L. (2011), "Anthropological Relocations and the Limits of Design," *Annual Review of Anthropology*, 40(1): 1–18.

Turner, V. (1969), *The Ritual Process: Structure and Anti-structure*, Rochester: Aldine de Gruyter.

SECTION IV

THE RELATIONALITY OF DESIGN

–11–

Generating Publics through Design Activity

Brendon Clark

THE PUBLIC NATURE OF PROJECT WORK

John Dewey (1954) argued that the public does not exist at large, but rather that *publics* are made up of individuals through face-to-face interaction brought into action around issues of importance to them. Publics are groups that form around matters of individual concern that fall outside the attention of present-day institutions. Dewey demonstrated a pragmatic approach that located the abstract concept of *public* in the lived experiences and practices of people. The difference between private and public refers to whether the actions of a *transaction* have implications that extend beyond the *interaction*. The formation of Deweyan *publics* depends upon the alignment between an understanding of an issue and its consequences. Ultimately, a public seeks to organize, gain resources, and appoint representatives that can ensure favorable actions to improve the implications.

Here I draw on the model of the formation of Deweyan publics to shed light on work practices at the intersection of design and anthropology. While anthropological ethnography has long been characterized as a descriptive practice examining past and present human behavior in writing with little regard for the future, design has been hailed as the practice of the future through material intervention and change. These distinctions become blurred when we shift the focus from output alone to include the working processes of each practice. Suchman has explored the interrelationship of social practice and technological development, taking focus away from the designed devices or networks of devices alone and locating the sites of technological production and use within larger complex sets of relationships. She defines "working relations" as the "sociomaterial connections that sustain the visible and invisible work required to construct coherent technologies and put them into use" (2002: 91).

This expanded and dynamic understating of technological development broadens who may be classified as participants in design and what may be included in the processes of design and implementation of technical products and services. The issues of individual concern that arise in the context of design anthropology may relate to the people included or excluded in design efforts, a topic of interest such as sustainable practices, or, as in the case examined in this chapter, a theoretical orientation to how a topic is approached. In invoking Dewey's conception of publics, I intend to link the activities of speculative, exploratory design and the development of working relations for addressing an issue, whether addressing the issue technologically, politically, with public or private services, or in combination.

To explore how the organization of collaborative project work can lead to the generation of publics, I first introduce a model of design practice that does not focus on "design for use," but rather seeks to draw on design traditions for instigating debate (see Mazé and Redström 2008). DiSalvo introduces "designerly means" for triggering Deweyan publics into action through raising awareness of the conditions and consequences of an issue (2009: 52). Unlike prescriptive design scenarios that use visualization of scenarios to suggest a desirable trajectory for product or service development, an approach used in commercial design, DiSalvo argues, design for the construction of publics involves the presentation of critical trajectories that leave the opportunity for multiple publics to form as a result. For example, to visualize a trajectory in a future when mining human waste for electricity is the norm, design researchers created a scenario with the product Poo Lunchbox, a plastic article of Tupperware with one side labeled "lunch" and the other side "poo" (DiSalvo 2009: 53). These trajectories do not prescribe how people will be triggered into action or take action, but rather confront people with a tangible, possibly undesirable option or experience that embraces the same design mechanisms as favorable scenarios.

While the Poo Lunchbox was part of an exhibit at the National Museum in London, other examples are experienced through a workshop format. For DiSalvo, linking design processes and practices with design research to the construction of publics in the Deweyan sense is based upon the influential nature of design output and how a critical future scenario provides reflection upon the absurdity of embellished views of technological development.

Anthropology has a long tradition of cultural critique, which plays a similarly provocative role for its audience, albeit through ethnographic description of "the other." A powerful form of anthropology as cultural critique has been the explicit or implicit use of descriptions of other ways of living for "disorienting the reader and altering perception" (Marcus and Fisher 1986: 111). In critical modes of research production, the galvanizing effect the output may have upon its audience depends greatly upon the values and perceptions of the audience. The output plays the role of a candidate scenario, something that could be reality, provoking reflections about how the future may unfold for people. As a candidate, it has the potential to motivate efforts toward embracing such a trajectory, working to prevent it, or no action.

This chapter builds upon DiSalvo's model of the construction of Deweyan publics as a mode of exploring favorable and unfavorable possibilities during the processes of design activities, rather than as an output of design alone. It is concerned with the experiences through which people turn understanding into collective action through interdisciplinary project work across sites of production and use, and how such a practice can be supported. I explore an approach to practicing design anthropology that focuses on the organization and unfolding of site-specific collaborative experiences. The work of combining various disciplinary, organizational, and personal traditions demands guidance. However, when working toward an undefined future with others whose working practices may be unfamiliar, it is difficult to make present not only the future objective, but also the means to get there. My aim here is to introduce a practice that focuses on making accessible possible future paths for addressing an issue, including the working relations, to the public sphere of the participants and potential participants. As candidate trajectories, these paths seek to provide reference points, whether favorable to people or unfavorable, for publics to form.

I draw on examples from a project exploring new options for supporting second language learning outside of the classroom setting. Positioning language learning as an interactional activity that benefits from contextualized interaction with others has prompted us to revisit how to support learning through technological development, potential learning resources, and the roles people play in different environments. I draw upon site-specific project explorations relating to sites of design and the practices of business, research, and use. Before introducing the case, I review some of the valuable organizational aspects of ethnographic fieldwork, the Scandinavian tradition of participatory design, and conceptions of performance.

THE ETHNOGRAPHER AS A RESEARCH INSTRUMENT

Ethnographic research has traditionally relied upon the ethnographer as a research instrument negotiating his or her way into an often messy entanglement of local activities as an approach to experiential subjective learning and data generation (Agar 1996; Powdermaker 1966; Rabinow 1977; Wolcott 1995). This process is based on being involved in shared experiences with members of a community with the ultimate goal of "grasp[ing] the native's point of view, his relation to life, to realise his vision of his world" (Malinowski 1932: 25). Ethnographic research and the Malinowskian model of participant observation introduced an experiential process that incorporated socialization into the life practices of others, as part and parcel of the researcher's endeavor. At this interactional level of learning to participate, breakdowns in the daily interactions between researchers and their hosts provide opportunities for meta-explanations by insiders or demonstrations of cultural norms to the ethnographer (Geertz 1973). These activities offer and become opportunities for new insight (Otto 1997). They also offer simultaneous and/or delayed documentation sought to develop an insider point of view by preserving the categorizations and perspectives of those studied. Agar suggests that the initial goal in ethnographic fieldwork is to be able to *paraphrase* what people are doing by the process of "decoding long sequences of verbal and nonverbal behaviour and then encoding our understanding of the meanings of those sequences into some utterances to check whether or not we understood what just occurred" (1996: 129).

When moving from individual fieldwork to interdisciplinary, interorganizational project work for purposes of designing sociomaterial practices, there is a similar messy, often clumsy organization of experiences in which project participants struggle to engage with each other's practices. In such cases, preservation of individual views and categorizations is not necessarily the desired outcome. Rather the goal is to develop shared practices and perspectives that combine various life histories, skills, and experiences. Drawing on experience and traditions of organizing ethnographic experiences for individual ethnographic research provides an outline for a model of taking and being given various roles in activities with and for those influencing and/or facing implications of project efforts. At the same time, the use of multiple methods of inquiry and juxtaposition of situations, points of view, and ways of working provide impetus to the organization of activity and experience rather than to written ethnography. However, while the ethnographer as a research instrument has proven invaluable for the individual researcher (as author), participatory design has a rich history with the researcher as a facilitator using the construction of physical materials to mediate collaborative activities. I now look to this tradition for a greater appreciation for organizing sociomaterial collaborative activities with a focus upon mutual learning.

MUTUAL LEARNING

The Scandinavian tradition of participatory design (PD) was born out of the workplace democracy movement of the 1960s with a focus on including the users of new technological systems in the development process. One of the original goals of PD was to develop technologies that supported skill building rather than developing expert technologies that replaced workers (Greenbaum and Kyng 1991). The model of mutual learning between designers and users is based on the premise that designers share the latest technological advancements as well as introduce the process of design to users, while the users share their skilled practices. Drawing on Wittgenstein, Ehn framed the activities of design between users and designers of new technical systems as *design language games* that seek to break the Cartesian separation of description and action. Coming from two separate language games, the goal is to develop a third *design language game* that has a *family resemblance* to each of the professional practices, but does not belong entirely to either (Ehn 1988).

Muller (2002) refers to these hybrid experiences as taking place in a "third space" between the context of system use and system design. Ehn's *designing-by-doing language games*, with the use of nonverbal artifacts such as mock-ups and cooperative prototyping techniques, allows both designers and users to identify a *family resemblance* to their own language games, while experiencing different possibilities of practice with the prototype in hand. This is an attempt to transcend what is known with what could be in the service of skill-building support systems. In this type of cooperative prototyping activity, breakdowns in understanding during use scenarios are used as triggers to reflect upon both practices of skilled use and of design, and for resolving conflict through adjusting the prototypes and the practices (Kyng 1995).

Whereas the PD facilitator has played a role in hosting collaborative activities for users and designers, the success of the ethnographer's (field)work has relied greatly upon his or her willingness to participate in the activities organized locally. Otto argues that taking part in role play activities in fieldwork is a political form of reciprocity. He suggests that, "[w]hereas local people will pursue their own interest in engaging the researcher in such a role-play, the latter may use it reflectively to experiment with means and interpretations and to gain a practical knowledge of cultural action" (1997: 99).

Exploring how others pursue their own interests through engagement is a fundamental feature of exploring future trajectories. I look to Goffman's theatrical framework for everyday behavior and performance theory for a greater appreciation for how to organize performances based on the everyday experiences of participants with an eye to the galvanizing mechanisms within the activities.

PROVIDING OCCASIONS TO PERFORM

Goffman's (1959) *impression management* during face-to-face encounters provides a vocabulary from theatrical performances, useful as a metaphor to blur the distinction between everyday interactions among people and staged productions:

> A performance, in the restricted sense in which I shall now use the term, is that arrangement which transforms an individual into a stage performer, the latter, in turn, being an object that can be looked at in the round and at length without offence, and looked to for engaging behaviour, by persons in an "audience" role (Goffman 1974: 124).

During ethnographic fieldwork, in daily office work activities such as meetings or presentations, or when facing a clerk in a store, we participate in arrangements that transform others or us into performers (to be looked at without offense). In asking others to perform in collaborative project settings, however, we draw on how people may interact when they perform together. Central to Goffman's dramaturgical framework is the idea of *front*, the *expressive equipment* employed during performances by individuals or the *performance team*. A *team* refers to those who "co-operate in staging a single routine" (1959: 79). While individuals and groups perform (or help perform) in a wide variety of routines on a daily basis, Goffman suggests people give special attention to those routines that influence their "*occupational reputation*" (1959: 33).

Overall, people and teams seek to illuminate some and diminish other characteristics in order to maintain a specific "definition of the situation" (Goffman 1959: 83), an image sustained with the audience's cooperation. Drawing on the PD ideal of mutual learning, attempting to surface potential interconnections among people from different practices and disciplinary orientations, upholding a favorable definition of the situation, at least for a moment, is a desired effect.

While Goffman provides a theatrical frame for the analysis of everyday behavior, performance theory explores the (greater) processes of organizing performances ranging from aesthetic performances to ritual ones (Schechner 1985). Schechner suggests that "[p]erformance is 'twice-behaved behaviour'" (1985: 36). For him, the most common performative circumstance is how the current focus determines what is drawn from the past experiences or projected into the past. It is through the specific goal of or interest in the upcoming performance that *strips of behavior* are called upon in performance. By isolating strips of behavior from everyday behavior, they can be deconstructed in workshop activities and redeveloped through rehearsals that build up new strips for the upcoming performance.

At the same time, the performance process can be viewed as a ritual process initiating a *liminal* period of new possibilities similar to the third space in PD. Turner argues that: "[T]he rules may 'frame' the performance, but the 'flow' of action and interaction within that frame may conduce to hitherto unprecedented insights and even generate new symbols and meanings, which may be incorporated into subsequent performances" (1982: 79). Following Schechner, the transformative nature of a performance, which is unpredictable, often arises from the audiences' stakes in the outcome and the attention given to the success of the performance.

Embracing performance as an organizing principle in collaborative project work brings focus to various activities intended for sharing knowledge and expertise with an eye for influencing how they can be arranged. However, asking for performances presupposes that a person is in a position to ask. Just as the ethnographer relies upon his or her own identity to negotiate access into the life worlds of others, the performative ethnographer negotiates influence over activities. This involves recruiting people to play various roles in different aspects of the performance process, whether a member of a specific group representing a particular expertise or merely a guest in the audience. It entails preparing materials, identifying stages, positioning audiences, and encouraging others to play along. Rather than a scripted act, however, it is inquiry in the sense that how a performance unfolds is unknown and may expose unanticipated results. There is a focus upon providing occasions for others to pursue their interests in a visible way.

SUPPORTING CONTEXTUALIZED LANGUAGE LEARNING

Språkskap is a language project focused on how to turn everyday situations between Swedish speakers and Swedish learners into "sites of language learning" through the development of information technology (IT) tools and educational concepts. The project arose out of a critique of the lack of technical and structural support for people to learn language outside of the classroom environment, specifically in Sweden. There remains a disconnect between what researchers of learning in general (Lave and Wenger 1991) and research in second language acquisition specifically (Firth and Wagner 2007) understand about situated, contextualized learning and how technological products and systems, public and private organizations, and citizen interactions support language learning. Simply put, a cognitive-dominant model of second language acquisition has a stranglehold on the initiatives for supporting language learning in education, technology development, and politics. This has stymied the exploration of contextualized learning support and places the burden of language learning predominantly on the shoulders of the learner.

Språkskap received a grant under an "everyday IT" program to demonstrate what could support contextualized learning activities.[1] The expected results were an IT demonstrator (something that demonstrates a concept), an idea catalog, and explorations in user-driven design methods. Three partner organizations represented commercial design and business, research, and the commercial practice of second language education. My role was that of project leader for the research organization. I was also the lead author of the funding proposal and had organized the coalition of partners. Once the project began, the challenges lay in how to explore the potential trajectories of the project through providing stages, audiences, and props for the various stakeholders to pursue their interests in an observable fashion.

THE BUSINESS OF DESIGN

The design consultancy was one of the three partners of the project. According to the project proposal, it was responsible for the design competence and engineering competence of the project and for the business development. At the outset of the Språkskap project collaboration, Madde, an interaction designer working with the design consultancy, and I organized a full-day sequence of activities involving the four core members of the project from the three main partner organizations: a pedagogue from the language school, an engineer from the design consultancy, Madde, and me. We referred to the workshop as a *project-in-a-day* (see Clark and Lahtivuori 2011) in which we intended to conduct some of the main phases of the project in a rough, fast-paced style at the early stage. We had two main areas of focus: potential product and service concepts that could support learning outside of the classroom context, and the potential business scenarios involved in turning the concepts into products and services available to the intended users.

In this case, the fifty-five employees of the design consultancy not only represented experience in a wide variety of commercial product and service design projects, but also their experiences as Swedish learners and Swedish speakers. Madde and I recruited six employees based on their experience to play different roles throughout the day, such as product users and business representatives.

COLLABORATIVE DESIGN

Cooperative prototyping in the PD tradition provides a format for exploring how to support interaction between people, through creating scenarios with mocked-up, malleable materials, *in hand* (Kyng 1995). A mock-up may combine paper, foam, and cardboard to provide a rough depiction of the functionalities of a concept. In this case, we asked the design teams to develop concepts that they found viable for supporting interaction between language speakers and learners outside of the classroom setting.

Similar to organizing interviews and observations in ethnographic fieldwork, here I was both part of organizing the activities and taking an active role in them. We split the four of us into two teams of two. Using pictures from everyday situations in which learners and speakers could meet, such as a parent dropping children at a kindergarten, and a learner waiting at the bus stop searching for bus information, we developed concepts and mock-ups to support interactions. The other team developed "The Beacon," a service supported by a device that connects subscribers in public spaces based on profile information. During the first prototype try-out activity, I played the role of a Swedish learner (which I was), while my teammate played a first-language speaker (which she was). They introduced us to the functions of The Beacon and asked us to act out a scenario in which the service prompted us to meet each other while traveling on the same bus. After exploring the concept with us, the design team readjusted its mock-up before a second session with the language learners and speakers recruited from the design consultancy who were unfamiliar with the project.

Latour argues that the role of the critic is no longer to deconstruct, but rather to assemble. He contends that once "something is constructed, then it means it is fragile and thus in great need of care and caution" (2004: 246). The two mock-ups resulting from the morning activities represented the type of concepts that could result from the project, albeit they were hastily created as probes into the type of concepts that could arise from the project. They were developed with consideration of the sociomaterial practices of the potential users, but without consideration of the broader set of working relations that could be necessary to develop and sustain the commercial aspects of the service. Euchner (2004) claims that the "the myth of the brilliant idea" often dictates the organization of innovation efforts in industry. He decries the overemphasis on ideas themselves at the expense of focusing on the contexts and conditions for innovation. Coming from outside of industry, it easy to simplify the innovation process and to exaggerate the power of new concepts. As the Språkskap project partners were coming from organizations with different orientations, it was important to explore the potential working relations involved in business development. At the design consultancy, we approached the CEO and senior business strategist to bring insight to the potential business trajectories of the project. They agreed to contribute one hour of their time to the project.

SALES PITCH DRAMA

We staged a sales pitch drama as an activity that could best resemble how the project was expected to conclude. After a short introduction, the teams briefly presented the Language Magnifier and The Beacon concept with a strong emphasis on how they support interaction between learners and speakers (see Plate 29). I then split the six of us into two teams, one tasked with pitching the concepts to a venture capitalist, the other with playing the role of venture capitalists.

After each team prepared its arguments and questions for the role play, I introduced the drama activity and sat as a member of the pitch team as the role play began. The twenty-minute role play was predominantly a back-and-forth discussion between the two business representatives, in character, as the core project team members looked on. The representative presenting the project began by stating, "[A]s you saw, this is a service that you run on a digital device. And it can be used in many different ways to enhance communication between people learning a language. So even though we showed it on our own device, our goal is to develop a pure software application and it's gonna be a global version." He quickly departed from the characteristics of the concepts presented as prototypes by reformulating them as a commercially viable product and distribution channels, a software available on mobile phone app stores. He continued by identifying the intended markets: "We will start by rolling out Swedish, but we have a roll-out plan with English, Spanish, Mandarin." Whether the departure from original conceptions, such as a concept that would be adapted to multiple languages because of their market potential, would be considered a welcome addition to the concepts or a deviation from a valuable concept depends upon one's interests.

The commercialization role play, however, demonstrated a trajectory of how the working relationships could unfold. The business representatives were recruited based on their experience in similar situations and their ability to reproduce how such a negotiation process could unfold. When the investor character asked, "[H]ow do you know that they will buy this software?" the pitch character improvised a plausible answer to a question he has likely answered before: "[W]e actually don't know yet. In these target groups we have tested the product and we have conducted surveys about how they feel and if they would like to use it. And our numbers are based on those surveys." The core team was witness to the type of argumentation that may be needed to convince investors that such a concept is worthy of their resources.

The day did not end with a single output agreed upon by the core project team. Rather, the sales pitch drama was the last activity of the day. Each participant was left to his or her own interpretations and left to organize as he or she saw fit. As an organizer, facilitator, and participant vested in the issue of second language learning, I had my own interests in and concerns about what I experienced. While I was satisfied with how we managed to demonstrate possible directions of the project, I was left dumbfounded and physically drained by the end of the sales role play. I witnessed how quickly the project concepts could be stripped of their core characteristics that were dear to me in favor of a fast-selling product that would provide return on investment. I was confronted by a trajectory that was not desirable to me in its current form and that threatened my own agenda of exploring contextualized learning solutions. Similar to the other project partners, I was free to commit resources and negotiate for or against the trajectories I was exposed to.

USAGE-BASED LANGUAGE RESEARCH

Collaborative project work often seeks to incorporate the knowledge and skills of multiple people with varying relationships to an issue, varying interests and agendas, coming from different practice traditions, and positioned differently as members of various organizations and communities of practice. In multi-sited ethnographic research, Marcus describes the ethnographer as a "circumstantial activist" because of the various contradictory commitments he or she forges by taking various roles in numerous sites. In this case, however, I was explicitly interested in the language learning agenda beyond the scope of a single project. I sought to explore the project with people that held special interests and knowledge in the topic area or who could potentially contribute to contextual learning support services. The advocacy in this case is not based on a specific group of people, but rather a specific conception of how and where learning can take place and the potential roles of technology, educational conceptions, and services for supporting learning. However, knowledge alone is not the goal, but rather to build demonstrations of how knowledge from different perspectives and formats can manifest in active support of contextualized learning.

The second example took place with the language learning group at the University of Southern Denmark. The group was not an official partner in the project, but through conversations I had with one of the researchers, he became sufficiently interested in the project to warrant a workshop. Over the course of an afternoon, the four core members of the project team participated in presentations by two professors and two PhD students describing theoretical, methodological approaches and examples of language learning and teaching based on everyday activity. The approach of Conversation Analytic–Second Language Acquisition (CA-SLA) sees the interaction between two people in communication as the minimum unit of analysis. We were introduced to usage-based linguistics, its challenge to the cognitive-dominant field of Second Language Acquisition (SLA), and a detailed transcript of an audio recorded interaction between an Icelandic learner and a café clerk. Rather than a field of SLA that views language learning as a separate type of knowledge only accessible through SLA, these researchers are CA-SLA specialists in studying how language is accomplished in everyday interaction (Firth and Wagner 1997, 2007). A "language learning as social practice" perspective rejects the "deficiency" model of analyzing language learning as a closed system demanding a process of cognitive acquisition and therefore allows CA-SLA, for instance, to explore the richness of accomplishments when looking at what language novices do in interaction. After the first half-day of exposure to their expertise through presentations, our team was responsible for facilitating a workshop with the goal of using their knowledge in the content area with our design process and objectives. This was an opportunity for us to marry our own project agenda with that of years of detailed research practice specific to the interest of the project.

The following day, we brought prepared workshop materials such as sheets of paper divided into blank sections of "before, during, and after" an encounter between a learner and speaker, paper of various sizes, Post-It notes, scissors, and pens. We organized and I facilitated a three-hour workshop using the case presented the day before as material. In the case, a learner of Icelandic as a second language, living in Iceland, recorded her mundane daily interactions for thirty minutes a week for three years. One of her early recordings came from a local bakery while she was buying bread. The researcher's analysis highlighted how the data demonstrated both the business of the encounter, to buy baked goods, and language learning practices in the same conversation. This was exactly the type of contextualized learning practice our project sought to support.

I planned a performance process that sought to draw on the rich research example, the language learning expertise, and the design and pedagogic expertise culminating in team performances. After the language researcher took us through the details of the data, we split into three groups working with the transcript from the Icelandic café, then held a short discussion in plenum and finally went off into three new working groups.

Through work with paper, foam prototypes, whiteboard, and text explanations, the workshop concretized three design directions: (1) materials and concepts for influencing the structure of the encounter between the learner and bakery worker; (2) technological platforms for the learner to easily document and reproduce the interaction; and (3) time and places to attend to language matters. For example, in one of the final performances, Madde, the designer, and Gudrun, the researcher who provided the data, stood behind the table set up with a display of material in front of them. Madde described how their solutions focused on the preparation and interaction phases, demonstrated by the data. She picked up a large piece of paper and held it between her and Gudrun, introducing the countertop screen concept that enabled the learner to foresee and practice a likely sequence or scenario of the interaction with the clerk, using the natural pauses in communication while the clerk prepared her order. Madde stated, "If I am Anna and you are a clerk, this would be between us. And we have sort of replaced these," she said, pointing to the paper between them, "so this is the preparing phase and this is the understanding phase or section and it is facing both ways." The example highlights how the group adapted the prepared material Madde brought from Sweden to Denmark to accommodate the sequencing of interaction germane to the learner's interaction in the café. They clearly performed a mutual understanding for the audience and the camera, complementing each other's points and looking to the audience and each other to verify their comments.

PERFORMANCE AS AN ORGANIZING PRINCIPLE

In the shift from organizing individual ethnographic experiences to organizing ethnographic activities culminating in performances of candidate trajectories, the role of the organizer is no longer that of an individual carrier of specialized knowledge from site to site as is common in research. Rather, the role is one of asking for performances, looking for opportunities to organize performative processes, negotiating collaboration of participants, identifying and introducing local materials and spaces, and facilitating activities. The critical dimension is found in the organization of performance processes. The audience, the setting, and the team makeup are part of the organizers' equipment relied upon to provide an arrangement for performance.

In the context of the language project, we introduced a challenge that had not been addressed adequately by current public and private organizations. The project sought to explore sociomaterial relationships that were not accessible through the language school's efforts alone, or through design, business, or academic research. The missing dynamic of a public across these various contexts is that the issue and the potential public are not out there merely to be linked together or visited. Rather, the cause and consequences of the issue need exploration by differently positioned people and a mechanism of raising them, through a process, to a candidate position by exposing them to an audience who has the potential to form. We conducted a series of design activities with people positioned differently in relation to the topic to materialize the sociomaterial relationships involved in supporting contextualized learning.

One of the great challenges in collaborative project work is how to assess value and how to account for what has taken place. Strathern stresses that "what makes interdisciplinary work difficult is knowing how to recognise that it has happened, and beyond that knowing to what extent it has been productive—in short, how to pinpoint the value of the interaction" (2005: 82–83). Bødker (1996) suggests that one of the shortcomings of participatory design projects has been that the benefits of "collective experiences of participation" often do not extend beyond the direct participants into their peer groups and that the value does not extend beyond the life of the project. With a focus on triggering the formation of publics, involving a wide variety of participants in design activities, beyond those who may merely add their skills to the concept development, the pool of people with such collective experience increases. A greater focus on working relations involves exploring how to legitimately enroll people from the participants' peer groups. For instance, recruiting users and business representatives from the design consultancy for very short involvement increased the number of people at the consultancy with experience in the project.

Organizing performance processes that align to the expected or intended processes of collaboration is meant to allow the participants to observe and react to something. But what forms the basis of individual or group value? Dunne and Raby make a general distinction between *affirmative design* and *critical design*. Affirmative design reinforces current trends conforming to "cultural, social, technical and economic expectations." Critical design, on the other hand, "provides critique of the prevailing situation through design that embod[ies] alternative social, cultural, technological or economic values" (2011: 28).

I position a form of practicing design anthropology that does not inherently fall into either category, but integrates aspects of both directions. Debate is largely delegated to the experience and output of collaborative activity by those who form the current and potential audiences. The selection or negotiation of sites, participants, and materials for the collaborative project work and the organization of the performance processes determine greatly whether an activity may appear affirmative or critical and whether that is deemed attractive or unattractive.

The relative nature of assessment suggests that value assessment of this form of practice can only be organized out of a situated interest of individuals. Suchman draws on feminist theory to situate objectivity within the dynamic life words of people. She argues for a move from the "master perspective that bases its claims to objectivity in the closure of debate, to multiple, located, partial perspectives that find their objective character through on-going dialogue" (1994: 22). A focus on collaborative performances seeks to provide an experiential demonstration of what is possible as a basis for potential action. This contrasts an organization of activity that promotes individual perspectives and leaves speculation of how disciplines, organizations, or perspectives may be woven together through the actions of individuals.

As one example from my own position, over a year and a half after the research-based design workshop in Denmark, I was contacted by one of the participants who described her great inspiration from the workshop. She had since organized a coalition of partners and was seeking funding for a project that combines Icelandic language courses with a network of businesses in which learners can conduct their daily business in Icelandic. She invited me to be a partner in the Icelandic Village project, where I have since co-organized and facilitated design workshops for the partners in the project. To date, in the pre-pilot of the Icelandic Village, four Icelandic language courses taught by three different teachers have coupled daily participation in the Icelandic Village sites with structured classroom activities using the content of their interactions. The Icelandic Village has become a test bed for contextualized learning support, further design explorations, and research on language learning, in addition to an international network of interested participants.

PROVIDING OCCASIONS FOR ACTION

I suggest that asking for performances to give experiential answers lifts candidate project processes and project outcomes into the public sphere. This provides opportunities for publics to form. The creation of various outputs consolidated into performances draws as their audience not only those in the room, but also the potential for their transmission, potentially triggering action outside the room. They are candidates conceived as best as they can be at present, with the intent of being considered for action. They do not attempt to preserve individual points of view, but rather to display what integration of practices could look like. They are held up in performance to be looked at in the round. Additionally, they provide candidate demonstrations of how collaborative efforts could unfold. This focus contrasts from attempting to grasp the natives' point of view or from the multi-sited ethnographer who may struggle to reconcile contradictory perspectives and interests. Here I have located my own role as a facilitator with interests. However, it is precisely in understanding that people are positioned differently and hold different, often changing, interests in relation to my own and the issues I favor. Just as with Dewey's publics, stakes are generated through interaction with others. Projects begin and are formed in relation to those who are willing participants and who commit their personal resources to project efforts in one way or another, in the present. In this sense, the work toward generating publics takes place at the experience level in face-to-face activities.

NOTE

1. The project was funded by VINNOVA, the Swedish Governmental Agency for Innovation Systems (2009–2010).

REFERENCES

Agar, M. H. (1996), *The Professional Stranger: An Informal Introduction to Ethnography*, San Diego, CA: Academic Press.

Bødker, S. (1996), "Creating Conditions for Participation: Conflicts and Resources in Systems Development," *Human-Computer Interaction*, 11(3): 215–236.

Clark, B., and Lahtivuori, M. (2011), "Project-in-a-Day: From Concept Mock-ups to Business at Play," in *Participatory Innovation Conference Proceedings*, Sønderborg: University of Southern Denmark, 151–157.

Dewey, J. (1954), *Public and Its Problems*, Athens, OH: Swallow Press.

DiSalvo, C. (2009), "Design and the Construction of Publics," *Design Issues*, 25(1): 48–63.

Dunne, A., and Raby, F. (2011), "Designer as Author," in *Design Act*, Stockholm: Sternberg Press, 28–31.

Ehn, P. (1988), *Work-oriented Design of Computer Artifacts*, Stockholm: Arbetslivscentrum.

Euchner, J. (2004), *The Practice of Innovation: Customer-centered Innovation at Pitney Bowes,* Stamford, CT: Pitney Bowes Inc. Available at: http://web.ics.purdue.edu/~dsnethen/hdarticles/pitneybowesinnovation.pdf. Accessed October 21, 2012.

Firth, A., and Wagner, J. (1997), "On Discourse, Communication, and (Some) Fundamental Concepts," *Modern Language Journal*, 81(3): 285–300.

Firth, A., and Wagner, J. (2007), "Second/Foreign Language Learning as a Social Accomplishment: Elaborations on a Reconceptualized SLA," *Modern Language Journal*, 91(5): 800–819.

Geertz, C. (1973), *The Interpretation of Cultures (Selected Essays)*, London: Fountain Press.

Goffman, E. (1959), *The Presentation of Self in Everyday Life*, New York: Anchor Books.

Goffman, E. (1974), *Frame Analysis: An Essay on the Organization of Experience*, London: Harper & Row.

Greenbaum, J., and Kyng, M. (1991), *Design at Work: Cooperative Design of Computer Systems*, Hillsdale, NJ: Lawrence Erlbaum Associates.

Kyng, M. (1995), "Making Representations Work," *Communications of the ACM*, 38(9): 46–55.

Latour, B. (2004), "Why Has Critique Run out of Steam? From Matters of Fact to Matters of Concern," *Critical Inquiry*, 30(2): 225–248.

Lave, J., and Wenger, E. (1991), *Situated Learning: Legitimate Peripheral Participation*, Cambridge: Cambridge University Press.

Malinowski, B. (1932), *Argonauts of the Western Pacific: An Account of Native Enterprise and Adventure in the Archipelagoes of Melanesian New Guinea*, London and New York: Routledge.

Marcus, G. E., and Fischer, M.M.J. (1986), *Anthropology as Cultural Critique: An Experimental Moment in the Human Sciences*, Chicago, IL and London: University of Chicago Press.

Marcus, G. E. (1998), *Ethnography through Thick and Thin*, Princeton, NJ: Princeton University Press.

Mazé, R., and Redström, J. (2008), "Switch! Energy Ecologies in Everyday Life," *International Journal of Design*, 2(3): 55–70.

Muller, M. J. (2002), "Participatory Design: The Third Space in HCI," in J. Jacko and A. Sears (eds.), *The Human-Computer Interaction Handbook: Fundamentals, Evolving Technologies and Emerging Applications*, Hillsdale, NJ: Lawrence Erlbaum Associates, 1051–1068.

Otto, T. (1997), "Informed Participation and Participating Informants," *Canberra Anthropology*, 20(1–2): 96–108.

Powdermaker, H. (1966), *Stranger and Friend: The Way of an Anthropologist*, New York: W.W. Norton & Company Inc.

Rabinow, P. (1977), *Reflections on Fieldwork in Morocco*, Berkeley: University of California Press.

Schechner, R. (1985), *Between Theater and Anthropology*, Philadelphia: University of Pennsylvania Press.

Strathern, M. (2005), "Experiments in Interdisciplinarity," *Social Anthropology*, 13(1): 75–90.

Suchman, L. (2002), "Located Accountabilities in Technology Production," *Scandinavian Journal of Information Systems*, 14(2): 91–105.

Turner, V. (1982), *From Ritual to Theatre: Human Seriousness of Play*, New York: PAJ Publisher.

Wolcott, H. F. (1995), *The Art of Fieldwork*, Walnut Creek, CA: AltaMira Press.

12

Bridging Disciplines and Sectors: An Industry-Academic Partnership in Design Anthropology

Christina Wasson and Crysta Metcalf

As discussed in the introduction to this volume, design anthropology strad-dles two fields or research traditions with markedly different objectives, ori-entations, epistemic assumptions, and methods (see Otto and Smith, this volume). Combining the practices of anthropology and design across a univer-sity-industry partnership adds another layer of complexity to the equation for success. While other authors in this book speak to the challenges of combin-ing anthropology and design, in this chapter we speak to the challenges of combining anthropology and design across organizations.

Like designers and anthropologists, universities and for-profit industries often have different, sometimes competing, goals and purposes. For instance, collaboration between industry and universities can face obstacles because these organizations are driven by different incentive systems and different goals (Bruneel, D'Este, and Salter 2010). In some ways, these organizational differences overlap with the disciplinary differences between designers and anthropologists. While anthropology is present and past focused to develop a body of knowledge, design is future focused and the goal is to develop new products, services, and policies. Universities are usually producing knowledge for educational purposes, while industry is usually harnessing knowledge for profit. While universities emphasize the creation of public knowledge, corpo-rations often want to keep the knowledge they produce private. The goal of a for-profit organization is, like design, to create products, while the product of academic research is knowledge. The fact that the two partners in any joint work have differing goals and objectives can, sometimes significantly, reduce the likelihood of either side viewing the relationship as a success. Further-more, research has shown that effective collaboration is even more challeng-ing across organizations than across disciplines. For instance, a study by Cummings and Kiesler found that "projects with PIs [Principal Investigators] from more universities were significantly less well coordinated and reported fewer positive outcomes" than projects with PIs from one university but multiple disciplines (2005: 703).

There is significant evidence that university-industry partnerships have historically faced fairly high rates of failure, at least in the United States (see Baba 1988). This has prompted a change in how universities and industry are coordinating for collaboration. Since the 1980s, there has been more focus on creating institutional structures to help mitigate the challenges. According to Freitas, Geuna, and Rossi, "This qualitative change in the nature of the relationships between industry and academia has been accompanied by the emergence of visible new organizational forms such as university-industry liaison offices, technology licensing offices, technology transfer offices, industry-university research centres, research joint ventures, university spin-offs and technology consultancies" (2010: 3–4). And, despite the effort to formalize the collaborations, consulting work, and paid access to university research, success is still varied and occurs less often than all involved would hope (Freitas et al. 2010).

Two major types of barriers that hinder success have been identified by Bruneel and colleagues (2010) as orientation-related barriers and transaction-related barriers. Orientation-related barriers are due to the different goals and objectives of universities and industry. Transaction-related barriers come into play with the advent of new institutional structures for university-industry collaboration, such as the technology transfer offices and others listed earlier. The barriers come from administrative and legal issues, such as who will retain intellectual property rights under what conditions. The development of technology licensing offices, technology transfer offices, technology consultancies, and so forth has corresponded to an increase in transaction-related barriers. Universities use these new organizational forms to capitalize on the commercialization of knowledge and produce financial gain for the universities. In doing so, there is increased conflict over intellectual property rights and the terms of the research partnership (Bruneel et al. 2010). For example, joint ventures and research centers can encounter competing interests when attempting to structure their agreements so that both the university and the organizational partner profit from royalties. Pavese has suggested that successful industry-university partnerships require figuring out "the right value proposition" (2009).

Before the development of these new industry-academic partnership models, the prior model of university-industry collaboration had been based on "*personal contractual* collaborations between university researchers and firm engineers and researchers" (Freitas et al. 2010: 16; italics in original). In these cases, the relationships were not institutional as such; they were based on researchers' social networks and the development of trust between the parties involved. The term *contractual* is used metaphorically rather than literally. It is our assertion that this earlier model actually works better than the newer model, at least in design anthropology partnerships.

Ours is a case study of successful personal contractual joint research between a professor and her class at the University of North Texas and a research scientist and her team at Motorola Mobility, Inc. We conclude that five major factors contribute to successful university-industry design anthropology partnerships: 1) the multidisciplinary membership of the teams; 2) the close alignment between the interests and backgrounds of the lead researchers; 3) the high value students placed on these projects; 4) a strong commitment on the part of the lead researchers; and 5) their reliance on a personal contract model.

THE HISTORY OF OUR COLLABORATION AND ITS INTERDISCIPLINARY CONTEXT

In the period from 2005 to 2011, we conducted five collaborative class projects. In this section, we outline the history and practices of our collaboration and situate it in the context of multiple, intersecting forms of interdisciplinary practice(s). The two of us initially met at the spring 2004 annual meeting of the Society for Applied Anthropology. Immediately in our first conversation, we started to explore the possibility of developing a collaboration in which Crysta, and through her Motorola, would be the client for a class project in Christina's design anthropology course at the University of North Texas.[1] We remained in communication over the summer, and planned our first collaboration for fall 2005. Thereafter, we usually collaborated on a class project every fall semester, with some variation due to adjustments to course schedules.

Here is a list of project topics and when projects were conducted:

- Eco-Moto (Fall 2005). An investigation of how the physical design of a mobile phone could communicate to consumers that this line of phones was ecologically friendly.
- Social Television Peripherals (Spring 2008). Motorola had developed design guidelines for a product that enabled friends and family who were geographically distant from each other to watch television together virtually. The class examined the design of remote controls, input devices, and presence indicators.
- Supplemental Experiences (Fall 2008). A study of how people move back and forth between live experiences and on-screen experiences that supplement the live event by providing more information about it.
- Nonintrusive Notifications (Fall 2009). Another study related to social television, this time focusing on the design of notifications about people's buddies that would appear on the television screen. Research was conducted to understand people's perceptions of interruptions during leisure activities.
- Exploratory Kitchen Media Research (Fall 2011). An investigation of how people use media before, during, and after the cooking process.

During the first class project in fall 2005, we experimented with our collaborative process, exploring ways to work together effectively. We both ended up feeling that the process as well as the results satisfied our respective needs, and were motivated to continue. The leader of the business group inside Motorola who was our ultimate *client* was very pleased with our work, generating recognition for us both inside and outside of Motorola. Subsequently our collaboration process remained fairly consistent in its general outlines, although we continued to refine our approach and each project had unique aspects. It was undergirded by our mutual commitment to a partnership in which we played equal but different roles, our willingness to be flexible, and our readiness to invest a fair amount of time and energy into the project. When we started to plan a class project, Crysta usually suggested a few potential research topics that would contribute to ongoing activities within her organization, and together we selected the one that seemed like the best fit for the class. We both contributed to the study design, methods, and protocols, with Crysta taking a lead role in the overall study design, and Christina understanding better how to adapt a study design to the context and constraints of a semester-long course.

Our compatibility as collaborators was facilitated by the specific characteristics of the organizations in which we worked and our roles within those organizations. Crysta worked in a research lab setting within Motorola. While Motorola went through various restructurings during the time period described, as of spring 2012, Crysta's organization was called the Applied Research Center at Motorola Mobility, Inc. As a manager in a corporate research lab, Crysta's role was to lead research projects that would generate ideas for new products and services. So the research projects Crysta suggested for the class fit within a larger constellation of similar, ongoing research projects.

Christina was a professor in the department of anthropology at the University of North Texas (UNT). This department offered a master's degree in applied anthropology, with the goal of training students who would become practitioners rather than academics. Client projects were regarded as a valuable aspect of students' preparation for such careers. Furthermore, one of the specializations of the department was business anthropology, which included design and organizational anthropology. In fact, at the time of the writing of this chapter, UNT was the only university in the United States that offered a course on design anthropology within an anthropology department. So the master's program attracted students who were interested in design anthropology. In addition, UNT's design department had a significant focus on design research. Faculty encouraged students to take the design anthropology course.

Our collaboration is situated within multiple, intersecting types of partnerships, including partnerships across institutional sectors, disciplines, and people. It is productive to examine interactions between the fields of anthropology and design in more detail, as they played out in the context of the class projects. The two fields were brought into dialogue in at least four ways: through the topics of the research projects; the composition of the class; Crysta's team composition; and the partnership between the two of us.

First, while the research topics for each class project were unique, they all shared the overall goal of combining anthropological theories and methods with design theories and methods to create tangible product ideas. The research process was enriched by the multiple disciplinary backgrounds that students brought to it. The case study presented later in this chapter illustrates the process. Second, Christina strove to have each class consist of about half anthropology students and half design students. One of the pedagogical goals was to have design and anthropology students learn from each other and learn how to collaborate with each other. The class was primarily open to advanced undergraduates and master's students in anthropology and design (UNT did not offer a PhD in anthropology). Christina also accepted a few doctoral students from fields such as marketing and information science. Total class size ranged from thirteen to eighteen students. Third, the team Crysta managed, and to whose ongoing research activities the class projects contributed, was highly interdisciplinary. In addition to an anthropologist and several designers, the team included engineers, computer scientists, and human-computer interaction specialists. The team had developed a highly collaborative research process in which all members of the team, regardless of training, participated. Computer scientists, designers, and other team members went into the field and gathered and analyzed the data together with a trained fieldworker; anthropologists, engineers, and others participated in the design process with the designers; and while prototyping was usually the purview of the computer scientists and engineers, they regularly consulted with the entire team to ensure the research prototypes were designed as planned and would answer the next set of research questions. The team had developed an interdisciplinary dialectical process that acted as a catalyst to inspire a collaborative culture of working relationships and an understanding of how to utilize the strengths of diverse disciplines (Metcalf 2008).

Fourth, while both of us were trained in anthropology, we each had extensive histories of working with designers and contributing to the interdisciplinary area that has been labeled *design anthropology*. Christina worked for E-Lab, a design firm that was a pioneer in incorporating ethnography into design research practice, from 1996 to 1997 (Wasson 2000, 2002; Wasson and Squires 2012). She subsequently taught design anthropology in collaboration with clients ranging from the Field Museum to Microsoft to the Dallas-Fort Worth International Airport, as well as maintaining a modest consulting practice. Christina was also a founding member of the Ethnographic Praxis in Industry Conference (EPIC) Steering Committee, one of the original six people who together developed the first EPIC event (Anderson and Lovejoy 2005;

Wasson 2005). She remained on the steering committee until 2010; her roles included chair of academic relations. Crysta has worked for Motorola since 2000, where she pioneered an approach to the integration of ethnography, design, and engineering targeted to the specific context of Motorola products and services (Metcalf 2011). She both worked on and led cross-disciplinary teams for the entirety of her career at Motorola, mentoring and teaching others how to conduct successful interdisciplinary research and develop transdisciplinary teams.

These four areas of interdisciplinary interactions illustrate complex connections between people, disciplines, and institutions that overlap and intersect in multiple ways. Crysta and Christina were able to model their experience in cross-disciplinary partnerships to students; the students themselves learned about other disciplines from their classmates in the context of collaborating on a project that would be used by an interdisciplinary team. Furthermore, the fields of anthropology and design were not linked in a simple one-on-one dialogue surrounded by a vacuum; rather, they were connected to additional disciplines through the composition of the class as well as the membership of Crysta's team.

OBJECTIVES AND INCENTIVES

In this section, we describe ways in which our collaboration addressed the goals of Christina's class and Crysta's team, our own agendas, and the objectives of our organizations. With respect to class goals, it was an invaluable experience for students in an applied master's program to work on a real client project; they were highly motivated by the awareness that their findings would be used. Furthermore, they learned important skills in conducting client-centered research projects. While some of them had already conducted academic ethnographic research projects, they were new to the cultural logic of developing a research design targeted to the needs of a client organization, maintaining a focus on client priorities during the course of the fieldwork, and engaging in an ongoing communication process with the client during analysis to ensure findings were directed to the client's needs. The class project helped us to bring students into the design anthropology/design research community of practice. In terms of relationality, it provided a vehicle for us to form a mentoring relationship with the students.

The goals of the interactive media user research (IMUR) team, Crysta's team within the Applied Research Center at Motorola Mobility, Inc., are to develop a body of knowledge about how people interact with media, how they interact with each other around media, and how they communicate with each other through media. Most of the team's research concentrates on innovations in video consumption and curation experiences, but includes research on photos, music, blogs, and books as well. The team seeks to understand people's behavior with respect to professionally created content and user-generated content in order to invent and design compelling consumer experiences. For the IMUR team, the value of collaborating with universities is threefold. First, there are a certain number of people on the team, and thus the number of projects that can be completed in any given year is limited. But the list of projects that the team is interested in conducting is fairly close to unlimited. University partnerships can enhance the team's ability to acquire additional information about media behaviors through research partnerships. The second form of value obtained when partnering with a university is diversity of perspective. In spite of the fact that Crysta's team is highly cross-functional, university professors and students bring a fresh perspective to project definitions, research questions, and analysis that contributes greatly to innovative thinking. Third, the collaboration also establishes university ties that are respected in the larger research organization.

Our collaboration also contributed to Christina's educational, research, and practice goals. Conducting applied research projects was central to her vision of how to train applied anthropology master's students. At the same time, she enjoyed the opportunity to conduct research on particular aspects of sociality and technology use that she might not have previously encountered, but which fit within the framework of her theoretical interests. As a professor, Christina did not have as much time to engage in applied projects as she would have liked, so the class projects were a valued way to maintain a foot in the world of practice. In addition, our collaboration contributed to the goals of Christina's department, college, and university. As mentioned previously, the UNT Department of Anthropology had an applied focus and a business anthropology specialization; our class projects contributed to both of these areas (Jordan, Wasson, and Squires 2013; Wasson 2008). Furthermore, the department was housed in a unique college, the College of Public Affairs and Community Service. Essentially this was a school of applied social sciences; it included other departments such as criminal justice, public administration, and social work. Therefore the emphasis on providing students with applied experience was seen as a feather in the cap of the college, and the fact that the client was such a well-known company was regarded as an additional plus. Finally, the university administration placed a strong emphasis on partnerships between the university and outside organizations. One of the four goals of UNT's 2012 Strategic Plan was to "partner with businesses and community groups to build and deepen meaningful relationships" that would strengthen the institution.[2]

While universities most often regard university-industry partnerships as a benefit for financial reasons, our collaboration was somewhat different since it took place in the context of a class rather than a research grant or consultancy. The advantage for students and for the university was the experience that students obtained. We are often asked whether Motorola pays students for these class projects. The answer is no. Students should be motivated to take the class for the learning experience, not because they want to earn money. It would be unfair to compete with other classes where the client is a nonprofit organization that cannot afford to pay, or where there is no class project. At the same time, Motorola did spend some money on these class projects. It paid for Crysta's trips to Texas and the pizza party for students at the end of the semester, as described in the following section. In addition, Motorola paid the costs of data collection. For instance, study participants were always given an incentive to compensate them for their time, and on some projects we used a recruiting firm to find study participants.

Another question that often comes up is whether students are required to maintain secrecy about the research findings. Again, the answer is no, because the research was designed as a class project rather than a consultancy with a professor. On some projects, there was a legal agreement between Motorola and UNT, but it protected Motorola's right to profit from design ideas that emerged from the project. All legal agreements explicitly preserved the right to publish for Christina and the students. From Motorola's perspective, a number of benefits for the corporation stemmed from establishing a university-industry partnership of the type that we engaged in. As part of the Applied Research Center, Crysta's team has a number of mandates that result from its position within the larger corporation. Alongside developing design ideas that Motorola can profitably use, one of the main goals is to produce patents, or intellectual property, that can be leveraged by the corporation. The team has regularly used the class's research as the foundation for new product innovation. This is done without including the class in brainstorming activities and Motorola thus retains the value of any intellectual property that the IMUR team generates.

The IMUR team is also expected to create thought leadership within its respective communities of practice. This increases the visibility of Motorola and highlights the rigor and cutting edge nature of technology research in the company, and this in turn attracts talent to the organization. Dissemination of the team's research, specifically publishing and speaking at conferences, is encouraged. This is why there is no obligation for Christina or the students to keep the research findings secret; publication of research is seen as having value for the company.

In addition, research teams are expected to collaborate with other groups within the company, so the corporation can leverage their knowledge throughout the product development cycle. University-industry projects are always conducted with an eye to providing benefit for other groups in the organization.

CASE STUDY: KITCHEN MEDIA

With our respective goals in mind, and our history of successful collaborations, we decided to team up once again for a joint research project in the fall of 2011. This was a project examining how people use media in the kitchen, and serves as our case study of a successful university-industry partnership. From Crysta's perspective, the IMUR team had been studying how people engage in television viewing experiences for a number of years (see, for example, Basapur et al. 2011; Harboe et al. 2007). These studies mainly focused on research in the living room or family room and how people engaged with the media and with each other when the primary task was watching television. However, the team knew it was missing a significant amount of information on how people engage in media experiences when watching the screen is not the primary focus of attention. The team also wanted more information about media behaviors when the media experience was taking place in other contexts in the home and when more than one type of media was being used as part of an activity. Investigating how people use media in the cooking process, the IMUR team believed, would serve as a good first step in looking at different media consumption contexts within the home. Crysta's team proposed that media use in the cooking process would be interesting because in the United States many people have televisions in their kitchens, and people utilize their smartphones and tablets in the kitchen and during the cooking process as well. The kitchen is also a social location, and the process of cooking is a social process, which means that if people were engaging in media experiences, they would be likely to be engaging in social activities as well (Grimes and Harper 2008; Svensson, Hook, and Coster 2005). Finally, the cooking experience was selected because the IMUR team expected the primary focus of activity to change during the process. They expected more shifting back and forth between tasks and between different types of media than when someone sits down in the living room to watch a program.

Crysta and Christina discussed the possibility of ethnographic-style research exploring kitchen media use and agreed this project would be good for university collaboration because it was a new domain area of research for both Crysta's team and Christina's class. From Crysta's point of view, it was a good topic because the students would not need a deep and nuanced understanding of the space and history of IMUR research to come up with findings that would be new and interesting to Motorola. What were the patterns in how people used media in the cooking process? Did people use more than one device to create, curate, and/or consume media while in the kitchen? What types of media were consumed in the kitchen—were they food or kitchen specific? Answers to any of these questions would help Crysta's team understand this space better and help it devise follow-on research. From Christina's point of view, exploratory kitchen media research seemed like a great topic because she was confident that students would be able to connect with it easily and become enthusiastic conducting fieldwork. After all, food preparation and eating are fundamental human experiences. In most cultures, certainly in ours, they evoke powerful emotions and feelings of connection with family and community (Mintz and Du Bois 2002).

We developed plans for the kitchen media project during the summer of 2011. Crysta wrote drafts of the research design and interview guide; Christina suggested minor edits. Christina developed the course syllabus, which operationalized the research design into a series of specific assignments for students. Crysta hired the recruiting firm to find the participants and acquired the participant incentives. Once class had started, Christina worked with students to create a password-protected website for fieldwork data on WordPress. Crysta visited the class in person three times over the course of the semester. First was an introductory visit in the second week. Second was a midpoint check-in during week nine. The last visit was during finals week; students delivered an oral presentation of their findings and submitted a written report. Crysta expressed her appreciation to the class by throwing a pizza party at Christina's house afterward. The students in this class included:

- Five undergraduate anthropology majors
- Two undergraduate communication design majors
- One undergraduate interdisciplinary arts and design/anthropology double major
- Three MA students in anthropology
- Two MFA students and one MA student in communication design
- One PhD student in marketing
- One PhD student in education.

The class was therefore mainly a mix of anthropology and design students, with a few students from other fields included for additional diversity and insights. This mix produced a productive interdisciplinary collaboration. The project benefited from the expertise of each discipline.

The class met one night a week for three hours. The first half of each class meeting was dedicated to discussion of readings on the history, theory, and practice of design anthropology to ensure that students received an introduction to relevant literature. The second half of each class meeting was focused on project activities. Crysta participated in almost every class meeting. Since she was based in the Chicago area while students were meeting in the vicinity of Dallas, we used virtual communication technologies on the days when she was not physically present at UNT. A speakerphone sat in the middle of the circle of students, and we used desktop sharing to allow Crysta to see what was being shown on the computer in the classroom (visible to students through an LCD projector).

Christina taught students to follow E-Lab's model of collaboration between anthropologists and designers. E-Lab was a pioneering design firm that played a leading role in bringing together ethnographic research and design in the 1990s. Christina assigned two articles that described E-Lab's work practices and had the class discuss them at length (Wasson 2000, 2002). One useful tool for these class discussions was an image termed the "bow tie model" that illustrated a collaborative, interdisciplinary work process (Wasson 2002). According to this model, the first half of the work process focused more on ethnographic research. It moved from the collection of *instances*—bits of data—through *patterns* across the data, to the development of explanatory *frameworks*. The frameworks were the center point or pivot of the work process. They were followed by more design-focused activities, first the development of high-level design concepts and then actual prototypes. Christina explained that the class would not go as far along the design path as it could, because of time constraints; its work process would end with visualizations of design ideas. Christina also emphasized that a central principle of E-Lab's work practices was that both researchers and designers should be members of a project team from beginning to end. Although researchers might play a lead role in the first half, it was important for designers to participate in fieldwork first hand. And although designers might play a lead role in the second half, it was important for researchers to continue to assess emerging design ideas in light of the research findings.

The course lasted for sixteen weeks—fifteen weeks of class meetings followed by finals week (this is the standard semester length at American universities). The first four weeks were spent in orienting students and training them in ethnographic field methods. Then the students spent five weeks conducting fieldwork. Eight research participants who regularly used media to enhance their cooking experience were recruited. They were asked to take pictures documenting their media use and to draw a map of their kitchen showing the location of all media devices used during a particular cooking event. Then student researchers conducted open-ended, in-depth interviews with the research participants to learn more about their cooking-related media use. The students worked in pairs and video recorded the interviews. Interviews lasted one-and-a-half to two hours. The student researchers placed photos, maps, detailed field notes about each interview, and extensive video clips from the interviews on a WordPress site that they created for the class. This made field data available to the whole group for comparison and analysis.

All students working together as a group, with Christina as guide and facilitator, conducted much of the analysis during class time. The students presented findings from their research over the course of four weeks. Each team of students verbally narrated its fieldwork experience and illustrated key moments and insights with photos and video clips. Other students asked questions and discussed the fieldwork. During this process, Christina noted examples and emergent insights in a Word document visible to the whole class via an LCD projector. Initially, the Word document functioned somewhat like a more sophisticated and deep version of a flipchart. As the Word document became longer, students started to group the ideas by having Christina cut and paste bits of text. Information was organized into the categories of instances, patterns, and design ideas. This process was somewhat similar to creating an affinity diagram, moving to an increasingly sophisticated and abstract level of analysis. The class needed a *portable* analysis space because its meeting room was used by many other classes over the course of each week, so it could not store any data or analysis materials in the room. Over time topics emerged that became the chapters of a written report. Toward the end of the semester, students were asked to choose a chapter topic; chapter authors generally included a mix of anthropology and design students. They conducted further analysis of the data on their topic and developed design ideas based on the research findings. In addition, one student took on the task of preparing a PowerPoint presentation.

While there is not space in this chapter to describe all of the findings from the project, a few examples may be illuminating (Aiken et al. 2011). First, we found a strong connection between sociality, media use, and cooking. For instance, people built community by sharing recipes and pictures of dishes they prepared. Second, we developed an overall framework about the temporal cycle of cooking. The cooking experience could be understood as being composed of three stages: before, during, and after cooking; or, planning, execution, and celebration. Contrary to expectations, the use of media was most prevalent before cooking and after cooking. The *before* stage was characterized by the richest media use, as it included exploration activities that led to browsing and information searches. Furthermore, the *after* stage of one cooking experience was often *the before* stage of the next cooking experience, either for the same person or another person. Plate 30 shows one of the *trajectories* we mapped for the study participant, Michael. Third, we identified three common orientations toward cooking among people who use media: the foodie orientation, the efficiency orientation (often seen in parents of large families), and the health orientation. We termed these *orientations* rather than *segments* or *personas* because the same person might display different orientations or a mix of orientations depending on the circumstances (Aiken et al. 2011).

Based on these research findings, students developed a number of interesting design ideas. For instance, to support sociality they designed a media device that would encourage and facilitate both physical and virtual social interactions before, during, and after the cooking experience. Specifically, they developed a stationary kitchen computer with the following capabilities, as illustrated in Plate 31:

- The ability to mount the screen onto any flat surface (kitchen cabinet doors, refrigerators, walls, etc.) and to pivot it in different directions
- A touch screen interface system
- A wireless and waterproof keyboard for optional use
- A built-in camera on the computer screen
- A voice command option
- Ahe capability to sync the stationary or "main" computer with other media (phones, tablets, laptops, desktops) (Aiken et al. 2011).

CONCLUSIONS

This project was extremely successful from both Crysta's and Christina's perspectives. Crysta's team utilized the findings of the study to greatly enhance its understanding of media use in context and also disseminated the research to other groups within the company who were producing products geared toward the kitchen context. Immediately after the research project was over, others in Motorola Mobility's Applied Research Center were requesting the results, and one member of another team sat in on the final presentation. From the UNT perspective, indications of the project's success included the positive evaluations given to the course by students; the opportunity for several students to present a paper on the project at the next meeting of the American Anthropological Association; and encouragement from the leadership of the National Association for the Practice of Anthropology (NAPA) to apply for the NAPA Student Achievement Award.

We think a number of factors played into the success of this and previous design anthropology projects conducted jointly by UNT and Motorola. We also believe that taking into consideration these five factors, collaborative success can be replicated. First, both teams on the project were multidisciplinary. Both the class and the IMUR team had designers, social scientists, and others whose perspectives and goals needed to be understood and accommodated as part of the teaming process. This difference in perspectives and goals is similar to the differences in perspectives and goals of UNT and Motorola, as described in the introduction. Thus the students and researchers were already familiar with negotiating differences in product orientation versus knowledge production orientation, because they had to accommodate that in their team building. When it came to accommodating the differences in perspectives and goals among institutions, it was already familiar territory. Second, the two of us as project leaders have aligned interests and backgrounds. As described previously, our partnership meshes well with our professional priorities and our other work activities, as well as those of the organizations in which we work. We both have many years of working at the intersection of anthropology, business, design, and technology. In addition, our professional circles overlap quite a bit. For instance, Marietta Baba, who was Crysta's dissertation advisor, has also informally mentored Christina for many years. A third factor that contributes to our successful partnership is that students greatly value the experience of participating in client-oriented class projects. They see the benefits of gaining marketable skills in design research, being able to list the project on their resume, and, for the design students, adding the designs they create to their portfolios. They also appreciate the skills they learn with regard to teamwork, collaboration across disciplines, connecting research insights with design ideas, and organizing a research process around client needs. Thus the students are motivated to do well on the project. In addition, the interactions between the two of us model an effective and constructive client-consultant relationship. Many students have had little exposure to such relationships beforehand, or have primarily encountered negative interactions between clients and consultants. A fourth element in the success of our partnership is our willingness to dedicate quite a bit of time and energy to the collaboration. We both demonstrated a high level of commitment to the project, which was visible to each other. For instance, Crysta displayed dedication through her willingness to give up one evening a week of her personal time, for sixteen weeks running, to participate in class meetings. Christina put quite a bit of effort into project management, ensuring that students carried out their research responsibilities in a timely manner, guiding the analysis process, and encouraging constructive teamwork among students.

Finally, it is our assertion that the collaborative research effort was successful because we based it on the personal contract model. The problem with the transaction-based approach that uses institutional structures for knowledge transfer, according to Freitas et al., "is that it ignores the specificities of the socio-economic-institutional context and the fields of research" (2010: 13). Instead of relying on institutionalized structures and market-based contracts for knowledge transfer, we relied on our own long-standing personal relationship based upon feelings of trust and obligation, feelings that stemmed, in part, from belonging to the same social and professional networks. Our partnership was, and is, a personal, socially situated contract, not a market contract with its associated administrative and legal challenges. It is well known in psychology and economics that when people view an interaction in market terms, they are willing to pay a (literal) price for not meeting their obligations, and are more willing to end tasks (see, for example, Frey and Jegen 2001; Gneezy and Rustichini 2000). On the other hand, when people view their interaction as part of a personal contract, part of having a relationship with the other person, then their actions are regulated by social norms—in which not meeting obligations or ending a research collaboration has social consequences. In this case, we did not want to violate our personal contract by letting each other down. Thus we were motivated to put more effort into making the joint interorganizational research project successful as part of our personal obligations to one another.

It is our hope that this short description of our partnership can be useful to others seeking to initiate academic-industry collaborations in design anthropology. We recognize that each partnership has unique dimensions and that different models of industry collaboration have evolved across the various programs that offer a specialization in design anthropology, such as SPIRE at the University of Southern Denmark, Design at the Swinburne Institute of Technology, and Design Ethnography at the University of Dundee. These programs vary, among other things, in the degree to which they emphasize preparation for a career in application, their housing in different disciplinary contexts, and the national educational traditions within which they are situated. Nonetheless, we expect the industry collaborations that they consider most successful share considerable similarities with our own experiences.

NOTES

1. The most recent syllabus for the design anthropology course, as well as other course materials, can be viewed at http://courses.unt.edu/cwasson/ courses/design-anthropology.
2. See http://www.unt.edu/features/four-bold-goals/.

REFERENCES

Aiken, J., Burns, M., Brazell, B., Carranza, R., Dennis, R., Dubois, J., Hicks, J., Lomelin, M., Maxwell, M. L., Orange, E., Paquette, A., Reed, S., Roswinanto, W., Schlieder, V., Wilson, S. K., and Yang, X. H. (2011), "Exploratory Kitchen Media Research," Report for Crysta Metcalf, Applied Research Center, Motorola Mobility Inc., by Design Anthropology Class, University of North Texas.

Anderson, K., and Lovejoy, T. (eds.) (2005), *Proceedings of the Ethnographic Praxis in Industry Conference*, Redmond, WA, November 14–16.

Baba, M. L. (1988), "Innovation in University-industry Linkages: University Organizations and Environmental Change," *Human Organization*, 47(3): 260–269.

Basapur, S., Harboe, G., Mandalia, H., Novak, A., Vuong, V., and Metcalf, C. (2011), "Field Trial of a Dual Device User Experience for iTV," in *Proceedings of EuroITV*, Lisbon, Portugal, June 29–July 1, 127–136.

Bruneel, J., D'Este, P., and Salter, A. (2010), "Investigating the Factors that Diminish the Barriers to University-industry Collaboration," *Research Policy*, 39(7): 858–868.

Cummings, J. N., and Kiesler, S. (2005), "Collaborative Research across Disciplinary and Organizational Boundaries," *Social Studies of Science*, 35(5): 703–722.

Freitas, I. M. B., Geuna, A., and Rossi, F. (2010), "University-industry Interactions: The Unresolved Puzzle," Working Paper Series, Department of Economics, University of Torino.

Frey, B. S., and Jegen, R. (2001), "Motivation Crowding Theory," *Journal of Economic Surveys*, 15(5): 589–612.

Gneezy, U., and Rustichini, A. (2000), "A Fine Is a Price," *Journal of Legal Studies*, 29(1): 1–17.

Grimes, A., and Harper, R. (2008), "Celebratory Technology: New Directions for Food Research in HCI," in *CHI 2008*, Florence, Italy, April 5–10, 467–476.

Harboe, G., Massey, N., Metcalf, C., Wheatley, D., and Romano, G. (2007), "Perceptions of Value: The Uses of Social Television," in *The 5th European Interactive TV Conference, 2007*, Amsterdam, May 24–25, 116–125.

Jordan, A., Wasson, C., and Squires, S. (2013), "Business Anthropology at the University of North Texas," in P. Sunderland and R. Denny (eds.), *Handbook of Anthropology in Business*, Walnut Creek, CA: Left Coast Press.

Metcalf, C. (2008), "Interdisciplinary Research, Anthropological Theory and Software Innovation: Bringing It All Together," paper presented at the Society for Applied Anthropology Meeting, Memphis, TN, March 28.

Metcalf, C. (2011), "Circulation of Transdisciplinary Knowledge and Culture in a High Tech Organization," *Anthropology News*, 52(2): 28.

Mintz, S. W., and Du Bois, C. M. (2002), "Anthropology of Food and Eating," *Annual Review of Anthropology*, 31: 99–119.

Pavese, K. E. (2009), *Introduction to The New York Academy of Sciences Web-seminar Academic-industry Collaboration: Best Practices*. Available at: www.nyas.org/Events/WebinarDetail.aspx?cid=d774f799-36cf-4982-87fa-ed2d9f6c9896. Accessed October 26, 2012.

Svensson, M., Hook, K., and Coster, R. (2005), "Designing and Evaluating Kalas: A Social Navigation System for Food Recipes," *ACM Transactions on Computer-Human Interaction*, 12(3): 374–400.

Wasson, C. (2000), "Ethnography in the Field of Design," *Human Organization*, 59(4): 377–388.

Wasson, C. (2002), "Collaborative Work: Integrating the Roles of Ethnographers and Designers," in S. Squires and B. Byrne (eds.), *Creating Breakthrough Ideas: The Collaboration of Anthropologists and Designers in the Product Development Industry*, Westport, CT: Bergin and Garvey, 71–90.

Wasson, C. (2005), "Celebrating the Cutting Edge," in *Ethnographic Praxis in Industry Conference*, Redmond, WA, November 14–16, 140–145.

Wasson, C. (2008), "A 'Dreamcatcher' Design for Partnerships," in E. K. Briody and R. T. Trotter (eds.), *Partnering for Organizational Performance: Collaboration and Culture in the Global Workplace*, Lanham, MD: Rowman and Littlefield, 57–73.

Wasson, C., and Squires, S. (2012), "Localizing the Global in Technology Design," in C. Wasson, M. O. Butler, and J. Copeland-Carson (eds.), *Applying Anthropology in the Global Village*, Walnut Creek, CA: Left Coast Press, 251–284.

13

Decolonizing Design Innovation: Design Anthropology, Critical Anthropology, and Indigenous Knowledge

Elizabeth (Dori) Tunstall

This chapter proposes the methodology of design anthropology as an answer to how one might create decolonized processes of design and anthropological engagement. I first set out the contexts for the need for decolonized anthropology and design innovation (for instance, the use of design principles and frameworks to generate new or improved business outcomes). I then go on to explore what design anthropology is, its intellectual foundations and its principles, and to describe the first phase of the Aboriginal Smart Art project as a case study of its principles in practice.

THE CONTEXT FOR DECOLONIZATION

In 1991, Faye Harrison published the edited volume, *Decolonizing Anthropology*, in which she and a group of "Third World peoples and their allies" sought: "To encourage more anthropologists to accept the challenge of working to free the study of humankind from the prevailing forces of global inequality and dehumanization and to locate it firmly in the complex struggle for genuine transformation" (Harrison 2010: 10).

In 1991, I had taken my first anthropology course at Bryn Mawr College in the United States. There I learned that the founding fathers of physical anthropology did not think I had the cranial capacity to even be in my class because I was an African American and thus of low intelligence. In spite of that first encounter with anthropology, I stuck with it because there was something powerful about a field devoted to investigating the expanding notions of what it means to be human. But the classical anthropological framing of my peoples, Africans and African Americans, as objects of anthropological inquiry required that I take seriously anthropology's role in the project of colonialism, and also the role of design innovation in continuing projects of neocolonialism and imperialism.

The phrase "handmaiden of colonialism" to describe anthropology is attributed to anthropologist Claude Lévi-Strauss (Asad 1973). The *Stanford Encyclopedia of Philosophy* (Kohn 2011) defines *colonialism* as "a broad concept that refers to the project of European political domination from the sixteenth to the twentieth centuries that ended with the national liberation movements of the 1960s." It distinguishes colonialism from imperialism: with colonialism theoretically aligned with settlement and direct control and imperialism aligned with economic exploitation and indirect control. A wide range of anthropologists in the 1960s and 1970s began to directly address anthropology's implication in colonialism and imperialism. While review of this literature is outside the scope of my chapter (see Uddin 2005 and Restrepo and Escobar 2005 for two exhaustive accounts), the points of criticism leveled against anthropology can be summarized as:

- classification of peoples, such that it overdetermined their characters and undermined their own self-definitions (Deloria Jr. 1988 [1969]; Hall 1992; Said 1978; Smith 1999);
- framing or representation of peoples as reduced "others" and outside the pale of time, civilization, and rationality (Fabian 1983; Smith 1999; Wolf 1982);
- evaluation of peoples in a hierarchy with European Caucasians in the top position of humanity and others ranked at various levels of subhumanness (Blakey 2010; Smith 1999); and
- lack of utility of its outputs, in the form of text-based ethnographies or films, for improving the quality of life of the peoples engaged as its anthropological objects/subjects (Deloria Jr. 1988 [1969]; Smith 1999, Tax 1975).

These four kinds of critique represent the hallmarks of colonial, imperialist, and neocolonial anthropology for many indigenous, minority, migrant, and other marginalized communities who have been "coded into the Western system of knowledge" (Smith 1999: 43). What does this have to do with design innovation and design anthropology? As I stated earlier, my personal engagement with the field of anthropology has been about trying to create a space for a decolonized anthropology in light of the discipline's history. It has now also become about securing a space for decolonized design innovation practices.

The Oslo Manual defines *innovation* as "the implementation of a new or significantly improved product (good or service) or process, a new marketing method, or a new organizational method in business practices, workplace organization, or external relations" (OECD 2005: 6). Embedded in this definition of innovation, which I argue is hegemonic in the field, are three assumptive paradigms as it relates to culture. First, individual elites or companies generate innovation (Brown and Ulijn 2004; Jostingmeier and Boeddrich 2005; Light 2008). There is a growing discussion of grassroots innovation that links sustainable consumption with community action (Seyfang and Smith 2007), but it represents only an emergent thread in the innovation discourse. Second, innovation promotes modernist values. Spanish philosopher Rosa Maria Rodriguez Magda (2004) states how innovation was "the very driving force of modernity," which sought to replace old ways of knowing. Third, innovation benefits individual companies, individual entrepreneurs and inventors, or the undifferentiated masses of society. Design innovation, even within the social sector, reflects the modernist agenda of OECD definitions of innovation.

In 2010, on his *Fast Company* blog, Bruce Nussbaum posed a question to the design community that had never been broached so directly: "Is humanitarian design the new imperialism?" The article raised provocative questions about the ethics of humanitarian design projects such as Project H, Acumen Fund's Water Project in India, and One Laptop Per Child: "Are designers the new anthropologists or missionaries, come to poke into village life, *understand* it and make it better—their *modern* way?" (Nussbaum 2010a: 1). The response from diverse sectors of the design community was swift as those such as Emily Pilloton of Project H (2010) dismissed Nussbaum's article as a gross oversimplification of their on-the-ground-work with communities. Niti Bhan, the only commentator whose non-Western voice in the debate was promoted in the *Design Observer* round up (Editors 2010), reminded people *from the OECD world* that, to paraphrase, mutual respect, reciprocity, and political history and reality were not acknowledged in the issues raised. How could it be otherwise? Who are the generators, what are the underlying values, and who are the beneficiaries of innovation remain the issues for design innovation as a subset of the innovation discourse. Nussbaum's two follow-up articles partly opened up these issues. The first one raised the specter of the "unintended consequences" of humanitarian design by probing the underlying values and the true beneficiaries of design innovations in the social sector (Nussbaum 2010b). The second one provocatively opened the issue of the origins of innovation by showing how humanitarian designers forge relationships with local elites (Nussbaum 2010c). This focus on local elites is important because it is they who determine, not those from the OECD world, whether design innovation is the handmaiden of colonialism or imperialism today. What is it that they say? What might be their critiques of design innovation?

Surprising, in the major academic journals on design (for example *Design Issues* and *Design Studies*), there is limited discussion by Asian, African, Middle Eastern, or Latin American scholars of design and imperialism or colonialism. Main critiques of imperialism and colonialism are written by Caucasian scholars in ex-colonial peripheries of Australia (Fry 1989) and South Africa (Van Eaden 2004). Exceptions are found in the 1989 *Design Issues* special issue on "Design in Asia and Australia" with the contributions of Shou Zhi Wang (1989) on modern Chinese design and Rajeshwari Ghose (1989) on design and development in Asia, with a focus on India. Ghose's article in particular outlines a critique of design and development's ideological biases in how it classifies, represents, models, and evaluates the Indian nation and people. She states:

> No wonder then that neither of the terms design nor development have natural equivalents in most of the Asian linguistic traditions, for they carry with them all the ideological underpinnings of First World associations, aspirations, and debates. This realization and, more recently, the deep dissatisfaction that has followed this realization, both from an ideological/cultural as well as a pragmatic point of view, has led to some very serious soul searching among the thinking designers of Asia in recent years. (1989: 39)

Outside of academic journals, one finds strong critical voices on design and development in blogs and conference presentations by design scholars and practitioners such as Arvind Lodaya, M. P. Ranjan, and Niti Bhan of India, Ravi Naidoo of South Africa, Adelia Borges of Brazil, and Benny Ding Leong of China. Their points of critique are similar to those against anthropology in terms of how hegemonic discourses of design and innovation:

- classify traditional craft as distinct from modern design, excluding the histories and practices of design innovation among Third World peoples (and their allies especially in regards to their responses to colonialism, imperialism, and neo-colonialism) (Borges 2007; Ghose 1989; Lodaya 2003; Ranjan and Ranjan 2005);
- frame design thinking as a progressive narrative of global salvation that ignores the alternative ways of thinking and knowing of Third World peoples and their allies (Leong and Clark 2003; Lodaya 2007);
- evaluate European, Euro-American, and Japanese design and innovation as the top of the design innovation hierarchy (Jepchumba 2009; Leong and Clark 2003; Lodaya 2006; Ranjan 2006); and
- utility of outputs because many design innovations are prototypes that have not been fully implemented, and thus have limited positive impact on communities.

A high-profile example of how design innovation can act in an imperialist way is the IDEO and the Rockefeller Foundation's Design for Social Impact initiative. The next section will briefly introduce the project and how it relates to the points of critique outlined previously.

THE IMPERIALISM OF DESIGN

In 2008, the Rockefeller Foundation invited IDEO, a global design consultancy, to explore how "design and how the design industry can play a larger role in the social sector" (IDEO and Rockefeller Foundation 2008a: 5). The first outcomes of this study were the *Design for Social Impact How-to Guide*

(2008a) and the *Design for Social Impact Workbook* (2008b). Both texts seek to demonstrate how design thinking as a human-centered design process can contribute to "transformation change in communities" (IDEO and Rockefeller Foundation 2008a: 2). Although the initiative is focused on communities, it follows the hegemonic paradigm of innovation in terms of its framing of who generates innovation, its underlying values, and who benefits.

In the Design for Social Impact initiative, Western design companies generate innovation, which places them at the top of the design innovation process. The texts are "intended for design companies of any size or type," to guide them so that they can sell their services to nongovernmental organizations (NGOs) and start-ups that operate in the social innovation sector, mostly in India and South Africa (IDEO and Rockefeller Foundation 2008a: 4). Through a content analysis of the photographic images, illustrations, and texts of the *Design for Social Impact How-to Guide*, I found that Western design companies are represented as active agents who guide, serve, embed, build, pay, and staff (the design processes). On the other hand, Indian and African institutions are represented as those to be passively guided and directed or to serve as sabbatical hosts, sites for capacity building, philanthropic tourist destinations, and support staff for projects (IDEO and Rockefeller Foundation 2008a). Why does it matter that Indian and African (not to mention Chinese, Brazilian, Mexican, and other non-OECD nations) design companies are not also the audiences for the *How-to-Guide*? Ghose discusses how Asian design is directly tied to issues of "technology/design transfers from the First World, as well as problems associated with adapting new or changing technology to diverse economic, social, cultural, and political conditions" (1989: 32). By framing non-Western design companies outside of the discourse of *Design for Social Impact*, the IDEO document positions Western design companies in a unique hierarchical position enabling them to guide non-Western institutions on how to solve problems. This elides the history of non-Western design innovation in which designers in India and Africa have creatively responded to the challenges posed to their communities, often in connection with processes of imperialism, colonialism, and neocolonialism.

In the Design for Social Impact initiative, values of design thinking draw from a progressive narrative of global salvation that ignores non-Western ways of thinking rooted in craft practices that predate yet live alongside modern manufacturing techniques. The general absence of Indian, African, Asian, Middle Eastern, or any other non-Western knowledge, with the exception of C. K. Prahalad, in the over twenty bibliographic and Internet resources at the end of the *How-to Guide* reflects the disregard for local knowledge and the intention to supplant it with Western design thinking as the dominant methodology (IDEO and Rockefeller Foundation 2008a). In a World Bank Institute article entitled "Design Thinking for Social Innovation: IDE," Tim Brown and Jocelyn Wyatt describe the specific contributions of design thinking to social challenges. "As an approach, design thinking taps into capacities we all have but that are overlooked by more conventional problem-solving practices . . . [It] relies on our ability to be intuitive, to recognize patterns, to construct ideas that have emotional meaning as well as being functional, and to express ourselves in media other than words or symbols" (2010: 30). Brown and Wyatt (2010) posit design thinking as an alternative to linear, rational, and conventional approaches to problem solving. In its human-centered approach, design thinking is said to respect local knowledge through its processes of gathering user needs and codesigning through iterative prototyping. Yet postcolonial and feminist critiques of Western models of linear and rationalist thinking have been well established since the 1960s and predate IDEO's design thinking. In fact, design thinking sounds similar to what Rajeshwari Ghose expressed in the late 1980s as the task of Asian designers: "Here too [Asian] designers have the dual task of documenting and understanding ethnicity and regional cultures, for understanding them is the essential first step to evolving a medium of visual communication and restoring local confidence in an age when traditional institutions are crumbling fast and benefits of industrialization are yet to trickle down" (1989: 40–41).

While design thinking represents an advance in Western business thought, what does it mean to bring design thinking to places that already have their own indigenous forms of thinking also critical of linear and rational models? Saki Mafundiwa raises this issue in his description of the epiphany that inspired him to create ZIVA, the Zimbabwe Institute for Vigital Arts:

> These were Afrikan-trained designers—unlike me, an Afrikan trained in the west. Soon I realized that force-feeding Afrikans design principles born in Europe, principles that were the product of the European experience, just doesn't work . . . Afrikans have their own palettes that have no kinship with the principles of color devised by such schools of thought as the Bauhaus. Why do we ignore those? The rest of the world would love to understand this Afrikan sense of color! Tapestries woven by "unschooled" craftspeople grace some of the world's major museums and private collections—stunning testimonials to the Afrikan creative genius. (Jepchumba 2009: sec. 1, par. 10)

Saki's efforts to train his Afrikan students in Afrikan ways of knowing expose how, notwithstanding the good intentions by IDEO, bringing design thinking and other nonnative principles to India, Africa, or China, for example, risks becoming another form of cultural imperialism that destabilizes and undermines indigenous approaches coming out of other creative traditions. To this last point, Rajeshwari Ghose makes an important statement: "If design is perceived as an ancient activity that has gone on for several centuries rather than as a brand new profession, then our whole perception of what constitutes Asian design begins to change and, thenceforth, issues pertaining to Asian design assume different forms" (1989: 36).

In the Design for Social Impact initiative introduced earlier, the main beneficiaries of innovation are the participating companies and individuals as well
as general society, while community benefits are limited by the lack of sustainable implementation of design prototypes. As outlined in the *How-to Guide*,
each strategic approach is evaluated against its "benefit to the company" and
"social impact" (IDEO and Rockefeller Foundation 2008a: 41). The benefits to
the company are all clearly enunciated through the listing of what happens to
each strategy when it works (for the company), both pros and cons. Although
they define *social impact* as the "capacity of this type of work to create positive social change on communities and individuals," it is represented only
as a graphical circle without descriptions of what that social impact might
be (IDEO and Rockefeller Foundation 2008a: 41). More important, the Design for Social Impact initiative explicitly seeks to transfer the resources of
philanthropic foundations and local NGOs to Western design companies. The
extent to which this places the initiative in direct competition with local design companies means that while its intentions may be good, it outcomes are
likely imperialistic. It resembles what Linda Smith refers to as the new wave
of imperialist processes that "enter with goodwill in their front pocket and patents in their back pocket" (1999: 24). Thus, IDEO's Design for Social Impact
initiative demonstrates how even a design innovation project with good intentions can be implicated in continuing practices of imperialism. While IDEO is
a good company representing *good* people-centered design processes, it fails
to respect the value systems of those communities it seeks to help. Design
anthropology is proposed as a methodology that can reframe both anthropology and design innovation as decolonized practices of cultural engagement.

DESIGN ANTHROPOLOGY: A DECOLONIZED METHODOLOGY

Over the last seven years, I have defined, promoted, and taught design anthropology as a field that seeks to understand how the processes and artifacts of design help to define what it means to be human and that focuses on
how design translates values into tangible experiences (Tunstall 2006, 2007,
2008a,b). I am proposing design anthropology as a methodology rather than
a method, because what is at stake for me are the principles and rules for
regulating the disciplines of design and anthropology to avoid neocolonization
and imperialism. By *decolonized*, I refer to the status of being "self-governing
or independent" (Dictionary.com). Thus, what I mean by a *decolonized methodology* is a system of methods, principles, and rules free from the biases
of the last five centuries of colonization and imperialism, and that thus
contributes to the self-definition and self-determination of those formerly colo-
nized. I seek to argue that design anthropology has great potential to become
a decolonized methodology for engaging with social issues.

This, of course, is not the only definition of design anthropology. Sper-schneider, Kjaersgaard, and Peterson define it as the bricolage of "making sense of what is there with remaking what is there to something new" (2001: 1). The University of Aberdeen in its Masters of Science (Design Anthropology) program defines it as "a novel and exciting interface where the speculative imagination of possible futures meets the comparative study of human ways of living and knowing" (Leach 2011: sec. 1). Joachim Halse suggests that de-sign anthropology is a provocation "that portrays the culture of use in terms of the culture of design" (2008: 31). Paula Gray defines it as "ethnographi-cally-informed design of new products, services and systems for consumers and businesses" (2010: 1). Two aspects of my definition of design anthropol-ogy distinguish it from others. The first is that my definition is not just about the application of anthropological theories and methods toward the better design of products, services, and systems. As I have stated elsewhere, "It allows for the possibility of saying stop to the design process" when the eth-ics of engagement are questioned (Tunstall 2008a: 28). The second is that "the outcomes of design anthropology include statements providing some deeper understanding of human nature as well as designed communications, products, and experiences" (Tunstall 2008b: sec. 1, par. 2). My definition of design anthropology draws from core sets of theoretical perspectives—the critical anthropology of "Third World peoples and their allies," indigenous and Scandinavian traditions of cooperative/participatory design, and indigenous, critical, feminist, ontological, and phenomenological knowledge traditions. In the following sections, I address how this particular methodological position-ing impacts the principles of design anthropology.

PRINCIPLES OF DECOLONIZED UNDERSTANDINGS OF VALUE SYSTEMS AND CULTURES

In an article written for *Adobe Think Tank*, I argued that "Design anthropol-ogy does not place separate emphasis on values, or design, or experience, which are the domains of philosophy, academic design research, and psychol-ogy, respectively. Rather, design anthropology focuses on the interconnecting threads among all three, requiring hybrid practices" (Tunstall 2008b: sec. 5, par. 2). As a methodology, I propose a design anthropology that adheres to a set of seven principles regarding how one understands and positively impacts on (1) human value systems; (2) the processes and artifacts of designing in making value systems tangible; and (3) the aligning of people's experiences with the values they prefer—all under conditions of unequal power relations. Fredrik Barth has been critical of how anthropologists have used the term *val-ues* without creating an "explicit theory and analysis of values" (1993: 31). I utilize the term *values* in my explanation of design anthropology because it highlights the different perspective that anthropologists have brought in their engagement with the design industries (Tunstall 2006) and it states what is at stake in processes of decolonization (Smith 1999: 74). In the edited volume, *Design Anthropology: Object Culture in the 21st Century*, Maria Bezaitis and Rick Robinson (2011) of E-Lab/Sapient argue that user research needs to get back to its emphasis on values as opposed to just being seen as valuable to industry. Thus, Bezaitis and Robinson contrast two of the three ways of talking about values noted by David Graeber. They promote what Graeber describes as values in the sociological sense "of what is ultimately good, proper, or desirable in human life" (Graeber 2001: 2) as opposed to the economic sense of measurement. What I have found most powerful about the role of anthropology in design is how it reveals the struggle over value systems as people seek to create meaning in their lives and pass them on to future generations. In this I share Barth's notion that studying values in and of themselves is not "a productive strategy . . . but [as part of social action] directs our attention to an area where collective institutions and representations articulate with individual behaviours" (1993: 44). Here Ton Otto's (2006) work about values and norms is illustrative. As the struggle over values affects people's identities, it also directly affects their ability to pass on those values to future generations. The collective creation of meaning and passing on to future generations is what can be defined as *culture*. As a decolonized methodology, design anthropology draws upon the concept of value systems, which can become cultures through consensus and transmission into the future, expressed in Cuban anthropologist Fernando Ortiz's theory of transculturation:

> I am of the opinion that the word transculturation better expresses the different phases of the process of transition from one culture to another because it does not consist merely in acquiring another culture (acculturation) . . . but the process also necessarily involves the loss or uprooting of a previous culture (deculturation) . . . and it carries the idea of new cultural phenomena (neoculturation). (1995 [1945]: 102–103)

The theory of transculturation helps to define three of eventually seven key principles I believe should guide the praxis of design anthropology when it comes to understanding and having positive impact on value systems:

- Value systems and cultures have to be accepted as dynamic, not static. Each generation goes through the process of negotiating the elements that make up its value systems and cultures.
- One needs to recognize the mutual borrowing that happens among value systems and cultures and to seek to mitigate or eliminate the unequal circumstances in which that borrowing takes place.
- One must look simultaneously at what is expressed as that to be gained, lost, and created new in the recombination of value systems and cultures by a group of people.

Adhering to these three principles addresses what Faye Harrison describes as the project of decolonizing anthropology by "demystifying hegemonic ideologies and producing/co-producing forms of knowledge that can be useful and potentially liberating for the world's dispossessed and oppressed" (2010: 8). The Aboriginal Smart Art project on which I am working provides an example of these principles in action.

THE ABORIGINAL SMART ART PROJECT

In 2011, Colin McKinnon Dodd of the Yamatji Aboriginal cultural group and the founder of the Aboriginal Artists Development Fund (AADF) asked me to conduct a project that would use technology to support Australian Aboriginal arts. The Koorie Heritage Trust, the peak Aboriginal institution in Victoria State, agreed to partner with the AADF and Swinburne University on a project focused on how indigenous knowledge belonging to Australian Aboriginal cultures can be used to create social, technological, and business innovations in the Victorian Aboriginal Art market that increase the holistic sustainability of Australian Aboriginal art-making communities. The project completed the first of three phases, focused on researching cultural values and codesigning innovation scenarios, in May 2012. This is to be followed by the implementation and then the roll-out and evaluation phases. The project's main aim embodies design anthropology's first principle by accepting the dynamic character of Australian Aboriginal culture. Lynnette Russell (2001) in her book *Savage Imaginings* discusses the way mainstream Australian society constructs Aboriginal culture as monolithic, located in the ancient past, and thus inauthentic if engaged with modernity. The Aboriginal Smart Art (ASA) project frames cultural diversity and hybridity as part of the dynamic nature of Aboriginal cultures. The contemporary living values of Australian Aboriginal storytelling and *their Dreamtime* (in other words lore guiding the interconnections between all things in the past and present) are not seen as anathema to modern technologies. The ASA project draws on the growing literature on Aboriginal communities and digital technologies that demonstrates the tremendous variability of intergenerational responses to technology in Aboriginal cultures (McCallum and Papandrea 2009; Samaras 2005; Verran and Christie 2007). As exemplified in the 2010 AIATSIS symposium on Information Technologies and Indigenous Communities, indigenous communities have been increasingly using information and communication technologies to support (1) cultural mapping, managing, and archiving; (2) cultural innovation, transmission, and communication; and (3) language revitalization (AIATSIS 2010). The Aboriginal Smart Art project extends these digital practices into the Aboriginal art market, thus also embodying the second principle of the design anthropology.

The borrowing of digital technologies by Aboriginal communities and the borrowing of indigenous visual representations by dealers, buyers, and viewers in the Aboriginal art market represents the mutual borrowing of cultures and values under unequal circumstances. For the Aboriginal Smart Art project, the main challenge is the commodification of Aboriginal artworks and exploitation of Aboriginal artists. Paraphrasing anthropologist Arjun Appadurai (2005: 34), I understand commodification as a process in which things are exchanged with minimal formation of social bonds and groups. The media's highlighting of the continued exploitation of Aboriginal artists by unscrupulous brokers, dealers, and gallery owners led to the development of the Indigenous Art Code in 2007. Yet the exploitation in the Aboriginal art market continues as manifested by the artwork being seen as objects for sale without connection to the artists, their families and communities, and the land. The Aboriginal Smart Art project seeks to eliminate the exploitation and commodification of Aboriginal artists by codesigning innovative technologies, business, and service models to embed story into Aboriginal artwork. People are less likely to exploit another person with whom they have established deep bonds through knowledge of the deeper meanings of the artwork to the artists and their communities. Artists are less likely to sell a painting on the roadside if it also carries story and ceremony for their future generations. The project seeks to use the values associated with Aboriginal storytelling to reduce the unequal circumstances of Aboriginal artists' participation in the Western art market by mainstreaming those values such that they change the business model for the market.

The Aboriginal Smart Art project embodies the third principle of design anthropology by examining what is gained, lost, and created anew by embedding story in Aboriginal art. Through the interviews with artists, art coordinators, gallery owners, wholesalers, and technical experts, the Aboriginal Smart Art team of researchers, students, and client partners learned about Aboriginal communities' loss of revenue, cultural practices including storytelling, and identity caused by the exploitation of Aboriginal artists and their communities as a continuation of imperialism. The team learned what communities felt they did or did not have to gain from using the technologies to record the story of art making and how it differed for urban and rural artists. Yet the team learned what could be created new by bringing Aboriginal storytelling values and Western technological values together, which was represented through three design concepts with related business models and technological requirements. The 1D concept (see Plate 32) demonstrates the students' understanding that communities are the first point of authenticating Aboriginal artists' use of specific motifs in the art and stories. The students explored how available technologies in Aboriginal communities such as smartphones could capture the art and story-making processes to be stored in a general database and embedded in the artwork itself through RFID chips and GPS image tracking. At the point of sale, viewers and buyers can access the story through a smartphone application.

PRINCIPLES FOR DECOLONIZED DESIGN INNOVATION

The *design* of *design anthropology* is theoretically indebted to two areas of design theory and practice. The first is the design thinking exemplified in the works of such indigenous/Third World scholar/practitioners as Indian M.P. Ranjan, Zimbabwean Saki Mafundikwa, and Native Hawaiian Herman Pi'ikea Clark. M.P. Ranjan clearly articulates a view of designing to which design anthropology seeks to speak directly:

> Here we are proposing that the design action takes into account the structure of society along with their macro aspirations, their histories and cultural preferences as a starting point and from here build imaginative approaches for products, services and systems that would include the meta-system, the infrastructure, the hardware, the software and the processware to ensure a perfect fit to the circumstances and requirements of the particular situation. (2011: sec. 1, par. 4)

The approaches advocated by these and other Third World scholars provide alternatives to the classifications and representations that see design primarily as a modern Western phenomenon by showing the long history of making in these communities. This provides another principle for design anthropology:

> One should seek to eliminate false distinctions between art, craft, and design in order to better recognize all culturally important forms of making as a way in which people make value systems tangible to themselves and others.

The second area of design thinking and practice is the Scandinavian cooperative and participatory design (Bødker, Ehn, Sjögren, and Sundblad 2000; Buur and Bagger 1999). The results of the 1980s Utopia project as described by Bødker et al. inform design anthropology's focus on "staging active design exercises such as the organisational tool-box and use of mock-ups and prototypes as a way to involve end users in design" (2000: 3). The work of Jacob Buur's SPIRE research group has advanced these ideas to define the praxis of participatory innovation. The principle that it provides to design anthropology is:

> Researchers and designers ought to create processes that enable respectful dialogue and relational interactions such that everyone is able to contribute their expertise equally to the process of designing and those contributions are properly recognized and remunerated.

These two principles can be glossed as ensuring processes of inclusion into the formation of design concepts, prototypes, and implementation such that the benefit of designing originates and ends with the groups involved, especially the most vulnerable group members. Here the Aboriginal Smart Art project again proves illustrative.

By seeking to embed the values of Aboriginal ways of visual culture as storytelling into a design project, the Aboriginal Smart Art project collapsed the distinctions between art, design, and craft (the fourth principle of design anthropology). Herman Pi'ikea Clark states that by creating the concept of art "no other pre-industrial society or culture in the world established a disassociated category for aesthetic objects as did Western European society" (2006: 3). While still using the term *art*, the Aboriginal Smart Art project attempts to transform aesthetic objects back to what Clark describes as their preindustrial roles as repositories, transmitters, and vehicles in the exploration and construction of knowledge (2006: 4). Aligning with the fifth principle of design anthropology, the project's two presentations and scenario codesign workshop created inclusive interactive forums in which Aboriginal artists, art coordinators, art collectors, business, technology, and design experts could contribute their knowledge to inform multiple scenarios for how the Aboriginal Smart Art processes might work. For the mid-semester presentations of learning from secondary research, the team used writing on sticky notes and directly on display banner posters to facilitate discussions of further directions for research to inform scenario planning. The scenario mapping and evaluation workshop demonstrated to the student team, the participating client, and the technical experts how complex and diverse were the possible solutions to the project's challenges. In the final semester presentation, participants, including Aboriginal artists, helped select which one of the three concepts the group will continue developing in phase two of the project. This process of inclusion will continue throughout phases two and three of the project.

PRINCIPLES FOR DECOLONIZED RESPECT FOR EXPERIENCES

Design anthropology, as I define it, comes directly out of my experiences of being an African American woman who has been trained in critical anthropology and applied that knowledge to the contexts of professional design and design education. It speaks to the heart of the atrocities of Western colonialism and imperialism, mainly the disrespect and disregard for the experiences of other people. Design anthropology enacts the critique of positionality and power articulated by Third World scholars, indigenous scholars, and second and third wave feminists by reframing the problem areas of social impact as within the value systems of imperialism. The design anthropology principle that emerges from this perspective is:

> Projects should use design processes and artifacts to work with groups to shift hegemonic value systems that are detrimental to the holistic well-being of vulnerable groups, dominant groups, and their extended environments.

Last, design anthropology requires that individuals and groups move beyond having empathy to acting with compassion. In an essay for the tenth anniversary of the ICOGRADA Design Education Manifesto, I combine Richard Sennett's (2003) definition of *respect* with Herbert Simon's (1969) definition of *design* to provide a definition of *respectful design* as "the creation of preferred courses of action based on the intrinsic worth of all human, animal, mineral, fauna and flora and the treatment of them with dignity and regard" (Tunstall 2011: 133). The acceptance of the intrinsic worth of everything and the treatment of them with dignity and regard characterizes compassion, which is a higher virtue than empathetic shared feelings advocated in design thinking. Design anthropology's final principle seeks a commitment to compassion from its students, scholars, and practitioners:

> The ultimate criteria for success of any design anthropological engagements are the recognized creation of conditions of compassion among the participants in a project and in harmony with their wider environments.

This may seem utopian, but it ensures that design anthropology understands its purpose as part of a spiritual system, not just an economic and social system. These last two principles require a longer time frame and greater scope for the praxis of design anthropology in order to build case studies. Yet at least anecdotally as I give presentations around the world, I am finding a shift already taking place in the ultimate purpose of design innovation and anthropology that closely aligns with these sentiments. Thus, I expect it will only be five years or so before we have these clear case studies.

CONCLUSION

By proposing design anthropology as a decolonized methodology, I return to where I began with Faye Harrison to advocate for design anthropology that frees its two parent fields from "the prevailing forces of global inequality and dehumanization and to locate it firmly in the complex struggle for genuine transformation" (2010: 10). Design innovation and anthropology have much that they can contribute to fighting global inequality, but first it should adhere to clear principles of respectful engagement with people's values, the translation of them through processes of inclusive codesign, and the evaluation of their effects on people's experiences from the perspective of the most vulnerable. The seven principles of design anthropology can assist in the evaluation of one's cultural interactions to ensure that one is avoiding the four imperialistic outcomes that others have critiqued in both anthropology and design innovation theories and practices. Having established these principles, I seek to focus on the implementation of design anthropology as a decolonized methodology through my projects and those of my allies and students. For what is needed now are clear case studies that demonstrate the creation of conditions of compassion as the true goal of any design anthropology engagement.

REFERENCES

AIATSIS (2010), *Program of 2010 Information Technologies and Indigenous Communities Research Symposium*, AIATSIS, Canberra, July 13–16. Available at: www.aiatsis.gov.au/research/docs/iticPrelimProg.pdf. Accessed June 10, 2012.

Appadurai, A. (2005), "Commodities and the Politics of Value," in M. M. Ertman and J.C. Williams (eds.), *Rethinking Commodification: Cases and Readings in Law and Culture*, New York: New York University Press, 34–44.

Asad, T. (ed.) (1973), *Anthropology and the Colonial Encounter*, Ithaca, NY: Ithaca Press.

Barth, F. (1993), "Are Values Real? The Enigma of Naturalism in the Anthropological Imputation of Values," in M. Hechter, L. Nadel, and R. Michod (eds.), *The Origin of Values*, Hawthorn, NY: Aldine de Gruyter, 31–46.

Bezaitis, M., and Robinson, R. (2011), "Valuable to Values: How 'User Research' Ought to Change," in A. Clarke (ed.), *Design Anthropology: Object Culture in the 21st Century*, New York: Springer Wien, 184–201.

Blakey, M. (2010), "Man, Nature, White and Other," in F. Harrison (ed.), *Decolonizing Anthropology*, 3rd edition, Arlington, VA: Association for Black Anthropologists, American Anthropological Association, 16–24.

Bødker, S., Ehn, P., Sjögren, D., and Sundblad, Y. (2000), *Co-operative Design: Perspectives on 20 Years with 'the Scandinavian Design Model*, Stockholm, Sweden: Centre for User Oriented IT Design (CID). Available at: http://cid.nada.kth.se/pdf/cid_104.pdf. Accessed May 6, 2012.

Borges, A. (2007), *Design for a World of Solidarity*. Available at: www.adeliaborges.com/wp-content/uploads/2011/02/12–17–2007-forming-ideas-design-solidario1.pdf. Accessed May 10, 2012.

Brown, T., and Ulijn, J. (2004), *Innovation, Entrepreneurship and Culture: The Interaction between Technology, Progress, and Economic Growth*, Cheltenham, UK: Edward Elgar Publishing.

Brown, T., and Wyatt, J. (2010), "Design Thinking for Social Innovation: IDE)," World Bank Institute, beta, July 12. Available at: http://wbi.worldbank.org/wbi/devoutreach/article/366/design-thinking-social-innovation-ideo. Accessed March 27, 2011.

Buur, J., and Bagger, K. (1999), "Replacing Usability with User Dialogue," *Communications of the ACM*, 42(5): 63–66.

Clark, H.P. (2006), "E Kūkulu Kauhale O Limaloa: Kanaka Maoli Education through Visual Studies," Paper presented at the Imaginative Education Research Symposium, Vancouver, BC. Available at: www.ierg.net/confs/viewabstract.php?id=254&cf=3. Accessed October 6, 2012.

Deloria Jr., V. (1988 [1969]), *Custer Died for Your Sins: An Indian Manifesto*, Oklahoma City: University of Oklahoma Press.

Editors (2010), "Humanitarian Design vs. Design Imperialism: Debate Summary," *Design Observer/Change Observer*, July 16. Available at: http://changeobserver.designobserver.com/feature/humanitarian-design-vs-design-imperialism-debate-summary/14498/. Accessed March 15, 2011.

Fabian, J. (1983), *Time and the Other: How Anthropology Makes Its Object*, New York: Columbia University Press.

Fry, T. (1989), "A Geography of Power: Design History and Marginality," *Design Issues*, 6(1): 15–30.

Ghose, R. (1989), "Design, Development, Culture, and Cultural Legacies in Asia," *Design Issues*, 6(1): 31–48.

Graeber, D. (2001), *Toward an Anthropological Theory of Value*, New York: Palgrave.

Gray, P. (2010), "Business Anthropology and the Culture of Product Managers," *AIPMM Product Management Library of Knowledge*, August 8. Available at: www.aipmm.com/html/newsletter/archives/000437.php. Accessed May 6, 2012.

Hall, S. (1992), "The West and the Rest," in S. Hall and B. Gielben (eds.), *Formations of Modernity*, Cambridge, UK: Polity Press and Open University, 276–320.

Halse, J. (2008), "Design Anthropology: Borderland Experiments with Participation, Performance and Situated Intervention," PhD dissertation, IT University, Copenhagen.

Harrison, F. (2010), "Anthropology as an Agent of Transformation," in F. Harrison (ed.), *Decolonizing Anthropology: Moving Further toward an Anthropology for Liberation*, third edition, Arlington, VA: Association of Black Anthropologists, American Anthropological Association, 1–14.

IDEO and Rockefeller Foundation (2008a), *Design for Social Impact How-to Guide*, New York, NY: IDEO and Rockefeller Foundation.

IDEO and Rockefeller Foundation (2008b), *Design for Social Impact: Workbook*, New York, NY: IDEO and Rockefeller Foundation.

Jepchumba (2009), "Saki Mafundikwa," *African Digital Art*, September. Available at: www.africandigitalart.com/2009/09/saki-mafundikwa/. Accessed October 6, 2012.

Jostingmeier, B. and Boeddrich, H. J. (eds.) (2005), *Cross-cultural Innovation: Results of the 8th European Conference on Creativity and Innovation*, Wiesbaden, Germany: DUV.

Kohn, M. (2011), "Colonialism," *The Stanford Encyclopedia of Philosophy*, Fall. Available at: http://plato.stanford.edu/archives/fall2011/entries/colonialism/. Accessed October 6, 2012.

Leach, J. (2011), "MSc Design Anthropology," Department of Anthropology, University of Aberdeen. Available at: www.abdn.ac.uk/anthropology/postgrad/MScdesignanthropology.php. Accessed October 6, 2012.

Leong, B. D., and Clark, H. (2003), "Culture-based Knowledge towards New Design Thinking and Practice—A Dialogue," *Design Issues*, 19(3): 48–58.

Light, P. (2008), *The Search for Social Entrepreneurship*, Washington, DC: Brookings Institute Press.

Lodaya, A. (2002), "Reality Check," *Lodaya.Webs.Com*. Available at: http://lodaya.webs.com/paper_rchk.htm. Accessed March 29, 2011.

Lodaya, A. (2003), "The Crisis of Traditional Craft in India," *Lodaya.Webs.Com*. Available at: http://lodaya.webs.com/paper_craft.htm. Accessed May 10, 2012.

Lodaya, A. (2006), "Conserving Culture as a Strategy for Sustainability," *Lodaya.Webs.Com*. Available at: http://lodaya.webs.com/paper_ccss.htm. Accessed May 10, 2012.

Lodaya, A. (2007), "Catching up; Letting Go," *Lodaya.Webs.Com*. Available at: http://lodaya.webs.com/paper_culg.htm. Accessed May 10, 2012.

Magda, R.M.R. (2004), *Transmodernidad,* Barcelona: Anthropos. Available at: http://transmoderntheory.blogspot.com/2008/12/globalization-as-transmodern-totality.html. Accessed October 15, 2010.

McCallum, K., and Papandrea, F. (2009), "Community Business: The Internet in Remote Australian Indigenous Communities," *New Media & Society*, 11(7): 1230–1251.

Nussbaum, B. (2010a), "Is Humanitarian Design the New Imperialism?" *Co.Design*, July 7. Available at: www.fastcodesign.com/1661859/is-humanitarian-design-the-new-imperialism. Accessed March 27, 2011.

Nussbaum, B. (2010b), "Do-gooder Design and Imperialism, Round 3: Nussbaum Responds," *Co.Design*, July 13. Available at: www.fastcodesign.com/1661894/do-gooder-design-and-imperialism-round-3-nussbaum-responds. Accessed March 27, 2011.

Nussbaum, B. (2010c), "Should Humanitarians Press on, If Locals Resist?" *Co. Design*, August 3. Available at: www.fastcodesign.com/1662021/nussbaum-should-humanitarians-press-on-if-locals-resist. Accessed March 27, 2011.

OECD and Eurostat (2005), *Oslo Manual: Guidelines for Collected and Interpreting Innovation Data*, 3rd edition, Oslo: OECD.

Ortiz, F. (1995 [1945]), *Cuban Counterpoint: Tobacco and Sugar*, Durham, NC: Duke University Press.

Otto, T. (2006), "Concerns, Norms and Social Action," *Folk*, 46/47: 143–157.

Pilloton, E. (2010), "Are Humanitarian Designers Imperialists? Project H Responds," *Co.Design*, July 12. Available at: www.fastcodesign.com/1661885/are-humanitarian-designers-imperialists-project-h-responds. Accessed March 27, 2011.

Ranjan, A., and Ranjan, M.P. (eds.) (2005), *Handmade in India*, New Delhi: National Institute of Design (NID), Ahmedabad, Council of Handicraft Development Corporations (COHANDS), New Delhi Development Commissioner (Handicrafts), New Delhi, and Mapin Publishing Pvt. Ltd.

Ranjan, M.P. (ed.) (2006), "Giving Back to Society: Towards a Post-mining Era," *IDSA Annual Conference*, Austin, TX, September 17–20.

Ranjan, M.P. (2011), "Design for Good Governance: A Call for Change," *Design for India Blog*, August 11. Available at: http://design-for-india.blogspot.com/2011/08/design-for-good-governance-call-for.html. Accessed November 14, 2011.

Restrepo, E., and Escobar, A. (2005), "Other Anthropologies and Anthropology Otherwise: Steps to a World Anthropologies Framework," *Critique of Anthropology*, 25(2): 99–129.

Russell, L. (2001), *Savage Imaginings*, Melbourne: Australian Scholarly Publishing.

Said, E. (1978), *Orientalism*, New York: Vintage Books.

Samaras, K. (2005), "Indigenous Australians and the 'Digital Divide,'" *Libri*, 55: 84–95.

Sennett, R. (2003), *Respect: The Formation of Character in an Age of Inequality*, New York: Norton.

Seyfang, G., and Smith, A. (2007), "Grassroots Innovation for Sustainable Development," *Environmental Politics*, 16(4): 584–603.

Simon, H. (1969), *The Sciences of the Artificial*, Cambridge, MA: MIT Press.

Smith, L.T. (1999), *Decolonizing Methodologies: Research and Indigenous Peoples*, London: Zed Books and Dunedin: University of Otago Press.

Sperschnieder, W., Kjaersgaard, M., and Petersen, G. (2001), "Design Anthropology—When Opposites Attract," First Danish HCI Research Symposium, PB-555, University of Aarhus, SIGCHI Denmark and Human Machine Interaction. Available at: www.daimi.au.dk/PB/555/PB-555.pdf. Accessed October 6, 2012.

Tax, S. (1975), "Action Anthropology," *Current Anthropology,* 16(4): 514–517.

Tunstall, E. (2006), "The Yin Yang of Ethnographic Praxis in Industry," in Ethnographic Praxis in Industry Conference Proceedings, Portland, OR: National Association for the Practice of Anthropology and Berkeley: University of California Press, 125–137.

Tunstall, E. (2007), "Yin Yang of Design and Anthropology," Unpublished paper presented at NEXT: AIGA 2007 Annual Conference, Denver, CO.

Tunstall, E. (2008a), "Design and Anthropological Theory: Trans-disciplinary Intersections in Ethical Design Praxis," in *Proceedings of the 96th Annual Conference of the College Arts Association* [CD], Dallas, TX: College Arts Association.

Tunstall, E. (2008b) "Design Anthropology: What Does It Mean to Your Design Practice?" *Adobe Design Center Think Tank*, May 13. Available at: www.adobe.com/designcenter/thinktank/tt_tunstall.html. Accessed August 5, 2008.

Tunstall, E. (2011), "Respectful Design: a Proposed Journey of Design Education" in A. Bennett and O. Vulpinari (eds.), ICOGRADA Education Manifesto 2011, Montreal: ICOGRADA.

Uddin, N. (2005), "Facts and Fantasy of Knowledge Retrospective of Ethnography for the Future of Anthropology," *Pakistan Journal of Social Science,* 3(7): 978–985.

Van Eeden, J. (2004), "The Colonial Gaze: Imperialism, Myths, and South African Popular Culture," *Design Issues*, 20(2): 18–33.

Verran, H., and Christie, M. (2007), "Using/designing Digital Technologies of Representation in Aboriginal Australian Knowledge Practices," *Human Technology*, 3(2): 214–227.

Wang, S.Z. (1989), "Chinese Modern Design: A Retrospective," *Design Issues*, 6(1): 49–78.

Wolf, E. (1982), *Europe and the People without History*, Berkeley: University of California Press.

14

Epilogue: Ethnography and Design, Ethnography in Design . . . Ethnography by Design

Keith M. Murphy and George E. Marcus

It has become commonplace over the past several decades for anthropologists and designers to form partnerships of different sorts on collaborative projects. This is often done in the interest of enhancing the work that designers do in creating new *things* in the world—with an ecumenical definition of that term—or in transforming the world as it is into one that is at least slightly upgraded from what came before. Not until very recently, however, has there been much of an attempt to formalize this relationship as a cohesive field of its own, with a common body of knowledge, methods, and research assumptions shared by a like-minded community of practitioners. The chapters in this volume offer an ambitious, pioneering contribution to the emergent field of design anthropology. Taken individually they reveal an assortment of approaches for how to conceive of and implement an integration of anthropological methods and preoccupations with those of design, all in the service of creating something new, something that both enhances and critically challenges its original sources. From Ewart's thoughtful excavation of design as a cluster of related practices—ones that look little like design in nontraditional contexts—to Drazin's consideration of design concepts as social facts, to Hallam's exploration of the cognitive outcomes afforded by designed features of anatomical models, the chapters in this volume offer a range of possibilities for forging deep links between anthropology and design at both practical and conceptual levels.

Yet as varying as the approaches represented here might be, there is nonetheless a binding thread woven among them that preserves their integrity as a broader collective endeavor. While the specific goals and theoretical frameworks of the projects described are diverse, the general composition of their personnel and the trajectories of their work evidence considerable overlap, at least on the surface. Much of the work presented was carried out by teams made up of anthropologists, designers, engineers, end users, and other stakeholders of various kinds, often working on projects with specific identity labels, like *Digital Natives*, *Body Games*, and *Indoor Climate and Quality of Life*, to name just a few. The funding for these projects tends to come from private industry, government sources, or both, with some articulated outcome serving as a warrant for the project's very existence—even if that outcome is, at the start, fuzzy in its particulars. Thus while there may be no canonical way to carry out design anthropology, there does seem to be some tacit agreement as to the basic formations in which the fundamental work of design anthropology is ordered.

One of the most central characteristics of the design anthropology presented here is also an enduring one, namely a direct emphasis on the utility, and indeed, the necessity of ethnographic methods for a humanist kind of design that accounts for the lived cultural worlds inhabited by designed things and their users. As early partnerships between anthropologists and designers could attest, ethnography has a lot to offer design (see, for example, Suchman's [2011] critical reflections on her work at Xerox PARC). In one dominant strand of this kind of engagement, user-oriented ethnography furnishes design with a methodology for accessing aspects of reality that are usually foreclosed to designerly speculation and produces data, extracted from *actual* use within a range of relevant cultural practices, which is then put to work as crucial raw material in the design process. Another benefit of ethnography for design is a different kind of theoretical engagement than most designers are accustomed to, as we have seen in this volume with, for instance, Clark's use of Goffman in a project on second language learning, Halse's ruminations on speculation and imagination at the intersection of design and anthropology, and Gatt and Ingold's call for reconceiving design in a more prospectively hopeful mode. Finally, ethnography can also transform the nature of collaboration in design work by infusing an already well-developed orientation to participation—especially within the specific tradition of participatory design—with a more robust anthropological sensitivity to sociality, as Smith has demonstrated with her work on museum exhibition design.

Yet as critical as the relationship between anthropology and design has become, we cannot help but notice that this relationship has historically been, by and large, one-sided, with a predominant emphasis on the benefits of anthropology for design without much regard for any potential contributions of design for anthropology. In this arrangement, design—or perhaps more accurately, designing—is typically granted primary status while anthropology—usually reduced to its iconic method, ethnography—is introduced as a significant, but still supplementary, component of an overall goal-oriented design process. In other words, in most instances the relationship between anthropology and design is asymmetrical, with anthropology almost exclusively subordinated to the needs of design. This situation, in one sense, is not unlike the classic role of the anthropological perspective operating through ethnographic insight in development projects of the late twentieth century, but with an important difference. There has always been at least a flavor of eccentricity, if not subversion, of the internal critic who collaborates nonetheless in the kind of role that anthropologists have played in development projects, dominated usually by positivist approaches to knowledge and explicitly normative ideas of progress (see, most acutely, Mosse 2011). In design projects, however, anthropologists work alongside those charged with making something, or problem solving, who intellectually, at least, share the same purview that encourages nuanced, venturesome, humanistically inclined imaginaries of the social, even through quite different media and sensory skill preferences (for example, drawing more than writing; visualizing more than listening). While the cross-talk in working together may in some instances be more pleasantly exotic for anthropologists in design collaborations, especially in their unpredictable brainstorming moments, than in classic development ones, the tune is still very much called by the demands of the technical, the applied problem solvable, and often the marketable, that occasion the collaboration itself. The community of anthropologists remains the primary audience for the meta-critical ethnography of collaboration that most anthropologists who participate in are inclined to produce reflexively as surplus value to the roles they are expected to take within design projects. Though nobody is asking the anthropologist to make an object of reflexive critique, the collaboration itself in which she participates, usually as a cultural expert on users and environments that the project affects, she does so anyhow—formally or informally—as a report to her discipline, in its boundless ethnographic curiosity about all things social, including design projects themselves. Several of the pieces in this volume, including those by Halse, Clark, and Smith, as well as Mette Gislev Kjaersgaard's (2011) recent dissertation, provide useful accounts of this double agency (and bind!) that results from an ethnographer's collaboration within a design project and her growing critical ethnographic perspective upon it, without a constituency for the latter itself.

What is most important about the vibrant contemporary incarnations of design anthropology presented in this volume is that they provide a much needed rebalancing of the historically lopsided relationship between design and anthropology, and they do so without damaging the integrity of the existing alliance. Design, it seems, does in fact have a lot to offer anthropology. All of these chapters demonstrate in their own ways that ongoing partnerships and collaborations between anthropologists and designers are pushing and prodding, sometimes with a nudge and other times with a shove, some of the fundamental definitions that constitute the anthropological enterprise. Practically any and all of its aspects are up for potential revision, including, among many others, its conceptual infrastructure and its operationalization (Gatt and Ingold, Drazin), the politics of encounter (Tunstall), the tools used for handling knowledge and knowledge production (Kilbourn), the kinds and contours of the partnerships that anthropologists form (Wasson and Metcalf), and the effects and affects anthropological work can bring to the world (Smith). Most compelling is that these topics are not floating in isolation: though the authors may highlight one or two in particular over others, all of these ideas flow through and resonate in each of the chapters, stemming from diverse project frameworks and contextual backgrounds. This convergence as to where design anthropology is heading and the textures of its possibilities is one of its most potent qualities.

From our perspective, the most significant leverage point between design and anthropology is with ethnography itself, the complex mode of engagement that sits at anthropology's core and that has proven so useful to so many areas of design. Ethnography is the *sine qua non* of the field, both in the sense of anthropology as an academic field and the field as methodological construct. It is the primary point of contact between researchers and their objects and subjects of inquiry, where meaningful research relations are first formed and transformed and challenged. Ethnography opens up a space of transduction, where the materials and practices of life as lived are generatively reconstituted into a new kind of energy useful for the production of knowledge. To be sure, knowledge production is ongoing in many anthropological domains, but it often starts and is conditioned by contingencies implicit in ethnographic moments. And while ethnography is of course not restricted to data recovered from the practices, things, utterances, glances, and other situated design data that fieldworkers encounter, the speculative possibilities of ethnography are always somehow tethered to them. Because design is inherently stitched to the social world, so embedded in a nexus of objects—that is, a nexus of things of various materialities made to exist in and support the social world—and because it, like ethnography, is a point of contact, a space of transduction, it seems to us that placing the two alongside one another and tracing their parallels and divergences is as good a place as any to begin exploring how design can help reshape anthropology.

So this is what we have been doing at the Center for Ethnography at the University of California, Irvine.[1] The center was established in 2005 during a decade when there emerged an increasing and explicit recognition among anthropologists (for example, see Rabinow et al. 2008) of the new challenges of establishing projects of individually conceived and produced field research amid complex arrangements, new forms of governance, and organizations whose keynotes are collaboration and social impact. What is it for anthropology to produce research and scholarship—both in its apprentice dissertation and more advanced forms—in these frames? How do they affect disciplinary authority and agendas beyond older understandings of the interdisciplinary? The design-anthropology relationship has been one of the most productive sites to think about the conditions of collaboration that in turn define the conditions of fieldwork on which so much ethnographic inquiry depends. The implication for ethnography can be seen most clearly by the exercise of experimenting with design as a means—as a source of techniques, dispositions, and forms—for the production of contemporary ethnography in the classic concept of fieldwork. So in the remainder of this epilogue, stimulated by the ideas presented in this volume and our own work at the Center for Ethnography, we want to explore the possibilities for a new kind of ethnographic inquiry, which have evolved historically within the disciplinary ambitions of anthropology, as shaped by the insights, practices, and pedagogies of design.

ETHNOGRAPHY THEN AND NOW

Ethnographic fieldwork is not what it used to be (Faubion and Marcus 2009). The sites ethnographers now visit are not configured as they were when anthropology first emerged as a discipline. Even the traditional (and, to be sure, idealized) destinations of anthropologists, small-scale societies, are today deeply intertwined with global flows and transnational forces that originate far beyond village and regional borders. While much high-quality research is still conducted in such *traditional* contexts, it is simply untenable to expect that a robust ethnographic portrait is possible without accounting for phenomena of various sorts that do not emerge directly from on-the-ground participant observation, and that account for a practical constitution of a "field" for fieldwork that is not simply a function of the ethnographer's travel to sites of sustained inquiry. When one reads ethnographies today, one wants more access to what the process of inquiry itself produces along the way, in circumstances, contexts, and settings that are foregrounded rather than relinquished to the background of the primary *mise-en-scene* of the fieldwork encounter. This requires spaces of intervention, an active role in producing occasions for experimental, and indeed speculative thinking and the collective and material making of concepts—in other words, studio work, in its various guises, which is the kind of activity that designers of various kinds have forged as their own method.

And yet despite recognitions of the substantial and complex transformations that *the field* has undergone over the past several decades, the methods ethnographers now take for granted as staples of ethnographic inquiry have remained, in their most basic contours, largely unchanged (compare, for example, the classic *Notes and Queries on Anthropology* (1967 [1951]), and a new handbook of method on virtual ethnography, Boellstorff et al. 2012). Most of these originally emerged from the specific contingencies—both intellectual and material—of early fieldwork situations. The assiduous recording of everyday life through note taking, for instance, is still the centerpiece of contemporary ethnographic methodology, both inside and outside of academic anthropology. While the general practice of carefully detailing unexpected observations in visiting foreign lands long predates the disciplinary development of ethnography, in the late nineteenth century note taking was the best, most accurate form of inscription available for social scientists interested in documenting previously unknown sociocultural phenomena. Precise transcription of indigenous languages through interviews with native speakers, a practice championed in the United States by Franz Boas and his student Edward Sapir, was significantly motivated not only by a desire to understand cultural and linguistic diversity, but also by a need to salvage the rapidly disappearing linguistic heritage of many American Indian groups. And, perhaps most famously, Bronislaw Malinowski's contributions to the development of long-term participant observation was prompted as much by international politics during World War I as it was by the research questions he posed in the Trobriand Islands.

There are many more ethnographic methods than note taking, transcription, and participant observation, of course, some that have come and gone and others that have more recently surfaced. Moreover, anthropologists working alongside designers and engineers have historically been much more open to innovating new methods in their fieldwork than anthropologists more firmly embedded within the academy, so there are some notable differences between the general contexts in which ethnographic work is conducted. Nonetheless the fundamental building blocks of contemporary ethnographic practice, the DNA of doing fieldwork, remains widely shared and largely unchanged since the inception of the formalized anthropological endeavor.

But as we said, times have changed. Most ethnographers still travel far from home, but many also work in their own communities. Advances in audio and video technology have made recording devices smaller, cheaper, and extremely powerful, and this has in turn allowed ethnographers to generate new kinds of data in previously unimaginable quantities. Constantly improving computer hardware and software allow us to innovate ways to analyze this data and derive not only novel research questions, but also novel *kinds* of research questions. Meanwhile, the nature of participation in ethnographic practice has shifted significantly to include not only a host of new collaborators besides our traditional *informants*, but also a much more complex web of ethical entanglements than ethnography's progenitors had imagined—or at least had chosen to acknowledge. It would seem that *where* and *with whom* we work has changed at a much faster rate than *how* we work. What this means is that conventional forms of ethnographic research inhabit a research terrain quite different from the ones in which they were brought into being. While this is by no means a fatal flaw, it may, in our view, actually inhibit the continued development of ethnography as a distinct sort of inquiry attuned to the details of social reality. There is a deep-seated (but lively and largely self-admitted) conservatism in anthropology's emblematic professional culture of method, which has the effect of slowing innovation down to a glacial pace. Change happens, but it usually comes from within and unfolds through tweaks and small-scale adjustments to the status quo. What we would like to do instead is to look outside of anthropology, beyond ethnography itself, to find other developed systems of thought and practice that when placed alongside and within ethnographic work can help us substantially reconfigure the fundamental building blocks of what ethnographers do, so as to better match the conditions shaping research that we now inhabit. From our point of view, design is one such system of thought and practice, not only because there is already a working relationship between design and anthropology, but for more specific reasons concerning the overlap between ethnography as mode and practice and design as mode and practice. Design seems to us a key domain for ethnography to explore critically, and perhaps absorb into its own process of inquiry.

ETHNOGRAPHY AND DESIGN

When we talk about design, we are conscious that our formulation relies in large part on an idealization and amalgamation of a number of related, but often quite disparate fields. This can lead to an invocation of specific *design principles* and *design practices* that may seem overly abstract or even inapplicable when compared with the specifics of any single design discipline. Architecture, industrial design, graphic design, interaction design, information architecture, software engineering, furniture design, urban planning, and scores of other design-oriented fields all work with different materials and at different scales, and in some respects their students undergo distinct kinds of training. Nonetheless there is enough in common among these various design fields to talk about *design* in general terms, in an idealized form, without distorting the overall nature of either *design* as a unified endeavor or any specific design-oriented field.

In broad strokes design actually shares a number of qualities with ethnography. There is, to repurpose Gatt and Ingold's (this volume) phrasing, a *correspondence* between the two. They are not, of course, instances of the same thing done differently, nor are they even variants of a kind. Instead they are imperfect analogs of one another, traversing overlapping territories at variable rates and prodded by their own motivations. Here is a sketch of such analogs, a compass for thinking about the absorption of design practices, or their influence, by ethnographic ones.

Both design and ethnography exist as product and process. The terms *design* and *ethnography* share a kind of (am)bivalent reference when used by their practitioners, simultaneously denoting what they make and what they do. *Design*, for instance, is often used to describe a thing in the world, or perhaps more accurately, a set of things that all fall under a single purview. We say *design is*, *design does*, and *design has* as if design operates as an autonomous entity in possession of consistent *qualia* across its various instantiations.

So, too, do we discuss ethnography, which, like design, is also more accurately comprised of individual ethnographies, singular contributions to a larger whole. In practice designers and ethnographers craft a design or an ethnography in their work, bringing forth into the world tangible products stemming specifically from putting learned principles and methods into action.

At the same time *design* and *ethnography* refer not just to the output produced by designers and ethnographers, but also the complex processes by which that output is made—processes almost entirely obscured by the form of their products. In both cases these processes rely on specific sets of (more or less) inviolable principles and core methods that students are exposed to from their introduction to the disciplines. Moreover, while the end products of both design and ethnography tend to receive most of the attention from those who consume them, practitioners understand that the processes and practices by which designed objects and ethnographic texts are brought into being are the *sine qua non* of what they do, even if those processes are largely invisible to the publics to whom they are accountable.

Both design and ethnography are focused on research. Training in both design and ethnography is heavily based in cultivating an understanding of what has come before, including the names and work of influential predecessors who have influenced their fields in some way—though both traditions employ techniques to narrow down both who and what count as relevant. For both, finding out "what has already been said" and "what has already been done" is not only crucial for producing innovative work, but also signals familiarity with a body of knowledge that is relevant to fellow practitioners. Both designers and ethnographers are also urged to employ a careful observation of the world around them and a purposeful inscription of what they observe. This is quite clearly a central aspect of ethnographic practice, but designers, too, are typically engaged in observational inquiry. Such research often involves investigations of new materials and construction techniques, or the work produced by other designers, or in some cases, as the many of the contributions to this volume demonstrate, how people use, think about, and feel about objects in specific contexts. We could say, then, that neither designers nor ethnographers take for granted that the minute operations of the world around them matter for conceiving and carrying out their work. That both ethnographers and designers do, in fact, often overlook or misrecognize the details of social reality is a nettlesome aspect shared by both fields—one that can possibly be addressed in their continued collaborations.

Both design and ethnography are anxiously people-centered. In different ways, design and ethnography maintain a nominal (if not always substantive) relationship to *the social*. Even for designers who treat people—often relabeled *users*—as merely one component of a complex system, the conclusion that almost all designed things in some way impinge upon and often reorganize interactions between people, either directly or indirectly, is unavoidable.

However as critical as people are to design and ethnography, both fields often fall victim to a tendency toward abstraction—for design in the process; for ethnography in the product—and thus a removal from material realities, despite the seemingly self-evident attunement to observations of real-world conditions.

Both design and ethnography are at the service of more than the thing itself. Though both design and ethnography often operate in practice with relatively small-bore goals—creating a comfortable chair or explaining a particular ritual—they are always linked into larger, less immediate symbolic processes, and their position in such processes often produces a range of different, unpredictable consequences. For instance design is deeply entrenched in a capitalist system of production, and most designers (excluding, perhaps, the most famous and elite) concentrate on creating designs that will, in one way or another, *sell*. This means that some concept of *success* is featured prominently in the design imaginary, with some designs succeeding while others are ignored or left behind. How this success is measured varies—money obviously dominates, but different design fields also barter in other kinds of symbolic capital. Traditionally ethnography is less concerned with success in the ways that design is. While some ethnographic texts are more influential than others and only a fraction of research proposals receive funding, success is not foregrounded as a notable aspect of the ethnographic imaginary. Instead concerns like *ethical entanglements* are much more highly pronounced, and ethnographic products are often judged according to universal and community standards for conducting ethical research. Our point here is that both cases—*success* in design and *ethics* in ethnography—reveal different ways in which design and ethnography are always from the start embedded in consequential contexts beyond the things—and processes—themselves.

Both design and ethnography are reflexive; or perhaps it is better to say they are both open to reflexivity. Since the 1980s, anthropologists have taken to incorporating a strong reflexive stance in their ethnographic fieldwork and writing. This entails, among many other things, an open acknowledgment of the role played by the ethnographer in the events described, ruminations on the limitations of particular methods, and often an openly political stance in relation to the framing of the research. As such, ethnographers spend quite a bit of time describing not only what they have observed, but also why they make the choices they do in carrying out their fieldwork. While most design fields do not typically count reflexivity among their core qualities, many designers do spend a great deal of time talking, thinking, and writing about what they do. Journals like *Design Studies* and *Design Issues*, and many others in more specialized fields, devote a tremendous amount of space to exploring design (most notably *design process*) from multiple perspectives, and the recent trend in *design thinking* is predicated on a precise identification, repackaging, and commodification of design's most basic practices. To be sure, the kinds of reflexivity ethnographers and designers engage in are not the same and they are implemented in different ways. Nonetheless both fields demonstrate at least some inclination toward critical self-evaluation.

There are many other points of correspondence between design and ethnography (for example both are simultaneously conceptually inflected while being grounded in a material reality; both are steeped in romanticism) that we will forego elaborating here. We hope that the several parallels we have presented at least begin to substantiate the argument that the relationship between ethnography and design is not as unidirectional as it is often made out to be. By highlighting the overall family resemblances between design and ethnography, rather than only the features of ethnography that benefit design, we are establishing a framework for treating their connections as dynamic and more fully reciprocal than is generally the case in design anthropology.

However, for balance, we should also sketch *some relevant dissimilarities and divergences between ethnography and design.* As we have mentioned, designers and ethnographers face different economic contingencies in their work, which affects the way the work is able to proceed. Their ethical entanglements—and the presence of those entanglements in their respective processes—are also differently ordered. Design is more target-focused, while ethnography is more open-ended. To start a project with a specific result in mind is the default position for most design projects, but for an ethnographer to do so would violate one of the most basic premises of field-based research. Indeed, the fundamental rationale for undertaking fieldwork instead of conducting laboratory experiments is to uncover previously unknown information about how the real world works. Both designers and ethnographers are well prepared to carry out their respective processes, but designers tend to have a better idea of where they will end up at the end.

Another way of describing this divergence is that design is more obviously creative, while ethnography is more obviously documentary. In fact, as we discuss later, ethnography (especially in the way that it is taught) is allergic to most kinds of creativity, preferring instead to stick with its own style of empiricism. It is unclear why this is the case, but one possible explanation is a perception that *making things* is unnervingly close to *making things up*, which, combined with the nature of fieldwork, leaves ethnographers open to possible critiques of fabricated data from particularly ungenerous readers. Whatever the reason, creativity is generally not rewarded in contemporary ethnography.

In their idealized forms design is more collaborative in nature, while ethnographic work is usually quite solitary. As most of the chapters in this book have demonstrated, this view of ethnography is of course not true in all instances, and in practice all kinds of ethnographic fieldwork are deeply collaborative along many dimensions. However, in academic anthropology, ethnographic projects, especially first projects conducted as dissertation research, are still fundamentally treated as the exclusive work of individual ethnographers. Even ethnographers currently working in nonacademic settings have most likely crafted and carried out their own self-directed projects before joining a collaborative team.

Finally, design and ethnography are built upon and facilitated by different pedagogical infrastructures. Design education is highly structured, usually organized around completing specific projects, especially in a student's later years. Many design traditions also involve a fair amount of critique, from professors, external critics, and fellow students. In contrast there are no commonly established ways to teach ethnography, at least in U.S. anthropology departments. Some graduate programs require students to take multiple courses in ethnographic methods, while others require none. In as much as these courses are practice based, rarely are the assigned projects usefully connected to the students' actual research interests or central projects—more often than not, they are simply exercises intended for students to *get the feel* of doing consequential, question-driven fieldwork. And meaningful critique is all but absent in contemporary ethnographic training.[2]

Another significant contrast in pedagogical infrastructures is the relationship between contexts of learning and contexts of practice. Design education most often takes place in studio environments, which are generally configured with the right kinds of equipment to support students in doing design work. Moreover, these studios are structured to anticipate the kinds of professional studios in which students will eventually work, thus maintaining a continuous flow between contexts of learning and contexts of practice. Again, such arrangements are all but absent in most ethnographic training. Learning both about ethnography and how to do ethnography usually follows a traditional seminar format common across many academic disciplines. Seminar rooms are set up to facilitate discussions and lectures, and thus tend to function poorly as environments for working through the details of ethnographic problems.

WHY USE DESIGN AS A TEMPLATE FOR REWORKING ETHNOGRAPHY?

By drawing inspiration from the correspondences between design and ethnography, and confronting the frictions caused by their basic differences, we hope to exploit some of the advantages of design to enhance or transform ethnographic pedagogy and practice. Our intention, quite simply, is to dismantle ethnography's aging frame, tear it down to its most basic elements, and then reconstruct something new using parts and assembly techniques shamelessly scavenged from design, with the goal of rebuilding the core engine of anthropology—and in so doing clear a space for further transformations of the anthropological apparatus. The design process, insofar as it can be reduced to a single entity, is generally oriented toward transforming (or cooking) "raw" information into "useful knowledge," a guided mutation of "mere ideas" into "workable concepts" or a "feasible design" that then becomes an "object" in the world. The design process inherently consists of techniques for "working out" and "working through" different kinds of materials. Rather than unfolding in a strict and predictable linear form, the design process continuously moves back and forth between activities and modes of action that stimulate creativity and that afford a kind of critical thinking rarely achieved through simple discussions. In our view, ethnography could benefit from the ways designers handle their material and the creativity they bring to their work. There is also room for infusing more speculative engagement in ethnography, as Halse (this volume) has pointed out.

Motivating this project is a belief that, through the application of design methods and thinking, various aspects of ethnography—from research design to methods to writing and representation and beyond—can be prospectively and productively remade to better suit the continuously shifting contingencies of contemporary anthropological research. By carefully integrating elements of design into ethnography, we hope to inject ethnography with a newfound creativity, new ways of thinking, new kinds of collaboration, new pedagogical techniques, new raw materials, and new kinds of outputs.

The ultimate results of this project are still unclear, but we have several aspirational goals. The most general is to find ways to update and modernize both the regulative norms and actual range of techniques in classic ethnographic practice, to make ethnography more adaptable to the contemporary world. While the mere application of design to ethnography may not itself accomplish this modernization, perhaps a solution can be discovered somewhere in their ongoing working relationship. Part of this modernization involves recognizing that contemporary ethnography is useful for many different purposes, and as such should be more flexible overall so as to better accommodate its attendant implementations. Moreover, this integration may also help ethnographers to reconstitute not only the way they do fieldwork, but also what actually counts as the "field," which for as long as it has existed has been defined foremost as something close to "not here." This may even include reconfiguring the roles played by informants in helping to formulate, carry out, and analyze on-the-ground fieldwork. Most important, we hope that bringing together design and ethnography in this way will help generate new, previously unforeseen forms of knowledge.

ETHNOCHARRETTE: AN EXPERIMENT IN ETHNOGRAPHIC ENGAGEMENT

In order to put these ideas into action, under the auspices of the Center for Ethnography at the University of California, Irvine, we have developed an ongoing series of events that we call *ethnocharrettes*. In design a *charrette* is an organized and highly focused stretch of time devoted to what amounts to quick and dirty designing. Charrettes are common in many design fields, including architecture, industrial design, and urban planning. In a way a charrette—which can last for a few hours or a few days—is a condensed version of a long-term design process. It is usually highly collaborative, bringing groups of people together, in some cases involving users and other nondesigners, to work on specific design problems with the goal of devising one or several solutions to the initial problem. There is no one way to run a charrette, though to work most effectively they should offer a good balance of structure and flexibility, with the intention of providing enough structure to foster focused creativity. In a way charrettes are like elaborate brainstorming sessions, but with a few more rules and expectations.

The *ethnocharrette* is an augmentation of the charrette form tailored to the needs of ethnographers. The idea behind initiating the ethnocharrette was simple enough: What happens if we ask ethnographers to run ethnographic material through a design studio process? How would they think? What would they produce? For our initial events we decided to use published ethnographic texts as our stimulus material, treating the contents contained in a familiar textual format as the basic information to discuss, think through, and transform. Our participants were graduate students, most of whom were working toward a PhD in anthropology, and all of whom had some amount of training in ethnographic fieldwork.

Our first two ethnocharrettes were day-long events. They were both divided into three stages, each of which lasted several hours, followed by a discussion period. For each ethnocharrette we instructed the participants to arrive having read the assigned book-length ethnography and to be prepared to discuss it as they would in a traditional seminar setting. For the second event (though not for the first) we provided a prompt several days prior, with a list of provocations for the participants to consider, including "Remake or reinvent the ethnography—explore roads that it didn't take, or how it might be differently animated or reanimated," and "Juxtapose the ethnography to something else, as a probe to engage it from a different angle."

Upon their arrival the participants were assigned to groups of three or four members and given their instructions. For the first stage, participants were required to decompose the assigned texts into whatever elements they individually or collectively felt were worthy of drawing attention to by writing them down in the form of small chunks that easily fit on post-it notes, which were then affixed to a whiteboard. This resulted in a vast array of seemingly random ideas, notes, and phrases jotted down and haphazardly arranged in front of the group. The goal of this exercise was to compel the participants to confront the traditional ethnographic product in a new, even uncomfortable way, to get them to manipulate the text to reveal—or perhaps conjure—an underlying composition of the ethnography. Participants were actively discouraged from thinking too much during this stage, and instead were told to force themselves to toss all ideas up on the wall, rendering both small and large details co-equal, tangible things that could later be called upon for closer scrutiny.

If the first stage concerned extracting and compiling raw information presented in the ethnography, the second stage required the participants to begin engaging more seriously in speculative, comparative, and synthetic thinking. The collages of post-it notes created during the first stage represented each group's collective understanding of the ethnography, though in a new, atomized form. The groups were now asked to identify clusters of concepts within their collages that could form new and potentially unexpected ethnographic categories and concepts. Our expectation was that these categories and concepts would not replicate what is already known, but would emerge though group discussion—and that they would not (and ideally, should not) match how the book's author had framed the project. The hope was that this exercise would allow the participants to draw connections that might not have been visible when they first read the ethnography. Toward the end of this stage participants were asked to select the clusters that they felt (individually and collectively) were useful for generating possible new avenues for speculation.

The final stage was dedicated to innovation. The groups were asked to develop a "rapid prototype" for a new ethnographic form, method, or mode, using the clusters of concepts they had identified as interesting and useful for speculation. They were instructed to stick relatively close to the original source material, but were allowed to let their discussions take them in whichever directions they wished. Their prototypes did not have to be concrete in any way, nor were they required to be aesthetically pleasing, but they did have to demonstrate some deep thinking about possibilities for how ethnographic material can be analyzed, argued, collected, or presented and needed to be something more than a verbal description. Participants were asked to present their prototypes in a slideshow format, and a group discussion followed the presentations. We will not spend time here discussing the specifics of what the groups produced during the initial events (an Internet search for "ethnocharrette" will lead to the project's website, which has the details), however the groups participating in both events worked hard to produce some very stimulating preliminary ideas that, if carried forward and developed in other forums, could prove interesting for advancing ethnographic inquiry.

In devising and conducting these initial ethnocharrettes we had two broad goals, one more conceptual in scope, the other more pedagogical. We were—and continue to be—quite hopeful that these events will, in time, help to generate the seeds of new ethnographic forms of a sort that can push ethnographic inquiry in new and useful directions. As we have conceived the ethnocharrette thus far, we have brought participants together to evaluate critically the kinds of ethnographic forms currently active in and vital to the ongoing pursuit of ethnographic inquiry. Our overriding objective has been to determine if by tweaking or reworking these forms, pathways for developing new practices, conceptual frameworks, and methods might emerge. From the start we had no expectations that any single event would produce some new ethnographic panacea. Instead the idea we have worked with has been to use established ethnographic texts as springboards for contemplating ethnography's possibilities—or, if not the possibilities for ethnography writ large, then at least for the participants themselves as they develop their own ethnographic projects and prepare to enter the field. After all, the future of all ethnographic inquiry will unfold through the work of its practitioners.

Following from this, our second goal has been to provide opportunities for our students to orient to ethnographic materials—and learning about and with and through them—in new and unexpected ways. This includes some very basic augmentations of traditional learning experiences, including, for instance, abandoning the seminar structure; relying on collaboration between students; and working in open, transformable spaces.

REFLECTIONS ON DESIGN IN ETHNOGRAPHY . . . SO FAR

Not surprising, there has been some friction in our attempts to blend design studio practices with ethnography, much of which surfaces at precisely the points of noncorrespondence we earlier identified. While there are plenty of reasons for this, ranging from minute practicalities of how we structured the events to broader conceptual mismatches, there are at least three dimensions that need further refinement.

First, studio techniques are more obviously goal directed than the work ethnographers do. This does not mean that ethnographic fieldwork is not goal oriented, but rather that the end results are not as clearly defined from the start as they are for design. Designers (and design students) tend to work with design briefs, descriptions of the end products that their clients (or professors) have asked them to make, and most design work is oriented toward achieving results that satisfactorily fit those descriptions. Briefs may be more or less specific, but regardless of their level of detail they serve as the primary device for organizing the trajectory of the design process. As such, a design process without a brief (or something like a brief) will rarely yield anything of much value. The constraint of the brief, while quite generative for practices geared toward producing specific products, in many ways seems unnecessarily restrictive and antithetical to the free exploration of ideas seen as underpinning traditional seminar interactions. Merging our goals as ethnographers with the kinds of goals design processes are adept at reaching is a critical challenge to confront moving forward. Related to this, a second mismatch between design and ethnography stems from, as we have stated, the different ways creativity is positioned and valued in the two disciplines. Creativity is quite obviously foregrounded as a necessary and often constituent component of design practice, and most studio techniques uncritically presume creative work—however one defines it—to be the most basic building block of any design process. This differs significantly from ethnographic instruction, especially within anthropology, in several ways. First, while almost all the work entailed in *doing* ethnographic research is in some way creative—for instance devising research questions, crafting grant applications, orchestrating fieldwork, writing up results—such creativity is rarely described or treated as such, nor is it explicitly articulated as valuable to the institution.

Second, on a much more practical level, the mundane work of design is centrally concerned with *making things*. While ethnographers do make things during certain stages of their practices, the orientation to making is quite different, and predominantly restricted to textual (and in some cases audiovisual) forms. In contrast to the seminar room or most home offices, studios are full of raw materials designers use to work through their ideas—they use markers and pencils to sketch, they make computer drawings on their laptops, they build prototypes with foam and cardboard, a kind of engagement with diverse materials that is rarely found in anthropology. We can summarize all of this by saying that in most instances studio techniques entail working within an infrastructure that both materially and ideologically supports and affords creative projects, a condition that does not fit with the current state of most ethnographic training.

Finally, and in some ways most crucially, studio pedagogy recognizes *critique* as a necessary and generative element of design education in ways that contemporary graduate training in anthropology does not. Embedded in studio practice is the expectation that design ideas are (more or less) always subject to assessment and open critique from peers, and in educational contexts, from instructors. Students are trained to articulate and explain the choices they have made in their work and to respond to what might be perceived as bad news when their instructors offer critical evaluation (a handy skill to have when they are eventually making presentations to paying clients). Indeed these moments of criticism, in which instructors identify the *problems* in a student's work (as well as the positive details), are where a great deal of the pedagogical work is accomplished in design education. In fact, critique is so embedded and expected in this institutional context that if a student were *not* to receive some amount of negative assessment, it would most likely be read as a sort of assault on her abilities. This, quite clearly, is the opposite of what is expected in academic anthropological training, on the part of both students and instructors. While critique is more acceptable in certain private formats, like paper comments, or at certain obvious stages, like oral exams or dissertation defenses, a regularized public performance of directed, individualized critique, no matter how constructive it might be, is generally no longer a preferred pedagogical practice in anthropology.

CONCLUDING REMARKS

In fulfilling our tasks as epilogists for a rich and exploratory volume setting parameters for the still nascent field of design anthropology, it would seem that in appreciating the volume collectively, we have produced another contribution to it, another ingredient to the stew. Rather than an integrative, programmatic meta-commentary on it—in essence a review and forecast—we instead have produced a further dialogic engagement with it, according to our own stakes, not unrelated to the hopes—both imaginative and partially enacted—expressed in each paper in its own idiom for the state of evolving collaborations between anthropologists, designers, and all of the other stakeholders with whom we interact. There can be no more appropriate epilogic tribute to a volume, and the arena of work that it reflects, than to have "joined in" rather than to have indulged the "meta." Like the volume itself it is a promissory of things to come.

NOTES

1. See www.ethnography.uci.edu
2. Note that there are national and regional differences in the way anthropology is taught. The tradition in Denmark, for instance, is more centered on collaboration and critique than the U.S. model with which we are more familiar. Given this, it is not surprising that design anthropology is more strongly emergent in Scandinavia than in other parts of the world.

REFERENCES

Anonymous. (1967 [1951]), *Notes and Queries on Anthropology*, sixth edition, revised and rewritten by a committee of the Royal Anthropological Institute of Great Britain and Ireland, London: Kegan Paul.

Boellstorff, T., Nardi, B., Pearce, C., and Taylor, T. L. (2012), *Ethnography and Virtual Worlds: A Handbook of Method*, Princeton, NJ: Princeton University Press.

Faubion, J. and Marcus, G. E. (2009), *Fieldwork Is Not What It Used to Be: Learning Anthropology's Method in a Time of Transition*, Ithaca, NY: Cornell University Press.

Kjaersgaard, M. G. (2011), "Between the Actual and the Potential: The Challenges of Design Anthropology," PhD dissertation, Faculty of Arts, Department of Culture and Society, University of Aarhus.

Mosse, D. (2011), *Adventures in Aidland: The Anthropology of Professionals in International Development*, London: Berghahn Books.

Rabinow, P., and Marcus, G. E., with Faubion, J.D., and Rees, T. (2008), *Designs for an Anthropology of the Contemporary*, Durham, NC: Duke University Press.

Suchman, L. A. (2011), "Anthropological Relocations and the Limits of Design," *Annual Review of Anthropology*, 40(1): 1–18.

Index

process and, 131
tangible, 104, 220, 258
theoretical processes and, 79
product development, 5–6, 9, 200–1
production
design and, 85–7
familiarity and, 87
professionals
users and, 123
Project H, 234
pterygopalatine ganglion anatomical
models, 111–12
publics
action occasions for, 212–13
components of, 199
design
collaboration in, 206–7
consultancy for, 200
formation of, 185
generation of, 200
innovations and, 19
prescriptive scenarios for,
200
language learning, 205
Språkskap project, 205, 207
usage-based research, 208–10
PD for, 202–3
performance with
opportunities, 203–5
as organizing principle, 210–12
teams, 204
theory, 204
sales pitches for, 207–8
workshop formats for, 200
see also Dewey, John
purpose-made anatomical models,
104, 113–14
PVC anatomical models, 109

Rabinow, Paul, 10, 168, 180, 193, 254
Ranjan, M. P., 235, 243
real time anthropology
correspondence and, 141–4
design influences on, 139–41
environmental design, 144–6
fieldwork for, 149
participant observation, 147–50
reflexive turn in, 153–4
synchronicity and, 149

reception, 166
reflection, 3, 11–12, 65, 71, 102, 125,
141–2, 165, 200
contextual and political, 174
critical, 8, 112, 185
see also Dourish, Paul;
reflection-in-action
on design in ethnography, 265–7
during future making processes,
192
embodied experience and, 194
and embodied practice, 16
theoretical, 1
theoretically informed, 173
reflection-in-action, 10, 71
reframe, 118, 238
design practice, 54
relations, 70–1, 163
research questions, 172
see also research
social imaginary, 70
reflexive turn, 153–4
relational thinking, 90
see also Bourriaud, Nicolas
research, 147
agenda, 52
assumptions, 251
collaborative, 229
as a collaborative process, 5, 76
see also design anthropology
conditions of, 131, 153
see also conditions
design, 225, 239
as a design process, 180
embeddedness of, 70
frame, 70–71, 78
interdisciplinary, 221
multi-sited ethnographic, 209
see also Marcus, George
packaging of, in design
anthropology, 72
partnerships, 222
practice-based inquiry and, 68
relations, 254
for style of knowing, 69
survey-based, 166
traditions, 216
transition to design, 64
user, 240